Learning Conversational Vietnamese

VIETNAMESE
FOR BEGINNERS

With special thanks to:
Nga B. Nguyen & Jeffrey M. Rocero (Audio Recordings)
Tuyet Nguyen – UnoDay Studio (Illustrations)

Learning Conversational Vietnamese

VIETNAMESE FOR BEGINNERS

By **Tri C. Tran**, PhD
University of California, Irvine

TUTTLE Publishing

Tokyo | Rutland, Vermont | Singapore

Table of Contents

Introduction

Welcome to *Vietnamese for Beginners*! This book has been carefully designed to provide you with a structured, engaging and comprehensive approach to mastering the Vietnamese language. Whether you are a complete beginner or seeking to strengthen your existing knowledge, this resource will guide you step by step toward fluency.

The book consists of fourteen chapters, the first two of which are dedicated to the introduction of the Vietnamese alphabet and its sound system.

Introduction to the alphabet

A strong foundation begins with understanding the building blocks of the language. In Chapter 1, you will be introduced to the alphabet and its corresponding letters. You will also find examples of letter combinations and their usage in words. By practicing the alphabet, you will build confidence in reading and writing from the very start.

Introduction to the sound system

Pronunciation is key to being understood in any language. Chapter 2 introduces you to the sound system, including vowels, semivowels, consonants and the tone system. You will learn the correct articulation of each sound through simple examples and audio recordings. Tips for mastering tricky sounds and pronunciation practice exercises will help you develop clear and natural speech.

Structure of the remaining chapters

Each of the remaining chapters in this book is structured to provide a balanced mix of essential skills, engaging content and cultural insights. Here is what you can expect:

1. Thematic dialogues

Each chapter includes two dialogues that reflect real-life situations and language usage. The dialogues are accompanied by comic strips that break down the conversations into manageable parts, making them easier to follow and understand.

2. Vocabulary lists

A vocabulary list accompanies each of the two dialogues, introducing key words and expressions related to the dialogue themes. The list helps you focus on relevant vocabulary that you can use immediately in practice and conversation.

3. Idiomatic expressions

Languages come alive through idioms. Each dialogue includes common idiomatic expressions that are explained in a section following it. These phrases will help you sound more natural and understand cultural nuances in everyday conversations.

4. Cultural notes
Learning a language means immersing yourself in its culture. Following each dialogue are cultural notes that explore traditions, customs and insights into daily life. These sections bridge the gap between language learning and cultural understanding.

5. Grammar sections
Two grammar sections in each chapter introduce and explain essential grammatical structures. These sections are presented in a clear, accessible manner with examples that link to the chapter themes, helping you see grammar in action.

6. Reading with illustration and comprehension questions
To improve your reading skills, each chapter includes one engaging reading passage accompanied by an illustration. The passage is followed by comprehension questions that challenge you to understand and analyze the text.

7. Proverb with explanation and discussion
Proverbs are a window into the soul of a culture. Each chapter introduces a traditional proverb, explained with an illustration and discussion prompts. This will help you reflect on the meaning and cultural significance of the saying.

8. Practice sections
Practice makes perfect! Each chapter provides a variety of exercises to strengthen your skills. These include:

- Listening exercises to sharpen your ear for the language
- Writing exercises to improve your written expression
- Translation exercises to develop accuracy and understanding between languages
- Vocabulary exercises to put in context the words just learned in the chapter

9. Comprehensive vocabulary list
At the end of each chapter, you will find a comprehensive list of all the vocabulary introduced. This allows for quick review and reinforcement of your learning.

10. Appendices
To further support your learning, this textbook includes several helpful appendices:

- Pronunciation guide – Charts of English-based transcriptions of Vietnamese words, including pronunciations of vowels, semivowels, diphthongs, triphthongs and consonants. The six tones in the language are represented using numbers for precise pronunciation of every word.
- Listening comprehension scripts – Complete scripts of the recordings for this type of practice exercise, accompanied by English translations to help you double check your listening skill.

- Answer key – A full set of answers for all exercises to help you self-assess and track your progress.
- Comprehensive glossary – A complete alphabetical glossary of words introduced in the textbook.

Additional resources are available online:

- Vocabulary flash cards – Printable flash cards for quick vocabulary practice.
- Audio recordings – Recordings of dialogues, vocabulary lists, and exercises to improve your listening and pronunciation skills.

Vivid manga-style illustrations accompany the dialogues, readings and proverbs to make the learning process more enjoyable.

Learning a language is a rewarding and transformative experience. It opens the door to new cultures, friendships and opportunities. As you progress through this textbook, remember to be patient with yourself and practice regularly. Each chapter has been designed to build your confidence, deepen your understanding and make learning enjoyable.

We hope this book becomes a valuable companion on your journey to mastering *Vietnamese for Beginners*. Let's get started!

Tri C. Tran

How to Download the Online Audio and Flash Cards for this Book:

1. Check to be sure you have an Internet connection.
2. Type the URL below into to your web browser.

https://www.tuttlepublishing.com/vietnamese-for-beginners

For support you can email us at info@tuttlepublishing.com.

CHAPTER 1

The Vietnamese Alphabet

Bảng Chữ Cái Tiếng Việt

I. The alphabet 

The Vietnamese alphabet consists of 29 letters:

A	Ă	Â	B	C	D	Đ	E	Ê	G
H	I	K	L	M	N	O	Ô	Ơ	P
Q	R	S	T	U	Ư	V	X	Y	

II. The names of the letters

The following charts present the names of the letters with pronunciation guides. Some letter names correspond with how the letter is pronounced, while others do not. The superscript numbers accompanying each letter name indicate their tones. Of the six tones in Vietnamese (see Chapter 2), only three are used for letter names. Number 1 indicates a mid-high, level tone, which is roughly equivalent to a normal-pitched monosyllabic word in English pronounced in isolation. Number 2 indicates a high-rising tone and Number 5 indicates a mid-low falling tone. A complete pronunciation guide chart, including tone numbers, is provided in the Appendix.

A. Vowels 

LETTER	NAME	NOTE
A	[a^{1}]	Like "a" in "father."
Ă	[a^{2}]	Like "a" as above, with a higher pitch.
Â	[uh^{2}]	Like "a" in "about," with a higher pitch.
E	[e^{1}]	Like "e" in "pen."
Ê	[eh^{1}]	Like "a" in "apron," without the "y" sound.
I	[ee^{1}]	Like "ee" in "bee."
O	[ah^{1}]	Like "o" in "hot."
Ô	[oh^{1}]	Like "oh," without the "w" sound.
Ơ	[uh^{1}]	Like "a" in "about."
U	[oo^{1}]	Like "oo" in "shoo."
Ư	[ŭ^{1}]	Like "oo" in "shoo," with lips unrounded.
Y	[ee^{1} grek^{2}]	Like "ee" in "bee," followed by "Greco," without "o."

Note:

Three diacritics (also called "vocalic marks") are used with vowels:

a. The breve (˘) used with letter **ă** indicates that this vowel sounds shorter and is produced with the mouth slightly more closed than **a**.

b. The circumflex (ˆ) used with letters **ê** and **ô** indicates that these two vowels sound more closed than **e** and **o**, respectively.

c. The hook (ʼ) used in letters **ơ** and **ư** indicates that the vowels they represent are "central vowels" (produced neither in the front nor back of the oral cavity).

B. Consonants

LETTER	NAME	
B	[beh^{1}]	Like "bay," without the "y" sound.
C	[seh^{1}]	Like "say," without the "y" sound.
D	[yeh^{1}]	Like "yay," without the final "y" sound.
Đ	[deh^{1}]	Like "day," without the "y" sound.
G	[zheh^{1}]	Like "s" in "measure," followed by "ay," without the "y" sound.
H	[hat^{2}]	Like "heart" without the "r" sound.
K	[ka^{1}]	Like "ca" in "calm."
L	[e^{1} luh^{5}]	Like "Ella."
M	[e^{1} muh^{5}]	Like "Emma."

LETTER	NAME	
N	[e^1 nuh^5]	Like "Anna."
P	[peh^1]	Like "pay," without the "y" sound.
Q	[koo^1]	Like "coo."
R	[e^1 ruh^5]	Like "era."
S	[es^2]	Like "es" in "estate."
T	[teh^1]	Like "tail" without "il."
V	[veh^1]	Like "veil" without "il."
X	[eets^2]	Like "eats."

C. Double and triple consonants 

The eight double consonants (also known as "digraphs") and the one triple consonant (or "trigraph") bear the names of each letter in the cluster said together, as shown in the previous section.

LETTER	NAME
CH	[seh^1 hat^2]
GH	[zheh^1 hat^2]
GI	[zheh^1 ee^1]
KH	[ka^1 hat^2]
NG	[en^1 zheh^1]
NGH	[en^1 zheh^2 hat^2]
NH	[en^1 hat^2]
PH	[ef^2]
TH	[teh^1 hat^2]
TR	[teh^1 e^1 ruh^5]

III. The sounds of the letters

For simplicity's sake, the pronunciation examples below include words bearing only two of the six tones. The mid-high, level tone (Number 1) has no tone mark and the high-rising tone (Number 2) has the [´] tone mark.

A. Vowels

A vowel letter can represent one or more vowel sounds, depending on what other letter(s) appears before or after it in a word. Some vowel sounds are denoted with one symbol, but this symbol is shown differently in the pronunciation guides according to how it is pronounced together with other sounds in a combination. For example, the letter Â is generally shown as [u] (as in "sân" [shun^1]), but when it comes before Y, the combined pronunciation is shown as [ay], as in "mây" [may^1].

RECORDING	LETTER	SOUND	EXAMPLES
1	A	[a]	**ba** [*ba*^{1}] "three" – **ai** [*ie*^{1}] "who" – **lan** [*lan*^{1}] "orchid"
2		[ă]	**tay** [*tăy*^{1}] "hand" – **mau** [*măw*^{1}] "fast" – **banh** [*bănh*^{1}] "ball"
3		[uh]	**cua** [*koouh*^{1}] "crab" – **bia** [*beeuh*^{1}] "beer" – **mưa** [*mŭuh*^{1}] "rain"
4	Ă	[ă]	**ăn** [*ăn*^{1}] "to eat" – **lăn** [*lăn*^{1}] "to roll" – **bắt** [*băt*^{2}] "to catch"
5	Â	[u]	**sân** [*shun*^{1}] "yard" – **mây** [*may*^{1}] "cloud" – **nấp** [*nup*^{2}] "to hide"
6	E	[e]	**đen** [*den*^{1}] "black" – **nét** [*net*^{2}] "trait" – **neo** [*new*^{1}] "anchor"
7	Ê	[eh]	**êm** [*ehm*^{1}] "smooth" - **ếch** [*ehch*^{2}] "frog" – **kêu** [*kehw*^{1}] "to call"
8	I	[ee]	**im** [*eem*^{1}] "quiet" – **đi** [*dee*^{1}] "to go" – **xinh** [*seenh*^{1}] "pretty"
9		[y]	**hai** [*hie*^{1}] "two" – **nói** [*nahy*^{2}] "to say" – **tiên** [*tyehn*^{1}] "fairy"
10	O	[ah]	**ót** [*aht*^{2}] "nape" – **to** [*tah*^{1}] "big" – **lon** [*lahn*^{1}] "can"
11		[w]	**hoa** [*hwa*^{1}] "flower" – **cao** [*kahw*^{1}] "tall" – **toán** [*twan*^{2}] "math"
12	Ô	[oh]	**ôn** [*ohn*^{1}] "to review" – **xô** [*soh*^{1}] "pail" – **tốt** [*toht*^{2}] "good"
13	Ơ	[uh]	**ơn** [*uhn*^{1}] "favor" – **cơm** [*kuhm*^{1}] "rice" – **lớp** [*luhp*^{2}] "class"
14	U	[oo]	**cú** [*koo*^{2}] "owl" – **vui** [*vooy*^{1}] "happy" – **vua** [*voouh*^{1}] "king"
15		[w]	**qua** [*kwa*^{1}] "to pass" – **quên** [*kwehn*^{1}] "to forget"
16	Ư	[ŭ]	**sư** [*shŭ*^{1}] "monk" – **cưa** [*kŭuh*^{1}] "to saw" – **tươi** [*tŭuhy*^{1}] "fresh"
17	Y	[ee]	**ly** [*lee*^{1}] "glass" – **quý** [*kwee*^{2}] "precious" – **suýt** [*shweet*^{2}] "nearly"
18		[y]	**đây** [*day*^{1}] "here" – **cay** [*kăy*^{1}] "spicy" – **yên** [*yehn*^{1}] "peaceful"

B. Consonants

The pronunciation of consonants in Vietnamese varies depending on dialect. The chart below shows the most common ways of pronouncing the letters, including simple, double and triple letters. Sound equivalents in English in the note column are only approximate.

Some consonant letters appear only at the beginning of words, some only at the end, and some in both positions.

RECORDING	LETTER	SOUND	NOTE	EXAMPLES
1	B	[b]	Like "b" in "boy."	**bi** [*bee*^{1}] "marble" – **bán** [*ban*^{2}] "to sell" – **bao** [*bahw*^{1}] "bag"
2	C	[k]	Like "c" in "cat," unaspirated.	**cá** [*ka*^{2}] "fish" – **xác** [*sak*^{2}] "corpse" – **vác** [*vak*^{2}] "to carry"

RECORDING	LETTER	SOUND	NOTE	EXAMPLES
3	**CH**	[ch]	Like "ch" in "chin," with tongue body against hard palate.	**cho** [*chah*^{1}] "to give" – **sách** [*shăch*^{2}] "book"
4	**D**	[y]	Like "y" in "yes."	**da** [*ya*^{1}] "skin" – **dai** [*yie*^{1}] "chewy"
5	**Đ**	[d]	Like "d" in "day."	**đo** [*dah*^{1}] "to measure" – **đinh** [*deenh*^{1}] "nail"
6	**G**	[g]	Like "g" in "good."	**ga** [*ga*^{1}] "station" – **gói** [*gahy*^{2}] "packet" – **gai** [*gie*^{1}] "thorn"
7	**GH**	[g]	Like "g" in "ghetto," appearing before **e**, **ê**, **i**.	**ghe** [*ge*^{1}] "boat" – **ghi** [*gee*^{1}] "to record" – **ghế** [*geh*^{2}] "chair"
8	**GI**	[y]	Like "y" in "year."	**giá** [*ya*^{2}] "price" – **giây** [*yay*^{1}] "second" – **gió** [*yah*^{2}] "wind"
9	**H**	[h]	Like "h" in "high."	**hai** [*hie*^{1}] "two" – **ho** [*hah*^{1}] "to cough" – **hang** [*hang*^{1}] "cave"
10	**K**	[k]	Like "k" in "kid."	**kem** [*kem*^{1}] "cream" – **kênh** [*kehnh*^{1}] "canal"
11	**KH**	[kh]	Like "k" in "kid," strongly aspirated.	**khô** [*khoh*^{1}] "dry" – **khách** [*khăch*^{2}] "guest"
12	**L**	[l]	Like "l" in "lake."	**la** [*la*^{1}] "to yell" – **lân** [*lun*^{1}] "unicorn" – **lớn** [*luhn*^{2}] "large"
13	**M**	[m]	Like "m" in "man."	**ma** [*ma*^{1}] "ghost" – **mơ** [*muh*^{1}] "to dream" – **đêm** [*dehm*^{1}] "night"
14	**N**	[n]	Like "n" in "no."	**nai** [*nie*^{1}] "deer" – **sơn** [*shuhn*^{1}] "paint" – **tên** [*tehn*^{1}] "name"
15	**NG**	[ng]	Like "ng" in "song."	**ngai** [*ngie*^{1}] "throne" – **ngon** [*ngahn*^{1}] "delicious"
16	**NGH**	[ng]	Like "ng" in "song," appearing before **e**, **ê**, **i**.	**nghe** [*nge*^{1}] "to hear" – **nghi** [*ngee*^{1}] "to suspect"
17	**NH**	[nh]	Like "ny" in "canyon."	**nho** [*nhah*^{1}] "grape" – **nhanh** [*nhănh*^{1}] "quick"
18	**P**	[p]	Like "p" in "hop."	**đáp** [*dap*^{2}] "to reply" – **xếp** [*sehp*^{2}] "to fold" – **bếp** [*behp*^{2}] "kitchen"
19	**PH**	[f]	Like "ph" in "phone."	**pha** [*fa*^{1}] "to mix" – **phai** [*fie*^{1}] "to fade" – **phấn** [*fun*^{2}] "chalk"
20	**Q**	[k]	Like "q" in "quick."	**quai** [*kwie*^{1}] "strap" – **quê** [*kweh*^{1}] "countryside"
21	**R**	[r]	Like "r" in "red."	**rơi** [*ruhy*^{1}] "to fall" – **rắn** [*răn*^{2}] "snake" – **run** [*roon*^{1}] "to quiver"
22	**S**	[sh]	Like "s" in "sugar."	**sai** [*shie*^{1}] "wrong" – **số** [*shoh*^{2}] "number" – **sâu** [*shohw*^{1}] "deep"

RECORDING	LETTER	SOUND	NOTE	EXAMPLES
23	T	[t]	Like "t" in "stay," unaspirated.	**tây** [*tay*^{1}] "west" – **tai** [*tie*^{1}] "ear" – **mát** [*mat*^{2}] "cool"
24	TH	[th]	Like "t" in "time," strongly aspirated.	**thu** [*thoo*^{1}] "autumn" – **thơm** [*thuhm*^{1}] "scented"
25	TR	[tr]	Like "tr" in "tree."	**trai** [*trie*^{1}] "boy" – **tro** [*trah*^{1}] "ash" – **trăm** [*trăm*^{1}] "hundred"
26	V	[v]	Like "v" in "van."	**vớ** [*vuh*^{2}] "sock" – **vai** [*vie*^{1}] "shoulder" – **van** [*van*^{1}] "to beg"
27	X	[s]	Like "s" in "sun."	**xa** [*sa*^{1}] "far" – **xe** [*se*^{1}] "car" – **xanh** [*sănh*^{1}] "blue"

PRACTICE

A. Vowel letter recognition 

Listen to the recording and mark the letters you hear in the correct order.

	a	ă	â	e	ê	i	o	ô	ơ	u	ư	y
1												
2												
3												
4												
5												
6												
7												
8												
9												
10												
11												
12												

B. Single consonant letter recognition.

Listen to the recording and circle the letters you hear below:

1.	m	n	l
2.	b	p	v
3.	t	đ	c

4.	g	d	r
5.	x	s	c
6.	h	k	g
7.	n	r	m
8.	đ	b	t
9.	r	l	d
10.	p	v	đ

C. Double and triple consonant letter recognition

Listen to the recording and write the letters you hear in the correct order:

1. ______________ 2. ______________

3. ______________ 4. ______________

5. ______________ 6. ______________

7. ______________ 8. ______________

9. ______________ 10. ______________

D. Word recognition 

Listen to the recording and write the words you hear. All the words bear the mid-high, level tone, so no tone marks will be needed.

1. ______________ 2. ______________ 3. ______________

4. ______________ 5. ______________ 6. ______________

7. ______________ 8. ______________ 9. ______________

10. ______________ 11. ______________ 12. ______________

13. ______________ 14. ______________ 15. ______________

16. ______________ 17. ______________ 18. ______________

19. ______________ 20. ______________

CHAPTER 2

The Sound and Tone System of Vietnamese

Hệ Thống Âm Và Thanh Tiếng Việt

I. The sound system

Like all other languages, Vietnamese speech includes three types of sound: vowels, semi-vowels and consonants.

A. The vowels 

There are eleven vowel sounds in Vietnamese. Of these sounds, nine correspond to one letter each and two correspond to two letters each. The phonetic transcriptions shown in brackets below are based on common word-to-sound correspondence in American English. Sound comparisons between Vietnamese and English are approximate. For simplicity, the examples below all bear the mid-high, level tone (without a tone mark).

	SOUND	LETTER	NOTE	EXAMPLES
1	[a]	**a**	Like "a" in "father."	**ba** [*ba*[1]] "three" – **la** [*la*[1]] "to yell"
2	[ă]	**a, ă**	Like [a], with lips slightly closed.	**lau** [*lăw*[1]] "to wipe" – **lăn** [*lăn*[1]] "to roll"
3	[u]	**â**	Like "u" in "fun."	**sân** [*shun*[1]] "yard" – **nâu** [*nohw*[1]] "brown"
4	[e]	**e**	Like "e" in "pen."	**xe** [*se*[1]] "car" – **quen** [*kwen*[1]] "familiar"
5	[eh]	**ê**	Like "a" in "apron," without the "y" sound.	**dê** [*yeh*[1]] "goat" – **đêm** [*dehm*[1]] "night"
6	[ee]	**i, y**	Like "ee" in "bee."	**đi** [*dee*[1]] "to go" – **ly** [*lee*[1]] "glass"
7	[ah]	**o**	Like "o" in "hot."	**to** [*tah*[1]] "big" – **lon** [*lahn*[1]] "can"
8	[oh]	**ô**	Like "oh," without the "w" sound.	**tô** [*toh*[1]] "bowl" – **hôn** [*hohn*[1]] "to kiss"

	SOUND	LETTER	NOTE	EXAMPLES
9	[uh]	ơ	Like "a" in "about."	**nơ** [*nuh*¹] "bow" – **cơm** [*kuhm*¹] "rice"
10	[oo]	u	Like "oo" in "shoo."	**xu** [*soo*¹] "cent" – **mun** [*moon*¹] "black"
11	[ŭ]	ư	Like [oo], with lips unrounded.	**sư** [*shŭ*¹] "monk" – **lưng** [*lŭng*¹] "back"

Notes:

- Two of the vowels occur only in closed syllables (followed by a consonant): **[ă]** (letter **ă**): **tắm** [*tăm*²] "to bathe," **cắt** [*kăt*²] "to cut;" and **[u]** (letter **â**): **lân** [*lun*¹] "unicorn," **mâm** [*mum*¹] "tray." The rest of the vowels occur in both open syllables (not followed by a consonant) and closed syllables.
- The vowel **[ă]** is written with the letter **ă** in most contexts (**ăn** [*ăn*¹] "to eat," **răng** [*răng*¹] "tooth," **năm** [*năm*¹] "year"), except when it comes before the letters **u**, **y**, **nh** or **ch**, when it is written as **a**: **lau** [*lăw*¹] "to wipe," **may** [*măy*¹] "to sew," **chanh** [*chănh*¹] "lemon," **xách** [*săch*²] "to carry."
- The vowel sound **[ee]** is written with the letter **i** when:
  a. appearing as one syllable in a reduplicative word: **âm ỉ** [*um*¹ *ee*⁴] "smoldering," **í ới** [*ee*² *uhy*²] "boisterously," **ì ầm** [*ee*⁵ *um*⁵] "roaring"
  b. appearing before consonant letters: **xinh** [*seenh*¹] "pretty," **tim** [*teem*¹] "heart," **lính** [*leenh*²] "soldier," **mít** [*meet*²] "jackfruit"
  c. appearing alone after the letters **b**, **ch**, **d**, **đ**, **g**, **m**, **n**, **ngh**, **nh**, **r**, **s**, **th**, **tr**, **v** and **x**: **bi** [*bee*¹] "marble," **di** [*yee*¹] "to move," **đi** [*dee*¹] "to go," **mi** [*mee*¹] "eyelashes," **chi** [*chee*¹] "to spend"
  d. appearing before another vowel letter: **hiu** [*heew*¹] "gloomy," **tia** [*teeuh*¹] "ray," **xíu** [*seew*²] "tiny."
- The vowel sound **[ee]** is usually written with the letter **y** when:
  a. appearing alone as a word: **ý** [*ee*²] "idea," **y** [*ee*¹] "exactly," **ỷ** [*ee*⁴] "to rely"
  b. it is the full vowel in a diphthong (to be discussed in detail later in this chapter): **quý** [*kwee*²] "precious," **tuy** [*twee*¹] "although," **quỳnh** [*kweenh*⁵] "Queen of the Night flower"
- After the letters **h**, **k**, **l**, **m**, and **t**, the letter **i** is usually used with Vietnamese native words and the letter **y** is used with words of Chinese origin:

LETTER	VIETNAMESE NATIVE WORDS	WORDS OF CHINESE ORIGIN
h	**hủ hỉ** [*hee*⁴ *hee*⁴] "to talk intimately"	**hỷ sự** [*hee*⁴ *shŭ*⁶] "joy"
k	**kì cọ** [*kee*⁵ *kah*⁶] "to scrub"	**kỳ dị** [*kee*⁵ *yee*⁵] "exotic"
l	**li ti** [*lee*¹ *tee*¹] "tiny"	**ly dị** [*lee*¹ *yee*⁶] "to divorce"
m	**mì** [*mee*⁵] "egg noodles"	**mỹ thuật** [*mee*³ *thwut*⁶] "arts"
t	**tỉ ti** [*tee*⁴ *tee*¹] "(to cry) softly"	**tỷ lệ** [*tee*⁴ *leh*⁶] "ratio"

B. The semi-vowels 

Semi-vowels are vowels partially pronounced when they go with a full vowel in diphthongs and triphthongs (see the next section for a detailed discussion of these sound combinations). Vietnamese has four semi-vowels as follows:

	SOUND	LETTER	EXAMPLES
1	[uh]	a	**đĩa** [*deeuh³*] "plate" – **múa** [*moouh²*] "to dance" – **mưa** [*mŭuh¹*] "rain"
2	[y]	i, y	**yêu** [*jehw¹*] "to love" – **tiền** [*tyehn⁵*] "money" – **voi** [*vahy¹*] "elephant" – **truyện** [*trwyehn⁶*] "story" – **hay** [*hăy¹*] "interesting" – **lấy** [*lay²*] "to take"
3	[w]	o, u	**hoa** [*hwa¹*] "flower" – **xoè** [*swe⁵*] "to spread (wings)" – **quà** [*kwa⁵*] "gift" – **tuỷ** [*twee⁴*] "bone marrow"
4	[ŭ]	ư	**trường** [*trŭuhng⁵*] "school" – **cười** [*kŭuhy⁵*] "to laugh" – **rượu** [*rŭuhw⁶*] "alcohol"

Notes:

- The semi-vowel **[uh]** (letter **a**) appears in the combinations **ia**, **ua** and **ưa**.
- The semi-vowel **[y]** is written as letter **i** when:
  a. appearing in the combination **iê: chiên** [*chyehn¹*] "to fry," **phiên** [*fyehn¹*] "turn"
  b. appearing in the combination **ai**, **oi**, **ôi**, **ơi**, **ui** and **ưi: sai** [*shie¹*] "wrong," **coi** [*kahy¹*] "to watch," **tôi** [*tohy¹*] "I," **nơi** [*nuhy¹*] "place," **núi** [*nooy²*] "mountain," **ngửi** [*ngŭy⁴*] "to smell."
- The semi-vowel **[y]** is written as letter **y** when:
  a. appearing at the beginning of a word in the combination **yê: yên** [*yehn¹*] "peaceful," **yếu** [*yew²*] "weak"
  b. appearing in the combination **ay** and **ây: tay** [*tăy¹*] "hand," **đây** [*day¹*] "here"
  c. appearing in the combination **uyê: tuyết** [*twyeht²*] "snow," **quyền** [*kwyehn⁵*] "right."
- The semi-vowel **[w]** is written as letter **o** when appearing in the combinations **oa**, **oă** and **oe**, after the letters **d**, **đ**, **g**, **h**, **kh**, **l**, **ng**, **nh**, **t**, **th** and **x: khoá** [*khwa²*] "key," **thoăn thoắt** [*thwăn¹ thwăt²*] "quick," **loe** [*lwe¹*] "flare."
- **[w]** is always written as **u** in combinations beginning with **q: qua**, **quă**, **quâ**, **que**, **quê**, **quô**, **quơ** and **quy: quần** [*kwun⁵*] "pants," **quét** [*kwet²*] "to sweep," **quốc** [*kwohk²*] "nation," **quỳ** [*kwee⁵*] "to kneel."
- **[w]** is also written as **u** when following other consonant letters in the combinations **uê**, **uô**, **uơ** and **uy: thuê** [*thweh¹*] "to rent," **muốn** [*mwohn²*] "to want," **thuở** [*thwuh⁴*] "period," **thuỷ** [*thwee⁴*] "water."

C. The diphthongs 

A diphthong is a combination of a full vowel and a semi-vowel. Two orders are possible: [full vowel + semi-vowel] and [semi-vowel + full vowel]. There are 28 diphthongs in Vietnamese.

RECORDING	SOUND	SPELLING	NOTE	EXAMPLES
1	[ie]	ai	Like "ie" in "tie."	**hai** [*hie¹*] "two" – **mai** [*mie¹*] "tomorrow"

RECORDING	SOUND	SPELLING	NOTE	EXAMPLES
2	[ahw]	**ao**	Like “ow” in “now.”	**sao** [*shahw*^{1}] “star” – **bao** [*bahw*^{1}] “bag”
3	[ăy]	**ay**	Like “i” in “write.”	**bay** [*băy*^{1}] “to fly” – **may** [*măy*^{1}] “to sew”
4	[ăw]	**au**	Like “ou” in “clout.”	**sau** [*shăw*^{1}] “after” – **đau** [*dăw*^{1}] “painful”
5	[ay]	**ây**	Like “ay” in “say.”	**cây** [*kay*^{1}] “tree” – **lây** [*lay*^{1}] “contagious”
6	[ohw]	**âu**	Like “ow” in “show.”	**đâu** [*dohw*^{1}] “where” – **nâu** [*nohw*^{1}] “brown”
7	[ew]	**eo**	Like “e” in “pen” followed by “w.”	**leo** [*lew*^{1}] “to climb” – **neo** [*new*^{1}] “anchor”
8	[ehw]	**êu**	Like “ew” in “ew.”	**kêu** [*kehw*^{1}] “to call” – **rêu** [*rehw*^{1}] “moss”
9	[eeuh]	**ia**	Like “e” in “here,” without “r.”	**kia** [*keeuh*^{1}] “there” – **đĩa** [*deeuh*^{3}] “plate”
10	[yeh]	**iê, yê**	Like “ye” in “yet.”	**kiếm** [*kyehm*^{2}] “sword” – **yên** [*yehn*^{1}] “peaceful”
11	[iw]	**iu**	Like “ee” followed by “w.”	**níu** [*neew*^{2}] “to hold on” – **xỉu** [*seew*^{4}] “to faint”
12	[ahy]	**oi**	Like “oi” in “hoist.”	**coi** [*kahy*^{1}] “to watch” – **voi** [*vahy*^{1}] “elephant”
13	[ohy]	**ôi**	Like “oi,” “o” pronounced closed.	**xôi** [*sohy*^{1}] “sticky rice” – **nôi** [*nohy*^{1}] “cradle”
14	[uhy]	**ơi**	Like “a” in “again,” followed by “y.”	**nơi** [*nuhy*^{1}] “place” – **bơi** [*buhy*^{1}] “to swim”
15	[oouh]	**ua**	Like “ure” in “sure,” without “r.”	**cua** [*koouh*^{1}] “crab” – **mua** [*moouh*^{1}] “to buy”
16	[wa]	**oa, ua**	Like “wa” in “watt.”	**loa** [*lwa*^{1}] “loudspeaker” – **quan** [*kwan*^{1}] “mandarin”
17	[wă]	**oă, uă**	Like “wa,” pronounced closed.	**xoăn** [*swăn*^{1}] “curly” – **quăng** [*kwăng*^{1}] “to throw”
18	[wu]	**uâ**	Like “ua” in “kumquat.”	**xuân** [*swun*^{1}] “spring” – **quân** [*kwun*^{1}] “soldier”
19	[we]	**oe, ue**	Like “we” in “wet.”	**khoe** [*khwe*^{1}] “to show off” – **quen** [*kwen*^{1}] “familiar”
20	[weh]	**uê**	Like “wa” in “way.”	**thuê** [*thweh*^{1}] “to rent” – **quên** [*kwehn*^{1}] “to forget”

RECORDING	SOUND	SPELLING	NOTE	EXAMPLES
21	[wee]	**uy**	Like "wee" in "weed."	**suy** [*shwee*[1]] "to decline" – **quýt** [*kweet*[2]] "tangerine"
22	[ooy]	**ui**	Like "u" in "thru" followed by "y."	**xui** [*sooy*[1]] "unlucky" – **vui** [*vooy*[1]] "happy"
23	[woh]	**uô**	Like "w" followed by a closed "o."	**luôn** [*lwohn*[1]] "always" – **chuông** [*chwohng*[1]] "bell"
24	[wuh]	**uơ**	Like "w" followed by "a" in "again."	**thuở** [*thwuh*[4]] "period" – **quơ** [*kwuh*[1]] "to wave"
25	[ŭuh]	**ưa**	Like "u" in "thru," unrounded, followed by "a" in "again."	**cưa** [*kŭuh*[1]] "to saw" – **xưa** [*sŭuh*[1]] "old times"
26	[ŭuh]	**ươ**	Like unrounded "u" as above, followed by "a" in "again."	**lươn** [*lŭuhn*[1]] "eel" – **bước** [*bŭuhk*[2]] "step"
27	[ŭy]	**ưi**	Like unrounded "u," followed by "y."	**ngửi** [*ngŭy*[4]] "to smell" – **cửi** [*kŭy*[4]] "loom"
28	[ŭw]	**ưu**	Like unrounded "u," followed by "w."	**hưu** [*hŭw*[1]] "retirement" – **lưu** [*lŭw*[1]] "to keep"

Notes:

- Diphthongs are divided into three groups according to syllable structure:
  a. Group 1: Diphthongs that appear only in open syllables (not followed by a consonant); 1, 2, 3, 4, 5, 6, 7, 8, 9, 11, 12, 13, 14, 15, 22, 25, 27 and 28 in the chart above: **tai** [*tie*[1]] "ear," **cao** [*kahw*[1]] "tall," **say** [*shăy*[1]] "drunk," **mau** [*măw*[1]] "fast," **đâu** [*dohw*[1]] "where," **mèo** [*mew*[5]] "cat," **nếu** [*nehw*[2]] "if," **mía** [*meeuh*[2]] "sugar cane," **níu** [*neew*[2]] "to hold on," **nói** [*nahy*[2]] "to say," **môi** [*mohy*[1]] "lip," **mới** [*muhy*[2]] "new," **thua** [*thoouh*[1]] "to lose," **núi** [*nooy*[2]] "mountain," **chưa** [*chŭuh*[1]] "not yet," **ngửi** [*ngŭy*[4]] "to smell," **cừu** [*kưw*[5]] "sheep."
  b. Group 2: Diphthongs that appear both in open syllables (not followed by a consonant) and in closed syllables (followed by a consonant); 16, 19, 20, 21 and 24 in the chart above: **qua** [*kwa*[1]] "to pass" & **quan** [*kwan*[1]] "mandarin," **que** [*kwe*[1]] "stick" & **quen** [*kewn*[1]] "familiar," **quê** [*kweh*[1]] "rustic" & **quên** [*kwehn*[1]] "to forget," **quỳ** [*kwee*[5]] "to kneel" & **quỳnh** [*kweenh*[5]] "Queen of Night flower," **thuở** [*thwuh*[4]] "period" & **huởn** [*hwuhn*[4]] "idle."
  c. Group 3: Diphthongs that appear only in closed syllables (always followed by a consonant); 10, 17, 18, 23 and 26 in the chart above: **tiền** [*tyehn*[5]] "money," **hoặc** [*hwăk*[6]] "or," **tuần** [*twun*[5]] "week," **thuốc** [*thwohk*[2]] "medication," **nước** [*nưuhk*[2]] "water."
- For lack of a better pronunciation guide, the diphthongs in (25) and (26) are shown as the same, and sound similar. However, in (25), the full vowel is **[ŭ]** and the semi-vowel is **[uh]**, which is spelled **ưa**. In (26) **[ŭ]** is the semi-vowel and **[uh]** is the full vowel, which is spelled **ươ**. Compare the words **nứa** (containing Diphthong 25) [*nŭuh*[2]] "a kind of bamboo," and **nước** (containing Diphthong 26) [*nŭuhk*[2]] "water."

D. The triphthongs

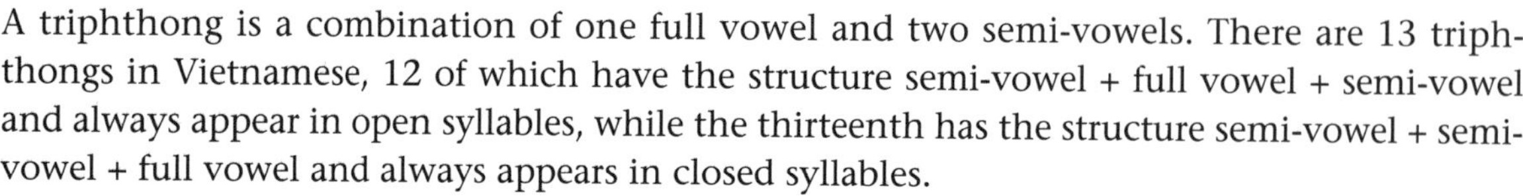

A triphthong is a combination of one full vowel and two semi-vowels. There are 13 triphthongs in Vietnamese, 12 of which have the structure semi-vowel + full vowel + semi-vowel and always appear in open syllables, while the thirteenth has the structure semi-vowel + semi-vowel + full vowel and always appears in closed syllables.

	SOUND	SPELLING	NOTE	EXAMPLES
1	[yehw]	**yêu, iêu**	Like "yie" in "yield," followed by "w."	**yêu** [*yehw*^{1}] "to love" – **tiêu** [*tyehw*^{1}] "black pepper"
2	[wohy]	**uôi**	Like "w" followed by closed "o" and "y."	**đuôi** [*dwohy*^{1}] "tail" – **nguôi** [*ngwohy*^{1}] "to subside"
3	[ŭuhy]	**ươi**	Like unrounded "u" followed by "a" in "again" and "y."	**tươi** [*tŭuhy*^{1}] "fresh" – **rươi** [*rŭuhy*^{1}] "sandworm"
4	[ŭuhw]	**ươu**	Like unrounded "u" followed by "a" in "again" and "w."	**hươu** [*hŭuhw*^{1}] "stag" – **rượu** [*rŭuhw*^{6}] "alcohol"
5	[weeuh]	**uya**	Like "wi" in "with," followed by "a" in "again."	**khuya** [*khweeuh*^{1}] "late at night"
6	[weew]	**uyu**	Like "wi" in "with" followed by "w."	**khuỷu** [*khweew*^{4}] "elbow" – **khuỵu** [*khweew*^{6}]"to stoop"
7	[wie]	**oai, uai**	Like "wi" in "wide."	**khoai** [*khwie*^{1}] "yam" – **quai** [*kwie*^{1}] "strap"
8	[wăy]	**oay, uay**	Like "ui" in "quite."	**xoáy** [*swăy*^{1}] "to whirl" – **quay** [*kwăy*^{1}] "to spin"
9	[way]	**uây**	Like "uai" in "quail."	**khuây** [*khway*^{1}] "solace" – **quây** [*kway*^{1}] "to enclose"
10	[wahw]	**uao**	Like "wow."	**quơ quào** [*kwuh*^{1} *kwahw*^{5}] "to scratch"
11	[wăw]	**uau**	Like "wow" with a shorter vowel.	**quạu** [*kwăw*^{6}] "sullen"
12	[wew]	**oeo, ueo**	Like "we" in "wet," followed by "w."	**ngoằn ngoèo** [*ngwăn*^{5} *ngwew*^{5}] "winding"
13	[wyeh]	**uyê**	Like "wi" in "with," followed by "e" in "yet."	**khuyên** [*khwyehn*^{1}] "to advise"

Notes:

The triphthongs might look overwhelming, but almost half of them are uncommon, appearing in only a few words (4, 5,6, 10, 11 and 12 in the chart above).

E. The consonants 

There are 22 consonants in Vietnamese. As in the previous sections, the notes comparing their pronunciation with English sounds are approximate.

	SOUND	LETTER	NOTE	EXAMPLES
1	[b]	b	Like "b" in "boy."	**ba** [*ba*[1]] "three" – **bao** [*bahw*[1]] "bag"
2	[k]	c, k, q	Like "c" in "cat" or "k" in "kit," pronounced without aspiration.	**cao** "tall" [*kahw*[1]] – **kem** [*kem*[1]] "cream" – **que** [*kwe*[1]] "stick"
3	[ch]	ch	Like "ch" in "chair," with tongue against hard palate.	**chai** [*chie*[1]] "bottle" – **chua** [*choouh*[1]] "sour"
4	[y]	d, gi	Like "y" in "yes."	**dao** [*yahw*[1]] "knife" – **giá** [*ya*[2]] "price"
5	[d]	đ	Like "d" in "do."	**đau** [*dăw*[1]] "pain" – **đi** [*dee*[1]] "to go"
6	[g]	g, gh	Like "g" in "go," pronounced softly.	**gan** [*gan*[1]] "liver" – **ghe** [*ge*[1]] "boat"
7	[h]	h	Like "h" in "hat."	**hai** [*hie*[1]] "two" – **heo** [*hew*[1]] "pig"
8	[kh]	kh	Like "k" in "key," pronounced very aspirated.	**khỉ** [*khee*[4]] "monkey" – **khó** [*khah*[2]] "difficult"
9	[l]	l	Like "l" in "love."	**lon** [*lahn*[1]] "can" – **ly** [*lee*[1]] "glass"
10	[m]	m	Like "m" in "mother."	**mưa** [*mŭuh*[1]] "rain" – **nam** [*nam*[1]] "south"
11	[n]	n	Like "n" in "name."	**nai** [*nie*[1]] "deer" – **lan** [*lan*[1]] "orchid"
12	[ng]	ng, ngh	Like "ng" in "long."	**ngai** "throne" [*ngie*[1]] – **nghe** [*nge*[1]] "to hear"
13	[ny]	nh	Like "ny" in "canyon."	**nhanh** [*nhănh*[1]] "fast" – **nhai** [*nhie*[1]] "to chew"
14	[p]	p	Like "p" in "cap."	**họp** [*hahp*[6]] "to meet" – **hẹp** [hep[6]] "narrow"
15	[f]	ph	Like "ph" in "phone."	**phao** [*fahw*[1]] "buoy" – **pha** [*fa*[1]] "to brew"
16	[r]	r	Like "r" in "rice."	**rau** [*răw*[1]] "vegetable" – **rêu** [*rehw*[1]] "moss"
17	[sh]	s	Like "s" in "sugar."	**sai** [*shie*[1]] "wrong" – **sâu** [*shohw*[1]] "deep"
18	[t]	t	Like "t" in "tea," pronounced without aspiration.	**tai** [*tie*[1]] "ear" – **tô** [*toh*[1]] "bowl"
19	[th]	th	Like "th" in "thyme," pronounced very aspirated.	**thu** [*thoo*[1]] "autumn" – **thăm** [*thăm*[1]] "to visit"
20	[tr]	tr	Like "tr" in "try."	**trai** [*trie*[1]] "boy" – **trên** [*trehn*[1]] "above"
21	[v]	v	Like "v" in "van."	**vui** [*vooy*[1]] "happy" – **voi** [*vahy*[1]] "elephant"
22	[s]	x	Like "s" in "sun."	**xa** [*sa*[1]] "far" – **xu** [*soo*[1]] "cent"

Notes:

- Consonants are divided into three groups according to their position in words:
  a. Group 1: Consonants that appear only at the beginning of a word (1, 4, 5, 6, 7, 8, 9, 15, 16, 17, 19, 20, 21 and 22 in the chart above): **bốn** [*bohn*[2]] "four," **da** [*ya*[1]] "skin," **đá** [*da*[2]]

"rock," **gái** [*gie*^{2}] "girl," **hai** [*hie*^{1}] "two," **khô** [*khoh*^{1}] "dry," **lau** [*lăw*^{1}] "to wipe," **phở** [*fuh*^{4}] "noodle soup," **ra** [*ra*^{1}] "to exit," **sôi** [*shohy*^{1}] "to boil," **thơm** [*thuhm*^{1}] "scented," **trái** [*trie*^{2}] "left," **và** [*va*^{5}] "and," **xa** [*sa*^{1}] "far."

b. Group 2: Only one consonant, **[p]**, letter **p**, (14) appears exclusively at the end of words: **nếp** [*nehp*^{2}] "sticky rice," **lớp** [*luhp*^{2}] "class," **sáp** [*shap*^{2}] "wax." Note that the spelling **ph** is for the consonant **[f]**, which appears at the beginning of words (**phía** [*feeuh*^{2}] "side," **pháo** [*fahw*^{2}] "firecracker").

c. Group 3: Consonants that appear both at the beginning and the end of words (2, 3, 10, 11, 12, 13 and18 in the chart above): **cá** [*ka*^{2}] "fish" & **hạc** [*hak*^{6}] "crane," **chó** [*chah*^{2}] "dog" & **ếch** [*ehch*^{2}] "frog," **mèo** [*mew*^{5}] "cat" & **bướm** [*bŭuhm*^{2}] "butterfly," **nai** [*nie*^{1}] "deer" & **ngan** [*ngan*^{1}] "Muscovy duck," **nghé** [*nge*^{2}] "buffalo calf" & **lang** [*lang*^{1}] "wolf," **nhện** [*nhehn*^{6}] "spider" & **tinh tinh** [*teenh*^{1} *teenh*^{1}] "chimpanzee," **tôm** [*tohm*^{1}] "shrimp" & **vịt** [*veet*^{6}] "duck."

- Final consonants in Vietnamese are "unreleased," meaning they are barely audible at the end of words.
- The letters **d** and **gi** are commonly pronounced **[y]** (4) in southern Vietnam and most of the central region. In the northern part of central Vietnam and in northern Vietnam, these letters are pronounced **[z]**. In this book, the sound **[y]** is used throughout for words beginning with the letters **d** or **gi**.

  Since **d** and **gi** share the same sound, context can help distinguish between pairs of words such as **dây** [*yay*^{1}] "string" and **giây** [*yay*^{1}] "second (60th of a minute)" when they are spoken.
- There are two "secondary consonants," **[m]** and **[p]**, that appear at the end of several words but are not shown in the spelling. These sounds occur in the following cases and are indicated in the pronunciation guides:

  a. When a word ends with the consonant **[ng]** (letter **ng**) and contains one of the "round vowels" represented by the letters **o**, **ô** and **u**, the secondary consonant **[m]** is added at the end of the word: **mong** [*mahngm*^{1}] "to expect," **không** [*khohngm*^{1}] "no, not," **chung** [*choongm*^{1}] "common."

  b. When a word ends with the consonant **[k]** (letter **c**) and contains one of the round vowels represented by the letters **o**, **ô** and **u**, the secondary consonant **[p]** is added at the end of the word: **học** [*hahkp*^{6}] "to learn," **dốc** [*yohkp*^{2}] "slope," **chúc** [*chookp*^{2}] "to wish."

II. The tone system 

Vietnamese is a tonal language. A tone is a fixed pitch assigned to a word to give it a distinct meaning. There are six tones in Vietnamese, each indicated with a superscript number in the pronunciation guides that corresponds to the chart below:

	TONE DESCRIPTION	TONE MARK	MARK NAME	EXAMPLES
1	Mid-high, level	N/A	N/A	**la** [*la*^{1}] "to shout" **ma** [*ma*^{1}] "ghost"
2	High, rising	´	**sắc** "sharp"	**lá** [*la*^{2}] "leaf" **má** [*ma*^{2}] "cheek"

	TONE DESCRIPTION	TONE MARK	MARK NAME	EXAMPLES
3	Mid-high, rising, glottalized	~	**ngã** "tumble"	**lã** [*la*^{3}] "water" **mã** [*ma*^{3}] "horse"
4	Mid-low, rising	?	**hỏi** "asking"	**lả** [*la*^{4}] "exhausted" **mả** [*ma*^{4}] "tomb"
5	Mid-low, falling	`	**huyền** "deep"	**là** [*la*^{5}] "to be" **mà** [*ma*^{5}] "but"
6	Low-falling, glottalized	.	**nặng** "heavy"	**lạ** [*la*^{6}] "strange" **mạ** [*ma*^{6}] "to gild"

The tones can be grasped more easily in the following chart that shows their relative pitches:

1	2	3	4	5	6
Mid-high, level	High, rising	Mid-high, rising, glottalized	Mid-low, rising	Mid-low, falling	Low-falling, glottalized
la	**lá**	**lã**	**lả**	**là**	**lạ**

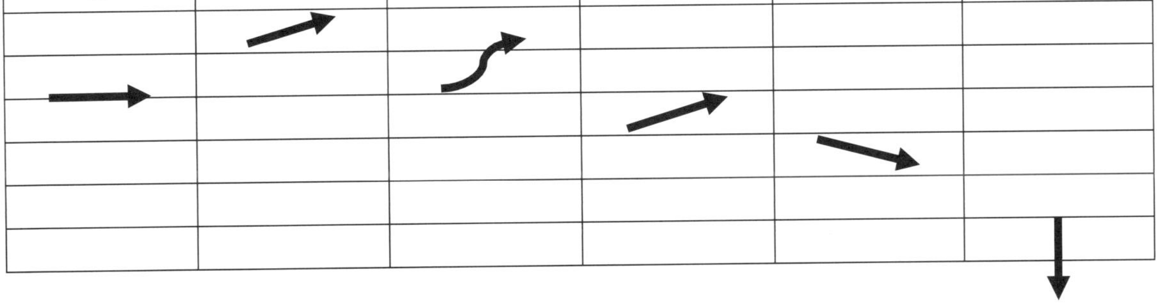

Notes on tones:

- Only in most northern dialects do all six tones exist, with a clear distinction between the mid-high, rising and glottalized tone (as in **lã**) and the mid-low, rising tone (as in **lả**). In the central and southern regions, these two tones normally merge into one resembling the latter tone.
- The tones heard in the audio recordings are made in a non-dialectal register for practical purposes. Tone patterns in regional dialects can differ anywhere from slightly to greatly.
- Pay attention to the fact that the mid-high, level tone is a "tone" in its own right, although there is no accent mark for it. In other words, this is an "unmarked" tone.
- A word can be pronounced with up to six different tones, yielding six different meanings. However, not every word has all six tones. When a word is associated with a tone but contains no meaning, it is called an "accidental gap" in the language. For example, only three of the following six forms are real "words" (with a meaning): **cua** [*koouh*^{1}] "crab," **cúa** [*koouh*^{2}] "palate," ***cũa** [*koouh*^{3}] (no meaning), **của** [*koouh*^{4}] "of," ***cùa** [*koouh*^{5}] (no meaning), ***cụa** [*koouh*^{6}] (no meaning).

- Vietnamese has a great number of monosyllabic words but also some multisyllabic words. Syllables are written separately, with a space between them, as in **mắc cỡ** "embarrassed." Separately, **mắc** can mean "expensive" and **cỡ** can mean "size," but in this word, the syllables do not have these meanings. In multisyllabic words, syllables can have the same tone or different tones. For examples, in **vi vu** "the sound made by the wind," both have the high-level tone, while in **xí xọn** "talkative," a high-rising tone is followed by a low-falling, glottalized tone.
- If a syllable or a word ends in a *stop consonant* (**c**, **ch**, **p**, or **t**), only two tones are possible, namely the high-rising tone (Number 2 in the chart) and the low-falling, glottalized tone (Number 6 in the chart). Some examples are **cóc** [*kahkp*[2]] "toad," **cọc** [*kahkp*[6]] "stake," **sách** [*shăch*[2]] "book," **sạch** [*shăch*[6]] "clean," **lớp** [*luhp*[2]] "class," **lợp** [*luhp*[6]] "to roof," **hát** [*hat*[2]] "to sing," **hạt** [*hat*[6]] "seed."

Notes on tone marks:

- The Vietnamese term for "mark" is **dấu**. To name the tone marks, one will say (from Number 2 to Number 6 in the chart), "**dấu sắc, dấu ngã, dấu hỏi, dấu huyền, dấu nặng.**" When referring to the tones themselves, for which the term is **thanh**, one should say, "**thanh ngang** (1), **thanh sắc** (2), **thanh ngã** (3), **thanh hỏi** (4), **thanh huyền** (5), **thanh nặng** (6)."
- Tone marks, also known as *diacritics*, are placed over a vowel letter to indicate its tone (or under, for the low-falling, glottalized tone). In a diphthong, the tone mark is placed over (or under) the vowel that represents a full vowel, not on the vowel letter that represents a semi-vowel. A difference in the position of tone marks can be observed in the words **quả** [*kwa*[4]] "fruit," where **a** is a full vowel (thus bearing the tone mark) and **u** is a semi-vowel, and **của** [*koouh*[4]] "of," where **u** is a full vowel (bearing the tone mark) and **a** is a semi-vowel. The same rule applies to words containing triphthongs: **người** [*ngŭuhy*[5]] "person" (**ơ** represents a full vowel), **truyện** [*trwyehn*[6]] "story," etc.
- A *tone mark* can co-occur with the three *vocalic marks* (Chapter 1) in many instances. While the arrangement of the marks is automatic with word processing on a computer, it should be properly done when hand-writing words. For example, the "sharp" mark should be placed to the right of the circumflex, as in the word **tốt** [*toht*[2]] "good," or right above the breve, as in **đắng** [*dăng*[2]] "bitter." Take care to note the position of diacritics when learning words.

PRACTICE

A. Vowel recognition 

Listen to the recording and circle the word with the vowel you hear:

1	ban	băn	bân	bơn
2	con	cân	côn	cơn
3	lung	lưng	long	lông
4	minh	manh	măn	mân
5	sen	sên	sinh	sanh

B. Diphthong recognition 

Listen to the recording and circle the word with the diphthong you hear:

1	cai	cay	cây	coi
2	mau	mao	mâu	môi
3	nêu	nao	neo	nâu
4	hiên	heo	hêu	hiu
5	tưa	tua	tuôn	tuân

C. Triphthong recognition 

Listen to the recording and circle the word with the triphthong you hear:

1	quai	quay	quây	quau
2	nghiêu	ngươu	ngoao	người
3	khoeo	khuyu	khuya	khuyên
4	liêu	luyên	loai	loay
5	tươi	tuôi	tiêu	tuyên

D. Consonant recognition 

Listen to the recording and circle the word with the consonant you hear:

1	sai	chai	dai	xai
2	bai	phai	mai	vai
3	hai	khai	cai	gai
4	tai	thai	đai	lai
5	nai	nhai	ngai	mai

E. Tone recognition 

Listen to the recording and circle the word with the tone you hear:

1	tiên	tiền	tiến	tiện
2	bông	bổng	bỗng	bống
3	đai	đài	đãi	đại
4	lâu	lầu	lẩu	lậu
5	lánh	lành	lãnh	lạnh
6	tình	tỉnh	tĩnh	tính

Chào anh chị. Tôi tên là Huy. Tôi là người Việt. Hello, guys. My name is Huy. I'm Vietnamese.

Chào hai bạn, tôi là Rosa, từ Tây Ban Nha đến. Hello, friends. I'm Rosa from Spain

Còn anh, anh tên là gì? And you, what's your name?

Tên tôi là Laurent và tôi là người Pháp. My name is Laurent and I'm French.

Rất hân hạnh được gặp hai bạn! Very pleased to meet you two.

Tôi cũng vậy. Me too.

Đến giờ rồi! Chúng ta cùng vào lớp nhé. It's time already. Let's go to our class together.

CHAPTER 3

Greetings and Introductions

Chào Hỏi Và Giới Thiệu

DIALOGUE 1

Huy is sitting in a campus cafeteria with two international students he's just found out are classmates in his political science class. They start their first encounter by introducing themselves to one another.

HUY **Chào anh chị. Tôi tên là Huy. Tôi là người Việt, còn anh chị là người nước nào?**
chahw^{5} ănh^{1} chee^{6} // tohy^{1} tehn^{1} la^{5} hwee^{1} // tohy^{1} la^{5} ngŭuhy^{5} vyeht^{6} // kahn^{5} ănh^{1} chee^{6} la^{5} ngŭuhy^{5} nŭuhk^{2} nahw^{5}
Hello "brother" (and) "sister" My name is Huy. I'm Vietnamese, and what nationality are you?

ROSA **Chào hai bạn, tôi là Rosa, từ Tây Ban Nha đến. Còn anh, anh tên là gì?**
chahw^{5} hie^{1} ban^{6} // tohy^{1} la^{5} Rosa tŭ^{5} tay^{1} ban^{1} nha^{1} dehn^{2} // kahn^{5} ănh^{1} ănh^{1} tehn^{1} la^{5} yee^{5}
Hello you two (friends), I'm Rosa, from Spain. And you, what's your name?

LAURENT **Chào Rosa và Huy. Tên tôi là Laurent và tôi là người Pháp.**
chahw^{5} rosa va^{5} hwee^{1} // tehn^{1} tohy^{1} la^{5} Laurent va^{5} tohy^{1} la^{5} ngŭuhy^{5} fap^{2}
Hello, Rosa and Huy. My name is Laurent and I am French.

HUY **Các bạn nói tiếng Việt giỏi lắm! Rất hân hạnh được gặp hai bạn!**
kak^{2} ban^{6} nahy^{2} tyehng^{2} vyeht^{6} yahy^{4} lăm^{2}// rut^{2} hun^{1} hănh^{6} dŭuhk^{6} găp^{6} hie^{1} ban^{6}
You guys speak Vietnamese very well! Very pleased to meet you two.

LAURENT **Tôi cũng vậy.**
tohy^{1} koongm^{3} vay^{6}
Me too.

ROSA **Đến giờ rồi! Chúng ta cùng vào lớp nhé.**
dehn^{2} yuh^{5} rohy^{5} // choongm^{2} ta^{1} koongm^{5} vah^{5} luhp^{2} nhe^{2}
It's time already. Let's go to (our) class together, eh.

KEY VOCABULARY 1

chào *v, interj*	to greet; hello	**Tây Ban Nha** *n, adj*	Spain; Spanish	**hân hạnh** *adj*	honored
tên *n*	name	**đến** *v*	to come, to arrive	**gặp** *v*	to meet
là *v*	to be	**gì** *pron*	what	**cũng vậy** *adv*	too
người *n*	person	**và** *conj*	and	**giờ** *n*	time; hour
Việt *adj*	Vietnamese	**Pháp** *n, adj*	France; French	**rồi** *adv*	already
còn *conj*	and, as for	**nói** *v*	to say, to speak	**cùng** *adv*	together
nước *n*	country	**tiếng** *n*	language	**vào** *v*	to enter
nào *adj*	which	**giỏi** *adj, adv*	good; well	**lớp** *n*	class
hai *n, adj*	two	**rất** *adv*	very		
từ *prep*	from	**được** *v*	to be; to be able to		

IDIOMATIC EXPRESSIONS 1

tên tôi là... This phrase means "My name is..." **Tôi tên là...** conveys the same meaning with a slightly different structure ("I am named...").

rất hân hạnh "Very honored" – a formal way of saying "very pleased" when introduced to someone. More informally, you can say **rất vui** "very pleased," as in **rất vui được nói chuyện với cô** "very pleased to get to talk to you." **Được** in this context expresses an opportunity for someone to do something.

tôi cũng vậy A common way to say "me too." It can also be used to mean "me neither," but to emphasize the negative sense, use **tôi cũng không** (**không** meaning both "no" and "not").

đến giờ rồi The noun **giờ** means "hour," "time," or "o'clock." **Đến giờ rồi** is "It's time already." **Mấy giờ rồi?** means "What time is it (already)?" **Tám giờ rồi** means "(It's) eight o'clock (already)." The word "already" is always included in the question and answer. To state "I need two hours to do this," say **Tôi cần hai giờ để làm việc này.**

CULTURE NOTES 1

In Vietnam, when people meet for the first time, they usually greet one another by saying **chào**, followed by a title or personal pronoun such as **ông** "sir," **bà** "ma'am," **cô** "miss," **anh** "brother," or **chị** "sister." There is no real equivalent to "How do you do?" or "How are you (doing)?" to follow up. However, in Vietnamese communities living abroad, an equivalent to those expressions has been coined and is becoming more common. You may hear people say **Ông/bà/anh/chị khoẻ không?** which literally means "Are you well?"

Normally, when two acquaintances or friends see each other, they ask perfunctory questions like **Anh đi đâu vậy?** "Where are you going?" or **Chị làm gì ở đây vậy?** "What are you doing here?"

If two speakers haven't seen each other for a long time, one usually asks the other **Dạo này cô ra sao?** "How have you been?"

GRAMMAR NOTES 1

The verb "là"

This is one of several verbs meaning "to be." It can be followed by a noun or an adjective.

(1) a. **Huy là người Việt.**
hwee^{1} *la*^{5} *ngŭuhy*^{5} *vyeht*^{6}
Huy is Vietnamese.

b. **Họ của Rosa là González.**
hah^{5} *koouh*^{4} *Rosa la*^{5} *González.*
Rosa's last name is González.

When **là** is followed by an adjective, it is mostly kept in writing, but habitually omitted in casual speech, unless the speaker wants to emphasize the adjective:

(2) a. **Vấn đề này là quan trọng.**
vun^{2} *deh*^{5} *năy*^{5} *la*^{5} *kwan*^{1} *trahngm*^{6}
This issue is important.

b. **Tiếng Việt Ø dễ quá!**
tyehng^{2} *vyeht*^{6} *yeh*^{3} *kwa*^{2}
Vietnamese is so easy!

c. **Giáo sư đó là khó tính lắm!**
yahw^{2} *shŭ*^{1} *dah*^{2} *la*^{5} *khah*^{2} *teenh*^{2} *lăm*^{2}
That professor is (indeed) very difficult.

In the negative form, **không phải là** appears before a noun and **là không** appears before an adjective, although **là** is usually omitted in the latter construction, especially in the spoken language:

(3) a. **Tôi không phải là sinh viên du học.**
tohy^{1} *khohngm*^{1} *fie*^{4} *la*^{5} *sheenh*^{1} *vyehn*^{1} *yoo*^{1} *hahkp*^{6}
I am not an international ("studying abroad") student.

b. **Câu này là không đúng.**
kohw^{1} *năy*^{5} *la*^{5} *khohngm*^{1} *doongm*^{2}
This sentence is not correct.

c. **Căn nhà này Ø không lớn.**
kăn^{1} *nha*^{5} *năy*^{5} *khohngm*^{1} *luhn*^{2}
This house is not big.

In a yes-or-no question containing a noun as the element being asked about, the frame construction **có phải là ... không** is used:

(4) **Ông có phải là người Mỹ không?**
ohngm^{1} *kah*^{2} *fie*^{4} *la*^{5} *ngŭuhy*^{5} *mee*^{3} *khohngm*^{1}
Are you (an) American?

If the question contains an adjective, the construction is reduced to **có... không**:

(5) **Tiếng Việt có khó không?**
tyehng^{2} *vyeht*^{6} *kah*^{2} *khah*^{2} *khohngm*^{1}
Is Vietnamese difficult?

NHÀ SÁCH
Chào cô Hồng! Cô đi đâu đó? Hello, Miss Hong! Where are you going?
Chào giáo sư Nam. Tôi đi mua cà-phê. Hello, Professor Nam. I'm going to get some coffee.

Đây là anh Thanh. Anh là kỹ sư điện toán. This is Thanh. He is a computer engineer.

Hân hạnh được biết anh! Pleased to meet you!

Chào cô Hồng! Hello, Miss Hong!
Cô Hồng là luật sư gia đình. Miss Hong is a family attorney.

DIALOGUE 2

Professor Nam is talking with a friend in front of a bookstore when another friend passes by. Nam says hi to her and introduces her to his friend.

NAM **A, chào cô Hồng! Cô đi đâu đó?**
a^{1} chahw^{5} koh^{1} hohngm^{5} // koh^{1} dee^{1} dohw^{1} dah^{2}
Ah, hello, Miss Hong! Where are you going (there)?

HỒNG **Chào giáo sư Nam. Tôi đi mua cà-phê.**
chahw^{5} yahw^{2} shŭ^{1} nam^{1} // tohy^{1} dee^{1} moouh^{1} ka^{5} feh^{1}
Hello Professor Nam. I'm going to get (buy) some coffee.

NAM **Cô Hồng ơi, tôi xin giới thiệu với cô: Đây là anh Thanh. Anh là kỹ sư điện toán.**
koh^{1} hohngm^{5} uh^{1} // tohy^{1} seen^{1} yuhy^{2} thyehw^{6} vuhy^{2} koh^{1} // day^{1} la^{5} ănh^{1} thănh^{1}// ănh^{1} la^{5} kee^{3} shŭ^{1} dyehn^{6} twan^{2}
Hey, Miss Hong, let me introduce you: This (here) is (brother) Thanh. He is a computer engineer.

HỒNG **Hân hạnh được biết anh Thanh!**
hun^{1} hănh^{6} dŭuhk^{6} byeht^{2} ănh^{1} thănh^{1}
(It's) nice meeting (knowing) you, (brother) Thanh.

THANH **Chào cô Hồng!**
chahw^{5} koh^{1} hohngm^{5}
Hello, Miss Hong!

NAM **Cô Hồng là luật sư gia đình, anh Thanh à.**
koh^{1} hohngm^{5} la^{5} lwut^{6} shŭ^{1} ya^{1} deenh^{5} // ănh^{1} thănh^{1} a^{5}
Thanh, Miss Hong is a family attorney.

KEY VOCABULARY 2

cô *n*	Miss, Ms.	**giới thiệu** *v*	to introduce
anh *n*	older brother	**với** *prep*	with
đi *v*	to go	**đây** *adv*	here
đâu *adv*	where	**kỹ sư** *n*	engineer
đó *adv, part*	there	**điện toán** *n*	computer
giáo sư *n*	professor	**biết** *v*	to know
mua *v*	to buy	**à** *part*	hey
ơi *part*	hey	**luật sư** *n*	lawyer

IDIOMATIC EXPRESSIONS 2

[*Name*] **ơi!** The particle **ơi** following a person's name is meant to call for their attention. However, it should only be used with family members or friends your age or younger, not normally with superiors or strangers. When someone is looking for a person, they can emphasize their call by adding another particle with the same effect, for example, **Anh Nam ơi! Anh Nam à**!

Tôi xin [*verb*] Literally meaning "to ask, to beg," the verb **xin** is used after **tôi** "I" or other first-person singular or plural pronouns to mean "let me" or "may I." For example, **Tôi xin hỏi ông một câu** "Let me ask you a question."

CULTURE NOTES 2

Vietnamese people usually address one another with a title or a term of address followed by a first name, not a last name like in the English-speaking world. Take Dr. Nguyễn Huy Tâm, for example (the order of the names being last + middle + first). In Vietnamese this would be **Bác sĩ Tâm**. Since there are only a few dozen last names in Vietnam, it is a person's first name that is their "identity."

Kinship terms are also used before first names among acquaintances: **anh Tuấn**, **cô Hoa**, **ông Bình**, **bà Thuý**, etc.

First names without a title or term of address are only used by parents addressing children, older siblings addressing younger ones, or between friends.

GRAMMAR NOTES 2

Personal pronouns

Most personal pronouns in Vietnamese are not true pronouns, but instead come from common nouns and/or kinship terms. One of the pronouns for "I" or "me," for example, is **tôi**, a noun meaning "servant" (to show humbleness on the speaker's part). Through time, however, **tôi** has lost its original meaning and become a neutral term that is even considered disrespectful in certain contexts. While it is normally used in the workplace or social settings (showing a sense of equality on the speaker's part), **tôi** is never used by children when speaking to their parents or other older family members, or even to older strangers. Children usually refer to themselves as **con** "child" when speaking to their parents and as **cháu** "nephew/niece" when speaking to older strangers.

On the other hand, a pronoun can have more than one reference. The word **anh** ("older brother") can be used to mean "I" (by a man speaking to someone he considers a younger brother), "you" (by a speaker addressing a man they consider their older brother), or even "he," when a speaker or writer refers to a man. Because of this openness of reference, the meaning of a pronoun should be carefully determined based on context.

PRONOUN	LITERAL MEANING	REFERENCE	USAGE
tôi	servant	I – me	Neutral – Professional – Could be considered disrespectful
anh	older brother	you	Addressing a man same age or slightly older
		I – me	Self-addressed toward younger people – Could be considered condescending
		he – him	Formal – In writing
chị	older sister	you	Addressing a woman same age or slightly older
		I – me	Self-addressed toward younger people – Could be considered condescending
		she – her	Formal – In writing
cô	Miss, Ms., aunt	you	Addressing a young or middle-aged woman
		I – me	Self-addressed toward children or young people
		she – her	Formal – In writing
ông	grandfather, Mr.	you	Addressing a middle-aged or older man
		he – him	Formal – In writing
bà	grandmother, Mrs.	you	Addressing a middle-aged or older woman
		she – her	Formal – In writing
em	younger sibling	You	Addressing a younger person – Could be considered condescending
		I – me	Self-addressed toward people slightly older than the speaker
		he – him she – her	Referring to young people or children
con	child (in the family)	you	A parent or any child addressing a child
		I – me	Self-addressed toward a parent or an adult
nó	that thing/person	it – he – him she – her	Referring to an object, an animal or a child – Considered disrespectful for adults
họ	relatives	they – them	Referring to two or more adults – Aloof

Speakers also use the adjective **ấy** "that" after a second-person pronoun to turn it into a third-person pronoun. Thus, if **cô** means "you" (second person), then **cô ấy** means "she." However—as shown in the chart above—when the person being referred to is present during a conversation, a speaker might simply use **cô** to mean "she" or "her," since in this situation **cô ấy** might sound formal, or even aloof in certain contexts. Note that pronouns in Vietnamese do not change their forms for different grammatical functions; the same word is used for she/her, he/him, etc.

Parents informally refer to their son or daughter as **nó** "he/him/she/her," but to sound polite, they also use **cháu** "niece/nephew" to refer to them when speaking with other people.

To form plural pronouns, two particles (or "markers") are used: **các** and **chúng**. Two pronouns, **tôi** and **nó**, go with **chúng**: **chúng tôi** "we/us," **chúng nó** "they/them" (for children or disrespectfully for adults). **Các** goes with the other pronouns: **các anh** "you" (pl., males), **các anh chị** "you" (pl., mixed genders), **các cô ấy** "they/them" (females), etc.

READING

VIỆT NAM

One-Pillar Pagoda in Hanoi

Việt Nam là một nước nhỏ ở vùng Đông Nam Á với dân số gần một trăm triệu người. Phía bắc của Việt Nam là Trung Quốc, phía tây là Lào, phía tây nam là Cam Bốt và phía đông là Biển Đông. Ba miền địa lý chính là miền Bắc, miền Trung và miền Nam. Các thành phố lớn là Hà Nội, Huế, Đà Nẵng và Sài Gòn.

Việt Nam có nhiều tài nguyên thiên nhiên và phong cảnh đẹp. Người Việt Nam cần cù, thông minh và hiếu khách.

vyeht^6 nam^1 la^5 moht^6 nŭuhk^2 nhah^4 uh^4 voongm^5 dohng^1 nam^1 a^2 vuhy^2 yun^1 shoh^2 gun^5 moht^6 trăm^1 tryehw^6 ngŭuhy^5 // feeuh^2 băk^2 koouh^4 vyeht^6 nam^1 la^5 troongm^1 kwohk^2 // feeuh^2 tay^1 la^5 lahw^5 // feeuh^2 tay^1 nam^1 la^5 kam^1 boht^2 va^5 feeuh^2 dohngm^1 la^5 byehn^4 dohngm^1 // ba^1 myehn^5 deeuh^6 lee^2 cheenh^2 la^5 myehn^5 băk^2 myehn^5 troongm^1 va^5 myehn^5 nam^1 // kak^2 thănh^5 foh^2 luhn^2 la^5 ha^5 nohy^6 hweh^2 da^5 năng^3 va^5 shie^5 gahn^5 // vyeht^6 nam^1 kah^2 nhyehw^5 tie^5 ngwyehn^1 thyehn^1 nhyehn^1 va^5 fahngm^1 kănh^4 dep^6 // ngŭuhy^5 vyeht^6 nam^1 kun^5 koo^5 thohngm^1 meenh^1 va^5 hyehw^2 khăch^2

Temple of the Celestial Lady in Hue

VIETNAM

Vietnam is a small country in Southeast Asia with a population of nearly 100 million. North of Vietnam is China, to the west is Laos, to the southwest is Cambodia and to the east is the East Sea. The three main geographical regions are the Northern Region, the Central Region and the Southern Region. The major cities are Hanoi, Hue, Danang and Saigon.

Vietnam has many natural resources and beautiful landscapes. The Vietnamese people are hard-working, smart and hospitable.

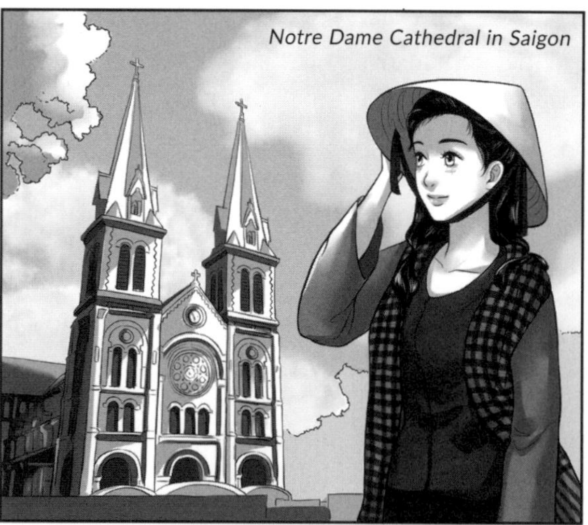

Notre Dame Cathedral in Saigon

COMPREHENSION QUESTIONS

Answer the following questions in complete sentences, first orally, then in writing. In general, answering a specific question in Vietnamese is rather easy. Simply repeat the whole question and replace the interrogative word (underlined) with the correct information.

Question: **Việt Nam nằm ở vùng nào?** *In what region is Vietnam located?*
Answer: **Việt Nam nằm ở vùng Đông Nam Á.**

1. **Dân số của Việt Nam là bao nhiêu?** *What is the population of Vietnam?*

   ____

2. **Phía bắc của Việt Nam là nước nào?** *Which country is north of Vietnam?*

   ____

3. **Phía tây và tây nam của Việt Nam là hai nước nào?** *Which two countries are to the west and the southwest of Vietnam?*

   ____

4. **Biển phía đông của Việt Nam tên là gì?** *What's the name of the sea to the east of Vietnam?*

   ____

5. **Việt Nam có mấy miền địa lý?** *How many geographical regions does Vietnam have?*

   ____

PRACTICE

A. Listening comprehension

Listen to the following welcome speech from the director of Vina Company and fill in the cells below with the correct information from the list:

Professions: **giám đốc - bác sĩ - kỹ sư - luật sư - giáo sư**

Hometowns: **Nha Trang - Sài Gòn - Huế - Tây Ninh - Đà Lạt**

	Name	*Profession*	*Hometown*
1	**Bà Thuý**		
2	**Ông Long**		
3	**Anh Vinh**		
4	**Cô Vy**		
5	**Ông Minh**		

B. The verb "là"

The following sentences give information about Mr. Nguyễn Thanh Nam. Fill in the blanks with the words from the list that fit the sentences grammatically and logically.

vui tính (funny) **giáo sư** **họ** **tên đệm** (middle name) **người Việt**

1. ____________________ **của ông Nam là Nguyễn.**

2. ____________________ **của ông là Thanh.**

3. **Ông Nam không phải là người Hoa mà** (but) **là** ____________________.

4. **Ông là** ____________________ **đại học.**

5. **Ông là người thông minh** (smart) **và** ____________________.

C. Personal pronouns

Mrs. Tâm is talking about herself and her family. Complete the sentences below with the correct personal pronouns for each context.

tôi **cháu** **chúng tôi** **các cháu** **anh ấy**

1. ______________ **tên là Tâm và họ của tôi là Trần.**
2. **Chồng tôi** (my husband) **tên là Khoa.** ______________ **là kỹ sư hoá học** (chemistry).
3. **Khoa và tôi,** ______________ **sống** (live) **ở Nha Trang.**
4. **Con gái** (daughter/girl) **của tôi tên là Thảo.** ______________ **là chuyên viên tâm lý** (psychologist).
5. **Con trai** (son/boy) **của tôi tên là Huy.** ______________ **là sinh viên năm thứ hai** (second-year).
6. **Tôi rất thương con cái** (children) **của tôi.** ______________ **ngoan** (well-behaved) **lắm!**

D. Vocabulary

Complete the following paragraph with the correct words from the list. Use each word only once.

dạy **người** **khó** **học** **chào** **nói** **là** **sinh viên**

______________ **các bạn! Tôi tên** ______________ **Dennis. Tôi là** ______________ **Mỹ. Tôi là** ______________ **tại trường đại học Quốc Gia Sài Gòn** (Saigon National University). **Tôi đang** ______________ **tiếng Việt và** ______________ **tiếng Anh** (English) **cho các sinh viên người Việt ở đây** (here). **Tiếng Việt rất hay** (very interesting) **nhưng** ______________ **quá, nên** (so) **tôi** ______________ **chưa giỏi lắm** (not very well yet).

PROVERB

MIẾNG TRẦU LÀ ĐẦU CÂU CHUYỆN.

myehng^{2} trohw^{5} la^{5} dohw^{5} kohw^{1} chwyehn^{6}

"A betel quid is the start of a conversation."

Chewing betel nut is a practice found in Vietnam and a number of other South and Southeast Asian countries, as well as in a few other regions of the world. A "quid" consists of a betel leaf wrapped around a slice of areca nut and a small amount of slaked lime. The quid is chewed for a certain amount of time and then spat out. Chewing betel nut is addictive, considered unhealthy, and becoming less popular in modern Vietnam.

In the past, people would offer one another a betel quid when they met up and were ready to start a chat. It was their way of saying "How are you?" or offering hospitality in the way a cup of tea might be offered in the West.

Betel leaves and areca nuts are traditionally used in wedding ceremonies to symbolize the union between a man and a woman. This custom is based on a legend about a couple that were separated by a misunderstanding. They eventually died of broken hearts, one becoming an areca tree and the other, a betel leaf vine. The vine grew around the tree, depicting a touching image that defies the saying "Till death do us part."

 FUNCTIONAL VOCABULARY

NOUNS - DANH TỪ

tên	(first) name
họ	last name
tên đệm	middle name
sinh viên	college student
học sinh	pupil
giáo viên	teacher
gia đình	family
đại học	university
nhà	house
trường	school
miền	region
miền Bắc	the Northern Region (of Vietnam)
miền Trung	the Central Region (of Vietnam)
miền Nam	the Southern Region (of Vietnam)
thành phố	city
tỉnh	province
thủ đô	capital
phía/hướng	direction
biển	sea
Biển Đông	the East Sea

ADJECTIVES - TÍNH TỪ

lớn	large
nhỏ	small
khó	difficult
dễ	easy
vui tính	funny
thông minh	smart
bắc	northern
nam	southern
đông	eastern
tây	western
ngoan	well behaved
đẹp	beautiful

VERBS - ĐỘNG TỪ

nói	to say; to speak
hiểu	to understand
nghe	to hear; to listen
đọc	to read
viết	to write
dạy	to teach
học	to learn

DỰ BÁO THỜI TIẾT MỘT SỐ TỈNH, THÀNH PHỐ TRONG NƯỚC
HÀ NỘI
26°C
20°C
SÀI GÒN
35°C
30°C
VŨNG TÀU
32°C
27°C
Hôm nay nóng đến 35 độ C ở Sài Gòn! Today's temperature is 35 degrees Celsius in Saigon.

Năm nay khí hậu khác hơn năm ngoái nhiều. This year's weather is so different from last year's.

Năm nào em cũng nói câu đó! You say the same thing every year!

Anh thích thời tiết nóng lắm, phải không? You like warm weather, don't you?
Còn phải nói! Obviously!

Em thích trời nắng với nhiệt độ mát mẻ. I like the weather to be sunny and mild.

CHAPTER 4

Climate and Weather

Khí Hậu Và Thời Tiết

DIALOGUE 1

Huy and Lan, brother and sister, are watching a weather forecast program on TV and chatting about the weather.

HUY **Hôm nay nóng đến 35 độ C ở Sài Gòn mà trời lại đang mưa ở Vũng Tàu!**
hohm^1 năy^1 nahngm^2 dehn^2 ba^1 mŭuhy^1 lăm^{1}doh^6 seh^1 uh^4 shie^5 gahn^5 ma^5 truhy^5 lie^6 dang^1 mŭuh^1 uh^4 voongm^3 tăw^5
Today's temperature is 35 degrees Celsius in Saigon, but it's raining in Vũng Tàu!

LAN **Năm nay khí hậu khác hơn năm ngoái nhiều.**
năm^1 năy^1 khee^2 hohw^6 khak^2 huhn^1 năm^1 ngwie^2 nhyehw^5
This year's weather is so different from last year's.

HUY **Năm nào em cũng nói câu đó!**
năm^1 nahw^5 em^1 koongm^3 nahy^2 kohw^1 dah^2
You say the same thing every year!

LAN **Anh thích thời tiết nóng lắm, phải không?**
ănh^1 theech^2 thuhy^5 tyeht^2 nahngm^2 lăm^2 fie^4 khohngm^1
You like warm weather, don't you?

HUY **Còn phải nói!**
kahn^5 fie^4 nahy^2
Obviously!

LAN **Em thì thích trời nắng với nhiệt độ mát mẻ.**
em^1 thee^5 theech^2 truhy^5 năng^2 vuhy^2 nhyeht^6 doh^6 mat^2 me^4
Personally, I like the weather to be sunny and mild.

KEY VOCABULARY 1

nóng *adj*	hot	**nói** *v*	to say, to speak
độ *n*	degree	**câu** *n*	sentence
mà... lại... *conj*	yet	**thích** *v*	to like
trời *n*	sky, heaven	**thời tiết** *n*	weather
mưa *n/v*	rain; to rain	**lắm** *adv*	very, very much
mà *conj*	but	**nắng** *n/adj*	sun rays; sunny
khí hậu *n*	climate	**với** *prep*	with
khác *adj*	different	**nhiệt độ** *n*	temperature
hơn *adv*	more	**mát mẻ** *adj*	cool, mild

IDIOMATIC EXPRESSIONS 1

Trời [mưa] The noun **trời** means "sky" or "heaven." In weather expressions, **trời** is grammatically equivalent to "it" in English. Thus, for example, "It is so sunny" would be **Trời nắng quá.**

Phải không? The full version is **phải hay không?** "right or not?" This phrase is used at the end of a statement to turn it into a *tag question*, like the English "right?" **Hôm nay trời đẹp thật, phải không?** "It's a really nice day today, isn't it?"

[...] nào cũng... A noun followed by the adjective **nào** (with or without one or more intervening elements) and the adverb **cũng** is equivalent to the English construction "every + [noun]...", **Người nào cũng than là hôm nay trời lạnh quá** "Everyone was complaining that it was so cold today."

Còn phải nói! "(Why did you) still have to say (it)?" A reply when something obvious is said.

CULTURE NOTES 1

Vietnamese people regard natural phenomena as acts of **trời**, or "heaven." Besides using **trời** in weather expressions for this reason, they also use this noun in many other expressions such as **Trời ơi!** "Heavens!" **Có trời biết!** "Only heaven knows," **Lạy trời mưa xuống** "Pray to heaven that it will rain," **Nhờ trời** "Thank heaven," and **Đứng như trời trồng** "Standing still as if planted by heaven."

Ever since Buddhism was introduced in Vietnam as early as the first century BCE, **Phật** "Buddha" has been a common word in everyday speech. It appears together with **trời** in several expressions: **Trời thương Phật độ** "Loved by heaven and saved by Buddha," **Trời Phật ơi!** "O heaven and Buddha!" **Có Trời Phật làm chứng** "Witnessed by heaven and Buddha."

The opposite concept of **trời** "heaven" is **đất** "earth." The following expressions can be heard often in everyday speech: **Trời đất ơi!** "O heaven and earth!" (An exaggerated version is **Trời đất quỷ thần ơi!** "O heaven, earth, demons and genies!"), **Trời cao đất dày ơi!** "O high heaven and thick earth!" **than trời trách đất** "to blame everything on heaven and earth," **trời không dung, đất không tha** "neither tolerated by heaven nor forgiven by earth" (referring to a tremendous sin or wrongdoing).

GRAMMAR NOTES 1

I. Weather expressions

To talk about the weather, you can use the nouns **thời tiết** "weather" or **trời**, as mentioned in the Idiomatic Expressions and Culture Notes sections. Both of these nouns can function as the subject of the sentence. Depending on the construction, these nouns can be used interchangeably or not.

a. **Hôm nay thời tiết (là) như thế nào?**
hohm^{1} năy^{1} thuhy^{5} tyeht^{2} (la^{5}) nhŭ^{1} theh^{2} nahw^{5}
What is the weather like today?

b. **Hôm qua thời tiết (or trời) rất đẹp.**
hohm^{1} kwa^{1} thuhy^{5} tyeht^{2} (truhy^{5}) rut^{2} dep^{6}
The weather was very nice yesterday.

The noun **trời** is usually followed by the verb **có** "to have" plus a noun referring to the weather or other natural phenomena.

a. **Mùa này trời thường có bão.**
moouh^{5} năy^{5} truhy^{5} thŭuhng^{5} kah^{2} bahw^{3}
There usually are storms in this season.

b. **Đêm nay trời có trăng đẹp quá!**
dehm^{1} năy^{1} truhy^{5} kah^{2} trăng^{1} dep^{6} kwa^{2}
What a beautiful moonlit night it is tonight!

c. **Ngày mai trời có gió nhiều không?**
ngăy^{5} mie^{1} truhy^{5} kah^{2} yah^{2} nhyehw^{5} khohng^{1}
Will it be very windy tomorrow?

Trời is also accompanied by adjectives with the help of a linking verb (**là** "to be," **thì** "to be," **có vẻ** "to appear," **trông** "to look," **dường như** "to seem," **[cảm] thấy [như]** "to feel [like]," etc.). In most cases, however, the verbs **thì** and **là** are habitually omitted.

a. **Trời thường (là) ấm áp vào mùa xuân.**
truhy^{5} thŭuhng^{5} la^{5} um^{2} ap^{2} vahw^{5} moouh^{5} swun^{1}
The weather is usually mild in spring.

b. **Sáng nay trời có vẻ u ám.**
shang^{2} năy^{1} truhy^{5} kah^{2} ve^{4} oo^{1} am^{2}
It seems overcast this morning.

c. **Trời thấy như càng lúc càng ẩm thấp.**
truhy^{5} thay^{2} nhŭ^{1} kang^{5} lookp^{2} kang^{5} um^{4} thup^{2}
It feels more and more humid.

Tôi đang may một bộ áo tắm mới đó! I'm making myself a new bathing suit.

Đừng quên là chúng ta cũng về miền quê chơi nữa. Don't forget that we'll go to the countryside, too.

 DIALOGUE 2

The school year is drawing to an end. Hồng and Thuý are really looking forward to the summer and what they will be doing during every student's favorite time of year.

THUÝ **Mấy hôm nay ngày nào cũng thật đẹp trời. Mùa hè sắp đến rồi!**
may^2 hohm^1 năy^1 ngăy^5 nahw^5 koongm^3 thut^6 dep^6 truhy^5 // moouh^5 he^5 shăp^2 dehn^2 rohy^5
The weather has been nice these last few days. Summer is around the corner!

HỒNG **Tôi chỉ mong kỳ thi mau kết thúc. Thuý đã ôn hết bài chưa?**
tohy^1 mahngm^1 kee^5 thee^1 măw^1 keht^2 thookp^2 // thwee^2 da^3 ohn^1 heht^2 bie^5 chŭuh^1
I can't wait for exams to be over. Have you reviewed all the material?

THUÝ **Cũng gần xong rồi. Nhưng chúng ta nên nói về mùa hè thì vui hơn.**
koongm^3 gun^5 sahngm^1 rohy^5 // nhŭng^1 choongm^2 ta^1 nehn^1 nahy^2 veh^5 moouh^5 he^5 thee^5 vooy^1 huhn^1
Pretty much. But it's more fun to talk about summer.

HỒNG **Mình sẽ đi tắm biển với nhau hằng ngày nhé!**
meenh^5 she^3 dee^1 tăm^2 byehn^4 vuhy^2 nhăw^1 hăng^5 ngăy^5 nhe^2
We'll go swimming in the sea every day, won't we?

THUÝ **Nhất định rồi. Tôi đang may một bộ áo tắm mới đó!**
nhut^2 deenh^5 rohy^5 // tohy^1 dang^1 măy^1 moht^6 boh^6 ahw^2 tăm^2 muhy^2 dah^2
Absolutely. I'm making myself a new bathing suit.

HỒNG **Thích quá há! Đừng quên là chúng ta cũng về miền quê chơi nữa.**
theech^2 kwa^2 ha^2 // dŭng^5 kwehn^1 la^5 choongm^2 ta^1 koongm^3 veh^5 myehn^5 kweh^1 chuhy^1 nŭuh^3
How nice! Don't forget that we'll go to the countryside, too.

KEY VOCABULARY 2

mấy hôm nay *adv*	the last few days	**nên** *v*	should
đẹp trời *adj*	nice (weather)	**vui** *adj*	fun
mùa hè *n*	summer	**tắm biển** *v*	to swim in the sea
đến *v*	to come; to arrive	**với nhau** *adv*	together
mong *v*	to hope, to expect	**hằng ngày** *adv*	every day
kỳ thi *n*	exam period	**nhất định** *adv*	absolutely, certainly
mau *adv*	quickly	**may** *v*	to sew
kết thúc *v*	to end	**áo tắm** *n*	bathing suit
ôn *v*	to review	**quên** *v*	to forget
xong *adj*	finished	**miền quê** *n*	countryside

IDIOMATIC EXPRESSIONS 2

đã... chưa? Use this construction with a verb to ask whether an action has taken place or not. **Các bạn đã nghỉ hè chưa?** "Have you started your summer vacation yet?"

nên... thì hơn This expression is equivalent to the English construction "had better + verb." **Sắp thi rồi, con nên dành thì giờ để ôn bài thì hơn** "The exams are coming up. You'd better spend time reviewing all the material."

[...] quá há! Commonly used in the spoken language, an adjective followed by the adverb **quá** "so" and the particle **há** "huh" expresses a heartfelt remark about something. **Khí hậu ở đây dễ chịu quá há!** "How pleasant the climate is here!" **Gió mát quá há!** "The breeze is pretty cool, huh?"

CULTURE NOTES 2

For Vietnamese students, the three-month summer vacation is the most awaited time of the year, signaled in particular by the colorful blooms of the royal poinciana trees and the cicadas' signature songs. Every year when summer arrives, most areas from the city to the countryside are brightly graced with orange-red flowers against the lush green leaves of royal poinciana trees. The Vietnamese name for this flower is **phượng vĩ** "tail of the phoenix."

Almost simultaneously, cicadas start chirping away from every tree, an incessant and melancholy soundtrack to the hot days of summer. In Vietnamese, a cicada is called **ve** or **ve sầu**. It is not entirely clear whether the word **sầu**, meaning "sad," refers to these winged insects' somber chirping, or simply is an arbitrary, coincidental part of their name.

One of the most popular summer songs, by the famous songwriter Hùng Lân, starts with these lyrics: **Trời hồng hồng, nắng trong trong, ngàn phượng rung nắng ngoài song** "The sky is dyed pink, the sunrays translucent, and thousands of royal poinciana flowers are dancing in the sun outside the windows."

GRAMMAR NOTES 2

II. Verbal aspects

Unlike many other languages, verbs in Vietnamese come in invariable forms and therefore do not show tenses—i.e., past, present, future—or any other grammatical features. The concept of tense is instead expressed through context or time expressions.

(4) a. **Mùa hè nào tôi cũng <u>đi</u> câu cá.** (*The present tense of the verb* **đi** *is construed through the time expression* **mùa hè nào**.)
moouh^5 he^5 nahw^5 tohy^1 koongm^3 dee^1 kohw^1 ka^2
I go fishing every summer.

b. **Tuần trước trời <u>có</u> nhiều sương mù.** (*The past tense of the verb* **có** *is construed through the time expression* **tuần trước**.)
twun^5 trŭuhk^2 truhy^5 kah^2 nhyehw^5 shŭuhng^1 moo^5
It was very foggy last week.

c. **Mấy giờ chiều nay các bạn sẽ ghé nhà tôi?** (*The future tense of the verb* **ghé** *is construed through the time expression* **chiều nay**.)
may^{2} yuh^{5} chyehw^{5} năy^{1} kak^{2} ban^{6} she^{3} ge^{2} nha^{5} tohy^{1}
What time will you guys stop by my house this afternoon?

While lacking grammatical markers for tense, however, Vietnamese verbs can be accompanied by markers expressing "aspect." This is a grammatical concept that describes how an action, event or state extends over time. For instance, an action can be viewed as completed (it has been done), ongoing (it is being done) or planned (it will be done).

In Vietnamese, five verbal aspects are recognized through the following *aspect markers*: **đã** (expressing a completed action), **vừa** (expressing a recently completed action), **đang** (expressing an ongoing action), **sắp** (expressing an action about to take place) and **sẽ** (expressing an action planned or predicted to take place). Note, however, that these markers are optional in most contexts, and speakers can use other expressions to express verbal aspects.

ASPECT	MARKER	EXAMPLE
Completed	**ĐÃ**	(5) **Bên chị trời đã bớt nóng chưa?** *behn^{1} chee^{6} truhy^{5} da^{3} buht^{2} nahngm^{2} chŭuh^{1}* Is it already less warm where you live?
Recently completed	**VỪA**	(6) **Ở đây tuyết vừa bắt đầu rơi.** *uh^{4} day^{1} twyeht^{2} vŭuh^{5} băt^{2} dohw^{5} ruhy^{1}* It has just started snowing here.
Ongoing	**ĐANG**	(7) **Trời đang mưa lớn lắm.** *truhy^{5} dang^{1} mŭuh^{1} luhn^{2} lăm^{2}* It is raining very hard.
About to take place	**SẮP**	(8) **Thời tiết có vẻ sắp thay đổi.** *thuhy^{5} tyeht^{2} kah^{2} ve^{4} shăp^{2} thăy^{1} dohy^{4}* The weather seems to be about to change.
Predicted	**SẼ**	(9) **Ngày mai trời sẽ có nhiều mây.** *ngăy^{5} mie^{1} truhy^{5} she^{3} kah^{2} nhyehw^{5} may^{1}* It will be very cloudy tomorrow.

 **READING**

MÙA GIÓ CHƯỚNG

Việt Nam nằm trong vùng nhiệt đới gió mùa. Việc phân chia bốn mùa xuân, hạ, thu, đông không rõ rệt bằng hai mùa—mùa mưa (từ tháng Sáu đến tháng Mười Một) và mùa khô (từ tháng Mười Hai đến tháng Năm). Gió mùa tây nam thổi vào mùa mưa, còn gió mùa đông bắc hoạt động vào mùa khô.

Đặc biệt, ở miền Tây Nam, người ta gọi gió mùa đông bắc là *gió chướng*, vì loại gió này gây ra nhiều thiệt hại về nông nghiệp và ngư nghiệp cho các vùng ven biển. Ở những vùng này, người dân có nhiều ao hồ nuôi các loại thuỷ hải sản và những vùng trồng nông sản. Một trong những ảnh hưởng xấu của gió chướng là làm cho việc xâm nhập mặn từ biển vào sâu hơn trong hệ thống sông ngòi ở miền này, làm tổn thất việc thu hoạch sản phẩm của người nuôi trồng.

vyeht^{6} nam^{1} năm^{5} trahngm^{1} voongm^{5} nhyeht^{6} duhy^{2} yah^{2} moouh^{5} // vyehk^{6} fun^{1} cheeuh^{1} bohn^{2} moouh^{5} swun^{1} ha^{6} thoo^{1} dohngm^{1} khohngm^{1} rah^{3} reht^{6} băng^{5} hie^{1} moouh^{5} // moouh^{5} mŭuh^{1} tŭ^{5} thang^{2} shăw^{2} dehn^{2} thang^{2} mŭuhy^{5} moht^{6} va^{5} moouh^{5} khoh^{1} tŭ^{5} thang^{2} mŭuhy^{5} hie^{1} dehn^{2} thang^{2} năm^{1} // yah^{2} moouh^{5} tay^{1} nam^{1} thohy^{4} vahw^{5} moouh^{5} mŭuh^{1} // kahn^{5} yah^{2} moouh^{5} dohngm^{1} băk^{2} hwat^{6} dohngm^{6} vahw^{5} moouh^{5} khoh^{1}

dăk^{6} byeht^{6} // uh^{4} myehn^{5} tay^{1} nam^{1} // ngŭuhy^{5} ta^{1} gahy^{6} yah^{2} moouh^{5} dohngm^{1} băk^{2} la^{5} yah^{2} chŭuhng^{2} // vee^{5} lwie^{6} yah^{2} năy^{5} gay^{1} ra^{1} nhyehw^{5} thyeht^{6} hie^{6} veh^{5} nohngm^{1} ngyehp^{6} va^{5} ngŭ^{1} ngyehp^{6} chah^{1} kak^{2} voongm^{5} ven^{1} byehn^{4} // uh^{4} nhŭng^{3} voongm^{5} năy^{5} // ngŭuhy^{5} yun^{1} kah^{2} nhyehw^{5} ahw^{1} hoh^{5} nwohy^{1} kak^{2} lwie^{6} thwee^{4} hie^{4} shan^{4} va^{5} nhŭng^{4} voongm^{5} trohngm^{5} nohngm^{1} shan^{4} // moht^{6} trahngm^{1} nhŭng^{3} ănh^{4}

hŭuhng^4 sohw^2 koouh^4 yah^2 chŭuhng^2 la^5 lam^5 chah^1 vyehk^6 sum^1 nhup^6 măn^6 tŭ^5 byehn^4 vahw^5 shohw^1 huhn^1 trahngm^1 heh^6 thohngm^2 shohngm^1 ngahy^5 uh^4 myehn^5 năy^5 // lam^5 tohn^4 thut^2 vyehk^6 thoo^1 hwăch^6 shan^4 fum^4 koouh^4 ngŭuhy^5 nwohy^1 trohngm^5

THE SEASON OF INOPPORTUNE WINDS

Vietnam is located in a tropical monsoon region. The four seasons—spring, summer, fall and winter—are not as distinct as the rainy season (from June to November) and the dry season (from December to May). Southwest winds blow in the rainy season and northeast winds in the dry season.

Notably, in the Southwest, people call the northeast winds "inopportune winds" because they typically cause damage to the agriculture and aquaculture of coastal regions. In these areas, many people own farmland or ponds where they raise freshwater and saltwater seafood. One of the negative effects of the "inopportune winds" is that they worsen soil salination, caused by salt water moving from the ocean into local rivers, which leads to large crop losses.

COMPREHENSION QUESTIONS

Answer the following questions in complete sentences, first orally, then in writing:

1. **Việt Nam nằm ở vùng khí hậu nào?** *In what climate region is Vietnam located?*

   ____

2. **Hai mùa chính ở Việt Nam là gì?** *What are the two main seasons in Vietnam?*

   ____

3. **Gió đông bắc thổi từ tháng mấy đến tháng mấy?** *From what month to what month do the northeast winds blow?*

   ____

4. **Tại sao người ta gọi gió đông bắc là gió chướng?** *Why do people call the northeast winds "inopportune"?*

   ____

5. **Gió chướng có ảnh hưởng gì đến việc xâm nhập mặn?** *What effect do "inopportune winds" have on soil salination?*

   ____

PRACTICE

A. Listening comprehension

Listen to the TV weather report and complete the chart below by circling the correct information in each category:

Report location	a. Sapa	b. Sa Đéc	c. Sài Gòn	d. Trường Sa
Morning temperature	a. 23°C	b. 13°C	c. 33°C	d. 30°C
Cloudiness	a. none	b. a lot	c. a little	d. not mentioned
Wind	a. light	b. strong	c. cool	d. stormy
Sun	a. scorching	b. warm	c. bright	d. dry
Afternoon weather	a. sunny	b. rainy	c. overcast	d. windy
Evening weather	a. clear	b. breezy	c. cold	d. warm
Night sky	a. cloudy	b. starry	c. moonlit	d. not mentioned

B. Weather expressions

Based on the given descriptions, write sentences about the weather using the words listed below. A verb and one or more words are provided in each sentence. Pay attention to word order.

nắng **ẩm ướt** **lạnh** **sương mù** **bão** **u ám** **mưa**

Ex: *The current temperature is 37°C.* (**là/hôm nay/quá**)
☞ **Hôm nay trời (là) nóng quá!**

1. *There is thunder and lightning now.* (**có vẻ/sắp/phải không**)

____

2. *The hygrometer shows a 90% RH (relative humidity).* (**thì/thường/vào mùa này**)

____

3. *It was hard driving in the city with limited visibility.* (**có/hôm qua/nhiều**)

____

4. *Strong winds are blowing in gusts.* (**dường như/sẽ/có/lớn**)

____

5. *The sky is covered with dark clouds.* (**trông/chiều nay/thật**)

____

6. *My sister is wearing a sweater.* (**thấy/tối nay/khá**)

____

7. *The sun is high in the sky.* (**Ø/sáng nay/đẹp**)

____

C. Aspect markers

Translate the English sentences. Include an appropriate aspect marker (**đã**, **vừa**, **đang**, **sắp** or **sẽ**) in each sentence. Refer to the Functional Vocabulary section or use a dictionary when necessary.

1. The weather forecast program is going to be on soon. [about to take place]

____

2. Is it snowing in Minnesota now? [ongoing]

____

3. It will be very cloudy tomorrow afternoon. [predicted to take place]

____

4. Have you checked the thermometer for today's temperature yet? [completed]

____

5. It was just drizzling. [recently completed]

____

D. Vocabulary

Fill in the blanks with words from the list below. Use each word only once.

khí hậu **đẹp trời** **dự báo thời tiết** **tuyết** **nhiệt độ** **thời tiết**

1. ______________ **ở tiểu bang California rất dễ chịu.**

   The ______________ in California is very pleasant.

2. **Tôi hy vọng ngày mai sẽ ______________ để chúng ta đi biển.**

   I hope tomorrow will be ______________ so we can go to the beach.

3. **Vào mùa này, ______________ thường thay đổi khá bất ngờ.**

   The ______________ often changes rather unexpectedly.

4. **Hôm nay ______________ cao nên tôi phải mở máy lạnh.**

   Today's ______________ is high, so I had to turn on the air conditioner.

5. **Việc ______________ không phải lúc nào cũng chính xác.**

   ______________ is not always precise.

6. **Nhiều vùng cao nguyên miền Bắc có ______________ vào mùa đông.**

   Several highland regions in the North have ______________ in the winter.

PROVERB

THÁNG BẢY HEO MAY, CHUỒN CHUỒN BAY THÌ BÃO.

thang² bảy⁴ hew¹ mảy¹ chwohn⁵ chwohn⁵ bảy¹ thee⁵ bahw³

"[In] the seventh month, [there are] autumn winds [and] dragonflies, [which forewarn] a storm."

Gió heo may is the name for the light winds of fall. In the old days, people relied on natural phenomena to forecast the weather. Dragonflies, abundant in the Vietnamese countryside, are believed to be a sign that a storm is imminent.

Farmers and peasants usually use the lunar calendar for their agricultural and cultural activities. **Tháng Bảy**, literally "Month Seven" according to the lunar calendar, is equivalent to August.

FUNCTIONAL VOCABULARY

DANH TỪ

nhiệt độ	temperature
khí hậu	climate
thời tiết	weather
trời	sky, heaven
mây	cloud
gió	wind
nắng	sunrays
mặt trời	sun
mặt trăng	moon
sao	star
bão	storm
sương mù	fog
tuyết	snow
mưa	rain
đất	earth, soil
mùa	season

TÍNH TỪ

nóng	hot, warm
ấm áp	temperate
lạnh	cold
sáng	bright
tối	dark
quang đãng	clear, cloudless
mát	cool, mild
u ám	overcast
ẩm thấp	humid
đẹp	nice, beautiful
xấu	bad
khô	dry
ướt	wet
nắng	sunny

ĐỘNG TỪ

có	to have
có vẻ	to appear
dường như	to seem
trông	to look
(cảm) thấy	to feel
rơi	to fall
thổi	to blow
dự báo	to forecast

Tôi là Hoa, trưởng phòng nhân sự của công ty. I'm Hoa, our company's head of Human Resources.

Tôi rất vui được có cuộc phỏng vấn hôm nay. I'm very glad to have this interview today.

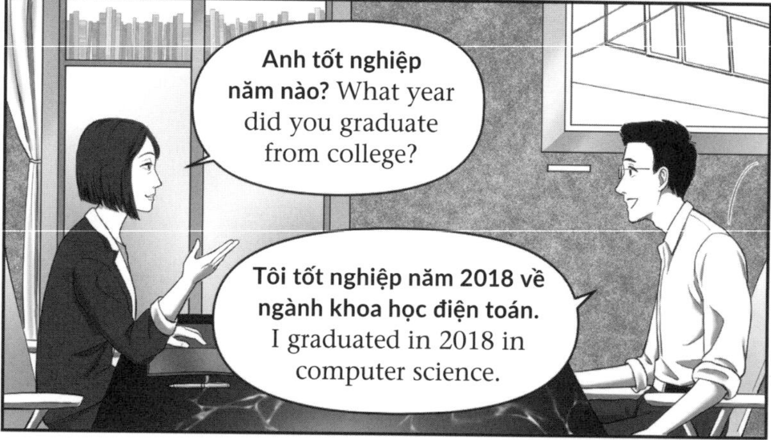
Anh tốt nghiệp năm nào? What year did you graduate from college?
Tôi tốt nghiệp năm 2018 về ngành khoa học điện toán. I graduated in 2018 in computer science.

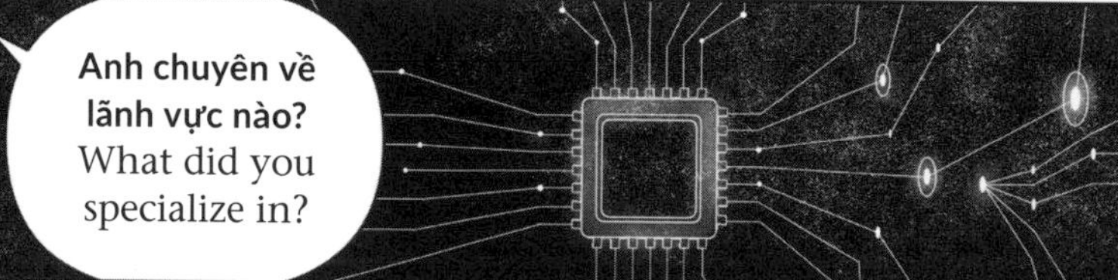
Anh chuyên về lãnh vực nào? What did you specialize in?

Tôi học về lập trình. I studied programming.

Tôi có thể tìm hiểu thêm về nhiều việc khác. I can learn other types of work, too.

CHAPTER 5

The Professional World

Thế Giới Nghề Nghiệp

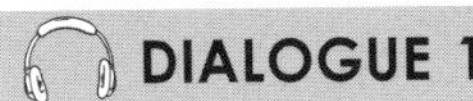

DIALOGUE 1

Tân is interviewing with Mrs. Hoa for a position in computer programming at a big IT company. This is the first part of the interview.

BÀ HOA **Chào anh Tân! Tôi là Hoa, trưởng phòng nhân sự của công ty.**
chahw^5 ănh^1 tun^1 // tohy^1 la^5 hwa^1 // trŭuhng^4 fahngm^5 nhun^1 shŭ^6 koouh^4 kohngm^1 tee^1
Hello Mr. Tan. I'm Hoa, our company's head of Human Resources.

TÂN **Chào bà. Tôi rất vui được có cuộc phỏng vấn hôm nay. Tôi không ngờ có ngày được ngồi trong toà nhà này của công ty ITCom.**
chahw^5 ba^5 // tohy^1 rut^2 vooy^1 dŭuhk^6 kah^2 kwohk^6 fahngm^4 vun^2 hohm^1 năy^1 // tohy^1 khongm^1 nguh^5 kah^2 ngăy^5 dŭuhk^6 ngohy^5 trahngm^1 twa^5 nha^5 năy^5 koouh^4 kohngm^1 tee^1 IT-Com
Hello ma'am. I'm very glad to have this interview today. I would never have guessed I would be sitting here one day in this ITCom building.

BÀ HOA **Chúng ta bắt đầu bằng một số chi tiết cá nhân của anh nhé. Anh tốt nghiệp đại học năm nào và về ngành gì?**
choongm^2 ta^1 băt^2 dohw^5 băng^5 moht^6 shoh^2 chee^1 tyeht^2 ka^2 nhun^1 koouh^4 ănh^1 nhe^2 // ănh^1 toht^2 ngyehp^6 die^6 hahkp^6 năm^1 nahw^5 va^5 veh^5 ngănh^5 yee^5
Let's start with some of your personal information, OK? What year did you graduate from college and what was your major?

TÂN **Tôi tốt nghiệp năm 2018 về ngành khoa học điện toán.**
tohy^1 toht^2 ngyehp^6 năm^1 hie^1 ngan^5 mŭuhy^5 tam^2 veh^5 ngănh^5 khwa^1 hakp^6 dyehn^6 twan^2
I graduated in 2018 in computer science.

BÀ HOA **Anh chuyên về lãnh vực nào?**
ănh^1 chwyehn^1 veh^5 lănh^3 vŭk^6 nahw^5
What did you specialize in?

TÂN **Tôi học về lập trình, nhưng tôi học hỏi rất nhanh. Tôi có thể tìm hiểu thêm về nhiều việc khác công ty cần tôi làm.**

tohy[1] hakp[6] veh[5] lup[6] treenh[5] // nhŭng[1] tohy[1] hakp[6] hahy[4] rut[2] nhănh[1] // tohy[1] kah[2] theh[4] teem[5] hyehw[4] thehm[1] veh[4] nhyehw[5] vyehk[6] khak[2] kohngm[1] tee[1] kun[5] tohy[1] lam[5]

I studied programming, but I am a quick learner. I can learn other types of work that the company needs me to do.

KEY VOCABULARY 1

trưởng *n*	head (of a unit)	**khoa học** *n*	science
phòng *n*	office	**chuyên về** *v*	to specialize in
nhân sự *n*	personnel	**lãnh vực** *n*	field
cuộc phỏng vấn *n*	interview	**lập trình** *n*	programming
hôm nay *adv*	today	**học hỏi** *v*	to learn (in general)
bắt đầu *v*	to start	**nhanh** *adj, adv*	fast
một số *adj*	a few, a number of	**có thể** *v*	to be able to, can
chi tiết *n*	detail; information	**thêm** *adv*	more
cá nhân *adj*	personal, individual	**việc** *n*	work; job
tốt nghiệp *v*	to graduate	**khác** *adj*	other; different
năm *n*	year	**công ty** *n*	company

IDIOMATIC EXPRESSIONS 1

Tôi rất vui được... "I am very happy to..." Use this expression when you get to do something favorable or desirable. The adjective **vui** can be replaced with others such as **hân hạnh** "honor," **mừng** "glad," **xúc động** "emotional," **hào hứng** "excited," etc. Complete the expression with a verb (and its complement and modifier[s]) indicating the situation: **Tôi rất mừng được gặp cô** "I'm very glad to meet you," **Tôi rất hào hứng được cộng tác với các anh chị** "I'm very excited to collaborate with you guys."

học hỏi **Học** means "to learn" or "to study," as in **Tôi đang học tiếng Việt** "I am learning Vietnamese." This verb is combined with other verbs to form compound verbs with a more general meaning: **học hỏi** "to learn and inquire," **học tập** "to learn and drill," **học hành** "to learn and practice," etc. An example is **Cô Lan rất thích học hỏi** "Miss Lan loves learning."

CULTURE NOTES 1

In the dialogue above, Tân is younger than Mrs. Hoa, but she still addresses him as "older brother Tân" to sound polite and professional. On his part, Tân addresses her using only the term **bà** "Mrs." without her first name. In many parts of the country, people use only a term of address when speaking with a person older than they are, avoiding the inclusion of their first name out of respect. When referring to them, however, it is acceptable to use their name: **Bà Hoa là trưởng phòng nhân sự** "Mrs. Hoa is the head of Human Resources."

GRAMMAR NOTES 1

I. Classifiers

Certain terms in Vietnamese are used before concrete nouns to indicate their category or "class," hence the name "classifiers." The classes include humans, objects, animals, fruits, flowers, dwelling units, means of transportation, and others.

CLASSIFIER	NOUN CLASS	EXAMPLES
cái	objects, items	**cái bàn** "table," **cái điện thoại** "telephone"
người	humans	**người đàn ông** "man," **người đàn bà** "woman"
đứa	children	**đứa con trai** "boy," **đứa con gái** "girl"
con	animals	**con mèo** "cat," **con cá** "fish," **con chim** "bird"
trái	fruits	**trái xoài** "mango," **trái cam** "orange"
cây	trees, plants	**cây táo** "apple tree," **cây chuối** "banana tree"
hoa	flowers	**hoa hồng** "rose," **hoa lan** "orchid"
chiếc	means of transportation	**chiếc xe hơi** "car," **chiếc thuyền** "boat"
dây	strings, cords	**dây chuyền** "necklace," **dây nịt** "belt"
bài	written texts	**bài học** "lesson," **bài thơ** "poem," **bài hát** "song"
bức	constructed works	**bức tượng** "statue," **bức tường** "wall"
cuốn/quyển	bound sheets	**cuốn sách** "book," **quyển vở** "notebook"
căn	small dwelling units	**căn phòng** "room," **căn nhà** "house"
ngôi	large homes, temples	**ngôi nhà** "mansion," **ngôi đền** "temple"
toà	large buildings	**toà thị chính** "city hall," **toà lâu đài** "palace"

Some classifiers denote shape or number, and in some cases are randomly assigned:

con **con người** "human beings," **con trai** "boy/son," **con gái** "girl/daughter," **con đường** "road, street," **con dao** "knife," **con tem** "stamp," **con mắt** "eye," **con sông** "river"

trái **trái banh** "ball," **trái đất** "Earth," **trái bong bóng** "balloon," **trái cầu** "shuttlecock"

cây **cây viết** "pen," **cây thước** "ruler," **cây gậy** "cane," **cây cầu** "bridge," **cây dù** "umbrella"

cuốn **cuốn phim** "movie, film roll," **cuốn chả giò** "eggroll," **cuốn truyện** "fiction book"

chiếc **chiếc nhẫn** "ring," **chiếc giày** "shoe" (in a pair), **chiếc đũa** "chopstick" (in a pair), **chiếc vớ** "sock" (in a pair)

đôi **đôi giày** "pair of shoes," **đôi dép** "pair of flip-flops," **đôi đũa** "pair of chopsticks," **đôi găng tay** "pair of gloves," **đôi mắt** "eyes," **đôi tay** "hands," **đôi chân** "feet," **đôi bạn** "the two friends," **đôi tình nhân** "the two lovers," **đôi vợ chồng** "husband and wife"

bộ **bộ quần áo** "suit," **bộ phim** "sequential movies," **bộ tách trà** "tea set," **bộ sưu tập** "collection," **bộ bài** "deck of cards"

A noun is usually preceded by a classifier when there is also a numeral/indefinite adjective or a demonstrative adjective accompanying it:

(1) a. **Tôi vừa mua mấy cuốn tiểu thuyết tiếng Việt.**
tohy^{1} vŭuh^{5} moouh^{1} may^{2} kwohn^{2} tyehw^{4} thwyeht^{2} tyehng^{2} vyeht^{6}
I've just bought a couple of novels in Vietnamese.

b. **Cô có thích cuốn tiểu thuyết này không?**
koh^{1} kah^{2} theech^{2} kwohn^{2} tyehw^{4} thwyeht^{2} năy^{5} khohngm^{1}
Do you like this novel?

However, classifiers are not used when the reference is general (which also implies a plural sense):

(2) a. **Anh có thích đọc Ø tiểu thuyết không?**
ănh^{1} kah^{2} theech^{2} dahkp^{6} tyehw^{4} thwyeht^{2} khohngm^{1}
Do you like reading novels?

b. **Anh ấy đọc nhiều Ø tiểu thuyết lắm.**
ănh^{1} ay^{2} dahkp^{6} nhyehw^{5} tyehw^{4} thwyeht^{2} lăm^{2}
He reads lots of novels.

A number of compound nouns and nouns containing two or more syllables are habitually used without a classifier:

(3) a. **Ø Thành phố này có nhiều hãng sản xuất đồ điện tử.**
thănh^{5} foh^{2} năy^{5} kah^{2} nhyehw^{5} hang^{3} shan^{4} swut^{2} doh^{5} dyehn^{6} tŭ^{4}
This city has several electronics factories.

b. **Ø Công viên kia đang được tu bổ.**
kohngm^{1} vyehn^{1} keeuh^{1} dang^{1} dŭuhk^{6} too^{1} boh^{4}
That park over there is being renovated.

c. **Ø Câu lạc bộ này là của các kiến trúc sư về hưu.**
kohw^{1} lak^{6} boh^{6} năy^{5} la^{5} koouh^{4} kak^{2} kyehn^{2} trookp^{2} shŭ^{1} veh^{5} hŭw^{1}
This club belongs to retired architects.

When a noun is specifically modified by one or more words, it doesn't require a classifier. Compare the sentences below, where the noun **trường** "school" is modified by another noun **đại học** "university" in (4b) and **phòng** "office" is modified by **hành chánh** "administrative" in (5b):

(4) a. **Ngôi trường này đẹp quá!**
ngohy^{1} trŭuhng^{5} năy^{5} dep^{6} kwa^{2}
How beautiful this school is!

b. **Ø Trường đại học này đẹp quá!**
trŭuhng^{5} die^{6} hahkp^{6} năy^{5} dep^{6} kwa^{2}
How beautiful this university is!

(5) a. **Căn phòng đó còn trống.**
kăn^{1} fahngm^{5} dah^{2} kahn^{5} trohngm^{2}
That office is still unoccupied.

b. **Ø Phòng hành chánh ở đâu vậy, cô?**
fahnm^{5} hănh^{5} chănh^{2} uh^{4} dohw^{1} vay^{6} koh^{1}
Miss, where is the administrative office?

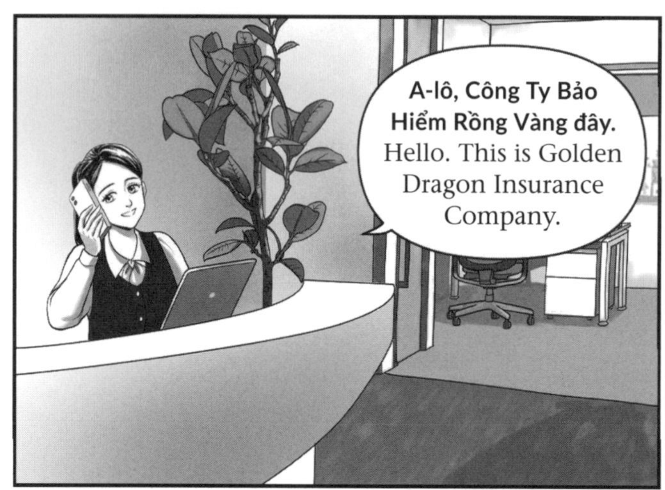

A-lô, Công Ty Bảo Hiểm Rồng Vàng đây.
Hello. This is Golden Dragon Insurance Company.

Chào chị. Tôi là Vân.
Hello. My name's Vân.
Chị cần gì ạ?
How can I help you?

Tôi muốn hỏi thêm chi tiết về đợt tuyển dụng phụ tá văn phòng.
I'd like to ask for more information about the office assistant job opening.
Công việc này bắt đầu là bán thời gian...
This position will start as part-time...

Đơn xin việc có cần kèm theo thư giới thiệu không ạ?
Does the application need to come with letters of recommendation?

Có chứ. Chị nhớ gửi cả bản tóm tắt cá nhân nữa nhé.
Of course. Please remember to send in a resumé as well.

DIALOGUE 2

Vân is calling an insurance company for information about a job opening.

THƯ KÝ **A-lô, Công Ty Bảo Hiểm Rồng Vàng đây.**
a1 loh1 // kohngm1 tee1 bahw4 hyehm4 rohngm5 vang5 day1
Hello. This is Golden Dragon Insurance Company.

VÂN **Chào chị. Tôi là Vân.**
chahw5 chee6 // tohy1 la5 vun1
Hello (sister). My name's Vân.

THƯ KÝ **Chào chị Vân. Chị cần gì ạ?**
chahw5 chee6 vun1 // chee6 kun5 yee5 a6
Hello, Vân. How can I help you?

VÂN **Tôi muốn hỏi thêm chi tiết về đợt tuyển dụng việc phụ tá văn phòng. Công việc này là toàn thời gian hay bán thời gian vậy, chị?**
tohy1 mwohn2 hahy4 thehm1 chee1 tyet2 veh5 duht6 teyehn4 yoongm6 vyehk6 foo6 ta2 văn1 fahngm5 // kohngm1 vyehk6 năy5 la5 twan5 thuhy5 yan1 hăy1 ban2 thuhy5 yan1 vay6 chee6
I'd like to ask for more information about the job opening for an office assistant. Is this position full-time or part-time?

THƯ KÝ **Công việc này bắt đầu là bán thời gian, nhưng có thể trở thành toàn thời gian sau một năm.**
kohngm1 vyehk6 năy5 băt2 dohw5 la5 ban2 thuhy5 yan1 // nhũng1 kah2 theh4 truh4 thănh5 twan5 thuhy5 yan1 shăw1 moht6 năm1
This position will start as part-time, but can become full-time after a year.

VÂN **Đơn xin việc có cần kèm theo thư giới thiệu không hở, chị?**
duhn1 seen1 vyehk6 kah2 kun5 kem5 thew1 thũ1 yuhy2 thyehw6 khohngm1 huh4 chee6
Does the application need to be accompanied by letters of recommendation?

THƯ KÝ **Có chứ. Chị nhớ gửi cả bản tóm tắt cá nhân nữa nhé.**
kah2 chũ2 // chee6 nhuh2 gũỹ ka4 ban4 tom2 tăt2 ka2 nhun1 nũuh3 nhe2
Of course. Please remember to send in a resumé as well.

KEY VOCABULARY 2

bảo hiểm *n*	insurance	**bắt đầu** *v*	to start
cần *v*	to need	**bán thời gian** *adj*	part-time
muốn *v*	to want	**toàn thời gian** *adj*	full-time
hỏi *v*	to ask	**đơn**	form; application
thêm *adv*	more	**đơn xin việc** *n*	job application
hay *conj*	or	**kèm theo** *v*	to accompany
tuyển dụng *v*	to hire	**thư giới thiệu** *n*	letter of recommendation

phụ tá *n*	assistant	**nhớ** *v*	to remember
văn phòng *n*	office	**gửi** *v*	to send
thư *n*	letter	**bản tóm tắt cá nhân**	resumé

IDIOMATIC EXPRESSIONS 2

[*Question*] **vậy** [*name/pronoun*] To tone down a question that would otherwise sound like an "interrogation," speakers usually add the particle **vậy**, and optionally use the interlocutor's name or personal pronoun to show friendliness or respect. **Vậy** can be replaced by **hở**, which sounds more informal or intimate. **Hạn chót nộp đơn là khi nào vậy, ông?** "When is the application submission deadline, sir?"

[*Command*] **nhé** A command (imperative sentence) can also be toned down in several ways, one of which is by adding the friendly-sounding particle **nhé** at the end. **Cô nhớ gọi lại tôi nhé** "Remember to call me back, will you?"

CULTURE NOTES 2

In the English-speaking world, a customer is usually welcomed with "How may I help you?" expressing the speaker's willingness to help. In Vietnam, the focus is on the customer, who might need help with something, hence the question **Ông/bà cần gì ạ?** "What do you need?" Notice that the particle **ạ** is added to make the speaker sound polite or respectful.

GRAMMAR NOTES 2

II. Demonstrative adjectives

This category of adjective indicates the degree of distance between a speaker and the person or thing they are referring to, either spatially or perceptually. Demonstrative adjectives follow the noun they modify.

	NEAR	FAR	VERY FAR
NOUN	**này**	**đó**	**kia**
	this	*that*	*that... over there*

If one or more descriptive adjectives are used with a noun, they will precede a demonstrative adjective. A "full" noun phrase can contain several types of modifiers in the following order with regards to the noun:

NUMERAL/ INDEFINITE ADJECTIVE/ PLURAL MARKER	CLASSIFIER	NOUN	DESCRIPTIVE ADJECTIVE	DEMONSTRATIVE ADJECTIVE
ba	**cuốn**	**từ điển**	**cũ**	**này**
three	*(for books)*	*dictionaries*	*old*	*these*
these three old dictionaries				
mấy	**cái**	**máy điện toán**	**mới**	**đó**
several	*(for objects)*	*computers*	*new*	*those*
those new computers				
những	**bức**	**thư**	**quan trọng**	**kia**
(plural)	*(for letters)*	*letters*	*important*	*those... over there*
those important letters over there				

Parallel to the demonstrative adjectives are the demonstrative adverbs, which are used for the same effects as the former, but with an adverbial function (modifying verbs).

NEAR	FAR	VERY FAR
đây	**đó**	**kia**
here	*there*	*over there*

These adverbs are usually used after the preposition **ở** "in, on, at." **Kia** is often preceded by the noun **đằng** "direction, way":

(6) a. **Văn phòng của ông giám đốc là ở đây.**
văn[1] fahngm[5] koouh[4] ohngm[1] yam[2] dohkp[2] la[5] uh[4] day[1]
The manager's office is here.

b. **Ở đó cô sẽ thấy nhiều nhà máy dệt.**
uh[4] dah[2] koh[1] she[3] thay[2] nhyehw[5] nha[5] măy[2] yeht[6]
You will see many textile mills there.

c. **Các anh chị đã đến thăm viện bảo tàng ở đằng kia chưa?**
kak[2] ănh[1] chee[6] da[3] dehn[2] thăm[1] vyehn[6] bahw[4] tang[5] uh[4] dăng[5] keeuh[1] chŭuh[1]
Have you guys visited the museum over there?

In sentences that identify objects or people, demonstrative adverbs can replace a classifier plus demonstrative adjective. Compare:

(7) a. **Cái này là bảng tên nhân viên, phải không?**
kie[2] năy[5] la[5] bang[4] tehn[1] nhun[1] vyehn[1] fie[4] khohngm[1]
This is an employee's name tag, isn't it?

b. → **Đây là bảng tên nhân viên, phải không?**

(8) a. **Người đó không phải là giám thị của tôi.**
ngŭuhy^5 dah^2 khohnm^1 fie^4 la^5 yam^2 thee^6 kooh^4 tohy^1
That's not my supervisor.

b. → **Đó không phải là giám thị của tôi.**

(9) a. **Chiếc kia là xe vận tải.**
chyehk^2 keeuh^1 la^5 se^1 vun^6 tie^4
That's a truck.

b. → **Kia không phải là xe vận tải.**

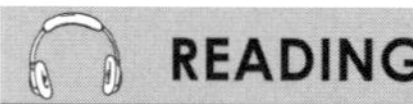

READING

NGHỀ KHẢM XÀ CỪ

Nghề khảm xà cừ là một trong những nghề thủ công lâu đời ở Việt Nam nhờ vào vị trí của đất nước trải dài theo bờ biển Đông. Xà cừ là lớp óng ánh lấy từ vỏ của những động vật nhuyễn thể sống dưới biển như trai, ốc hay bào ngư. Sau khi được biến chế kỹ càng, các mảnh xà cừ được gắn vào tranh ảnh, đồ trang sức, đồ gỗ trong nhà, v.v. Tất cả các giai đoạn đều được thực hiện tỉ mỉ bằng tay. Kết quả là những tác phẩm nghệ thuật nổi bật như có ba chiều, lóng lánh và đủ màu sắc tự nhiên của xà cừ.

Ngày nay, kỹ thuật tân tiến đã cho phép máy móc làm một số giai đoạn trong việc khảm xà cừ. Tuy vậy, không có máy móc nào thay thế được bàn tay khéo léo và tài tình của những nghệ nhân sống về nghề này qua bao đời nay.

ngeh^5 kham^4 sa^5 kŭ^5 la^5 moht^6 trahngm^1 nhŭng^3 ngeh^5 thoo^4 kohngm^1 lohw^1 duhy^5 uh^4 vyeht^6 nam^1 nhuh^5 vahw^5 vee^6 tree^2 loouh^4 dut^2 nŭuhk^2 trie^4 yie^5 thew^1 buh^5 byehn^4 dohngm^1 // sa^5 kŭ^5 la^5 luhp^2 ahngm^2 ănh^2 lay^2 tŭ^5 vah^4 koouh^4 nhŭng^3 dohngm^6 vut^6 nhwyehn^3 theh^4 shohngm^2 yŭuhy^2 byehn^4 nhŭ^1 trie^1 ohkp^2 bahw^5 ngŭ^1 // shăw^1 khee^1 byehn^2 cheh^2 kee^3 kang^5 // kak^2 mănh^4 sa^5 kŭ^5 dŭuhk^6 găn^2 vahw^5 trănh^1 ănh^4 doh^5 trang^1 shŭk^2 doh^5 goh^3 trahngm^1 nha^5 vun^1 vun^1 // tut^2 ka^4 kak^2 yie^1 dwan^6 dehw^5 dŭuhk^5 thŭk^6 hyehn^6 tee^4 mee^4 băng^5 tăy^1 // keht^2 kwa^4 la^5 nhŭng^3 tak^2 fum^4 ngeh^6 thwut^6 nohy^4 but^6 nhŭ^1 kah^2 ba^1 chyehw^5, lahngm^2 lănh^2 va^5 doo^4 măw^5 shăk^2 tŭ^6 nhyehn^1 koouh^4 sa^5 kŭ^5//

ngăy^5 năy^1 kee^3 thwut^6 tun^1 tyehn^2 da^3 chah^1 fep^2 măy^2 mahkp^2 lam^5 moht^6 shoh^2 yie^1 dwan^6 trahngm^1 vyehk^6 kham^4 sa^5 kŭ^5 // twee^1 vay^6 khohngm^1 kah^2 măy^2 mahkp^2 nahw^5 thăy^1 theh^2 dŭuhk^6 ban^5 tăy^1 khew^2 lew^2 va^5 tie^5 teenh^5 koouh^4 nhŭng^3 ngeh^6 nhun^1 shohngm^2 veh^5 ngeh^5 năy^5 kwa^1 bahw^{1}duhy^5 năy^1

NACRE INLAY HANDICRAFTS

Nacre (mother-of-pearl) inlay art is one of Vietnam's long-standing handicrafts, thanks to the country's location stretching along the East Sea. Nacre is the iridescent layer taken from the shells of various types of marine mollusk such as oysters, snails and abalones. After careful processing, pieces of nacre are inlaid into paintings, jewelry, wood furniture, and other items. All the steps are meticulously done by hand. The result is artistic work that appears almost three-dimensional, glistening and naturally colorful with nacre.

Nowadays, modern technology has allowed machinery to take over some steps in nacre inlay. However, no machine can replace the skilled and talented hands of the artists who have made their living from this craft for generations.

COMPREHENSION QUESTIONS

Answer the following questions in complete sentences, first orally, then in writing.

1. **Xà cừ là gì?** *What is nacre?*

 ____

2. **Các mảnh xà cừ được gắn vào đâu?** *Where are the pieces of nacre inlaid?*

 ____

3. **Tại sao nghề khảm xà cừ được gọi là nghề thủ công?** *Why is nacre inlay art called a handicraft?*

 ____

4. **Các sản phẩm khảm xà cừ trông như thế nào?** *How do nacre-inlaid products look?*

 ____

5. **Máy móc có thể thay thế nghệ nhân trong việc khảm xà cừ không?** *Can machines replace artists in the nacre-inlaying process?*

 ____

PRACTICE

A. Listening comprehension

Based on the following audio about a job opening, circle the correct information in the chart below.

	a.	b.	c.
Company	điện tử	điện thoại	điện thư
Position	thư ký	giám thị	giám đốc
Job type	toàn thời gian	bán thời gian	tạm thời
Document NOT needed	thư giới thiệu	bản tóm tắt	bản điểm
Send application to	trưởng phòng	giám đốc	thư ký
Send application via	điện thư	bưu điện	tin nhắn
Deadline	cuối tuần	cuối tháng	cuối năm

B. Classifiers

Fill in the blanks in the following sentences with the correct classifiers from the list.

cái chiếc cây bài căn trái con người cuốn toà

1. _____________ **phòng này rất thích hợp để làm phòng họp.**
   This room is very suitable for using as a conference room.

2. **Giám đốc của tôi là _____________ đàn bà mặc đồ đen.**
   My manager is the woman in black.

3. **Tôi muốn _____________ ghế này cho văn phòng mới của tôi.**
   I want this chair for my new office.

4. **Mua cho tôi hai _____________ viết và một _____________ từ điển.**
   Buy me two pens and a dictionary.

5. **Cô có thể để _____________ địa cầu đó trên bàn làm việc của cô.**
   You can put that globe on your office desk.

6. **Anh cần bao nhiêu _____________ tem để gửi thư?**
   How many stamps do you need to mail your letters?

7. **Công ty của chúng tôi là ở trong _____________ nhà cao đó.**
   Our company is in that tall building.

8. ______________ **xe màu vàng kia là của cô thư ký.**
That yellow car over there belongs to the secretary.

9. **Ông chủ tịch công ty sẽ đọc một** ______________ **diễn văn khai mạc.**
The company president will give an opening speech.

C. Demonstrative adjectives

Choose the correct demonstrative adjectives (**này**, **đó** or **kia**) according to the distance between the pointing hand and the objects, then build sentences based on the given information and the model below.

	GẦN *Near*	**XA** *Far*	**RẤT XA** *Very far*
ĐIỆN THOẠI – cái – đen – là của ai? *Whose black telephone is that?*			
0. **Cái điện thoại đen đó là của ai?**			
SÁCH – cuốn – nhỏ – không mắc lắm. *This small book is not very expensive.*			
1.			
VIẾT – cây – mới – không phải là của tôi. *That new pen over there is not mine.*			
2.			
MÈO – con – lớn – tên là Mimi. *That big cat's name is Mimi.*			
3.			
XE ĐẠP – chiếc – cũ – giá bao nhiêu? *How much is that old bike over there?*			
4.			

	GẦN *Near*	**XA** *Far*	**RẤT XA** *Very far*
☞	🏠		
NHÀ - ngôi - đẹp - ở gần biển. *This beautiful house is close to the beach.*			
5.			

D. Vocabulary

Complete the paragraph below with the correct words given in the list. Use each word only once.

thư ký   đi làm   toà   đi dạo   nhà   người   lớn   sống   xe   chó

(1) ________________ **đàn bà đó tên là Vân. Bà làm** (2) ________________ **ở một công ty trong**

(3) ________________ **nhà kia. Bà lái một chiếc** (4) ________________ **màu trắng để** (5)

________________**. Bà** (6) ________________ **với gia đình trong một căn** (7) ________________

ở gần biển. Nhà của bà không (8) ________________ **lắm nhưng rất đẹp. Vào cuối tuần, bà thường**

(9) ________________ **với chồng và con** (10) ________________ **tên là Lulu.**

PROVERB

TRĂM HAY KHÔNG BẰNG TAY QUEN.

trăm¹ hăy¹ khohngm¹ băng⁵ tăy¹ kwen¹

"A hundred good [workers] are not equal to a skilled pair of hands."

Hay "good" in this context refers to people who have been trained or certified to do something. Still, they are not necessarily as skilled as those who have long experience doing the same thing without training or certification.

In old Vietnam, workers were valued not by formal training or education but by how long they had been on the job. The use of the word "hands" tells us the proverb is about manual work, which was prevalent in the past, rather than about today's white-collar jobs.

FUNCTIONAL VOCABULARY

DANH TỪ

phòng	room
chi tiết	detail; information
(công) việc	work; job
công ty	company
hãng	firm; factory
khoa học	science
lãnh vực	field
bảo hiểm	insurance
văn phòng	office
phụ tá	assistant
thư	letter
đơn	form; application
ngành	major
xe	car, vehicle
nhà	house
viết	pen
sách	book
giám đốc	manager
thư ký	secretary

TÍNH TỪ

nhanh	quick
chậm	slow
mới	new
cũ	old
khác	different; other
cao	tall, high
thấp	short, low
bán thời gian	part-time
toàn thời gian	full-time
tạm thời	temporary

ĐỘNG TỪ

chuyên về	to specialize in
phỏng vấn	to interview
tốt nghiệp	to graduate
bắt đầu	to start
có thể	to be able to
cần	to need
nhớ	to remember
gửi	to send

Tôi cần thuê hai trăm miếng bọc lưng ghế màu hồng...
I'll need to rent two hundred pink chair back covers...

Chị cho tôi đặt năm trăm hoa hồng vàng.
And let me order five hundred yellow roses.

CHAPTER 6

Numbers, Telling Time and Dates

Số Đếm – Giờ Giấc – Ngày Tháng

 **DIALOGUE 1**

Hoa, a wedding planner, is having a video call with Hồng, the owner of a wedding supplies store, about what she needs for an upcoming event she is planning.

HOA **Chào chị Hồng! Dạo này chị thế nào?**
chahw^5 chee^6 hohngm^5 // yahw^6 năy^5 chee^6 theh^2 nahw^5
Hello Hồng! How have you been?

HỒNG **A, chị Hoa! Lâu ngày quá! Chúng tôi bận rộn lắm, còn chị thì sao?**
a^1 chee^6 hwa^1 // lohw^1 ngăy^5 kwa^2 // choongm^2 tohy^1 bun^6 rohn^6 lăm^2 // kahn^5 chee^6 thee^5 shahw
Ah, Hoa! It's been a while! We're so busy, how about you?

HOA **Tôi cũng vậy. Tôi đang chuẩn bị cho một đám cưới vào tháng tới. Chị cho tôi đặt và thuê một số món nhé.**
tohy^1 koongm^3 vay^6 // tohy^1 dang^1 chwun^4 bee^6 chah^1 moht^6 dam^2 kŭuhy^2 vahw^5 thang^2 tuhy^2 // chee^6 chah^1 tohy^1 dăt^6 va^5 thweh^1 moht^6 shoh^2 mahn^2 nhe^2
Me too. I'm preparing for a wedding next month. Let me order and rent a few things, OK?

HỒNG **Dạ được. Chị cần những gì?**
ya^6 dŭuhk^6 // chee^6 kun^5 nhŭng^3 yee^5
Of course. What did you need?

HOA **Tôi cần thuê hai trăm miếng bọc lưng ghế màu hồng, hai mươi cái khăn trải bàn cùng màu, ba mươi lăm bình cắm hoa nhỏ và bốn cái lớn.**
tohy^1 kun^5 thweh^1 hie^1 trăm^1 myehng^2 bahkp^6 lŭng^1 geh^2 măw^5 hohngm^5 // hie^1 mŭuhy^2 kie^1 khăn^1 trie^4 ban^5 koongm^5 măw^5 // hie^1 mŭuhy^1 beenh^5 kăm^2 hwa^1 nhah^4 va^5 ba^1 kie^2 luhn^2
I'll need to rent two hundred pink chair back covers, twenty tablecloths, same color, thirty-five small flower vases and four big ones.

HỒNG **Chị muốn hoa gì?**

chee[6] mwohn[2] hwa[1] yee[5]

What kind of flowers would you like?

HOA **Chị cho tôi đặt năm trăm hoa hồng vàng cho các bàn tiệc. À, chị làm cho tôi một cái vòm hoa hình bán nguyệt, cao hai mét, phủ một tấm màn voan hồng nhạt, một trăm hoa hồng trắng lẫn với một trăm hoa màu hồng cùng với nhiều lá bạch đàn nhé.**

chee[6] chah[1] tohy[1] dăt[6] năm[1] trăm[1] hwa[1] hohngm[5] vang[5] chah[1] kak[2] ban[5] tyehk[6] // a[5] chee[6] lam[5] chah[1] tohy[1] moht[6] kie[1] vahm[5] hwa[1] heenh[5] ban[2] ngwyeht[6] kahw[1] hie[1] met[2] // foo[4] moht[6] tum[2] man[5] vwan[1] hohngm[5] nhat[6] // moht[6] trăm[1] hwa[1] hohngm[5] trăng[2] lun[3] vuhy[2] moht[6] trăm[1] hwa[1] măw[5] hohngm[5] koongm[5] vuhy[2] nhyehw[5] la[2] băch[6] dan[5] nhe[2]

Let me order five hundred yellow roses for the banquet tables. Ah, please make me a two-meter-tall halfmoon floral arch, covered with a light pink veil curtain, one hundred white roses mixed with another hundred pink ones and a lot of eucalyptus leaves.

KEY VOCABULARY 1

bận (rộn) *adj*	busy	**hoa** *n*	flower
chuẩn bị *v*	to prepare	**tiệc** *n*	party; banquet
đám cưới *n*	wedding ceremony	**vòm hoa** *n*	floral arch
tháng *n*	month	**hình bán nguyệt** *n*	halfmoon shape
đặt *v*	to place; to order	**mét** *n*	meter
thuê *v*	to rent	**tấm** *n, cl*	sheet
món *n*	item	**màn** *n*	drape, curtain
miếng *n*	piece	**voan** *n*	veil
bọc *v*	to cover; to wrap	**nhạt** *adj*	light (color)
màu *n*	color	**trắng** *adj*	white
hồng *adj*	pink	**nhiều** *adj*	many
khăn trải bàn *n*	tablecloth	**lá** *n*	leaf
bình cắm hoa *n*	flower vase	**bạch đàn** *n*	eucalyptus

IDIOMATIC EXPRESSIONS 1

Lâu ngày quá! "It's been quite a while!" Notice that this expression does not contain a verb but is rather an idiomatic phrase. **Lâu** means "(for) a long time" and **lâu ngày** translates as "many days."

Còn [chị] thì sao? This is the equivalent of "How about you?" Use it to ask someone about the same situation shared by both speakers. Replace the pronoun in the brackets with an appropriate pronoun addressing the interlocutor.

CULTURE NOTES 1

In general, Vietnamese people superstitiously avoid black and white, especially for decorations on occasions such as birthdays and weddings (except for the bride's and groom's clothing, of course). When it comes to flowers, some white is acceptable as long as it is mixed with other bright colors. **Đen**, the color black, is usually associated with negative things. The expression **Đen bạc, đỏ tình** (literally "black in gambling, red in love") is equivalent to the English "unlucky at cards, lucky in love." **Trắng**, the color white, on the other hand, is associated with emptiness or nothingness, as expressed in **Anh ấy mất trắng tài sản** "'He has lost all his assets" or **trắng tay** "empty-handed."

GRAMMAR NOTES 1

I. Plural markers, numbers

The plural of a noun in Vietnamese is not shown with an attached suffix like the **-s** in English, for example, but expressed in other ways, one of which is the use of *plural markers*: **các** and **những.** These two markers come before a noun, or before a classifier if the noun takes one. **Các** refers to all the things or people in a given group, while **những** refers to some of the things or people in a group.

(1) a. **Những cái đồng hồ này rất đắt tiền.**
nhŭng^{3} kie^{2} dohngm^{5} hoh^{5} năy^{5} rut^{2} dăt^{2} tyehn^{5}
These watches are very expensive.

b. **Các tấm lịch năm mới đâu rồi?**
kak^{2} tum^{2} leech^{6} năm^{1} muhy^{2} dohw^{1} rohy^{5}
Where are all the New Year calendars?

Plural markers, however, do not appear every time a noun is expressed in a plural sense. There are other ways to give a noun a plural meaning:

- Bare form of the noun: In many contexts, the mere mention of a countable noun implies that it is plural:

(2) a. **Máy điện toán càng ngày càng tinh vi.**
măy^{2} dyehn^{6} twan^{2} kang^{5} ngay^{5} kang^{5} teenh^{1} vee^{1}
Computers are more and more intricate every day.

b. **Nhiều người không thích dùng điện thoại thông minh.**
nhyehw^{5} ngŭuhy^{5} khohngm^{1} theech^{2} yoongm^{5} dyehn^{6} thwie^{6} thohngm^{1} meenh^{1}
Many people don't like using smartphones.

- Compound nouns: A number of nouns are combined with another one, either a synonym or one in the same category, for a plural reference:

(3) a. **Nhà cửa dạo này khan hiếm quá!**
[**nhà** "house" + **cửa** "door" = **nhà cửa** "houses"]
nha^{5} *kŭuh*^{4} *yahw*^{6} *năy*^{5} *khan*^{1} *hyehm*^{2} *kwa*^{2}
How scarce houses are nowadays!

b. **Giao lộ đó lúc nào cũng đông đúc xe cộ.**
[**xe** "vehicle" + **cộ** "cart" = **xe cộ** "vehicles"]
yahw^{1} *loh*^{6} *dah*^{2} *lookp*^{2} *nahw*^{5} *koongm*^{3} *dohngm*^{1} *dookp*^{2} *se*^{1} *koh*^{6}
That junction is always crowded with vehicles.

- When not appearing as a bare form, accompanied by a plural marker or in a compound, a noun can be interpreted in the plural sense with the help of a *numeral adjective* or a *quantifier* (also known as an *indefinite adjective*):

(4) a. **Tôi cần ba cái bàn tròn.**
[Numeral adjective + (Classifier) + Plural noun]
tohy^{1} *kun*^{5} *ba*^{1} *kie*^{2} *ban*^{5} *trahn*^{5}
I need three round tables.

b. **Sẽ có nhiều khách đến buổi tiệc.**
[Quantifier + Plural noun]
she^{3} *kah*^{2} *nhyehw*^{5} *khăch*^{2} *dehn*^{2} *bwohy*^{4} *tyehk*^{6}
There will be a lot of guests coming to the party.

A *cardinal number* is a noun that denotes quantity. When a number comes before a noun to indicate the quantity of the things or people represented by the noun, it becomes a *numeral adjective*. The following are cardinal numbers in Vietnamese (**số** is the Vietnamese noun for "number"):

không	*zero*	**mười**	*ten*
một	*one*	**mười một**	*eleven*
hai	*two*	**mười hai**	*twelve*
ba	*three*	**mười ba**	*thirteen*
bốn	*four*	**mười bốn**	*fourteen*
năm	*five*	**mười lăm**	*fifteen*
sáu	*six*	**mười sáu**	*sixteen*
bảy	*seven*	**mười bảy**	*seventeen*
tám	*eight*	**mười tám**	*eighteen*
chín	*nine*	**mười chín**	*nineteen*

hai mươi	*twenty*	ba mươi	*thirty*
hai mươi mốt	*twenty-one*	bốn mươi	*forty*
hai mươi hai	*twenty-two*	năm mươi	*fifty*
hai mươi ba	*twenty-three*	sáu mươi	*sixty*
hai mươi bốn	*twenty-four*	bảy mươi	*seventy*
hai mươi lăm	*twenty-five*	tám mươi	*eighty*
hai mươi sáu	*twenty-six*	chín mươi	*ninety*
hai mươi bảy	*twenty-seven*	một trăm	*one hundred*
hai mươi tám	*twenty-eight*	một trăm lẻ một	*one hundred one*
hai mươi chín	*twenty-nine*	một trăm mười	*one hundred ten*

The Vietnamese words in italics in the chart above have irregular forms, albeit in a consistent way. **Năm** "five" becomes **lăm** after **mười** "ten" and its irregular form **mươi**, which appears in numbers from twenty on. **Một** "one" becomes **mốt** after **mươi**.

Chục is a synonym of **mười/mươi**, used colloquially. This term is used alternatively with **mươi** in counting, especially for (i) age (although this could make a person sound "old"): **ba chục tuổi** instead of **ba mươi tuổi** "thirty years old"; (ii) money: **năm chục đồng** instead of **năm mươi đồng** "fifty dong" (the Vietnamese currency); (iii) percentages: **chín chục phần trăm** instead of **chín mươi phần trăm** "ninety per cent"; (iv) measurements: **sáu chục kí-lô** instead of **sáu mươi kí-lô** "sixty kilograms."

To ask a person in their teens or older their age, use **bao nhiêu** "how much, how many":

(5) **Anh bao nhiêu tuổi?**
ănh[1] bahw[1] nhyehw[1] twohy[4]
How old are you?

If asking for a child's age, use **mấy** "how many":

(6) **Cháu mấy tuổi?**
chăw[2] may[2] twohy[4]
How old are you?

Use **bao nhiêu** and **mấy** similarly for other kinds of questions based on the estimated/expected quantity in the answers:

(7) a. **Chiếc xe đó giá bao nhiêu (đô-la)?**
chyehk[2] se[1] dah[2] ya[2] bahw[1] nhyehw[1]
How much (in dollars) does that car cost?

b. **Cái bánh này (là) mấy đồng vậy?**
kie[2] bănh[2] năy[5] la[5] may[2] dohngm[5] vay[6]
How many dong is this cake?

Chục is used only with numbers ending in zero: **một chục** "ten," **hai chục** "twenty," **ba chục** "thirty," etc. There is only one way to say (and write) a number like "forty-two": **bốn mươi hai**, where **chục** would be incorrect.

As seen in the chart, the word **lẻ** is used to indicate a zero between the hundreds and ones place. **Lẻ** also means "odd" or "decimal," as in **số lẻ** "odd number" or "decimal number," as opposed to **chẵn** "even" or "whole," as in **số chẵn** "even number" or "whole number."

The chart below lists larger numbers:

hai trăm	*two hundred*	**một ngàn**	*one thousand*
ba trăm	*three hundred*	**mười ngàn**	*ten thousand*
bốn trăm	*four hundred*	**một trăm ngàn**	*one hundred thousand*
năm trăm	*five hundred*	**một triệu**	*one million*
sáu trăm	*six hundred*	**một tỷ**	*one billion*
bảy trăm	*seven hundred*	**một ngàn tỷ**	*one trillion*
tám trăm	*eight hundred*	**một triệu tỷ**	*one quadrillion*
chín trăm	*nine hundred*	**một ngàn tỷ tỷ tỷ**	*one quintillion*

Punctuation for numbers is different in Vietnamese than in English. A comma (**phẩy**) separates a whole number from a fractional part. Thus, while English speakers use a decimal point in 2.56 (two point fifty-six), Vietnamese speakers will write the same number as **2,56** and read it as **hai phẩy năm mươi sáu.**

On the other hand, the period (**chấm**) is used for whole numbers with four or more digits. While English speakers write 1,000 for "one thousand," Vietnamese speakers write **1.000** for **một ngàn.** 5,400,000 would be **năm triệu bốn trăm ngàn**, written as **5.400.000.**

In a rather large number with some zeros beside other digits, the zeros are read as **không**, except when when they are in the tens place with a number 1 through 9 to the right, where they are read as **lẻ**. For example, **2.035.406.002** (written in the Vietnamese style) would be read as **hai tỷ KHÔNG trăm ba mươi lăm triệu bốn trăm LẺ sáu ngàn KHÔNG trăm LẺ hai.**

For *ordinal numbers*, the term **thứ** (short for **thứ tự** "order") is used before a cardinal number, with the three exceptions of "first," "second" and "fourth": **thứ nhất** "first," **thứ nhì** "second" (but **thứ hai** is also acceptable), **thứ ba** "third," **thứ tư** "fourth," **thứ năm** "fifth," etc. The rest are regular, with **thứ** preceding all other numbers: **thứ một trăm** "one hundredth," **thứ hai ngàn** "two thousandth," etc.

With all the numbers shown above, you now can do some basic math in Vietnamese! The four main operations are **cộng** "to add; plus," **trừ** "to subtract; minus," **nhân** "to multiply; times" and **chia** "to divide; by." Three prepositions are usually (but optionally) used with these terms: **cộng (với)** "plus," **trừ (đi)** "minus," **nhân (với)** "times; multiplied by" and **chia (cho)** "divided by."

(8) a. **5 + 10 = 15 → Năm <u>cộng (với)</u> mười bằng/là mười lăm.**
năm¹ kohngm⁶ vuhy² mũuhy⁵ băng⁵/la⁵ mũuhy⁵ lăm¹
Five plus ten equals/is fifteen.

b. **31 - 17 = 14 → Ba mươi mốt trừ (đi) mười bảy bằng/là mười bốn.**
ba^{1} mŭuhy^{1} moht^{2} trŭ^{5} dee^{1} mŭuhy^{5} băy^{4} băng^{5}/la^{5} mŭuhy^{5} bohn^{2}
Thirty-one minus seventeen equals/is fourteen.

c. **11 x 5 = 55 → Mười một nhân (với) năm bằng/là năm mươi lăm.**
mŭuhy^{5} moht^{6} nhun^{1} vuhy^{2} năm^{1} băng^{5}/la^{5} năm^{1} mŭuhy^{1} lăm^{1}
Eleven times five equals/is fifty-five.

d. **204 ÷ 4 = 51 → Hai trăm lẻ bốn chia (cho) bốn bằng/là năm mươi mốt.**
hie^{1} trăm^{1} le^{4} bohn^{2} cheeuh^{1} chah^{1} bohn^{2} băng^{5}/la^{5} năm^{1} mŭuhy^{1} moht^{2}
Two hundred four divided by four equals/is fifty-one.

TRUYỀN HÌNH
SÀI GÒN MỚI
Kính chào quý vị. Đây là bản tin buổi chiều. Greetings, ladies and gentlemen. This is our evening news.

Cô có tin gì đặc biệt cho khán giả của chúng ta đây? What special news do you have for our viewers?

Đội tuyển Việt Nam đã lọt vào vòng chung kết của giải Túc Cầu Thế Giới 2026. Team Vietnam has qualified for the 2026 FIFA World Cup.

Thật là một tin đáng mừng. That's good news indeed.
Một hội nghị quốc tế về biến đổi khí hậu sẽ diễn ra vào tháng tới tại Đà Lạt. An international conference on climate change will take place next month in Dalat.
Hy vọng hội nghị sẽ tìm được một số giải pháp cho vấn đề nghiêm trọng này. Hopefully the conference will find some solutions to this grave issue.

DIALOGUE 2

Two TV newscasters are presenting the evening news and interacting with each other during the broadcast. This is the first part of their presentation.

NEWSCASTER 1 **Kính chào quý vị. Đây là bản tin buổi chiều của đài truyền hình Sài Gòn Mới vào 7 giờ 30 phút.** *(To Newscaster 2)* **Chào cô Trang, cô có tin gì đặc biệt cho khán giả của chúng ta đây?**

keenh2 chahw5 kwee2 vee6 // day1 la5 ban4 teen1 bwohy4 chyehw5 koouh4 die5 trwyehn5 heenh5 shie5 gahn5 muhy2 vahw5 băy4 yuh5 ba1 mŭuhy1 foot2 // chahw5 koh1 trang1 // koh1 kah2 teen1 yee5 dăk6 byeht6 yănh5 chah1 khan2 ya4 koouh4 choongm2 ta1 day1

Greetings, ladies and gentlemen. This is New Saigon TV Channel's 7:30 evening news. Hello, Miss Trang! What special news do you have for our viewers?

NEWSCASTER 2 **Xin chào quý vị và chào anh Hưng. Hôm nay là thứ Bảy, ngày 6 tháng 12 năm 2025. Chúng tôi có một tin rất vui: đội tuyển Việt Nam đã lọt vào vòng chung kết của giải Túc Cầu Thế Giới 2026.**

seen1 chahw5 kwee2 vee6 va5 chahw5 ănh1 hŭng1 // hohm1 năy1 la5 thŭ2 băy4 ngăy5 shăw2 thang2 mŭuhy5 hie1 năm1 hie1 ngan5 khohngm1 trăm1 hie1 mŭuhy1 lăm1 // choohngm2 tohy1 kah2 moht6 teen1 rut2 vooy2 // dohy6 twyehn4 vyeht6 nam1 da3 laht6 vahw5 vahngm5 choong1 keht2 koouh4 yie4 tookp2 kohw5 theh2 yuhy2 hie1 ngan5 hie1 mŭuhy1 shăw2

Greetings to all of you and Mr. Hưng. Today is Saturday, the sixth of December, 2025. We have some quite good news: Team Vietnam has qualified for the 2026 FIFA World Cup.

NEWSCASTER 1 **Cám ơn cô Trang. Thật là một tin đáng mừng vì đây là lần đầu tiên chúng ta có mặt trong giải túc cầu lớn nhất thế giới này. Tin kế tiếp chúng tôi gửi đến quý vị là một hội nghị quốc tế về biến đổi khí hậu sẽ diễn ra vào tháng tới tại thành phố cao nguyên Đà Lạt.**

kam2 uhn1 koh1 trang1 // thut6 la5 moht6 teen1 dang2 mŭng5 vee5 day1 la5 lun5 dohw5 tyehn1 choongm1 ta1 kah2 măt6 trahngm1 yie4 tookp2 kohw5 luhn2 nhut2 theh2 yuhy2 năy5 // teen1 keh2 tyehp2 choongm2 tohy1 gŭy4 dehn2 kwee2 vee6 la5 moht6 hohy6 ngee6 kwohk2 teh2 veh5 byehn2 dohy4 khee2 hohw6 she3 yehn3 ra1 vahw5 thang2 tuhy2 tie6 thănh5 foh2 kahw1 ngwyehn1 da5 lat6

Thank you, Miss Trang. That's good news indeed because this is the first time we will be present at the world's biggest soccer tournament. The next news we relay to you is that an international conference on climate change will take place next month in the highland city of Dalat.

NEWSCASTER 2 **Hy vọng hội nghị sẽ tìm được một số giải pháp cho vấn đề nghiêm trọng này, phải không anh Hưng?**

hee1 vahngm6 hohy6 ngee6 she3 teem5 dŭuhk6 moht6 shoh2 yie4 fap2 chah1 vun2 deh5 ngyehm1 trahngm6 năy5 // fie4 khohngm1 ănh1 hŭng1

(I) hope the conference will find some solutions to this grave issue, right, Mr. Hưng?

 KEY VOCABULARY 2

kính *adj, adv*	respectful(ly)	**lớn nhất** *adj*	biggest
quý vị *n*	(esteemed) you	**kế tiếp** *adj*	next
(bản) tin *n*	news (report)	**có mặt** *v*	to be present
buổi chiều *n*	late afternoon	**hội nghị** *n*	conference
đài truyền hình *n*	television station	**quốc tế** *adj*	international
đặc biệt *adj*	special	**biến đổi khí hậu** *n*	climate change
khán giả *n*	viewer, audience	**diễn ra** *v*	to take place
đội tuyển *n*	team	**tháng tới** *adv*	next month
lọt vào *v*	to reach (a stage)	**thành phố** *n*	city
vòng chung kết *n*	final tournament	**cao nguyên** *n*	highlands
giải *n*	prize	**hy vọng** *v*	to hope
túc cầu *n*	soccer	**tìm** *v*	to look; to find
thế giới n	world	**một số** *adj*	a number (of)
đáng mừng *adj*	good (news)	**giải pháp** *n*	solution
lần *n*	time, occasion	**vấn đề** *n*	problem, issue
đầu tiên *adj*	first	**nghiêm trọng** *adj*	grave

IDIOMATIC EXPRESSIONS 2

Quý vị

Quý is an honorific prefix (**quý ông** "gentleman," **quý bà** "lady," **quý khách** "esteemed guest," etc.), while **vị** is a noun used to formally refer to people (**Vị đó là ông giám đốc công ty** "That person is the president of the company"). **Vị** also functions as a classifier before respected people with titles such as **vị tổng thống** "the (nation's) president," **vị giáo sư** "the professor," **vị tướng** "the general," etc.

Quý vị is habitually used as a plural reference to mean "ladies and gentlemen."

CULTURE NOTES 2

Kính chào/ Xin chào

Language used in social settings outside one's circle of family and friends is customarily formal, polite or respectful. The adverb **kính** "respectfully" usually precedes **chào** "to salute, to greet": **Kính chào quý vị** "Hello, ladies and gentlemen." Another respectful greeting uses the verb **xin** "to ask for" before the verb. Thus, **xin chào bà** literally means "(I'm) asking for your permission to say hello, ma'am."

GRAMMAR NOTES 2

II. Telling time and dates

The complete sentence for telling time is **Bây giờ là [...] giờ, [...] phút, [...] giây** "It is now (hour[s]), (minute[s]), (second[s])." For example, the time **2:35:10** is read (and written) as **hai giờ, ba mươi lăm phút, mười giây.**

A day consists of the following periods: **sáng** "morning" (12:01 a.m. – 10:59 a.m.), **trưa** "late morning/early afternoon" (11:00 a.m. – 1:00 p.m.), **chiều** "late afternoon" (1:01 p.m. – 6:59 p.m.), **tối** "evening" (7:00 p.m. – 9:59 p.m.), and **đêm** "night" (10:00 p.m. – 12:00 a.m.).

(9) a. 5:00 a.m. → **Năm giờ sáng.**
năm^1 yuh^5 shang^2

b. 12:00 p.m. → **Mười hai giờ trưa** or **Giữa trưa** "midday."
mŭuhy^5 hie^1 yuh^5 trŭuh^1 // yŭuh^3 trŭuh^1

c. 1 p.m. → **Một giờ trưa.**
moht^6 yuh^5 trŭuh^1

d. 4 p.m. → **Bốn giờ chiều.**
bohn^2 yuh^5 chyehw^5

e. 7 p.m. → **Bảy giờ tối.**
băy^4 yuh^5 tohy^2

f. 10 p.m. → **Mười giờ đêm.**
mŭuhy^5 yuh^5 dehm^1

g. 12:00 a.m. → **Mười hai giờ đêm** *or* **Nửa đêm** "midnight."
mŭuhy^5 hie^1 yuh^5 dehm^1 // nŭuh^4 dehm^1

Khuya is an adjective meaning "late at night" (**thức khuya** is "to stay up late"). It is also used to optionally replace **đêm** with night times such as **mười một giờ khuya** "11:00 p.m."

Here are some more examples:

(10) a. 8:15 → **Tám giờ mười lăm.** (***phút*** is often left out in everyday speech)
tam^2 yuh^5 mŭuhy^5 lăm^1

b. 9:30 → **Chín giờ ba mươi** *or* **Chín giờ rưỡi.**
cheen^2 yuh^5 ba mŭuhy // cheen^1 yuh^5 rŭuhy^3

c. 5:45 → **Năm giờ bốn mươi lăm** *or* **Sáu giờ kém mười lăm.**
năm^1 yuh^5 bohn^2 mŭuhy^1 lăm^1 // shăw^2 yuh^2 kem^2 mŭuhy^5 lăm^1

To indicate the time at which something is done or happens, the preposition **vào** is used. Redundantly, the noun **lúc** "time, while" also comes after **vào**, or replaces it:

(11) a. **Tôi thường dậy vào sáu giờ rưỡi.**
tohy^1 thŭuhng^5 yay^6 vahw^5 shăw^2 yuh^5 rŭuhy^3
I usually get up at six-thirty.

b. **[...] vào lúc sáu giờ rưỡi.**

c. **[...] lúc sáu giờ rưỡi.**

Ordinal numbers are used to name the first six days of the week, with the first one marked as "the second day": **thứ Hai** "Monday," **thứ Ba** "Tuesday," **thứ Tư** "Wednesday," **thứ Năm** "Thursday," **thứ Sáu** "Friday" and **thứ Bảy** "Saturday." "Sunday" is **Chủ Nhật**, literally "the Day of the Lord," which originates in Christianity brought to Vietnam by European missionaries in the early 17th century.

Cardinal numbers are used to name nine out of the twelve months of the lunar year, with three exceptions (the first and the last months have original names, and the fourth month uses an ordinal number instead of a cardinal one): **tháng Giêng**, **tháng Hai**, **tháng Ba**, **tháng Tư**, **tháng Năm**, **tháng Sáu**, **tháng Bảy**, **tháng Tám**, **tháng Chín**, **tháng Mười**, **tháng Mười Một**, **tháng Chạp**.

The terms for the solar months (also known as Gregorian) are the same as those for the lunar months, except for the first and the last months, which are cardinal numbers, i.e., **tháng Một** "January" and **tháng Mười Hai** "December." Typically, the lunar calendar is about one month behind the solar calendar.

The complete statement of a date has the following order: [*Day of the week*], [*Day of the month*], [*Month*] and [*Year*], for example:

(12) **Hôm nay là thứ Năm, ngày 25, tháng 12, năm 2025.**
hohm^{1} năy^{1} la^{5} thŭ^{2} năm^{1} ngăy^{5} hie^{1} mŭuhy^{1} lăm^{1} thang^{2} mŭuhy^{5} hie^{1} năm^{1} hie^{1} ngan^{5} khohngm^{1} trăm^{1} hie^{1} mŭuhy^{1} lăm^{1}
Today is Thursday, December 25, 2025.

The classifier **ban** is used in **ban ngày** "daytime" and **ban đêm** "nighttime." **Buổi** goes with the other periods: **buổi sáng** "the morning," **buổi trưa** "the afternoon," **buổi chiều** "the late afternoon" and **buổi tối** "the evening."

The following are common questions related to times and dates. Pay attention to the underlined interrogative phrases:

a. **Bây giờ là mấy giờ?**
bay^{1} yuh^{5} la^{5} may^{2} yuh^{5}
What time is it (now)?

b. **Anh thường dậy vào/lúc mấy giờ?**
ănh^{1} thŭuhng^{5} yay^{6} vahw^{5}/lookp^{2} may^{2} yuh^{5}
What time do you usually get up?

c. **Hôm nay là thứ mấy?**
hohm^{1} năy^{1} la^{5} thŭ^{2} may^{1}
What day is it today?

d. **Hôm nay là ngày mấy?**
hohm^{1} năy^{1} la^{5} ngăy^{5} may^{2}
What's the date today?

e. **Tháng này là tháng mấy?**
thang^{2} nay^{5} la^{5} thang^{2} may^{2}
What month is it?

f. **Năm nay là năm nào?**
năm^{1} năy^{1} la^{5} năm^{1} nahw^{5}
What year is it?

g. **Em sinh (vào) năm nào?**
em^{1} sheenh^{1} vahw^{5} năm^{1} nahw^{5}
What year were you born?

h. **Năm nay là năm gì?**
năm^{1} năy^{1} la^{5} năm^{1} yee^{5}
What lunar year is it?

i. **Năm nay là năm con gì?**
năm^{1} năy^{1} la^{5} năm^{1} kahn^{1} yee^{5}
What is the animal symbol for this year?

j. **Sinh nhật của cô là khi nào?**
sheenh^{1} nhut^{6} koouh^{4} koh^{2} la^{5} khee^{1}nahw^{5}
When's your birthday?

READING

ÂM LỊCH

Ở Việt Nam, người ta dùng cả dương lịch lẫn âm lịch. Dương lịch dùng trong các lãnh vực xã hội như công việc, giấy tờ, giáo dục, thương mại, kỹ thuật, v.v., còn âm lịch dùng cho các sinh hoạt văn hoá như lễ lạt truyền thống, phong tục dân gian hay tử vi đông phương.

Chữ âm chỉ về mặt trăng hay khái niệm "âm" đối nghịch với "dương". Âm lịch dựa vào chu kỳ và vị trí của mặt trăng. Mỗi năm âm lịch mang biểu tượng của một con vật. Có tất cả mười hai biểu tượng thú vật (gọi là "địa chi"), bên cạnh mười biểu tượng "thiên can" đi kèm theo mỗi năm, tạo thành một chu kỳ sáu mươi năm, theo khái niệm phong thuỷ. Ví dụ, năm 2026 là năm Bính Ngọ (với biểu tượng là con ngựa).

Ngày tháng dương lịch (hay còn gọi là "ngày tây") có thể chuyển sang ngày tháng âm lịch (còn gọi là "ngày ta") để đối chiếu khi cần thiết. Nhiều loại lịch ở Việt Nam có ghi cả ngày tây lẫn ngày ta, tiện lợi cho mọi sinh hoạt hằng ngày.

uh4 vyeht6 nam1 ngũuhy5 ta1 yoongm5 ka4 yũuhng1 leech6 lun3 um1 leech6 // yũuhng1 leech6 yoongm5 trahngm1 kak2 lănh3 vũk5 sa3 hohy6 nhũ1 kohng1 vyehk6 yay2 tuh5 yahw2 yookp6 thũuhng1 mie6 kee3 thwut6 vun1 vun1 // kahn5 um1 leech6 yoongm5 chah1 nhũng3 kak2 sheenh1 hwat6 văn1 hwa2 nhũ1 leh3 lak6 trwyehn5 thohngm2 fahngm1 tookp6 yun1 yan1 hăy1 tũ4 vee1

chũ3 um1 chee4 veh5 măt6 trăng1 hăy1 khie2 nyehm6 um1 dohy2 ngeech6 vuhy2 yũuhng1 // um1 leech6 yũuh6 vahw5 choo1 kee5 va5 vee6 tree2 koouh4 măt6 trăng1 // mohy3 năm1 um1 leech6 mang1 byehw4 tũuhng6 koouh4 moht6 kahn1 vut6 // kah2 tut2 ka4 mũuhy5 hie1 byehw4 tũuhng6 thoo2 vut6 // gahy6 la5 deeuh6 chee1 // behn1 kănh6 mũuhy5 byehw4 tũuhng6 thyehn1 kan1 dee1 kem5 thew1 mohy3 năm1 // tahw6 thănh5 moht6 choo1 kee5 shăw2 mũuhy1 năm1 // thew1 khie2 nyehm6 fahngm1 thwee4 // vee2 yoo6 năm1 hie1 ngan5 khohngm1 trăm1 hie1 mũuhy1 shăw2 la5 năm1 beenh2 ngah6 // vuhy2 byehw4 tũuhng6 la5 kahn1 ngũuh6

ngăy5 thang2 yũuhng1 leech6 // hăy1 kahn5 gahy6 la5 ngăy5 tay1 // kah2 theh4 chwyehn4 shang1 ngăy5 thang2 um1 leech6 (kahn5 gahy6 la5 ngăy5 ta1 // deh4 dohy2 chyehw2 khee1 kun5 thyeht2 // nhyehw5 lwie6 leech6 uh4 vyeht6 nam1 kah2 gee1 kah4 ngăy5 tay1 lun3 ngăy5 ta1 // tyehn6 luhy6 chah1 mahy6 sheenh1 hwat6 hăng5 ngăy5

THE LUNAR CALENDAR

In Vietnam, people use both a solar calendar and a lunar calendar. The solar calendar is used in situations such as work, documentation, education, business, and technology, while the lunar calendar is used for cultural activities including traditional holidays, popular customs and Eastern horoscopes.

The term **âm** refers to the moon or "yin," the opposite concept of "yang." The lunar calendar is based on the cycles and positions of the moon. Each lunar year bears the symbol of an animal. There are twelve animal symbols (known as "the terrestrial branches") in addition to "the ten celestial stems" accompanying each year, forming a sixty-year cycle, according to an ancient Chinese system referring to the time concept of heaven and earth. For example, the year 2026 is labeled *Bính Ngọ* (symbolized by the horse).

Solar dates (also called "Western dates" [**ngày tây**]) can be converted into lunar dates (also called "our dates" [**ngày ta**]) when necessary. Many calendars in Vietnam include both solar dates and lunar dates, to be convenient for all daily activities.

COMPREHENSION QUESTIONS

Answer the following questions in complete sentences, first orally, then in writing.

1. **Dương lịch dùng trong những lãnh vực nào?** *In what situations is the solar calendar used?*

___

2. **Âm lịch dùng cho những sinh hoạt gì?** *For what activities is the lunar calendar used?*

___

3. **Âm lịch dựa vào hiện tượng thiên nhiên nào?** *On what natural phenomenon is the lunar calendar based?*

___

4. **Hai thành phần trong tên của một năm âm lịch là gì?** *What are the two components in the name of a lunar year?*

___

5. **Ngày tháng âm lịch còn được gọi là gì?** *What are the lunar dates also called?*

___

PRACTICE

A. Listening comprehension

Listen to the following announcement from a Republic Radio broadcast about a gift-distribution event organized by a university on the occasion of the Mid-Autumn Festival. Complete the chart below with the correct information from the announcement. Write the numbers in digits where possible.

Event date (solar)	**thứ , ngày , tháng , năm**
Event date (lunar)	**ngày , tháng , năm**
Starting time	
Number of gift bags	
Number of traditional mooncakes	
Number of snow-skin mooncakes	
Number of lanterns	
Number of toys	

B. Basic math in Vietnamese!

Read the following math operations before writing them out in words.

0. 25 + 17 = 42
   Hai mươi lăm cộng (với) mười bảy bằng/là bốn mươi hai.

1. 140 + 39 = 179

____

2. 263 – 98 = 165

____

3. 72 x 41 = 2.952

____

4. 1.879.860 ÷ 15 = 125.324

____

5. 25,30 x 250 = 6.325

____

C. Telling time – Mấy giờ rồi?

Write out in words the times indicated on the following clocks, including the period of day. Where there are two ways of telling the time, (a) and (b) are indicated.

3:15 p.m.

0. **Ba giờ mười lăm (phút) chiều.**

8:45 a.m.

1a. ______________________________

1b. ______________________________

5:30 p.m.

2a. ______________________________

2b. ______________________________

1:25 p.m.

3. ______________________________

7:12 p.m.

4. ______________________________

12:00 a.m.

5a. ______________________________

5b. ______________________________

10:37 p.m.

6a. ______________________________

6b. ______________________________

D. Vocabulary

Fill in the blanks in the following sentences with the correct words from the list. Use each word only once.

gì ngày thế kỷ bao nhiêu dương lịch nào tuần (lễ) mấy

1. **Một tháng thường có bốn ____________________.**

   A month typically has four ____________________.

2. **Năm nay ông ấy ____________________ tuổi?**

   ____________________ *old is he (this year)?*

3. **Một năm có ba trăm sáu mươi lăm ____________________.**

   A year has 365 ____________________.

4. **Theo âm lịch, năm nay là năm ____________________?**

   According to the lunar calendar, what year is ____________________?

5. **Chúng ta sẽ gặp nhau lúc ____________________ giờ?**

   ____________________ *time will we meet up?*

6. **Cô ấy sinh vào năm ____________________?**

   ____________________ *year was she born?*

7. **Một ____________________ là một trăm năm.**

   A ____________________ *is one hundred years.*

8. **Ngày tây là ngày tính theo ____________________.**

   Western dates are the ones based on ____________________.

 **PROVERB**

THỜI GIỜ NGỰA CHẠY TÊN BAY.

thuhy^5 *yuh*^{5} *ngŭuh*^{6} *chăy*^{6} *tehn*^{1} *băy*^{1}

"Time (passes by like) galloping horses and flying arrows."

Vietnamese proverbs typically omit and imply some of their words. The expression above shows just that, with the verb equivalent to "passes by" and the preposition equivalent to "like" missing. A full version of it would be **Thời giờ trôi qua như ngựa chạy tên bay**.

Vietnamese has two nouns equivalent to the English "time." **Thời giờ** (also **thì giờ**) refers to the time used for doing something, while **thời gian** expresses the general concept of time. Compare the following sentences: **Tôi không có thì giờ để nghỉ ngơi** "I don't have time to relax" and **Thời gian chữa lành mọi vết thương** "Time heals all wounds."

This proverb clearly dates back to ancient times, suggesting an image of Vietnamese warriors riding horses and shooting arrows in battles, in addition to using swords or spears.

FUNCTIONAL VOCABULARY

DANH TỪ

số	number
ngày	day
đêm	night
sáng	morning
trưa	afternoon
chiều	late afternoon
tối	evening
tuần (lễ)	week
tháng	month
năm	year
thời gian	time
giờ	hour
phút	minute
giây	second
đồng hồ	watch; clock
tuổi	age
lịch	calendar
thì giờ/thời giờ	time (to use)
lễ	holiday
ngày nghỉ	day off

TÍNH TỪ

đúng giờ	punctual
sớm	early
trễ	late
khuya	late at night
trẻ	young
già	old
đầu (tiên)	first
cuối (cùng)	last
xưa	ancient
nay	present; modern
tới	next, upcoming

TRẠNG TỪ

hôm nay	today
ngày nay	nowadays
hôm qua	yesterday
hôm kia	day before yesterday
ngày mai	tomorrow
ngày mốt	day after tomorrow
tuần này	this week
tháng này	this month
năm nay	this year
năm ngoái	last year
năm tới	next year
bây giờ	now
sau	later
khi nào	when
bao nhiêu	how much/many
mấy	how many

ĐỘNG TỪ

sinh	to be born
xảy ra	to happen
diễn ra	to take place
đếm	to count
sống	to live
chết	to die
chuẩn bị	to prepare
chấm dứt	to end
có mặt	to be present
vắng mặt	to be absent
bằng	to equal
cộng	to add
trừ	to subtract
nhân	to multiply
chia	to divide

Cuối tuần này chúng ta có mục gì vui không?
Are we doing anything fun this weekend?
Thứ Bảy này chúng ta sẽ đi dự tiệc sinh nhật của Việt sao?
We're going to Việt's birthday party this Saturday right?
Bao giờ mình sẽ đi mua quà cho Việt với nhau đây?
When are we going to buy his presents?
Mình nên đặt hàng trên mạng cho tiện.
We should just order some things online.
An giúp gói quà cho đẹp nhé!
You'll help wrap the gifts nicely, right?

CHAPTER 7

Money and Banking

Tiền Tệ – Ngân Hàng

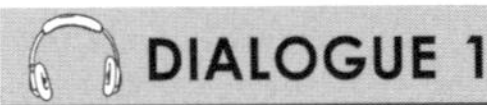

DIALOGUE 1

An and Khoa are talking on the phone about things they've been doing together and planning for the upcoming weekend.

AN **Khoa đã nhận được hai triệu đồng An gửi để trả lại tiền vé xem hoà nhạc rồi phải không?**
khwa^1 da^3 nhun^6 dŭuhk^6 hie^1 tryehw^6 dongm^5 an^1 gŭy^4 deh^4 tra^4 lie^6 tyehn^5 ve^2 sem^1 hwa^5 nhak^6 rohy^5 fie^4 khohngm^1
Khoa, you got the two million dong I sent to pay you back for the concert ticket, didn't you?

KHOA **Tôi nhận được rồi. Cám ơn An. Cuối tuần này chúng ta có mục gì vui không?**
tohy^1 nhun^6 dŭuhk^6 rohy^5 // kam^2 uhn^1 an^1 // kwohy^2 twun^5 năy^5 choongm^2 ta^1 kah^2 mookp^6 yee^5 vooy^1 khohngm^1
I did. Thank you, An. Are we doing anything fun this weekend?

AN **Khoa quên là thứ Bảy này chúng ta sẽ đi dự tiệc sinh nhật của Việt sao?**
khwa^1 kwehn^1 la^5 thŭ^2 băy^4 năy^5 choongm^2 ta^1 she^3 dee^1 yŭ^6 tyehk^6 sheenh^1 nhut^6 koouh^4 vyeht^6 shahw^1
Did you forget we're going to Việt's birthday party on Saturday?

KHOA **Ồ, tôi quên khuấy đi mất! Bao giờ mình sẽ đi mua quà cho Việt với nhau đây?**
oh^5 tohy^1 kwehn^1 khway^2 dee^1 mut^2 // bahw^1 yuh^5 meenh^5 she^3 dee^1 moouh^1 kwa^5 chah^1 vyeht^6 vuhy^2 nhăw^1 day^1
Oh, I totally forgot! When are we going shopping for his presents?

AN **An nghĩ là mình nên đặt hàng trên mạng cho tiện. Mỗi người chúng ta sẽ mua một món gì giá khoảng năm trăm ngàn đồng. Khoa có đồng ý không?**
an¹ ngee³ la⁵ meenh⁵ nehn¹ dăt⁶ hang⁵ trehn¹ mang⁶ chah¹ tyehn⁶ // mohy³ ngŭuhy⁵ choongm² ta¹ she³ moouh¹ moht⁶ mahn² yee⁵ ya² khwang⁴ năm¹ trăm¹ ngan⁵ dohngm⁵ // khwa¹ kah² dohngm⁵ ee² khohngm¹
I think we should just order some things online. Let's each buy something priced around 500,000 dong. Okay?

KHOA **Vậy cũng được. An giúp gói quà cho đẹp nhé!**
vay⁶ koongm³ dŭuhk⁶ // an¹ yoop² gahy² kwa⁵ chah¹ dep⁶ nhe²
That works, too. You'll help wrap the gifts nicely, right?

 KEY VOCABULARY 1

nhận *v*	to receive	**quà** *n*	gift
trả (lại) *v*	to pay (back)	**với nhau** *adv*	together
tiền *n*	money	**nghĩ** *v*	to think
vé *n*	ticket	**nên** *v*	should
hoà nhạc *n*	concert	**đặt** *v*	to place; to order
xem *v*	to watch	**hàng** *n*	merchandise, goods
cuối tuần *n*	weekend	**trên mạng** *adv*	online
mục *n*	plan	**tiện** *adj*	convenient
vui *adj*	fun; happy	**mỗi người** *n*	each person
quên *v*	to forget	**món** *n*	item
dự *v*	to attend	**giá** *n*	price
tiệc *n*	party	**khoảng** *adv*	approximately
sinh nhật *n*	birthday	**đồng ý** *v*	to agree
bao giờ *adv*	when	**giúp** *v*	to help
mua *v*	to buy	**gói** *v*	to wrap

IDIOMATIC EXPRESSIONS 1

Tôi quên khuấy đi mất! "I totally forgot (about it)!" **Khuấy** in this context takes on the meaning of "completely" when coming after the verb **quên** "to forget." As a verb, it means "to stir," as in **khuấy ly sữa** "to stir the glass of milk."

Vậy cũng được. "It's OK that way." **Được**, in this context, means "OK, acceptable." Say **Được rồi** when you mean "It's fine." Say **Không được** when you mean "It's not allowed."

CULTURE NOTES 1

In a conversation between people talking on a first-name basis, you can use the first name of your interlocutor to address them as "you," and your first name to mean "I." However, this is acceptable only if you are about the same age as your interlocutor(s).

The term **mình** (reduced from the informal **chúng mình** "we") is an "inclusive **we**," referring to everyone, including the speaker (the standard form is **chúng ta**). **Tối nay mình đi chơi nhé!** "Let's (all) go out tonight, OK?"

On the other hand, **chúng tôi** is an "exclusive **we**," used to refer to the speaker and some other people, but not the person(s) to whom they are speaking. **Chúng tôi không hiểu anh muốn nói gì** "We don't understand what you're trying to say."

GRAMMAR NOTES 1

I. Interrogative words

Interrogative words appear in *specific questions*, i.e., when you ask for some particular information. While in English all the interrogative words (the so-called Wh-words) appear at the beginning of questions (except for "echo questions," when they come at the end), Vietnamese interrogative words have various positions in a question, depending on different factors.

Most interrogative words occupy the positions normally reserved for their grammatical functions in a statement. Compare these examples:

(1) a. **Ông Tuấn là phó giám đốc của công ty.** [***Ông Tuấn*** *is the subject of the sentence*]
ohngm^1 twun^2 la^5 fah^2 yam^2 dohkp^2 koouh^4 kohngm^1 tee^1
Mr. Tuấn is the vice-president of the company.

b. **Ai là phó giám đốc của công ty?**
ie^1 la^5 fah^2 yam^2 dohkp^2 koouh^4 kohngm^1 tee^1
Who is the vice-president of the company?

c. **Chúng tôi thấy một toà nhà lớn cạnh hồ nước.** [***một toà nhà lớn*** *is the direct object of the verb* ***thấy***]
choongm^2 tohy^1 thay^2 moht^6 twa^5 nha^5 luhn^2 kănh^6 hoh^2 nŭuhk^2
We saw a large building next to the lake.

d. **Các anh thấy gì cạnh hồ nước?**
kak^2 ănh^1 thay^1 yee^5 kănh^5 hoh^5 nŭuhk^2
What did you guys see next to the lake?

e. **Gia đình tôi sống ở Sài Gòn**. [***ở Sài Gòn*** *is an adverbial modifier*]
ya^1 deenh^5 tohy^1 shohngm^2 uh^4 shie^5 gahn^5
My family lives in Saigon.

f. **Gia đình chị sống ở đâu?**
ya^1 deenh^5 chee^6 shognm^2 uh^4 dohw^1
Where does your family live?

Some interrogative words express a nuance when placed at the beginning or at the end of a question:

(2) a. **Cô nấu món này làm sao?**
koh^{1} nohw^{2} mahn^{2} năy^{5} lam^{5} shahw^{1}
How did you prepare this dish?

b. **Làm sao cô nấu được món này?**
lam^{5} shahw^{1} koh^{1} nohw^{2} dŭuhk^{6} mahn^{2} năy^{5}
How could you prepare this dish?

c. **Các anh chị về đây bao giờ?**
kak^{2} ănh^{1} chee^{6} veh^{5} day^{1}
When did you guys get back here?

d. **Bao giờ các anh chị về đây?**
bahw^{1} yuh^{5} kak^{2} ănh^{1} chee^{6} veh^{5} day^{1}
When are you going to come back here?

Tại sao "why" always appears at the beginning of a question:

(3) **Tại sao họ không gọi cho cô?**
tie^{6} shahw^{1} hah^{6} khohngm^{1} gahy^{6} chah^{1}koh^{1}
Why didn't they call you?

In the chart below, interrogative words are shown according to their grammatical categories:

INTERROGATIVE PRONOUNS	**ai**	who
	(cái) gì	what
INTERROGATIVE ADJECTIVES	**nào/gì**	which/what
	của ai	whose
INTERROGATIVE ADVERBS	**đâu**	where to
	ở đâu	where at
	mấy	how many
	bao nhiêu	how much/many
	bao xa	how far
	bao lâu	how long
	tại sao	why
	thế nào	how
	khi nào/bao giờ	when
	để làm gì	what for

There are a few points to remember about the interrogative **gì** "what." It can be used alone in a direct object position but is normally preceded by the generic classifier **cái** or the noun **điều** "thing" when functioning as the subject or object of a preposition:

(4) a. **Cô cần gì?** [***gì*** *is the direct object of* ***cần***]
koh^1 kun^5 yee^5
What do you need?

b. **Cái gì ở trên bàn vậy?** [***cái gì*** *is the subject*]
kie^2 yee^5 uh^4 trehn^1 ban^5 vay^6
What's on the table?

c. **Điều gì làm cho anh ấy buồn?** [***điều gì*** *is the subject*]
dyehw^5 yww^5 lam^5 chah^1 ănh^1 ay^2 bwohn^5
What makes him sad?

d. **Bà ấy đang nói về điều gì?** [***điều gì*** *is the object of the preposition* ***về***]
ba^5 ay^2 dang^1 nahy^2 veh^5 dyehw^5 yee^5
What is she talking about?

Sao is a synonym of **gì**, but is not always interchangeable with it:

(5) a. **Cô nói gì/sao?**
koh^1 nahy^2 yee^5/shahw^1
What did you say?

b. **Ông đang nghĩ gì vậy?**
ohngm^1 dang^1 ngee^3 yee^5 vay^6
What are you thinking about?

c. **Ông nghĩ sao?**
ohngm^1 ngee^3 shahw^1
What do you think?

Gì can also be used as an adjective, partly synonymous to **nào** but not always interchangeable with it. The choice between **nào** and **gì** is largely based on convention rather than rules:

(6) a. **Chị nói tiếng gì?**
chee^6 nahy^2 tyehng^2 yee^5
What language do you speak?

b. **Anh là người nước nào?**
ănh^1 la^5 ngŭuhy^5 nŭuhk^2 nahw^5
What's your nationality?

c. **Tháng nào cô sẽ rảnh để làm việc này?**
thang^2 nahw^5 koh^1 she^3 rănh^4 deh^4 lam^5 vyehk^6 năy^5
In what month will you be available to do this job?

When asking someone to choose between options, however, **nào** is the correct word to use:

(7) **Trong các món ăn này, các cô thích món nào nhất?**
trahngm^1 kak^2 mahn^2 ăn^1 năy^5 kak^2 koh^1 theech^2 mahn^2 nahw^5 nhut^2
Of all these dishes, which one do you like the most?

NGÂN HÀNG

Chào anh Tân.
Lâu ngày không gặp anh.
Hello, Mr. Tân. I haven't seen you in a while.

Cô cho tôi gửi vào trương mục tiết kiệm sáu triệu đồng.
Let me deposit six million dong into my savings account.

DIALOGUE 2

Tân is at a bank taking care of a few tasks. He is talking to a bank teller.

NHÂN VIÊN **Chào anh Tân. Lâu ngày không gặp anh. Hôm nay anh cần gì ạ?**
chahw^{5} ănh^{1} tun^{1}// lohw^{1} ngăy^{5} khohngm^{1} găp^{6} ănh^{1} // hohm^{1} năy^{1} ănh^{1} kun^{5} yee^{5} a^{6}
Hello, Mr. Tân. I haven't seen you in a while. What can I do for you today?

TÂN **Chào cô Trâm. Mọi việc bình thường cả chứ? Tôi cần cô giúp ba việc.**
chahw^{5} koh^{1} trum^{1} // mahy^{6} vyehk^{6} beenh^{5} thŭuhng^{5} kah^{4} chŭ^{2} // tohy^{1} kun^{5} koh^{1} yoop^{2} ba^{1} vyehk^{6}
Hello, Miss Trâm. I hope everything is going well for you. I need you to help me with three things.

NHÂN VIÊN **Dạ, được.**
ya^{6} dŭuhk^{6}
Yes, of course.

TÂN **Cô cho tôi gửi vào trương mục tiết kiệm của tôi sáu triệu đồng này.**
koh^{1} chah^{1} tohy^{1} gŭy^{4} vahw^{5} trŭuhng^{1} mookp^{6} tyeht^{2} kyehm^{6} koouh^{4} tohy^{1} shăw^{2} tryehw^{6} dohngm^{5} năy^{5}
Let me deposit these six million dong into my savings account.

NHÂN VIÊN **Xong rồi. Kế tiếp là gì nữa ạ?**
sahngm^{1} rohy^{5} // keh^{2} tyehp^{2} la^{5} yee^{5} nŭuh^{3} a^{6}
Done. How else can I help you?

TÂN **Tôi muốn rút năm trăm ngàn đồng từ trương mục ngân phiếu để mua một cái lệnh phiếu. Lệ phí được miễn, phải không cô?**
tohy^{1} mwohn^{2} root^{2} năm^{1} trăm^{1} ngan^{5} dongm^{5} tŭ^{5} trŭuhng^{1} mookp^{6} ngun^{1} fyehw^{2} deh^{4} moouh^{1} moht^{6} kie^{1} lehnh^{6} fyehw^{2} // leh^{6} fee^{2} dŭuhk^{6} myehn^{3} // fie^{4} khohngm^{1} koh^{1}
I wanted to withdraw five hundred thousand dong from my checking account to purchase a money order. The fee is waived, isn't it?

NHÂN VIÊN **Đúng vậy, cho khách hàng lâu năm như anh.**
doongm^{2} vay^{6} // chah^{1} khăch^{2} hang^{5} lohw^{1} năm^{1} nhŭ^{1} ănh^{1}
That's right, for a long-time customer like you.

TÂN **Hay lắm! Cuối cùng, nhờ cô chuyển giùm tôi ba triệu rưởi, lấy từ trương mục tiết kiệm của tôi, đến người có tên và số trương mục ghi trên mảnh giấy này.**
hăy^{1} lăm^{2} // kwohy^{2} koongm^{5} nhuh^{5} koh^{1} chwyehn^{4} yoom^{5} tohy^{1} ba^{1} tryehw^{6} rŭuhy^{3} // lay^{2} tŭ^{5} trŭuhng^{1} mookp^{6} tyeht^{2} kyehm^{6} koouh^{4} tohy^{1} // dehn^{2} ngŭuhy^{5} kah^{2} tehn^{1} va^{5} shoh^{2} trŭuhng^{1} mookp^{5} gee^{1} trehn^{1} mănh^{4} yay^{2} năy^{5}
Very good! Finally, please help me make a wire transfer of three and a half million dong from my savings account to the person whose name and account number are written on this piece of paper.

NHÂN VIÊN **Anh còn cần gì nữa không?**
ănh¹ kahn⁵ kun⁵ yee⁵ nũuh³ khohngm¹
Did you need anything else?

TÂN **Dạ không. Cám ơn cô Trâm nhiều!**
ya⁶ khohngm¹ // kam² uhn¹ koh¹ trum¹ nhyehw⁵
No. Thanks a lot, Miss Trâm.

 KEY VOCABULARY 2

gặp *v*	to see, to meet	**đúng vậy** *expr*	that's right
mọi việc *pron*	everything	**khách hàng** *n*	customer
bình thường *adj*	normal, OK	**hay lắm!** *expr*	Very good!
gửi vào *v*	to deposit	**cuối cùng** *adv*	finally
trương mục *n*	account	**nhờ** *v*	to ask for help
tiết kiệm *n*	savings	**giùm** *v*	to help with
xong rồi *expr*	it's done (already)	**chuyển** *v*	to transfer
kế tiếp *adj*	next	**lấy** *v*	to take
nữa *adv*	more	**từ** *prep*	from
rút *v*	to withdraw	**đến** *prep*	to
ngân phiếu *n*	bank check	**ghi** *v*	to write
lệnh phiếu *n*	money order	**mảnh** *n*	piece
lệ phí *n*	fee	**giấy** *n*	paper
miễn *v*	to waive, to exempt	**còn** *adv*	still

IDIOMATIC EXPRESSIONS 2

Lâu ngày This adverbial expression is used to mean "It's been a while." It is also found in the expression **lâu ngày chày tháng** "over a long period of time." **Lâu** means "long" and **chày** means "late."

Lâu năm Used as an adjective, this expression means "long-time" or "long-standing," describing things or people: **một người bạn lâu năm** "a long-time friend."

CULTURE NOTES 2

Dạ This word is a polite "yes," but it is also used as a polite particle with other words. Thus, **dạ không** is a polite "no" and **dạ phải** is a polite way of saying "that's right." The proverb **Gọi dạ, bảo vâng** means "Say 'yes' when you are called upon, and 'I will obey' when you are told (to do something)." **Vâng lời** is a compound verb meaning "to obey" (literally, "to obey words").

GRAMMAR NOTES 2

II. Types of questions

Yes-no questions
In this type of question, the words **có** "yes" and **không** "no" wrap around a verb (and its complement or modifiers, if any):

(8) a. **Cô có muốn biết tổng cộng số tiền trong trương mục không?**
koh^{1} kah^{2} mwohn^{2} byeht^{2} tohngm^{4} kohngm^{6} shoh^{2} tyehn^{5} trahngm^{1} trŭuhng^{1} mookp^{6} khohngm^{1}
Do you want to know your account balance?

b. **Dạ có. Tôi còn bao nhiêu tiền trong đó vậy anh?**
ya^{6} kah^{2} // tohy^{1} kahn^{5} bahw^{1} nhyehw^{1} tyehn^{5} trahngm^{1} dah^{2} vay^{6} ănh^{1}
Yes. How much money do I have left in it?

c. **Hôm nay chị có đi ngân hàng không?**
hohm^{1} năy^{1} chee^{6} kah^{2} dee^{1} ngun^{1} hang^{5} khohngm^{1}
Are you going to the bank today?

d. **Không. Ngày mai tôi mới đi.**
khohngm^{1} // ngăy^{5} mie^{1} tohy^{1} muhy^{2} dee
No. I won't go until tomorrow.

In a yes-no question with the verb **là** "to be," use **phải** right after **có**:

(9) a. Ông **có phải là nhân viên ngân hàng ở đây không?**
ohngm^{1} kah^{2} fie^{4} la^{5} nhun^{1} vyehn^{1} ngun^{1} hang^{5} uh^{4} day^{1} khohngm^{1}
Are you a bank teller here?

b. **Dạ phải.**
ya^{6} fie^{4}
Yes, I am.

c. **Tấm ngân phiếu này có phải là của bà không?**
tum^{2} ngun^{1} fyehw^{2} năy^{5} kah^{2} fie^{4} la^{5} koouh^{4} ba^{5} khohngm^{1}
Is this check yours?

d. **Dạ không.**
ya^{5} khohngm^{1}
No, it's not.

Choice questions
A choice question contains the conjunction **hay** "or" between the two parts. Note that **hoặc**, a synonym of **hay**, is used only in statements, never in this type of question.

(10) a. **Cô muốn mua ngân phiếu bảo chứng hay lệnh phiếu?**
koh^{1} mwohn^{2} moouh^{1} ngun^{1} fyehw^{2} bahw^{4} chŭng^{2} hăy^{1} lehnh^{6} fyehw^{2}
Did you want to buy a certified check or a money order?

b. **Ông cần đổi đô-la ra euro hay bảng Anh vậy?**
ohngm¹ kun⁵ dohy⁴ doh¹ la¹ ra¹ uh¹ roh¹ hăy¹ bang⁴ ănh¹ vay⁶
Did you need to exchange dollars for euros or English pounds?

Specific questions

A specific question contains an *interrogative word*. These questions are so called because they ask for specific information such as identification, location, reason, purpose, etc.

(11) a. **Giám đốc ngân hàng này là ai vậy?**
yam² dohkp² ngun¹ hang⁵ năy⁵ la⁵ ie¹ vay⁶
Who is the president of this bank?

b. **Tại sao chị không mua một chứng chỉ ký gửi để được lãi suất cao?**
tie⁶ shahw¹ chee⁶ khohngm¹ moouh¹ moht⁶ chŭng² chee⁴ kee² gŭy⁴ deh⁴ dŭuhk⁶ lie³ shwut² kahw¹
Why don't you buy a certificate of deposit to earn a high interest rate?

Tag questions

This type of question is formed with a statement followed by a "tag" (usually a particle or a short phrase).

(12) a. **Hôm nay hối suất đồng đô-la vẫn như cũ à?**
hohm¹ năy¹ hohy² shwut² dohngm⁵ doh¹ la¹ vun³ nhŭ¹ koo³ a⁵
The dollar's exchange rate is the same today, isn't it?

b. **Bà cần tái tài trợ cho tiền nợ nhà, phải không?**
ba⁵ kun⁵ tie² tie⁵ truh⁶ chah¹ tyehn⁵ nuh⁶ nha⁵ fie⁴ khohngm¹
You need to refinance your mortgage, don't you?

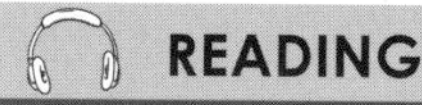

READING

ĐỒNG TIỀN VIỆT NAM

Đơn vị tiền tệ của Việt Nam là "đồng", dựa theo tên của kim loại chính dùng để đúc tiền ngày trước. Tiền tệ của Việt Nam bắt đầu xuất hiện từ giữa thế kỷ thứ X. Lúc đó, chỉ có loại tiền kim loại hình tròn, có lỗ vuông ở giữa. Trên mặt đồng tiền thường có ghi niên hiệu của nhà vua đang trị vì và mệnh giá của đồng tiền.

Tiền giấy được phát hành lần đầu tiên ở Việt Nam vào cuối thế kỷ thứ XIV. Tuy nhiên, các triều đại kế tiếp vẫn cho đúc tiền kim loại. Khi thực dân Pháp đặt nền đô hộ trên khắp Đông Dương (bao gồm Việt Nam, Lào và Cam Bốt) vào năm 1884, chính quyền thuộc địa cho phát hành tiền Đông Dương (tiếng Pháp gọi là *piastre*), lưu hành ở ba nước Đông Dương, song song với tiền tệ bản địa của từng nước, từ năm 1885 đến 1954.

Ngày nay, tên gọi "đồng" được dùng lại cho đơn vị tiền tệ của Việt Nam. Vì đất nước đã trải qua nhiều thời kỳ lịch sử khác nhau, có rất nhiều loại tiền, tiền đồng cũng như tiền giấy, ghi lại nhiều hình ảnh thú vị và ý nghĩa. Đây là một trong những điều thu hút giới sưu tầm tiền cổ tại Việt Nam cũng như trên khắp thế giới.

dohngm^5 tyehn^5 viyeht^6 nam^1

duhn^1 vee^5 tyehn^5 teh^6 koouh^4 vyeht^6 nam^1 la^5 dohngm^5 // yŭuh^6 thew^1 tehn^1 koouh^4 keem^1 lwie^6 cheenh^2 yoong^5 deh^4 dookp^2 tyehn^5 ngăy^5 trŭuhk^2 // tyehn^5 teh^6 koouh^4 vyeht^6 nam^1 băt^2 dohw^5 swut^2 hyehn^6 tŭ^5 yŭuh^3 theh^2 kee^4 thŭ^2 mŭuhy^5 // lookp^2 dah^2 chee^4 kah^2 lwie^6 tyehn^5 keem^1 lwie^6 heenh^5 trahn^5 kah^2 loh^3 vwohng^1 uh^4 yŭuh^3 // trehn^1 măt^6 dohngm^5 tyehn^5 thŭuhng^5 kah^2 gee^1 nyehn^1 hyehw^6 koouh^4 nha^5 voouh^1 dang^1 tree^6 vee^5 va^5 mehnh^6 ya^2 koouh^4 dohngm^5 tyehn^5

tyehn^5 yay^2 dŭuhk^5 fat^2 hănh^5 lun^5 dohw^5 tyehn^1 uh^4 vyeht^6 nam^1 vahw^5 kwohy^2 theh^2 kee^4 thŭ^2 mŭuhy^5 bohn^2 // twee^1 nhyehn^1 kak^2 tryehw^5 die^6 keh^2 tyehp^2 vun^3 chah^1 dookp^2 tyehn^5 keem^1 lwie^6 // khee^1 thŭk^6 yun^1 fap^2 dăt^6 nehn^5 doh^1 hoh^6 trehn^1 khăp^2 dohngm^1 yŭuhng^1 // bahw^1 gohm^5 vyeht^6 nam^1 lahw^5 va^5 kam^1 boht^2 vahw^5 năm^1 moht^6 ngan^5 tam^2 trăm^1 tam^2 mŭuhy^1 bohn^2 // cheenh^2 kwyehn^5 theohk^6 deeuh^6 chah^1 fat^2 hănh^5 tiehn^5 dohngm^1 yŭuhn^1 // tiyehng^2 fap^2 gahy^6 la^5 pee-astre // lŭw^1 hănh^5 uh^4 ba^1 nŭuhk^2 dohngm^1 yŭuhng^1 // shahngm^1 shahngm^1 vuhy^2 tyehn^5 teh^6 ban^4 deeuh^6 koouh^4 tŭng^5 nŭuhk^2 // tŭ^5 năm^1 moht^6 ngan^5 tam^2 trăm^1 tam^2 mŭuhy^1 lăm^1 dehn^2 moht^5 ngan^5 cheen^2 trăm^1 năm^2 mŭuhy^1 bohn^2

ngăy^5 năy^1 tehn^1 gahy^6 dohngm^5 dŭuhk^6 lie^6 chah^1 duhn^1 vee^6 tyehn^5 teh^6 kooh^4 vyeht^6 nam^1 // vee^5 dut^2 nŭuhk^2 da^3 trie^4 kwa^1 nhyehw^5 thuhy^5 kee^5 leech^6 shŭ^4 khak^2 nhăw^1 // kah^2 rut^2 nhyehw^5 lwie^6 tyehn^5 // tyehn^5 dohng^5 koong^3 nhŭ^1 tyehn^5 yay^2 // gee^1 lie^6 nhyehw^5 heenh^5 ănh^4 thoo^2 vee^6 va^5 ee^2 ngeeuh^3 // day^1 la^5 moht^6 trahngm^1 nhŭng^3 dyehw^5 thoo^1 hoot^2 yuhy^2 shŭw^1 tum^5 tyehn^5 koh^4 tie^6 vyeht^6 nam^1 koongm^3 nhŭ^1 trehn^1 khăp^2 theh^2 yuhy^2

THE VIETNAMESE DONG

The Vietnamese currency is the "dong," named after the principal metal used to mint coins in the old days. Vietnamese currency appeared for the first time in the middle of the tenth century. Back then, there existed only round metal coins with a square hole in the middle. On either side of a coin, the annual title of the current ruling king and its denomination were engraved.

Paper money was issued for the first time in Vietnam toward the end of the fourteenth century. However, coins were still minted by the ensuing dynasties. In 1884, when the French colonialists established their rule all over Indochina (consisting of Vietnam, Laos and Cambodia), the colonial government issued the Indochinese currency (known as *piastre* in French), circulating alongside the local currency in each of the three countries, from 1885 until 1954.

Nowadays, the name "dong" is again used for the Vietnamese currency. Because the country has undergone several historical periods, there are many types of currency, coins and notes featuring interesting and significant images. This is one of the things that attracts collectors of old money both in Vietnam and the world over.

COMPREHENSION QUESTIONS

Answer the following questions in complete sentences, first orally, then in writing.

1. **Tại sao tiền Việt Nam được gọi là "đồng"?** *Why is the Vietnamese currency called the "dong"?*

 ____

2. **Đồng tiền cổ là như thế nào?** *What did an old coin look like?*

 ____

3. **Tiền giấy xuất hiện lần đầu tiên vào thế kỷ thứ mấy?** *In which century did paper money first appear?*

 ____

4. **Tiền Đông Dương được dùng trong những nước nào?** *In what countries was the Indo-Chinese currency used?*

 ____

5. **Người Pháp đặt tên cho đồng tiền Đông Dương là gì?** *What did the French name the Indo-Chinese currency?*

 ____

PRACTICE

A. Listening comprehension

Listen to the questions (**câu hỏi**) in this interview and write the correct answers (**câu trả lời**) from the given list.

a. **Tôi học tiếng Pháp.**
 I'm learning French.

b. **Không, tôi không đi làm.**
 No, I don't work.

c. **Tôi học bài ở thư viện.**
 I'm studying at the library.

d. **Phải, tôi là người Mỹ.**
 Yes, I'm an American.

e. **Không, tôi đang học năm thứ hai.**
 No, I'm in my second year.

f. **Tôi mười chín tuổi.**
 I'm nineteen years old.

g. **Tôi sống ở Đà Nẵng.**
 I live in Danang.

h. **Tôi học ở Đại Học Quốc Gia.**
 I study at the National University.

Câu hỏi	Câu trả lời
1	
2	
3	
4	
5	
6	
7	
8	

B. Interrogative words

Ask specific questions using the correct interrogative words from the list, based on the underlined elements in the answers below. Change the perspective for the subject when necessary.

đâu gì nào ai mấy bao nhiêu tại sao bao xa bao lâu thế nào khi nào

Model:

☞ Câu hỏi: Anh làm việc ở **đâu**?

Câu trả lời: Tôi làm việc ở Nha Trang.

1. ______________________________?

Thư viện thành phố cách ngân hàng Chase **300 mét**.

The City Library is 300 meters away from Chase Bank.

2. ______________________________?

Cô ấy đi mua sắm với **các bạn**.

She went shopping with her friends.

3. ______________________________?

Con trai tôi ba tuổi.

My son is three years old.

4. ______________________________?

Ngày mai họ sẽ đi ăn với nhau.

They will be eating out together tomorrow.

5. ____?
Chúng tôi đi **biển**.
We're going to the beach.

6. ____?
Thành phố Tampa thuộc tiểu bang **Florida**.
The city of Tampa is in the state of Florida.

7. ____?
Anh ấy học tiếng Anh **vì cần thi TOEFL**.
He is learning English because he needs to take the TOEFL.

8. ____?
Chiếc xe này giá **ba chục ngàn đô-la**.
This car costs thirty thousand dollars.

9. ____?
Hôm nay tôi **bận lắm**.
I'm very busy today.

10. ____?
Trường đại học này tên là **Phan Bội Châu**.
This university's name is Phan Bội Châu.

11. ____?
Từ nhà tôi lái xe đến trường mất **ba mươi phút**.
It takes thirty minutes to drive from my house to school.

C. Types of questions

Make the types of questions suggested, based on the information given in parentheses.

Model:
Yes-no question (***Bà/có/tiền lẻ***)
☞ **Bà có tiền lẻ không?**

1. Specific question (***Ngân Hàng Thành Phố/nằm/trên/đường nào***)

____?

2. Choice question (***Cô/cần/đô-la/euro***)

____?

3. Yes-no question (***Hôm nay/hối suất đồng yen/cao***)

____?

4. Tag question (***Đồng nhân dân tệ/là/của/Trung Quốc***)

____?

5. Yes-no question (***Đây/là/quầy đổi ngoại tệ***)

____?

6. Specific question (***Anh/muốn/mua/lệnh phiếu/tại sao***)

____?

D. Vocabulary

Do the following **ô chữ** "crossword puzzle," referring to the Functional Vocabulary Section for help if needed. *Include all the necessary accent marks.*

ACROSS – NGANG	DOWN – DỌC
1. Paper form of payment issued by a bank, a post office or a money transfer service center.	1. Sum charged or paid for services.
4. Be present (*at an event*).	2. Financial institution.
5. Sum of money for which something is bought or sold.	3. Value of a currency determined for conversion to another.
6. Give support or aid to.	6. Piece of paper money.
7. Slip of paper for a fare or admission.	12. Place (*something on a surface*).
8. To bring into one's possession.	13. Formal form of address for a man.
9. Transfer in exchange for money.	15. Vietnamese currency.
10. White metallic element with symbol *Ag*.	17. Withdraw or take out.
11. Send or deposit.	20. Coins and bills used for paying.
14. Classifier for objects.	21. Antonym of 9 Across.
16. Banking record of money received or spent.	
18. Modal verb expressing that an action is a duty.	
19. Money accumulated by economy.	
22. Interesting or entertaining.	
23. Suitable or agreeable for the purpose.	

PROVERB

NÉN BẠC ĐÂM XOẠC TỜ GIẤY.

nen[2] bak[6] dum[1] swak[6] tuh[5] yay[2]

"A bar of silver can poke through a piece of paper."

This proverb satirically depicts an image of bribery, through which people can use the power of money to persuade corrupt officials to do illegal things for them. During the feudal periods in Vietnam, silver was used as money, even more commonly than gold, for everyday purchases or trade. For this reason, the general term referring to money is the compound noun **tiền bạc** "money and silver." Many expressions use **bạc** in that sense: **cờ bạc** or **bài bạc** "gambling" (**bài** is "playing cards" and **cờ** is "chess"), **đánh bạc** "to gamble," **giấy bạc** "banknote," etc. Another way to say "one million dong" is **một triệu bạc** instead of **một triệu đồng**.

FUNCTIONAL VOCABULARY

DANH TỪ

tiền	money
tiền tệ/tiền bạc	money (*in general*)
đồng	Vietnamese currency
tiền giấy	paper money
tiền đồng	coin
giấy bạc	banknote
tiền lẻ	change
ngân hàng	bank
nhân viên	employee
giá	price
trương mục	account
ngân phiếu	check, checking
tiết kiệm	savings
lệnh phiếu	money order
lệ phí	fee
lãi suất	interest rate
hối suất	exchange rate
khách hàng	customer
quà	gift
vé	ticket
sinh nhật	birthday
hoà nhạc	concert

TÍNH TỪ

bình thường	normal
vui	fun; happy
kế tiếp	next, following
hay	good, interesting
tiện	convenient
mỗi	each, every

ĐỘNG TỪ

nhận	to receive
gửi (vào)	to deposit (into)
quên	to forget
dự	to attend
mua	to buy
bán	to sell
nghĩ	to think
nên	should
đặt	to place; to order
đồng ý	to agree
giúp	to help
gặp	to see; to meet
rút	to withdraw
chuyển	to transfer
lấy	to take

Ồ, tôi ngủ chẳng biết trời trăng gì nữa!
Oh, I slept like a log!

Ở đây các bạn dậy sớm quá há.
You guys get up so early here, huh.

Ở thành phố này không ngày nào mà không kẹt xe.
In this city, there isn't a single day without traffic jams.

Thành phố này náo nhiệt quá!
What a busy city this is!

Tôi có cảm tưởng là Sài Gòn không bao giờ ngủ!
I get the impression that Saigon never sleeps!

CHAPTER 8

Daily Activities at Home

Ở Nhà – Sinh Hoạt Hằng Ngày

DIALOGUE 1

Vân, a computer technician living in Saigon, welcomes her pen pal Vanessa, a graduate student from California whose major is Vietnamese studies, to her home for a two-week stay. Vanessa is talking with Van, wanting to know everything about life in this bustling city.

VÂN **Đêm qua Vanessa ngủ ngon không?**
dehm^{1} kwa^{1} vanessa ngoo^{4} ngahn^{1} khohngm^{1}
Did you sleep well last night?

VANESSA **Ồ, tôi ngủ chẳng biết trời trăng gì nữa! Ở đây các bạn dậy sớm quá há.**
oh^{5} tohy^{1} ngoo^{4} chăng^{4} byeth^{2} truhy^{5} trăng^{1} yee^{5} nŭuh^{3} //uh^{4} day^{1} kak^{2} ban^{6} yay^{6} shuhm^{2} kwa^{2} ha^{2}
Oh, I slept like a log! You guys get up so early here, huh.

VÂN **Ở thành phố này không ngày nào mà không kẹt xe nên chúng tôi không dám ra khỏi nhà trễ.**
uh^{4} thănh^{5} foh^{2} năy^{5} khohngm^{1} ngăy^{5} nahw^{5} ma^{5} khohngm^{1} ket^{6} se^{1} nehn^{1} choongm^{2} tohy^{1} khohngm^{1} yam^{2} ra^{1} khahy^{4} nha^{5} treh^{3}
In this city, there's not a single day without traffic jams, so we don't dare leave our houses late.

VANESSA **Người đi làm ở đây có về nhà ăn trưa như ở Tây Ban Nha hay một số nước châu Mỹ La Tinh không?**
ngŭuhy^{5} dee^{1} lam^{5} uh^{4} day^{1} kah^{2} veh^{5} nha^{5} ăn^{1} trŭuh^{1} nhŭ^{1} uh^{4} tay^{1} ban^{1} nha^{1} hăy^{1} moht^{6} shoh^{2} nŭuhk^{2} chohw^{1} mee^{3} la^{1} teenh^{1} khohngm^{1}
Do workers here go home for lunch like in Spain and some Latin American countries?

VÂN **Ngày nay gần như không có chuyện đó nữa đâu. Chúng tôi thường ra ngoài ăn ở những tiệm gần chỗ làm hay đặt thức ăn để người ta mang đến.**

ngăy^5 năy^1 gun^5 nhŭ^1 khohngm^1 kah^2 chwyehn^6 dah^2 nŭuh^3 dohw^1 // choongm^2 tohy^1 thŭuhng^5 ra^1 ngwie^5 ăn^1 uh^4 nhŭng^3 tiehm^6 gun^5 choh^3 lam^5 hăy^1 dăt^6 thŭk^2 ăn^1 deh^4 ngŭuhy^5 ta^1 mang^1 dehn^2

That custom hardly exists nowadays. We usually go out to eat at places near our offices or order food to be delivered.

VANESSA **Thành phố này náo nhiệt quá! Ngồi trong nhà Vân mà mình có thể nghe tiếng xe cộ ngoài đường thật rõ. Tôi có cảm tưởng là Sài Gòn không bao giờ ngủ!**

thănh^5 foh^2 năy^5 nahw^2 nhyeht^6 kwa^2 // ngohy^1 trahng^1 nha^5 vun^1 ma^5 meenh^5 kah^2 theh^4 nge^1 tyehng^2 se^1 koh^6 ngwie^5 dŭuhng^5 thut^6 rah^3 // tohy^1 kah^2 kam^4 tŭuhng^4 la^5 shie^5 gahn^5 khohngm^1 bahw^1 yuh^5 ngoo^4

What a busy city this is! Sitting here in your apartment, I can hear the traffic in the street so clearly. I get the impression that Saigon never sleeps!

KEY VOCABULARY 1

ngủ *v*	to sleep	**ra ngoài** *v*	to go outside
ngon *adj*	delicious; sound	**tiệm** *n*	store, shop
dậy *v*	to get up	**chỗ làm** *n*	workplace
kẹt xe *n*	traffic jam	**thức ăn** *n*	food
dám *v*	dare	**mang đến** *v*	to bring, to deliver
ra khỏi *v*	to get out of	**náo nhiệt** *adj*	bustling
người đi làm *n*	worker	**ngồi** *v*	to sit
về nhà *v*	to go home	**tiếng** *n*	sound; language
ăn trưa *v*	to have lunch	**xe cộ** *n*	vehicles; traffic
châu Mỹ La Tinh *n*	Latin America	**rõ** *adj/adv*	clear; clearly
gần như *adv*	almost	**cảm tưởng** *n*	impression
chuyện *n*	matter; story	**không bao giờ** *adv*	never

IDIOMATIC EXPRESSIONS 1

ngủ chẳng biết trời trăng gì nữa Literally, "to sleep without being aware of heaven or the moon any longer." Another expression equivalent to the English "to sleep like a log/a baby" is **ngủ say như chết** "to sleep soundly like the dead."

tôi có cảm tưởng là/rằng... "I have an impression that..." **Là** in this construction is a conjunction, used colloquially instead of **rằng** (in formal speech or in writing).

CULTURE NOTES 1

As you will notice in the way the two friends address each other (and as mentioned briefly in Chapter 7), a person's first name can be used to mean "you" between friends or partners, more often among young speakers than older people. A first name can even be used to mean "I/me," either intimately or informally. Vân can say to Vanessa, for example, **"Vân không biết"** to mean "I don't know."

The pronoun **mình** is colloquially short for the plural informal/intimate **chúng mình** or **tụi mình** (inclusive "we," versus the formal **chúng ta**, and as opposed to the exclusive "we" **chúng tôi**). In the context of the dialogue above, **mình** is used like the general "you" in English or the formal pronoun "one." The sentence **Mình phải thật cẩn thận khi băng qua đường ở đây** means "We/you/one must be very careful when crossing the street here."

When used informally as a true singular pronoun, **mình** means "I/me": **Mình không biết bạn muốn gì** "I don't know what you want."

GRAMMAR NOTES 1

I. Negative expressions

In addition to the common negative adverb **không**, several other words and expressions can be used to express negation with various nuances. Sentence (1a) below can be paraphrased with alternative negative expressions such as:

(1) a. **Tôi không hiểu anh muốn nói gì.**
tohy^{1} *khohngm*^{1} *hyehw*^{4} *ănh*^{1} *mwohn*^{2} *nahy*^{2} *yee*^{5}
I don't understand what you mean.

b. **Tôi không hiểu anh muốn nói gì cả.** (*Emphatic*)

c. **Tôi không hề hiểu anh muốn nói gì.** (*Emphatic*)

d. **Tôi chẳng hiểu anh muốn nói gì.** (*Colloquial, emphatic*)

e. **Tôi đâu hiểu anh muốn nói gì.** (*Colloquial, emphatic*)

f. **Tôi có hiểu anh muốn nói gì đâu.** (*Colloquial, emphatic*)

Negation can also be emphasized by the use of a negative expression, followed by the particle **mà** and the negative adverbs **không/chưa** as follows (a double negative):

(2) a. **Không ai mà không thích xem tin tức trên truyền hình.**
khohngm^{1} *ie*^{1} *ma*^{5} *khohngm*^{1} *theech*^{2} *sem*^{1} *teen*^{1} *tŭk*^{2} *trehn*^{1} *trwyehn*^{5} *heenh*^{5}
Nobody dislikes watching the news on TV.

b. **Không có gì mà anh ấy không biết.**
khohngm^{1} *kah*^{2} *yee*^{5} *ma*^{5} *ănh*^{2} *ay*^{2} *khohngm*^{1} *byeht*^{2}
There's nothing he doesn't know.

c. **Không đâu mà chúng tôi chưa đến.**
khohngm^1 dohw^1 ma^5 choong^2 tohy^1 chŭuh^1 dehn^2
There is no place we haven't been to.

d. **Không làm sao mà tôi không cười được.**
khohngm^1 lam^5 shahw^1 ma^5 tohy^1 khohngm^1 kŭuhy^5 dŭuhk^6
There's no way I can help laughing.

e. **Không bao giờ mà họ không gọi trước khi đến.**
khohngm^1 bahw^1 yuh^5 ma^5 hah^6 khohngm^1 gahy^6 trŭuhk^2 khee^1 dehn^2
They never fail to call before coming.

The following pronouns and adverbs in Vietnamese have different meanings, depending on what grammatical functions they have in a sentence. Study the chart below and the examples that follow:

	AS INTERROGATIVE	AS INDEFINITE	AS NEGATIVE (WITH KHÔNG)
ai	who	somebody, anybody	nobody
gì	what	something, anything	nothing
làm sao	how	somehow, anyhow	no way
bao giờ	when	ever, any time	never
đâu	where	somewhere, anywhere	nowhere

(3) a. **Trong nhà anh ai là người cắt cỏ?** [**ai:** *interrogative pronoun*]
trahngm^1 nha^5 ănh^1 ie^1 la^5 ngŭuhy^5 kăt^2 kah^4
Who in your family mows the lawn?

b. **Cô có thấy ai đang rửa chén bát không?** [**ai:** *indefinite pronoun*]
koh^1 kah^2 thay^2 ie^1 dang^1 rŭuh^4 chen^2 bat^2 khohngm^1
Do you see anyone washing the dishes?

c. **Căn phòng này không ai dọn dẹp cả.** [**không ai:** *negative pronoun*]
kăn^1 fahngm^5 năy^5 khohngm^1 ie^1 yahn^6 yep^6 kah^4
Nobody cleans up this room at all.

d. **Chị thường ăn gì vào bữa sáng?** [**gì:** *interrogative pronoun*]
chee^6 thŭuhng^5 ăn^1 yee^5 vahw^5 bŭuh^3 shang^2
What do you usually eat for breakfast?

e. **Cô nấu gì tôi cũng thích.** [**gì:** *indefinite pronoun*]
koh^1 nohw^2 yee^5 tohy^1 koongm^3 theech^2
I like anything you cook.

f. **Sáng Chủ Nhật tôi không muốn làm gì cả.** [**không (...) gì:** *negative pronoun*]
shang^2 choo^4 nhut^6 tohy^1 khohngm^1 mwohn^2 lam^5 yee^5 ka^4
I don't want to do anything on Sunday mornings.

g. **Bà nướng bánh này làm sao?** [***làm sao:*** *interrogative adverb*]
ba^5 nüuhng^2 bănh^2 năy^5 lam^5 shahw^1
How did you bake this cake?

h. **Tôi lau chùi nền nhà làm sao cũng không bóng được.** [***làm sao:*** *indefinite adverb*]
tohy^1 lăw^1 chooy^5 nehn^5 nha^5 lam^5 shahw^1 koongm^3 khohngm^1 bahngm^2 dŭuhk^6
The floors will never be shiny, however much I scrub them.

i. **Cô ấy không làm sao ủi hết chỗ quần áo này được.** [***không làm sao:*** *negative adverb*]
koh^1 ay^1 khohngm^1 lam^5 shahw^1 ooy^4 heht^2 choh^3 kwun^5 ahw^2 năy^5 dŭuhk^6
There's no way she can iron all these clothes.

j. **Bao giờ em mới hút bụi trong phòng khách?** [***bao giờ:*** *interrogative adverb*]
bahw^1 yuh^5 em^1 muhy^2 hoot^2 booy^6 trahngm^1 fahngm^5 khăch^2
When will you vacuum the living room?

k. **Bao giờ con muốn giặt đồ cũng được.** [***bao giờ:*** *indefinite adverb*]
bahw^1 yuh^5 kahn^1 mwohn^2 yăt^6 doh^5 koongm^3 dŭuhk^6
Anytime you want to wash the clothes is fine.

l. **Các cô ấy không bao giờ thức khuya.** [***không bao giờ:*** *negative adverb*]
kak^2 koh^1 ay^2 khohngm^1 bahw^1 yuh^5 thŭk^2 khweeuh^1
They never stay up late.

m. **Anh thường đọc sách ở đâu?** [***ở đâu:*** *interrogative adverb*]
ănh^1 thŭuhng^5 dahkp^6 shăch^2 uh^4 dohw^1
Where do you usually read?

n. **Ông đặt cái chậu hoa này ở đâu cũng đẹp.** [***ở đâu:*** *indefinite adverb*]
ohngm^1 dăt^6 kie^2 chohw^6 hwa^1 năy^5 uh^4 dohw^1 koongm^3 dep^6
This pot of flowers will look nice anywhere you put it.

o. **Không ở đâu có loại gỗ quý để làm bàn ghế như ở vùng này.** [***không ở đâu:*** *negative adverb*]
khohngm^1 uh^4 dohw^1 kah^2 lwie^6 goh^3 kwee^2 deh^4 lam^5 ban^5 geh^2 nhŭ^{1}uh^4 voongm^5 năy^5
You can't find this precious wood for furniture-making anywhere like you can in this region.

Tôi vẫn tưởng rằng cuộc sống ở đây chậm rãi lắm.
I always thought life here was quite slow.

Hôm qua trên đường từ phi trường về nhà Vân...
Yesterday on the way to your home from the airport...

Tôi đã thấy Sài Gòn nhộn nhịp đến dường nào.
I got to see how lively Saigon is.

Ngày thường tôi phải vội vã lắm.
On weekdays I always have to be in a big hurry.

Tôi thường dậy lúc 6 giờ, đánh răng rửa mặt và tắm thật nhanh.
I usually get up at six o'clock, brush my teeth, wash my face and take a quick shower.

Tôi chỉ có thể ăn vội bữa sáng ở văn phòng.
I can only have a hasty breakfast in my office.

DIALOGUE 2

Today Vanessa and Van are getting ready to explore Saigon. They are talking over a relaxed breakfast.

VANESSA **Trước khi đến Việt Nam, tôi vẫn tưởng rằng cuộc sống ở đây chậm rãi lắm. Bây giờ tôi mới biết là mình lầm. Hôm qua trên đường từ phi trường về nhà Vân tôi đã thấy Sài Gòn nhộn nhịp đến dường nào.**
Trŭuhk2 khee1 dehn2 vyeht6 nam1 // tohy1 vun3 tŭuhng4 răng5 kwohk6 shohng2 uh4 day1 chum6 rie3 lăm2 // bay1 yuh5 tohy1 muhy2 byeht2 la5 meenh5 lum5 // hohm1 kwa1 trehn1 dŭuhng5 tŭ5 fee1 trŭuhng5 veh5 nha5 tohy1 da3 thay2 shie5 gahn5 nhohn6 nheep6 dehn2 yŭuhng5 nahw1
Before coming to Vietnam, I always thought life here was quite slow. It wasn't until now that I realized I was wrong. Yesterday on the way to your home from the airport I got to see how lively Saigon is.

VÂN **Hôm nay là Chủ Nhật nên Vanessa và tôi mới được ngồi thưởng thức bánh mì với trứng ốp-la và cà-phê sữa nóng một cách thư thả như thế này, chứ ngày thường tôi phải vội vã lắm.**
hohm1 năy1 la5 choo4 nhut6 nehn1 vanessa va5 tohy1 muhy2 dŭuhk6 ngohy5 thŭuhng4 thŭk2 bănh2 mee5 vuhy2 trŭng2 ohp2 la1 va5 ka5 feh1 shŭuh3 nahngm2 moht6 kăch2 thŭ2 tha4 nhŭ1 theh2 năy5 // chŭ2 ngăy5 thŭuhng5 tohy1 fie4 vohy6 va3 lăm2
Today is Sunday, so you and I get to relax and sit here enjoying some bread, fried eggs and coffee with milk, but on weekdays I always have to be in a big hurry.

VANESSA **Vậy một buổi sáng điển hình trong tuần của Vân ra sao?**
vay6 moht6 bwohy4 shang2 dyehn4 heenh5 trahngm1 twun5 koouh4 vun1 ra1 shahw1
So, what's a typical weekday morning like for you?

VÂN **Chắc cũng không khác gì mấy so với một buổi sáng của Vanessa ở bên Mỹ đâu. Tôi thường dậy lúc 6 giờ, đánh răng, rửa mặt và tắm thật nhanh. Tôi phải ra đường sớm để tránh bị kẹt xe. Tôi chỉ có thể ăn vội bữa sáng ở văn phòng.**
chăk2 koongm3 khohngm1 khak2 yee5 may2 shah1 vuhy2 moht5 bwohy4 shang2 koouh4 vanessa uh4 behn1 mee3 dohw1 // tohy1 thŭuhng5 yay5 lookp2 shahw2 yuh5 dănh2 răng1 rŭuh4 măt6 va5 tăm2 thut6 nhănh1 // tohy1 fie4 ra1 dŭuhng5 shuhm2 deh4 trănh2 bee5 ket6 se1 // tohy1 fie4 ăn1 vohy5 bŭuh3 shang2 uh4 văn1 fahngm5
Maybe not so different from yours in America. I usually get up at six, brush my teeth, wash my face and take a quick shower. I have to be on the road early to avoid getting stuck in traffic. I can only have a quick breakfast at my office.

 KEY VOCABULARY 2

vẫn *adv*	still; always	**thư thả** *adj*	relaxed
tưởng *v*	to suppose	**ngày thường** *n*	regular day
cuộc sống *n*	life	**vội vã** *adj*	hurried
chậm rãi *adj*	slow-paced	**điển hình** *adj*	typical
lầm *adj*	mistaken	**chắc** *adv*	maybe
phi trường *n*	airport	**so với** *conj*	than
nhộn nhịp *adj*	lively	**đánh răng** *v*	to brush one's teeth
thưởng thức *v*	to enjoy	**rửa mặt** *v*	to wash one's face
bánh mì *n*	bread	**tắm** *v*	to bathe, to shower
trứng ốp-la *n*	fried egg	**tránh** *v*	to avoid
sữa *n*	milk	**bữa sáng** *n*	breakfast

IDIOMATIC EXPRESSIONS 2

Tôi vẫn tưởng rằng... **Tưởng** is "to think," but this verb is usually used in the sense of "to think mistakenly or be under an illusion." For example, ***Đừng tưởng rằng anh là người duy nhất biết chuyện này*** "Don't think (incorrectly) that you are the only one who knows about this."

Còn... thì sao? Equivalent to "What/How about," this expression contains the conjunction **còn** "and," the verb **thì** "to be" and the interrogative pronoun **sao** "what," in addition to the subject in question. The blank is available for a noun (referring to a person or a thing), ***Còn vấn đề này thì sao?*** "What about this matter?" or a pronoun, ***Còn họ thì sao?*** "How about them?"

CULTURE NOTES 2

The French colonialists' 100-year presence in Vietnam—spanning the second half of the 19th century to the first half of the 20th century—resulted, among other things, in the presence of thousands of loanwords from the French language. In the dialogue above, you see **trứng ốp-la**, which came from *oeuf au plat* "fried egg" and **cà-phê**, from *café* "coffee." French loanwords, with modified spellings and pronunciations in accordance with Vietnamese grammar, are so popular that few people even realize that they often use them here and there in their speech. In **đổ xăng** "to fill up your gas tank," the noun **xăng** is from the French *essence* "gasoline," and **xì-căng-đan** came from *scandale* "scandal." **Xà-lách**, from *salade*, is an interesting case. This loanword has a different meaning in Vietnamese: Instead of meaning "salad" as in the original language, it now means "lettuce" for Vietnamese speakers.

On the gastronomic side, Vietnamese people's main staple is **cơm** "steamed rice"—also meaning in a general sense "food." **Cơm** is usually eaten with side dishes, typically **món xào** "stir-fried dish (with meat/seafood and vegetables)," **món kho** "braised dish (with pork or seafood)," and **món canh** "soup." For a quick meal without having to cook, you can stop by a take-out restaurant and take advantage of its **cơm chỉ** services—so called because **chỉ** means "to point at," whereby you simply point at any of the steaming hot dishes, deliciously and invitingly sitting behind the glass, and the server will readily scoop them up for you.

GRAMMAR NOTES 2

II. Adverbs of manner and degree

A. Adverbs of manner

An adverb modifies a verb to show how an action is performed. In Vietnamese, most adverbs of manner share the same form as their adjectival counterparts (i.e., you simply take an adjective and conveniently use it as an adverb). Compare the following pairs of sentences:

(4) a. **Cô ấy là một người nấu ăn giỏi.** [***giỏi*** *is an adjective, describing the noun* **người nấu ăn**]
koh^{1} ay^{1} la^{5} moht^{6} ngŭuhy^{5} nohw^{2} ăn^{1} yahy^{4}
She is a good cook.

b. **Cô ấy nấu ăn giỏi.** [***giỏi*** *is an adverb, modifying the verb* **nấu ăn**]
koh^{1} ay^{2} nohw^{2} ăn^{1} yahy^{4}
She cooks well.

c. **Điệu nhạc này nhanh quá!** [***nhanh*** *is an adjective, describing the noun* **điệu nhạc**]
dyehw^{6} nhak^{6} năy^{5} nhănh^{1} kwa^{2}
This tune is so fast!

d. **Anh ấy hát nhanh quá!** [***nhanh*** *is an adverb, modifying the verb* **hát**]
ănh^{1} ay^{2} hat^{2} nhănh^{1} kwa^{2}
He sings so fast!

Speakers can choose, however, to express the manner in which an action is performed by using the phrase **một cách** "in a manner," followed by an adjective. In this kind of expression, the adjective has to (i) contain at least two syllables, (ii) be used with another word, or (iii) come with a *reduplicating syllable*.

If an adjective is inherently *disyllabic*, it can be used with or without **một cách** when functioning as an adverb of manner:

(5) a. **Cô Hồng là một người rụt rè.** [***rụt rè*** *is a disyllabic adjective, describing the noun* **người**]
koh^{1} hohngm^{5} la^{5} moht^{6} ngŭuhy^{5} root^{6} re^{5}
Miss Hồng is a timid person.

b. **Cô Hồng rụt rè hỏi tôi.** [***rụt rè*** *is a disyllabic adverb, modifying the verb* **hỏi**]
koh^{1} hohng^{5}m root^{6} re^{5} hahy^{4} tohy^{1}
Miss Hồng timidly asked me a question.

c. **Cô Hồng hỏi tôi một cách rụt rè.** [***rụt rè*** *is a disyllabic adjective, used after* **một cách** *to form an adverb-of-manner phrase*]
koh^{1} hohngm^{5} hahy^{4} tohy^{1} moht^{6} kăch^{2} root^{6} re^{5}
Miss Hồng asked me a question in a timid way.

If an adjective is *monosyllabic*, when following **một cách** to form an adverb-of-manner phrase, it must be combined with another element in one of the three types as follows.

The first type is a *coordinate compound adjective*, in which the main adjective is combined with another adjective, either synonymous or semantically associated with it. Study the following examples:

(6) a. **Hôm ấy là một ngày vui của tôi.** [*vui is an adjective, describing the noun* **ngày**]
hohm^1 ay^2 la^5 moht^5 ngăy^5 vooy^1 koouh^4 tohy^1
It was a happy day for me.

b. **Anh ấy nói chuyện vui lắm.** [*vui is an adverb, modifying the verb* **nói chuyện**]
ănh^1 ay^2 nahy^2 chwyehn^6 vooy^1 lăm^2
He talks very pleasantly.

c. **Anh ấy chào đón chúng tôi một cách vui mừng.** [**vui mừng** *is a coordinate compound adjective (***mừng** *means "glad"), used after* **một cách** *to form an adverb-of-manner phrase*]
ănh^1 ay^2 chahw^5 dahn^2 choongm^2 tohy^1 moht^6 kăch^2 vooy^1 mŭng^5
He welcomed us in a cheerful way.

The second type is a *subordinate compound adjective*, in which the adjective is the head word, and the other word is a secondary element that can come from various parts of speech. Consider the sentences below:

(7) a. **Xe đang chạy với tốc độ nhanh.** (*nhanh is an adjective, describing the noun* **tốc độ**]
se^1 dang^1 chăy^6 vuhy^2 tohkp^2 doh^6 nhănh^1
The car was moving at a fast speed.

b. **Xe đang chạy nhanh.** (*nhanh is an adverb, modifying the verb* **chạy**]
se^1 dang^1 chăy^6 nhănh^1
The car was moving fast.

c. **Cậu bé trả lời một cách nhanh trí.** [**nhanh trí** *is a subordinate compound adjective (***trí** *means "brain"), used after* **một cách** *to form an adverb-of-manner phrase*]
kohw^6 be^2 tra^4 luhy^5 moht^6 kăch^2 nhănh^1 tree^2
The little boy replied in a witty way.

The third type is a *reduplicated adjective*, in which a *meaningless syllable* copies one or more phonetic features from the adjective itself:

(8) a. **Lúc chờ đợi ai, tôi thấy thì giờ chậm quá.** [*chậm is an adjective, describing the noun* **thì giờ**]
lookp^2 chuh^5 duhy^6 ie^1// tohy^1 thay^2 thee^5 yuh^5 chum^6 kwa^2
When waiting for someone, I find the time so slow.

b. **Thì giờ trôi qua sao chậm quá!** [*chậm is an adverb, modifying the verb* **trôi qua**]
thee^5 yuh^5 trohy^1 kwa^1 shahw^1 chum^6 kwa^2
How slowly is the time passing by!

c. **Thì giờ trôi qua một cách chậm chạp**. [***chậm chạp*** *is a reduplicated adjective (****chạp*** *copies the initial consonant sound and the low tone from* ***chậm****), used after* ***một cách*** *to form an adverb-of-manner phrase*]
Time is passing by in a slow manner.

B. Adverbs of degree

As their name suggests, these adverbs indicate the degree to which a descriptive adjective or an adverb of manner applies. Some adverbs of degree appear before the word they modify, some after it, and some even appear in both positions with some nuances. **Quá**, for example, makes the sentence sound more emphatic when it comes before the word it modifies than when it comes after.

ADVERB OF DEGREE		ADVERB OF DEGREE	MEANING
rất	DESCRIPTIVE ADJECTIVE or ADVERB OF MANNER		very
		lắm (*coll.*)	very, so
khá			considerably, rather
cũng (*coll.*); **hơi** (*coll.*)			pretty, kind of
thật		**thật** (*coll.*)	really
quá (*coll.*)		**quá** (*coll.*)	so, too

(9) a. **Đêm nào tôi cũng thức rất khuya.**
dehm^1 nahw^5 tohy^1 koongm^3 thŭk^2 rut^2 khweeuh^1
I stay up very late every night.

b. **Anh tôi cũng đi ngủ trễ lắm!**
ănh^1 tohy^1 koongm^3 dee^1 ngoo^4 treh^3 lăm^2
My older brother also goes to bed so late!

c. **Em trai tôi tập thể dục khá đều đặn.**
em^1 trie^1 tohy^1 tup^6 theh^4 yookp^6 kha^2 dehw^5 dăn^6
My younger brother exercises rather regularly.

d. **Dạo này cô ấy có vẻ hơi bận rộn.**
yahw^6 năy^5 koh^1 ay^2 kah^2 ve^4 huhy^1 bun^6 rohn^6
She seems to have been kind of busy lately.

e. **Lịch sinh hoạt hằng ngày của anh ấy thật dày đặc.**
leech^6 sheenh^1 hwat^6 hăng^5 ngăy^5 koouh^4 ănh^1 ay^2 thut^6 yăy^5 dăk^6
His daily schedule is really tight.

f. **Tôi rất bận mà chị tôi lại rảnh rang quá!**
tohy^1 rut^2 bun^6 ma^5 chee^6 tohy^1 lie^6 rănh^4 rang^1 kwa^2
I'm very busy yet my older sister never does anything!

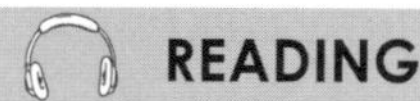

READING

TẬP THỂ DỤC BUỔI SÁNG TRONG CÔNG VIÊN

Từ nhiều thập niên gần đây, người dân thành phố đã có thói quen tụ tập ở những công viên gần nhà để tập thể dục buổi sáng, thay vì làm việc đó riêng lẻ ở nhà. Từ tinh mơ, nhiều người dân trong xóm đã vui vẻ gọi nhau ra công viên.

Khi đến nơi, người ta tụm năm tụm ba làm những điều theo sở thích. Có người thì thong thả tản bộ hay chạy quanh công viên, có người dùng những dụng cụ thể dục có sẵn ở đó để tập. Chỗ này một nhóm này tập Thái Cực Quyền, chỗ kia một nhóm khác đang làm những động tác thông thường như hít thở, vận động các bắp thịt ở tay, chân, bụng, v.v.

Vài thanh thiếu niên chơi vũ cầu hay ném dĩa nhựa. Nhiều trẻ em đạp xe, lớn thì đạp xe hai bánh, nhỏ thì đạp xe ba bánh. Ai ai cũng cả thấy sảng khoái vì cơ thể và đầu óc được thư thái trong bầu không khí trong lành của buổi sáng sớm.

Người ta đến công viên không những chỉ để tập thể dục mà còn để gặp gỡ, thăm hỏi và trao đổi với nhau những mẩu chuyện về đời sống tất bật hằng ngày. Công viên quả là nơi giúp mọi người thắt chặt thêm những mối quan hệ tốt đẹp trong cộng đồng.

tup^{6} theh^{4} yookp^{6} bwohy^{4} shang^{2} trahngm^{1} kohngm^{1} vyehn^{1}

tŭ^{5} nhyehw^{5} thup^{6} nyehn^{1} gun^{5} day^{1} // ngŭuhy^{5} yun^{1} thănh^{5} foh^{2} da^{3} kah^{2} thahy^{2} kwen^{1} too^{6} tup^{6} uh^{4} nhŭng^{3} kohngm^{1} vyehn^{1} gun^{5} nha^{5} deh^{4} tup^{6} theh^{4} yookp^{6} bwohy^{4} shang^{2} thăy^{1} vee^{5} lam^{5} vyehk^{6} dah^{2} ryehng^{1} le^{4} uh^{4} nha^{5} // tŭ^{5} teenh^{1} muh^{1} nhyehw^{5} ngŭuhy^{5} yun^{1} trahngm^{1} sahm^{2} da^{3} vooy^{1} ve^{4} gahy^{6} nhăw^{1} ra^{1} kohngm^{1} vyehn^{1}

khee^{1} dehn^{2} nuhy^{1} ngŭuhy^{5} ta^{1} toom^{6} năm^{1} toom^{6} ba^{1} lam^{5} nhŭng^{3} dyehw^{5} thew^{1} shu^{4} theech^{2} // kah^{2} ngŭuhy^{5} thee^{5} thahngm^{1} tha^{4} tan^{4} boh^{6} hăy^{1} chăy^{6} kwănh^{1} kohngm^{1} vyehn^{1} // kah^{2} ngŭuhy^{5} yoongm^{5} nhŭng^{3} yoongm^{6} koo^{6} theh^{4} yookp^{5} kah^{2} shăn^{3} uh^{4} dah^{2} deh^{4} tup^{6} // choh^{3} năy^{5} moht^{6} nhahm^{2} tup^{6} thie^{2} kŭk^{6} kwyehn^{5} // choh^{3} keeuh^{1} moht^{6} nhahm^{2} khak^{2} dang^{1} lam^{5} nhŭng^{3} dohngm^{6} tak^{2} thohng^{1} thŭuhng^{5} nhŭ^{1} heet^{2} thuh^{4} vun^{6} dohngm^{6} kak^{2} băp^{2} theet^{6} uh^{4} tăy^{1} chun^{1} boongm^{6} vun^{1} vun^{1}

vie^{5} thănh^{1} thyehw^{2} nyehn^{1} chuhy^{1} voo^{3} kohw^{5} hăy^{1} nem^{2} yeeuh^{3} nhŭuh^{6} // nhyehw^{5} tre^{4} em^{1} dap^{6} se^{1} // luhn^{2} thee^{5} dap^{6} se^{1} hie^{1} bănh^{2} // nhah^{4} thee^{5} dap^{6} se^{1} ba^{1} bănh^{2} // ie^{1} ie^{1} koongm^{3} kam^{4} thay^{2} shang^{4} khwie^{2} vee^{5} kuh^{1} theh^{4} va^{5} dohw^{5} ahkp^{2} dŭuhk^{6} thŭ^{1} thie^{2} trahngm^{1} bohw^{5} khohngm^{1} khee^{2} trahngm^{1} lănh^{5} koouh^{4} bwohy^{4} shang^{2} shuhm^{2}

ngŭuhy^{5} ta^{1} dehn^{2} kohngm^{1} vyehn^{1} khohngm^{1} nhŭng^{3} chee^{4} deh^{4} tup^{6} theh^{4} yookp^{6} ma^{5} kahn^{5} deh^{4} găp^{6} guh^{3} thăm^{1} hahy^{4} va^{5} trahw^{1} dohy^{4} vuhy^{2} nhăw^{1} nhŭng^{3} mohw^{4} chwyehn^{6} veh^{5} duhy^{5} shohngm^{2} tut^{2} but^{6} hăng^{5} ngăy^{5} // kohngm^{1} vyehn^{1} kwa^{4}la^{5} nuhy^{1} yoop^{2} mahy^{6} ngŭuhy^{5} thăt^{2} chăt^{6} thehm^{1} nhŭng^{3} mohy^{2} kwan^{1} heh^{6} toht^{2} dep^{6} trahngm^{1} kohnm^{6} dohngm^{5}

MORNING EXERCISE AT THE PARK

For the past few decades, people in the cities have been accustomed to gathering at nearby parks to do their morning exercise, instead of doing it individually at home. Starting at dawn, many people in the neighborhoods cheerfully call one another to come out to the parks.

Upon arriving, they get into groups to do things based on their interests. Some walk leisurely or jog around the park while others use the exercise equipment available there for their workouts. Over here a group is doing tai chi, over there another group is doing a routine including breathing exercises and moves to stimulate muscles in the arms, legs, abdomen, etc.

A few teenagers are playing badminton or throwing frisbees. Some kids are riding bicycles, the older ones on two wheels and the younger ones, on three. Everyone is feeling cheerful, because their bodies and minds are relaxed in the fresh air of the early morning.

People come out to the parks not only to exercise but also to meet up, check in and chat about their busy lives with one another. The parks are indeed places that help strengthen good relationships in the community.

COMPREHENSION QUESTIONS

Answer the following questions in complete sentences, first orally, then in writing.

1. **Người dân thành phố thường tập thể dục buổi sáng ở đâu?** *Where do city people usually exercise in the morning?*

   ____

2. **Một số động tác thể dục thông thường là gì?** *What are some of the usual exercise moves?*

   ____

3. **Vài thanh thiếu niên đang chơi gì?** *What are a few teenagers playing?*

____

4. **Ai đang đạp xe?** *Who's biking?*

____

5. **Ngoài việc tập thể dục, người ta còn đến công viên để làm gì?** *Besides exercising, what do people also come to the park for?*

____

PRACTICE

A. Listening comprehension

Listen to the recording about morning activities in Thảo's family. Write the names of the people in the boxes that match what they are doing.

People (and pets!) in the family

Ba – Mẹ – Huy – Thảo – Bảo – Con chó – Con mèo

ACTIVITY	PEOPLE/PETS
Ngủ trên xô-pha *Sleeping on the couch*	
Thay quần áo trong phòng ngủ *Changing in his bedroom*	
Rửa mặt trong buồng tắm *Washing her face in the bathroom*	
Đọc báo tại bàn ăn *Reading a newspaper at the dining table*	
Chơi với quả banh *Playing with a ball*	
Tập thể dục trong phòng gia đình *Exercising in the family room*	
Làm bữa ăn sáng trong nhà bếp *Preparing breakfast in the kitchen*	

B. Emphatic negative expressions

Change the following sentences to double negative constructions. Note that the expressions should be split up in some cases.

không ai mà không... không có gì mà không... không đâu mà không...
không thế nào mà không... không bao giờ mà không...

Model

a. **Ai cũng thích xem truyền hình vào buổi tối.**
Everyone likes to watch TV in the evening.

b. ☞ **Không ai mà không thích xem truyền hình vào buổi tối.**

1a. **Trong nhà tôi ai cũng đi ngủ sớm.**
In my family everyone goes to bed early.

1b. ______________________________

2a. **Cái gì trong nhà bếp cũng sạch sẽ và gọn gàng.**
Everything in the kitchen is clean and tidy.

2b. ______________________________

3a. **Ở đâu cũng có công viên để người dân đến chơi.**
There are parks everywhere for people to come and hang out.

3b. ______________________________

4a. **Thế nào tôi cũng ăn trái cây tráng miệng.**
I'll eat fruit for dessert anyway.

4b. ______________________________

5a. **Bao giờ em gái tôi cũng rửa chén sau bữa ăn.**
My younger sister always washes the dishes after meals.

5b. ______________________________

C. Adverbs of manner and degree

Rewrite each of the following sentences, (i) adding the phrase **một cách** before the underlined adverb, (ii) replacing the adverb with the *disyllabic form* given in parentheses and (iii) adding the *adverb of degree* (also given in parentheses) in its correct position.

Model

a. **Chị tôi quét nhà nhanh.** (*nhanh nhẹn - rất*)
My older sister is sweeping the floors very fast.

b. ☞ **Chị tôi quét nhà một cách rất nhanh nhẹn.**

1a. **Anh tôi giặt quần áo kỹ.** (*kỹ lưỡng - lắm*)
My older brother washes his clothes carefully.

1b. ☞ ____________________

2a. **Tôi thường phải nấu ăn vội.** (*vội vàng - hơi*)
I usually have to cook in a hurry.

2b. ☞ ____________________

3a. **Chị có tập thể dục đều không?** (*đều đặn - thật*)
Do you exercise regularly?

3b. ☞ ____________________

4a. **Các em của cô xếp quần áo gọn.** (*gọn gàng - quá*)
Your little siblings fold their clothes neatly.

4b. ☞ ____________________

5a. **Con chúng tôi luôn luôn học chăm.** (*chăm chỉ - khá*)
Our kids always study diligently.

5b. ☞ ____________________

D. Vocabulary

Choose the correct verb from the list below that's associated with each of the words in the Item column. Refer to the Functional Vocabulary section for the meanings of the verbs.

lau mặt đánh răng thức giấc đi ngủ tắm nấu ăn giặt đồ gội đầu cắt cỏ đổ rác gọi điện thoại nhắn tin đọc sách ủi đồ xem phim

Model

chổi "broom" ☞ **quét nhà**

	ITEM	ASSOCIATED VERB
1	**giường** "bed"	
2	**lời nhắn** "message"	
3	**điện thoại** "telephone"	
4	**khăn** "towel"	
5	**áo quần** "clothing"	
6	**đồng hồ báo thức** "alarm clock"	
7	**bãi cỏ** "lawn"	
8	**vòi hoa sen** "shower head"	
9	**thùng rác** "trash bin"	
10	**sách** "book"	
11	**bàn chải răng** "toothbrush"	
12	**nồi** "pot"	
13	**bàn ủi** "iron"	
14	**phim** "movie"	
15	**tóc** "hair"	

PROVERB

BÓI RA MA, QUÉT NHÀ RA RÁC.

bahy[2] ra[1] ma[1] kwet[2] nha[5] ra[1] rak[2]

"Fortune telling summons spirits, sweeping piles up rubbish."

By placing these two practices side by side—one spiritual and the other routine—the proverb points out the conspicuous results, with sarcasm implied toward the former.

Besides offering a humorous observation, the proverb, in its first part, also reveals that a considerable number of Vietnamese are fond of visiting fortune tellers to learn what the future holds for them—never mind the popular saying that goes, **Thầy bói nói láo ăn tiền** "Fortune tellers make their fortune by lying."

The second part depicts traditional Vietnam, in which most houses have concrete, brick or tiled floors that need to be swept every day with a broom. Brooms in Vietnam, especially in the countryside, are handmade with tiger grass, also known as Asian broom grass. The plant's round, solid stems are used to make the shaft of the broom while the narrow, leathery leaves serve as the brush.

FUNCTIONAL VOCABULARY

DANH TỪ

sinh hoạt	activity
người đi làm	working people
tiệm	store, shop
xe cộ	vehicles; traffic
đường	street
tin tức	news
thế giới	world
buổi sáng	morning
buổi trưa	early afternoon
buổi chiều	late afternoon
buổi tối	evening
ban đêm	night; nighttime
ban ngày	daytime
công viên	park
phòng ngủ	bedroom
phòng khách	living room
nhà bếp	kitchen
nhà xe	garage
buồng tắm	bathroom
điện thoại	telephone
lời nhắn	message

TÍNH TỪ

hằng ngày	daily
náo nhiệt	bustling
chậm rãi	slow-paced
thư thả	relaxed
vội vã	hurried

ĐỘNG TỪ

lau mặt	to wash one's face
đánh răng	to brush one's teeth
thức giấc	to wake up
đi ngủ	to go to bed
tắm	to wash oneself
nấu ăn	to cook
giặt đồ	to do laundry
gội đầu	to wash one's hair
cắt cỏ	to cut the grass
đổ rác	to take the trash out
gọi điện thoại	to make a phone call
nhắn tin	to send a message
đọc sách	to read
ủi đồ	to iron one's clothes
xem phim	to watch a movie

Đây là hãng Du Lịch An Nam.
This is An Nam Travel Agency.

Có chương trình du lịch giá đặc biệt nào đến Phú Quốc không ạ?
Are there any travel deals to Phu Quoc?

Chúng tôi đang có chương trình đặc biệt một tuần lễ ở Đông đảo.
We currently have a promotion for a one-week trip to Eastern Island.

Bãi biển nổi tiếng ở đó là bãi Dài, phải không cô?
Long Beach is a famous beach there, isn't it?

QUÁN CÀ PHÊ

Chúng tôi có thể chọn khách sạn chứ?
Can we choose our hotel?

CHAPTER 9

Travel and Vacations

Du Lịch - Nghỉ Mát

DIALOGUE 1

Hải is planning a trip to a beach resort with Hương, his girlfriend. He is talking on the phone with Xuân, a travel agent.

XUÂN **A-lô! Đây là hãng Du Lịch An Nam. Tôi là Xuân. Quý vị cần gì ạ?**
a[1] loh[1] day[1] la[5] hang[3] yoo[1] leech[5] an[1] nam[1] // tohy[1] la[5] swun[1] // kwee[1] vee[5] kun[5] yee[5] a[6]
Hello, this is An Nam Travel Agency. Xuân speaking. How may I help you?

HẢI **Chào cô Xuân. Tôi là Hải. Tháng tới có chương trình du lịch giá đặc biệt nào đến Phú Quốc không ạ?**
chahw[5] koh[1] swun[1] // tohy[1] la[5] hie[4] // thang[1] tuhy[2] kah[2] chŭuhng[1] treenh[5] dăk[6] byeht[6] nahw[5] dehn[2] foo[2] kwohk[2] khohngm[1] a[6]
Hello, Miss Xuân. I'm Hải. For next month, are there any travel deals to Phu Quoc?

XUÂN **Anh gọi thật đúng lúc! Chúng tôi đang có chương trình đặc biệt một tuần lễ ở Đông đảo, bao vé máy bay và khách sạn. Có bao nhiêu người đi, hở anh?**
ănh[1] gahy[6] thut[6] doongm[2] lookp[2] // choongm[2] tohy[1] dang[1] kah[2] chŭuhng[1] treenh[5] dăk[6] byeht[6] moht[6] twun[5] leh[3] uh[4] dohngm[1] dahw[4] // bahw[1] ve[2] măy[2] băy[1] va[5] khăch[2] shan[6] // kah[2] bahw[1] nhyehw[1] ngŭuhy[5] dee[1] huh[4] ănh[1]
You called at the right time! We currently have a special deal for a one-week trip to Eastern Island, airfare and hotel included. How many people are going?

HẢI **Hai người, cô ạ. Bạn gái tôi và tôi. Bãi biển nổi tiếng ở đó là bãi Dài, phải không cô?**
hie[1] ngŭuhy[5] koh[1] a[6] // ban[6] gie[2] tohy[1] va[5] tohy[1] // bie[3] byehn[4] nohy[4] tyehng[2] uh[4] dah[2] la[5] bie[3] yie[5] // fie[4] khohngm[1] koh[1]
Two of us, my girlfriend and me. Long Beach is a famous beach there, isn't it?

XUÂN **Dạ, đúng rồi. Anh chị muốn đi ngày nào?**
ya[6] doongm[2] rohy[5] // ănh[1] chee[6] mwohn[2] dee[1] ngăy[5] nahw[5]
That's correct. What day do you two want to leave?

HẢI **Thứ Bảy này, được không cô? Chúng tôi có thể chọn khách sạn chứ?**
thŭ^{2} băy^{4} năy^{5} dŭuhk^{6} khohngm^{1} koh^{1} // choongm^{2} tohy^{1} kah^{2} theh^{4} chahn^{6} khăch^{2} shan^{6} chŭ^{2}
This coming Saturday, is that okay? Can we choose our hotel?

XUÂN **Thứ Bảy được ạ, còn khách sạn thì chúng tôi đã có sẵn trong chương trình giảm giá này. Tổng cộng là 75 triệu đồng cho hai người, chỉ bằng 80% giá bình thường.**
thŭ^{2} băy^{4} dŭuhk^{6} a^{6}// kahn^{5} khăch^{2} shan^{6} thee^{5} choong^{2} tohy^{1} da^{3} kah^{2} shăn^{3} trahngm^{1} chŭuhng^{1} treenh^{5} yam^{4} ya^{2} năy^{5} // tohngm^{4} kohngm^{6} la^{5} băy^{4} mŭuhy^{1} tryehw^{6} dohngm^{5} chah^{1} hie^{1} ngŭuhy^{5} // chee^{4} băng^{5} tam^{2} mŭuhy^{1} fun^{5} tram^{811} ya^{2} beenh^{5} thŭuhng^{5}
Saturday is alright, but the hotel for this deal has already been selected. Your total is 75 million dong for two people, just 80% of the regular price.

KEY VOCABULARY 1

hãng *n*	agency	**đi** *v*	to go; to leave
du lịch *n*	traveling	**chọn** *v*	to choose
chương trình *n*	program	**có sẵn** *v*	to be included
nào *adj*	any	**còn** *conj*	as for
đến *prep*	to; until	**đã** *adv*	already
thật *adv*	really	**ạ** *part*	*polite word*
đúng lúc *adv*	well-timed	**giảm giá** *v*	to discount
giá đặc biệt *n*	special price	**tổng cộng** *n*	total
vé *n*	ticket	**cho** *prep*	for
máy bay *n*	airplane	**chỉ** *adv*	only
khách sạn *n*	hotel	**bằng** *adj*	equal
chứ *part*	*interrogative word*	**bình thường** *adj*	regular
bãi biển *n*	beach	**phần trăm** *adv*	percent
rồi *adv*	already	**tính** *v*	to calculate, to count
được *adj*	OK, acceptable	**thì** *part*	*emphatic word*
bạn gái *n*	girlfriend	**hở** *part*	*interrogative word*
bao *v*	to cover; to include	**chưa tính** *prep*	excluding

IDIOMATIC EXPRESSIONS 1

... thật đúng lúc! **Đúng** normally means "correct." The phrase **đúng lúc** refers to an opportune moment. **Các cô đến thật đúng lúc!** "You ladies have arrived exactly at the right time!"

Dạ, đúng rồi. "That's correct/right." (**Dạ** in this context is a respectful/polite particle.) **Rồi** "already" is an adverb used quite often at the end of phrases and sentences, almost as a filler (also seen in Chapter 6, **Mấy giờ rồi?** "What time is it?"). A few other examples are **Trời mưa rồi!** "It's raining!," **Hôm nay là thứ Sáu rồi** "Today is Friday (already)," **Anh nói sai rồi** "You said it wrong."

CULTURE NOTES 1

In Vietnamese, not only does a speaker have to speak correctly, they also need to sound either respectful or polite (except when interlocutors are on a first-name basis). In situations where respect or politeness is required, speakers use the particle **ạ** at the end of a phrase or a sentence in three cases: (i) when respectfully speaking to a superior (children to adults or adults to the elderly): **Cháu chào bác ạ** "Hello, Uncle!"(ii) when politely speaking to a peer or a stranger: **Không phải đâu ạ** "That's not right," and (iii) when speaking endearingly to a child: **Hôm nay mẹ sẽ về trễ, con ạ** "I'll be home late today" (a mother speaking to her child).

In a long conversation, however, speakers should not use **ạ** with every sentence. Instead, other polite/respectful terms can be chosen. The sentences above can be rephrased as **Kính chào bác** (**kính** means "respectfully"), **Không phải đâu, cô** (**cô** "miss"—or other terms of address—used at the end of a question or an answer can make a sentence sound polite, or at least less curt), and **Hôm nay mẹ sẽ về trễ đấy** (**đấy** means "there," used as a filler and to make a statement sound "fuller").

GRAMMAR NOTES 1

I. The verb "thì"

Thì is equivalent to the verb "to be," but is used only with adjectives, adverbs or prepositional phrases.

(1) a. **Mùa hè ở đây thì không nóng lắm.** [**nóng** is an adjective]
moouh^{5} he^{5} uh^{4} day^{1} thee^{5} khohngm^{1} nahngm^{2} lăm^{2}
The summer here is not very warm.

b. **Khu nghỉ mát đó thì khá xa.** [**xa** is an adverb]
khoo^{1} ngee^{4} mat^{2} dah^{2} thee^{5} kha^{2} sa^{1}
That resort is rather far away.

c. **Khách sạn Viettel thì ngay trước bãi biển** [**ngay trước bãi biển** is a prepositional phrase]
khăch^{2} shan^{6} viettel thee^{5} ngăy^{1} trŭuhk^{2} bie^{3} byehn^{4}
The Viettel Hotel is just in front of the beach.

When a sentence includes two contrasting clauses, **thì** is used only in the second one (just as "is" occurs only once in the English translation below):

(2) **Biển mùa này Ø lạnh vào buổi sáng nhưng buổi chiều thì ấm áp.**
byehn^{4} moouh^{5} năy^{5} lănh^{6} vahw^{5} bwohy^{4} shang^{2} nhŭng^{1} bwohy^{4} chyehw^{5} thee^{5} um^{2} ap^{2}
During this season, the sea is cold in the morning but lukewarm in the afternoon.

In general, speakers omit **thì** in most contexts:

(3) a. **Vịnh Hạ Long Ø rất nổi tiếng đối với du khách ngoại quốc.**
veenh^{6} ha^{6} lahngm^{1} rut^{2} nohy^{4} tyehng^{2} dohy^{2} vuhy^{2} yoo^{1} khăch^{2} ngwie^{6} kwohk^{2}
Ha Long Bay is very well known to foreign tourists.

b. **Khu thương xá Ø gần chỗ chúng tôi ở.**
khoo^{1} thŭuhng^{1} sa^{2} gun^{5} choh^{3} choong^{2} tohy^{1} uh
The shopping mall is close to where we are staying.

The verb **thì** is distinct from the particle **thì**, which appears in sentences for emphatic effect:

(4) a. **Hãng máy bay Air Vietnam thì tôi đi thường xuyên lắm.**
hang^{3} mǎy^{2} bǎy^{1} air vietnam thee^{5} tohy^{1} dee^{1} thŭuhng^{5} swyehn^{1} lăm^{2}
I fly Air Vietnam in particular very frequently.

b. **Nếu muốn ngắm cảnh đồng quê thì các bạn nên đi xe lửa.**
nehw^{2} mwohn^{2} ngăm^{2} kănh^{4} dohngm^{5} kweh^{1} thee^{5} kak^{2} ban^{6} nehn^{1} dee^{1} se^{1} lŭuh^{4}
If you guys want to enjoy the country scenery, then you should take the train.

Remember that the verb **là**, also equivalent to "to be" (Chapter 3), can be used either with nouns, **Nam là sinh viên** "Nam is a student," or adjectives **Vấn đề này là quan trọng** "This issue is important." By contrast, **thì** (only used with adjectives) gives more emphasis to the sentence: **Ba tôi thì khó tính lắm** "My dad is very difficult indeed." **Câu hỏi này thì khó là phải rồi** "It is true that this question is hard."

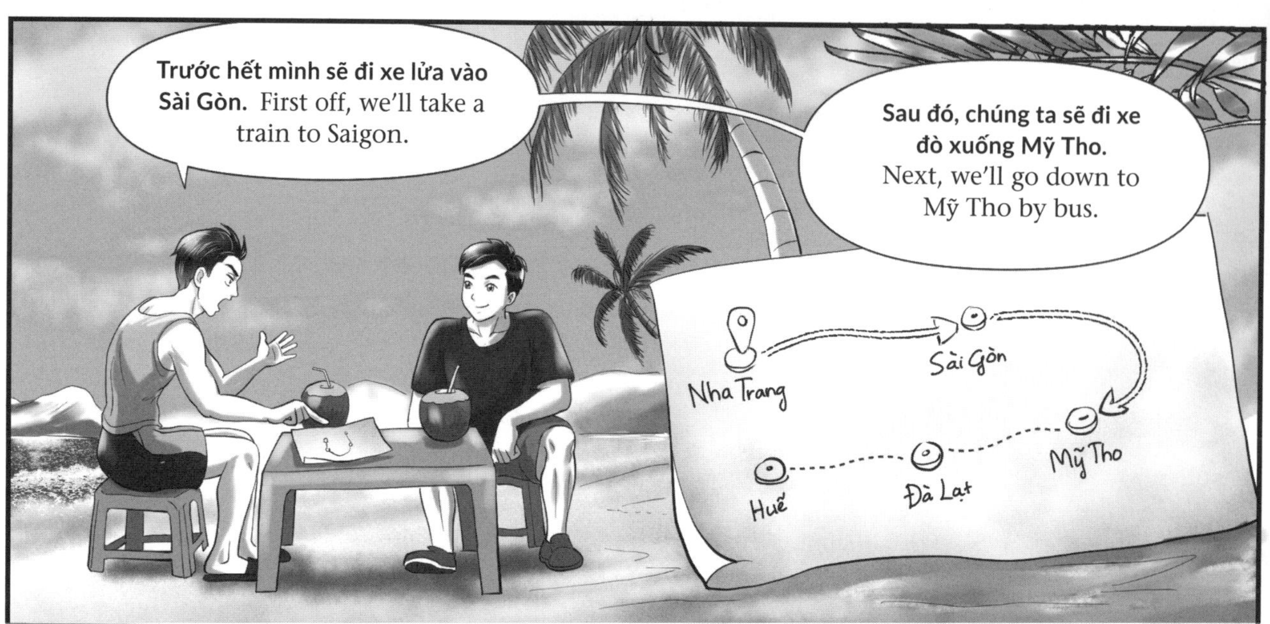
Trước hết mình sẽ đi xe lửa vào Sài Gòn. First off, we'll take a train to Saigon.
Sau đó, chúng ta sẽ đi xe đò xuống Mỹ Tho. Next, we'll go down to Mỹ Tho by bus.
Nha Trang
Sài Gòn
Mỹ Tho
Đà Lạt
Huế

Huế
Đà Lạt
Em thích rừng thông, hồ hay thác nước? Do you like pine forests, lakes or waterfalls?
Đà Lạt tràn ngập những loài hoa tuyệt đẹp. All of them! Dalat has tons ot beautiful flowers too.

Cuối cùng, mình sẽ bay ra Huế, cố đô của Việt Nam. Finally, we'll fly to Huế, Vietnam's former capital.
Anh đừng quên thưởng thức bún bò và cơm hến ở đó nhé! We can't forget to enjoy beef vermicelli and clam rice there!

DIALOGUE 2

Sơn and his brother Hà live in Nha Trang, a coastal city in Central Vietnam. As summer quickly approaches, they are excitedly discussing the itinerary of their trip and what they plan to do at each stop.

HÀ **Ở đây, chúng ta thấy biển quanh năm rồi. Mùa hè này anh em mình đi thăm thú những nơi khác bằng nhiều phương tiện khác nhau là có lý nhất.**
uh^{4} day^{1} choongm^{2} ta^{1} thay^{1} byehn^{4} kwănh^{1} năm^{1} rohy^{5} // moouh^{5} he^{5} năy^{5} ănh^{1} em^{1} meenh^{5} dee^{1} thăm^{1} thoo^{2} nhũng^{3} nuhy^{1} khak^{2} băng^{5} nhyehw^{5} fŭuhng^{1} tyehn^{6} khak^{2} nhăw^{1} la^{5} kah^{2} lee^{2} nhut^{2}
Here we see the sea all year round. This summer, it makes sense that we're going to visit other places using various means of transportation.

SƠN **Như đã quyết định, trước hết mình sẽ đi xe lửa vào Sài Gòn để viếng Nhà Thờ Đức Bà rồi ghé chợ Bến Thành. Sau đó, chúng ta sẽ đi xe đò xuống Mỹ Tho và thưởng thức trái cây tươi ở đó, phải không anh?**
nhŭ^{1} da^{3} kwyeht^{2} deenh^{6} // trŭuhl^{2} heht^{2} meenh^{5} she^{3} dee^{1} se^{1} lŭuh^{4} vahw^{5} shie^{5} gahn^{5} deh^{4} vyehng^{2} nha^{5} thuh^{5} dŭk^{2} ba^{5} rohy^{5} ge^{2} chuh^{5} behn^{2} thănh^{5} // shăw^{1} dah^{2} choongm^{2} ta^{1} she^{3} swohng^{2} mee^{3} thah^{1} va^{5} thŭuhng^{4} thŭk^{2} trie^{2} kay^{1} tŭuhy^{1} uh^{4} dah^{2} // fie^{4} khohngm^{1} ănh^{1}
Like we decided, first off, we'll take a train to Saigon to visit Notre Dame Cathedral, then stop by Bến Thành Market. Next, we'll go down to Mỹ Tho by bus, where we'll enjoy fresh fruits, right?

HÀ **Phải rồi. Chúng ta sẽ ở lại đó hai ngày rồi lên Đà Lạt. Thành phố cao nguyên này có nhiều cảnh đẹp lắm. Em thích rừng thông, hồ hay thác nước?**
fie^{4} rohy^{5} choongm^{2} ta^{1} she^{3} uh^{4} lie^{6} dah^{2} hie^{1} ngăy^{5} rohy^{5} lehn^{1} da^{5} lat^{6} // thănh^{5} foh^{2} kahw^{1} ngwyehn^{1} năy^{5} kah^{2} nhyehw^{5} kănh^{4} dep^{6} lăm^{2} // em^{1} theech^{2} rũng^{5} thohng^{1} hoh^{5} hăy^{1} thak^{2} nŭuhk^{2}
Right. We'll stay there for two days, then head up to Da Lat. The scenery is gorgeous in this highland city. Do you like pine forests, lakes or waterfalls?

SƠN **Cái gì em cũng thích! Đà Lạt không những có nhiều rau quả ngon mà còn tràn ngập những loài hoa tuyệt đẹp nữa.**
kie^{2} yee^{5} em^{1} koongm^{3} theech^{2} // da^{5} lat^{6} khohngm^{1} nhũng^{3} kah^{2} nhyehw^{5} răw^{1} kwa^{4} ngahn^{1} ma^{5} kahn^{5} tran^{5} ngup^{6} nhũng^{3} lwie^{5} hwa^{1} twyeht^{6} dep^{6} nũuh^{3}
I like everything! Da Lat doesn't just have delicious vegetables, it has tons of beautiful flowers, too.

HÀ **Cuối cùng, mình sẽ bay ra Huế, cố đô của Việt Nam. Nơi đó, chúng ta sẽ đi thăm cung điện và lăng tẩm của các vị vua chúa nổi tiếng trong lịch sử.**
kwohy^{2} koongm^{5} meenh^{5} she^{3} băy^{1} ra^{1} hweh^{2} koh^{2} doh^{1} koouh^{4} vyeht^{6} nam^{1} // nuhy^{1} dah^{2} choongm^{2} ta^{1} she^{3} dee^{1} thăm^{1} koongm^{1} dyehn^{6} va^{5} lăng^{1} tum^{4} koouh^{4} kak^{2} vee^{6} voouh^{1} choouh^{2} nohy^{4} tyehng^{2} trahngm^{1} leech^{6} shŭ^{4}
Finally, we'll fly to Huế, Vietnam's former capital. There, we'll pay a visit to the palaces and tombs of the famous kings of our history.

SƠN **Anh đừng quên hai món bún bò và cơm hến của xứ Huế nhé!**
ănh^{1} dũng^{5} kwehn^{1} hie^{1} mahn^{2} boon^{2} bah^{5} va^{5} kuhm^{1} hehn^{2} koouh^{4} sŭ^{2} hweh^{2} nhe^{2}
We can't forget the two famous dishes of Huế: beef vermicelli and clam rice!

 KEY VOCABULARY 2

quanh năm *adv*	all year round	**cảnh** *n*	scenery
thăm thú *v*	to visit	**rừng** *n*	forest
phương tiện *n*	means	**thông** *n*	pine
có lý *v*	to make sense	**hồ** *n*	lake
quyết định *v*	to decide	**thác nước** *n*	waterfall
trước hết *adv*	first of all	**rau quả** *n*	vegetables
xe lửa *n*	train	**ngon** *adj*	delicious
viếng *v*	to pay a visit	**tràn ngập** *v*	to be filled
nhà thờ *n*	church	**loài** *n*	species
Đức Bà *n*	Our Lady	**bay** *v*	to fly
ghé *v*	to stop by	**cung điện** *n*	palace
chợ *n*	market	**lăng tẩm** *n*	mausoleum
sau đó *adv*	afterwards	**vua chúa** *n*	kings and lords
xe đò *n*	charter bus	**nổi tiếng** *adj*	famous
trái cây *n*	fruit	**lịch sử** *n*	history
tươi *adj*	fresh	**bún bò** *n*	beef vermicelli
ở lại *v*	to stay	**cơm hến** *n*	clam rice

IDIOMATIC EXPRESSIONS 2

Cái gì tôi cũng thích! By using an indefinite word (**cái gì**) at the beginning of a sentence and the particle **cũng**, the speaker strongly emphasizes the idea expressed by that indefinite word. The normal, unemphatic way to express the same idea would be **Tôi thích mọi thứ** "I like everything." Another example with this emphatic construction is **Ai cũng muốn đến thăm ngôi đền này** "Everyone wants to visit this temple," as opposed to its unemphatic counterpart **Mọi người đều muốn đến thăm ngôi đền này**. (The adverb **đều** "equally" is habitually used after indefinite pronouns with **mọi** "every-" besides **mọi người: mọi nơi** "everywhere," **mọi thứ** "everything," **mọi lần** "every time": **Mọi nơi đều có hướng dẫn viên du lịch nói nhiều thứ tiếng** "Everywhere there are multilingual tour guides.")

không những... mà... Equivalent to the English "not only... but also...," this construction is used quite commonly. The positions of the words depend on the structure of the sentences they appear in. **Huế không những nổi tiếng về sông Hương mà còn về núi Ngự nữa** "Huế is famous not only for the Perfume River but also for Ngự Mountain." **Không những tôi thích biển Nha Trang mà các bạn tôi cũng vậy** "Not only do I like Nha Trang but so do my friends."

CULTURE NOTES 2

In informal or intimate conversations, speakers tend to collectively refer to themselves and their interlocutors using the common pronoun **mình** (Chapter 7). Two sisters, for example, will say **hai chị em mình** "we/us sisters." Note that it is customary for a number to be used with this kind of expression. A few other examples: **(hai) vợ chồng mình** "we/us husband and wife," **(hai) mẹ con mình** "we/us mother and daughter," **hai đứa mình** "we/us couple of friends," **ba tụi mình** "the three of us."

GRAMMAR NOTES 2

II. Verbs of movement

The most common verb of movement is **đi**, which means "to go" or "to leave." The general question for this verb is **Anh đi đâu vậy?** "Where are you going?" A preposition that goes with this verb is **đến** "to, toward" (or **tới**, in the central and southern dialects):

(5) a. **Đi từ nhà ga xe lửa đến chợ Bến Thành là bao xa?**
dee^1 tŭ^5 nha^5 ga^1 se^1 lŭuh^4 dehn^2 chuh^6 behn^2 thănh^5 la^5 bahw^1 sa^1
How far is it [to go] from the train station to Bến Thành Market?

b. **Xe đò này có đi tới Vĩnh Long không, anh?**
se^1 dah^5 năy^5 kah^2 dee^1 tuhy^2 veenh^3 lahngm^1 khohngm^1 ănh^1
Does this coach bus go all the way to Vĩnh Long?

More often than not, however, the preposition is omitted:

(6) a. **Khi nào chị đi Ø Đà Nẵng?**
khee^1 nahw^5 chee^6 dee^1 da^5 năng^3
When are you leaving for Da Nang?

b. **Chiều nay chúng ta có đi Ø biển không?**
chyehw^5 nay^1 choongm^2 ta^1 kah^2 dee^1 byehn^4 khongm^1
Are we going to the beach this afternoon?

Đến also functions as a verb meaning "to come, to arrive." Since this verb is a homonym of the preposition **đến**, they are never used together.

(7) a. **Mấy giờ máy bay đến vậy?**
may^2 yuh^5 măy^2 băy^1 dehn^2 vay^6
What time will the plane arrive?

b. **Tối nay anh đến nhà tôi chơi nhé.**
tohy^2 năy^1 ănh^1 dehn^2 nha^5 tohy^1 chuhy^1 nhe^2
Come hang out at my house tonight, OK?

When speakers want to indicate the direction of movement more specifically, they add a *particle of direction* to the verb **đi**: **đi ra** "to go out," **đi vào** "to go in," **đi lên** "to go up," **đi xuống** "to go down," **đi qua** "to go across," and **đi về** "to go back."

(8) a. **Hành khách lần lượt đi ra khỏi phi trường.**
hănh^{5} *khăch*^{2} *lun*^{5} *lŭuht*^{6} *dee*^{1} *ra*^{1} *khahy*^{4} *fee*^{1} *trŭuhng*^{5}
The passengers left [went out of] the airport one by one.

b. **Cô phải đi lên ba tầng lầu mới đến văn phòng du lịch.**
koh^{1} *fie*^{4} *dee*^{1} *lehn*^{1} *ba*^{1} *tung*^{5} *lohw*^{5} *muhy*^{2} *dehn*^{2} *văn*^{1} *fahngm*^{5} *yoo*^{1} *leech*^{6}
You have to go up three floors to get to the travel office.

c. **Nhiều người rất sợ đi qua cây cầu này.**
nhyehw^{5} *ngŭuhy*^{5} *rut*^{2} *shuh*^{6} *dee*^{1} *kwa*^{1} *kay*^{1} *kohw*^{5} *năy*^{5}
Many people are very scared of crossing this bridge.

In many instances, the particles of direction accompanying the verb of movement **đi** are conveniently converted to verbs and used independently: **Mấy giờ anh ra phi trường?** "What time are you going to the airport?," **Mời cô vào** "Please come inside."

When talking about movement from one city or country to another, speakers usually use these particles-turned-verbs to specify the direction of their movement:

(9) a. **Khi nào anh ra Hà Nội?** [**ra** is used for going northwards within Vietnam, lit. "to go out"]
khee^{1} *nahw*^{5} *ănh*^{1} *ra*^{1} *ha*^{5} *nohy*^{6}
When are you leaving for Hanoi?

b. **Tuần tới anh ấy sẽ vào Sài Gòn.** [**vào** is used for going southward within the country, lit. "to go in"]
twun^{5} *tuhy*^{2} *ănh*^{1} *ay*^{2} *she*^{3} *vahw*^{5} *shie*^{5} *gahn*^{5}
He will go to Saigon next week.

c. **Ai cũng thích lên Đà Lạt vào mùa xuân.** [**lên** is used for going from the lowlands to the highlands, lit. "to go up"]
ie^{1} *koongm*^{3} *theech*^{2} *lehn*^{1} *da*^{5} *lat*^{6} *vahw*^{5} *moouh*^{5} *swun*^{1}
Everyone likes to go up to Đà Lạt in the spring.

d. **Cô có định xuống Nha Trang với họ không?** [**xuống** is used for going from the highlands to the lowlands, lit. "to go down"]
koh^{1} *kah*^{2} *deenh*^{6} *swohng*^{2} *nha*^{1} *trang*^{1} *vuhy*^{2} *hah*^{6} *khohngm*^{1}
Are you planning to go down to Nha Trang with them?

e. **Việt đang ở Cần Thơ. Tối nay anh ấy sẽ lên Sài Gòn.** [**lên** is used for going northwards within southern Vietnam; **xuống** is used for the reverse]
vyeht^{6} *dang*^{1} *uh*^{4} *kun*^{5} *thuh*^{1} // *tohy*^{2} *năy*^{1} *ănh*^{1} *ay*^{2} *she*^{3} *lehn*^{1} *shie*^{5} *gahn*^{5}
Việt is in Cần Thơ now. He's going up to Saigon this evening.

f. **Tháng sau chúng tôi sẽ qua Mỹ thăm bạn bè.** [**qua** is used for going from one country to another, lit. "to go across"]
thang^{2} *shăw*^{1} *choongm*^{2} *tohy*^{1} *she*^{3} *kwa*^{1} *mee*^{3} *thăm*^{1} *ban*^{6} *be*^{5}
We will go to America to visit friends next month.

READING

VỊNH HẠ LONG

Vịnh Hạ Long là một thắng cảnh nổi tiếng ở Việt Nam, được tổ chức UNESCO công nhận là Di Sản Thiên Nhiên Thế Giới. Là một trong những địa điểm du lịch thu hút nhiều du khách trong cũng như ngoài nước, vịnh Hạ Long bao gồm gần 2.000 đảo lớn nhỏ, nằm ở phía tây của vịnh Bắc Phần, thuộc tỉnh Quảng Ninh.

Tên "Hạ Long" có nghĩa là "những con rồng đáp xuống", gợi lên vẻ đẹp uy nghi và tráng lệ của vùng vịnh này. Nước xanh biếc bao quanh các hòn đảo, bên cạnh những ngọn núi, hang động và bãi tắm. Tô điểm thêm cho vẻ đẹp tuyệt diệu ở đây là những chiếc thuyền buồm trôi lững lờ trên mặt biển bao la.

Ngoài sinh hoạt du lịch, vịnh Hạ Long còn là nơi cho các nhà nghiên cứu về thực vật và động vật khám phá và tìm hiểu thế giới thiên nhiên phong phú này. Vùng vịnh cũng mang lại một nguồn hải sản gần như bất tận cho người dân địa phương.

veenh^{5} ha^{6} lahngm^{1}

veenh^{6} ha^{6} lahnmg^{1} la^{5} moht^{6} thăng^{2} kănh^{4} nohy^{4} tyehng^{2} uh^{4} vyeht^{6} nam^{1} dŭuhk^{6} toh^{4} chŭk^{2} unesco kohngm^{1} nhun^{6} la^{5} yee^{1} shan^{4} thyehn^{1} nhyehn^{1} theh^{2} yuhy^{2} // la^{5} moht^{6} trahnm^{1} nhŭnh^{3} deeuh^{6} dyehm^{4} yoo^{1} leech^{6} thoo^{1} hoot^{2} nhyehw^{5} yoo^{1} khăch^{2} trahngm^{1} koongm^{3} nhŭ^{1} ngwie^{5} nŭuhk^{2} // veenh^{6} ha^{6} lahngm^{1} bahw^{1} gohm^{5} gun^{5} hie^{1} ngan^{5} dahw^{4} luhn^{2} nhah^{4} // năm^{5} uh^{4} feeuh^{2} tay^{1} koouh^{4} veenh^{5} băk^{2} fun^{5} thwohk^{4} teenh^{4} kwang^{4} neenh^{1}

tehn^{1} ha^{6} lahngm^{1} kah^{2} ngeeuh^{3} la^{5} nhŭng^{3} kahn^{1} rohngm^{5} dap^{2} swohng^{2} // guhy^{6} lehn^{1} ve^{4} dep^{6} wee^{1} ngee^{1} va^{5} trang^{2} leh^{6} koouh^{4} voongm^{5} veenh^{5} năy^{5} // nŭuhk^{2} săh^{1} byehk^{2} bahw^{1} kwănh^{1} kak^{2} hahn^{5} dahw^{4} // behn^{1} kănh^{6} nhŭng^{3} ngahn^{6} nooy^{2} hang^{1} dohngm^{5} va^{5} bie^{3} tăm^{2} // toh^{1} dyehm^{4} thehm^{1} chah^{1} ve^{4} dep^{6} twyeht^{6} yehw^{6} uh^{4} day^{1} la^{5} nhŭng^{3} chyehk^{2} thwyehn^{5} bwohm^{5} trohy^{1} lŭng^{3} luh^{5} trehn^{1} măt^{6} byehn^{4} bahw^{1} la^{1}

ngwie^5 sheenh^1 hwat^6 yoo^1 leech^6 // veenh^6 ha^6 lahngm^1 kahn^5 la^5 nuhy^1 chah^1 kak^2 nha^5 ngyehn^1 kŭw^2 thŭk^6 vut^6 va^5 dohngm^6 vut^6 kham^2 fa^2 va^5 teem^5 hyehw^4 theh^2 yuhy^2 thyehn^1 nhyehn^1 fahngm^1 foo^2 năy^5 // voongm^5 veenh^6 koongm^3 mang^1 lie^6 moht^6 ngwohn^5 hie^4 shan^4 gun^5 nhŭ^1 but^1 tun^6 chah^1 ngŭuhy^5 yun^1 deeuh^6 fŭuhng^1

HA LONG BAY

Ha Long Bay is a well-known destination in Vietnam, recognized by UNESCO as a World Heritage Site. A tourist site attracting many visitors, domestic and foreign alike, Ha Long Bay consists of nearly 2,000 islands, big and small, located west of the Gulf of Tonkin in Quảng Ninh province.

The name "Hạ Long" means "descending dragons," suggesting the majestic beauty of the bay area. Emerald waters surround the islands, next to mountains, caves and beaches. Enhancing the area's sublime splendor are sailboats slowly floating on the immense sea.

In addition to tourism, Ha Long Bay is a site for researching animals and plants to discover and study our rich natural world. The bay area also provides local residents with a near-endless sources of sea products.

COMPREHENSION QUESTIONS

Answer the following questions in complete sentences, first orally, then in writing.

1. **Vịnh Hạ Long được tổ chức nào công nhận là Di Sản Thiên Nhiên Thế Giới?** *Which organization recognizes Ha Long Bay as a World Heritage Site?*

   ____

2. **Vịnh Hạ Long nằm ở đâu?** *Where is Ha Long Bay located?*

   ____

3. **Tên "Hạ Long" có nghĩa là gì?** *What does the name "Hạ Long" mean?*

   ____

4. **Ngoài đảo và núi ra, vịnh Hạ Long còn có những gì khác?** *Besides islands and mountains, what else does Ha Long Bay have?*

   ____

5. **Vịnh Hạ Long mang lại tài nguyên thiên nhiên gì cho dân địa phương?** *What natural resources does Ha Long Bay provide local residents with?*

   ____

PRACTICE

A. Listening comprehension 

Listen to the recording about a tour to one of the best island cities in Vietnam and put a check mark above each correct answer in the following chart:

Tên công ty *Company's name*	**Việt Á** *Viet-Asia*	**Á Châu** *Asia*	**Á Việt** *Asia-Viet*
Thời gian du lịch *Tour length*	**2 ngày 3 đêm** *2 days & 3 nights*	**3 ngày 3 đêm** *3 days & 3 nights*	**3 ngày 2 đêm** *3 days & 2 nights*
Địa điểm du lịch *Travel destination*	**Phú Yên**	**Phú Quốc**	**Phú Nhơn**
Chuyến bay *Flight*	**khứ hồi** *round trip*	**một chiều** *one-way*	**quá cảnh** *layover*
Hãng hàng không *Airline*	**Nam Á** *Southeast*	**Nam Việt** *South Vietnam*	**Việt Nam** *Vietnam*
Khu nghỉ mát *Resort*	**5 sao** *five-star*	**4 sao** *four-star*	**3 sao** *three-star*
Phòng *Room*	**giường đôi** *double bed*	**giường chiếc** *single bed*	**hai giường** *two beds*
Bữa ăn bao *Meal included*	**bữa sáng** *breakfast*	**bữa trưa** *lunch*	**bữa tối** *dinner*
Nơi KHÔNG thăm viếng *Place NOT visited*	**đảo** *islands*	**chùa** *temples*	**sòng bài** *casinos*
Giá tổng cộng *Total price*	**3.353.000đ**	**3.535.000đ**	**3.335.000đ**

B. The verb "thì"

Translate the following sentences into Vietnamese using the verb **thì**. Use the Functional Vocabulary section and/or a dictionary if necessary.

1. The town of Sapa is famous for its rice terraces.

   ____

2. The climate in this area is ideal for tourism.

   ____

3. The local people are always friendly to foreign tourists.

   ____

4. Trans-Vietnam trains nowadays are very modern.

   ____

5. The weather in this coastal city is usually unpredictable, isn't it?

   ____

C. Verbs of movement

Instead of using the common verb **đi**, fill in the blanks with the correct verbs of movement **ra, vào, lên, xuống, qua** and **về**, based on the map. The names of highland locations are italicized.

1. **Ngày mai đoàn du khách ở Sapa sẽ __________ Hà Nội.**
   The tourist group in Sapa will go to Hanoi tomorrow.

2. **Từ Hà Nội __________ Huế bằng xe lửa mất bao nhiêu tiếng đồng hồ?**
   How many hours does it take to go by train from Hanoi to Huế?

3. **Giá vé máy bay từ Nha Trang __________ Pleiku thì không mắc lắm.**
   Air tickets from Nha Trang to Pleiku are not very expensive.

4. **Cuối tuần này chúng tôi sẽ __________ Cam Bốt và __________ lại Sài Gòn vào thứ Tư.**
   We will go to Cambodia this weekend and return to Saigon on Wednesday.

5. **Họ sẽ từ Cà Mau __________ Sài Gòn, rồi sau đó __________ Nha Trang bằng xe đò.**
   They will go by bus from Cà Mau to Saigon, then to Nha Trang afterwards.

D. Vocabulary

Choose the word best associated with each of the following sentences. Use the Functional Vocabulary section and/or a dictionary if necessary.

1. **Chúng tôi sẽ bay lên Kontum để xem Lễ Hội Đua Voi.**
   We will fly to Kontum to watch the Elephant Race Festival.
   a. **xe đò**
   b. **phi trường**
   c. **bãi biển**
   d. **sông**

2. **Tháng tới các bạn định du lịch ở đâu?**
   Where do you guys plan to travel next month?
   a. **ở nhà**
   b. **đi làm**
   c. **nghỉ hè**
   d. **đi học**

3. **Nhà tôi chỉ cách công viên Tự Do ba phút.**
   My house is only three minutes away from Freedom Park.
   a. **đi xe lửa**
   b. **đi xe đò**
   c. **đi tàu thuỷ**
   d. **đi bộ**

4. **Các anh chị sẽ ở lại đó trong bao nhiêu ngày?**
   How many days will you guys stay there for?
   a. **khu nghỉ mát**
   b. **công ty du lịch**
   c. **trạm xe buýt**
   d. **nhà ga xe lửa**

5. **Cả nhà tôi sẽ qua Pháp thăm bạn bè và mua sắm.**
   Our family will go to France to visit friends and do some shopping.
   a. **bằng lái xe**
   b. **thẻ căn cước**
   c. **giấy thông hành**
   d. **thẻ tín dụng**

6. **Du thuyền của chúng tôi sẽ ghé tổng cộng là 7 quốc gia.**
   Our cruise ship will stop in a total of seven countries.
   a. **chuyến bay**
   b. **chuyến xe**
   c. **chuyến xe lửa**
   d. **chuyến đi**

7. **Đoàn du khách đang thăm viếng nhiều cảnh đẹp trong vùng.**
   The tourist group is visiting several scenic spots in the area.
   a. **hướng dẫn viên**
   b. **nhân viên**
   c. **giám thị**
   d. **giám đốc**

8. Hành khách xếp hàng để lên chuyến bay đi Đà Nẵng.
The passengers were lining up to board the flight to Danang.

a. **vé máy bay**
b. **thẻ ngân hàng**
c. **thẻ lên máy bay**
d. **vé vào cửa**

 **PROVERB**

ĐI CHO BIẾT ĐÓ BIẾT ĐÂY, Ở NHÀ VỚI MẸ BIẾT NGÀY NÀO KHÔN.

dee[1] chah[1] byeht[2] dah[2] byeht[2] day[1]
uh[4] nha[5] vuhy[2] me[6] byeht[2] ngăy[5] nahw[5] khohn[1]

"Travel so you'll get to know different places—
when will you ever wise up if you always stay home with your mother?"

This proverb is actually a **ca dao**, or "short folk song." In fact, these "songs," which of course can be sung, are verses passed down orally from generation to generation. They most commonly take the form shown here, with six feet in the first verse and eight in the second. They can also take different poetic forms, but the six-eight form is the most popular. Each form involves rules related to tones, rhyming, and line length. **Truyện Kiều** "The Tale of Kieu" by **Nguyễn Du** (1766–1820)—often called Vietnam's Shakespeare—is a famous epic poem using the six-eight form and consisting of 3,254 verses.

FUNCTIONAL VOCABULARY

DANH TỪ

hãng	agency; factory
du lịch	travel, tourism
chương trình	program
máy bay	airplane
xe lửa	train
xe đò	coach bus
tàu thuỷ	ship
du thuyền	cruise ship
xe đạp	bicycle
xe gắn máy	motorcycle
xe hơi	car
khách sạn	hotel
khu nghỉ mát	resort
bãi biển	beach
phương tiện	means
rừng	forest
hồ	lake
thác nước	waterfall
cung điện	royal palace
lăng tẩm	mausoleums
lịch sử	history
du khách	tourist
hướng dẫn viên	guide
nhà thờ	church
chùa	Buddhist temple
đền	temple

ĐỘNG TỪ

đi	to go; to leave
đi bộ	to walk
đến	to come; to arrive
về	to return
lên	to go up
xuống	to go down
ra	to go out
vào	to go in
qua	to go across
thăm	to visit
ghé	to stop by
bay	to fly
ở lại	to stay
chọn	to choose
du ngoạn	to go sightseeing
quyết định	to decide

Em thấy trong người ra sao?
How are you feeling?
Cổ họng em đau lắm.
I have a bad sore throat.

Chà, em sốt khá cao đấy!
Oh, you have a rather high fever.
Lúc nào em cũng thấy buồn nôn. I feel queasy all the time.

Em nên uống nhiều nước và uống thuốc này cho hạ sốt.
Drink a lot of water and take this medicine to reduce the fever.
!

Em có thể ăn những thức ăn nào hở, bác sĩ?
What kind of food can I eat?
Thức ăn lỏng như xúp hay cháo và tráng miệng với trái cây.
Liquid food like soup or porridge and fruit for dessert.

CHAPTER 10

Health and Well-being

Sức Khoẻ Và An Khang

DIALOGUE 1

Vinh hasn't been feeling well for the past few days, so he decided to go to the doctor. He is being examined by Dr. Trâm, who's asking him several questions.

BÁC SĨ TRÂM **Em là Vinh, phải không? Em thấy trong người ra sao?**
em^1 la^5 veenh^1 fie^4 khohngm^1 // em^1 thay^2 trahngm^1 ngŭuhy^5 ra^1 shahw^1
You're Vinh, right? How are you feeling?

VINH **Dạ, em thấy mệt và choáng váng lắm, bác sĩ ạ. Cổ họng em cũng đau nữa.**
ya^6 em^1 thay^2 meht^6 va^5 chwang^2 vang^2 lăm^2 bak^2 shee^3 a^6 // koh^4 hahngm^6 em^1 koongm^3 dăw^1 nŭuh^3
Doctor, I feel very tired and lightheaded. My throat is sore, too.

BÁC SĨ TRÂM **Để tôi đo nhiệt độ cho em. Chà, em sốt khá cao đấy! Em có cảm giác gì khác nữa không?**
deh^4 tohy^1 dah^1 nhyeht^6 doh^6 chah^1 em^1 // cha^5 em^1 shoht^2 kha^2 kahw^1 day^2 // em^1 kah^2 kam^4 yak^2 yee^5 khak^2 nŭuh^3 khohngm^1
Let me take your temperature. Oh, you have a rather high fever. Any other symptoms?

VINH **Dạ, toàn thân em mỏi nhừ và em không muốn ăn uống gì cả. Lúc nào em cũng thấy buồn nôn.**
ya^6 twan^5 thun^1 em^1 mahy^4 nhŭ^5 va^5 em^1 khohngm^1 mwohn^2 ăn^1 wohng^2 yee^5 ka^4 // lookp^2 nahw^5 em^1 koongm^3 thay^2 bwohn^5 nohn^1
My whole body is fatigued, and I don't have any appetite. I feel queasy all the time.

BÁC SĨ TRÂM **Nãy giờ em ho cũng nhiều đấy. Tôi nghĩ là em bị cúm rồi. Em về nhà nghỉ ngơi, uống nhiều nước và uống thuốc này cho hạ sốt, một lần hai viên và cách nhau 6 tiếng đồng hồ nhé.**
năy^{3} yuh^{5} em^{1} hah^{1} nhyehw^{5} day^{2} // tohy^{1} ngee^{3} la^{5} em^{1} bee^{5} koom^{2} rohy^{5} // em^{1} veh^{5} nha^{5} ngee^{4} nguhy^{1} wohng^{2} nhyehw^{5} nŭuhk^{2} va^{5} wohng^{2} thwohk^{2} năy^{5} chah^{1} ha^{6} shoht^{2} // moht^{6} lun^{5} hie^{1} vyehn^{1} va^{5} kăch^{2} nhăw^{1} shăw^{2} tyehng^{2} dohngm^{5} hoh^{5} nhe^{2}
You've also been coughing a lot. I think you have the flu. Go home to rest, drink a lot of water and take this medicine to reduce the fever, two pills every six hours.

VINH **Em có thể ăn những thức ăn nào hở, bác sĩ?**
em^{1} kah^{2} theh^{4} ăn^{1} nhŭng^{3} thŭk^{2} ăn^{1} nahw^{2} huh^{4} bak^{2} shee^{3}
What kind of food can I eat?

BÁC SĨ **Em nên ăn những thức ăn lỏng như xúp hay cháo và tráng miệng với trái cây.**
em^{1} nehn^{1} ăn^{1} nhŭng^{3} thŭk^{2} ăn^{1} lahngm^{4} nhŭ^{1} soop^{2} hăy^{1} chahw^{2} va^{5} trang^{2} myehng^{6} vuhy^{2} trie^{2} kay^{1}
You should eat liquid food like soup or porridge and have fruit for dessert.

KEY VOCABULARY 1

bác sĩ *n*	doctor	**buồn nôn** *adj*	nauseated
mệt *adj*	tired	**nãy giờ** *adv*	so far
choáng váng *adj*	lightheaded, dizzy	**ho** *v*	to cough
cổ họng *n*	throat	**cúm** *n*	flu
đau *v*	to hurt	**về nhà** *v*	to go home
đo *v*	to measure	**nghỉ ngơi** *v*	to rest
chà *interj*	ah	**uống** *v*	to drink
sốt *n*	fever	**nước** *n*	water
cảm giác *n*	sensation	**thuốc** *n*	medication
toàn *adj*	entire	**viên thuốc** *n*	pill
thân *n*	body	**cho** *conj*	in order to
mỏi nhừ *adj*	fatigued	**hạ** *v*	to lower
lúc nào *adv*	anytime, all the time	**cách nhau** *adv*	apart

IDIOMATIC EXPRESSIONS 1

Em thấy trong người ra sao? "How do you feel [physically]?" **Người** means "person" in general and "body" in this context. **Tôi thấy lạnh cả người** "I feel chills through my body" refers to a physical reaction to something bizarre or scary.

The interrogative phrase **ra sao** asks for something to be described or recounted: **Bạn trai của chị ra sao?** "What's your boyfriend like?," **Đầu đuôi câu chuyện ra sao?** "What's the long and the short of it?"

CULTURE NOTES 1

Vinh refers to himself as **em** "younger brother," based on his estimate that the doctor is old enough to be his older sister. However, he doesn't call her **chị**, but instead **bác sĩ**. This professional title is also used to mean "you" by speakers (patients or otherwise) when addressing a physician: **Dạo này bác sĩ thế nào?** "How have you been, (doctor)?"

GRAMMAR NOTES 1

I. Health-related expressions

Several constructions are used to express health conditions, one of which is the verb **bị** "to be" followed by an adjective (which can be modified by a noun and become a compound adjective).

(1) a. **Tôi bị <u>bệnh</u> đã ba ngày nay.**
tohy¹ bee⁶ behnh⁶ da³ ba¹ ngăy⁵ năy¹
I've been sick for three days.

b. **Em gái tôi bị <u>đau bụng</u> vì ăn nhiều kẹo.**
em¹ gie² tohy¹ bee⁶ dăw¹ boongm⁶ vee⁵ ăn¹ nhyehw⁵ kew⁶
My little sister had a bellyache because she ate too much candy.

Compound adjectives such as **đau bụng,** lit. "painful in the abdomen" or **nhức đầu,** lit. "painful in the head" can be used without **bị**, when they grammatically become verbal phrases "(one's) belly aches," "(one's) head hurts," respectively:

(2) a. **Tôi nhức đầu quá!**
tohy¹ nhŭk² dohw⁵ kwa²
My head hurts so much!

b. **Hùng đang đau bụng nên không muốn ăn gì cả.**
hoongm⁵ dang¹ dăw¹ boongm⁶ nehn¹ khohngm¹ mwohn² ăn¹ yee⁵ ka⁴
Hung has a stomachache, so he doesn't want to eat anything.

When **bị** is followed by a noun referring to an illness, it functions as a verb meaning "to have" or "to suffer from":

(3) a. **Cô bị chứng trầm cảm từ bao lâu rồi?**
koh¹ bee⁶ chŭng² trum⁵ kam⁴ tŭ⁵ bahw¹ lohw¹ royh⁵
How long have you been suffering from depression?

b. **Anh ấy bị bệnh mất ngủ kinh niên.**
ănh¹ ay² bee⁶ behnh⁶ mut² ngoo⁴ keenh¹ nyehn¹
He has chronic insomnia.

Verbs expressing various types of pain such as **đau** "to feel pain, to hurt," **nhức** "to have a sharp pain," **mỏi** "to tire," **ê ẩm** "to ache," etc. are used as follows:

(4) a. **Em đau ở đâu?**
em[1] dăw[1] uh[4] dohw[1]
Where do you hurt?

b. **Bắp thịt chỗ này của tôi nhức lắm.**
băp[2] theet[6] choh[3] năy[5] koouh[4] tohy[1] nhŭk[2] lăm[2]
I feel a very sharp pain in my muscles here.

c. **Tay chân tôi đều mỏi.**
tăy[1] chun[1] tohy[1] dehw[5] mahy[4]
My arms and legs are getting tired.

d. **Toàn thân tôi ê ẩm.**
twan[5] thun[1] tohy[1] eh[1] um[4]
My whole body is aching.

These verbs, however, function as adjectives when they follow the verb **cảm thấy** (usually reduced to **thấy**) "to feel":

(5) a. **Em thấy đau ở đâu?**
em[1] thay[2] dahw[1] uh[4] dohw[1]
Where do you feel pain?

b. **Tôi thấy nhức ngay chỗ này.**
tohy[1] thay[2] nhŭk[2] ngăy[1] choh[3] năy[5]
I feel sharp pain right here.

c. **Tôi không thấy mỏi gì cả.**
tohy[1] khohngm[1] thay[2] mahy[4] yee[5] kah[4]
I don't feel tired at all.

d. **Em có thấy ê ẩm ở lưng không?**
em[1] kah[2] thay[2] eh[1] um[4] uh[4] lŭng[1] khohngm[1]
Does your back ache? (Lit. "Do you feel an ache in your back?")

Dạo này lúc nào em cũng thấy uể oải. Lately, I always feel sluggish.
Thói quen ăn uống của em ra sao? What are your eating habits like?

Em thường ăn trưa với bánh mì thịt hay mì ăn liền. I usually have a sandwich or instant ramen for lunch.
Hảo Hảo
Nhiều khi em chỉ ăn thức ăn đông lạnh vì đi làm về mệt quá. Oftentimes I just eat frozen food because I am so tired after work.

Z
Z
Z
Em đừng quên tập thể dục đều đặn cũng như ngủ đầy đủ nhé. Don't forget to exercise regularly as well as get enough sleep.

DIALOGUE 2

Thảo hasn't been feeling very energetic lately. Today she is visiting the office of Mr. Bảo, a nutritionist, to get some advice.

ÔNG BẢO **Chào Thảo. Hôm nay em thế nào?**
chahw^5 thahw^4 // hohm^1 năy^1 em^1 theh^2 nahw^5
Hello, Thảo. How are you today?

THẢO **Chào ông. Dạo này lúc nào em cũng thấy uể oải, không đủ sức để học hành hay làm việc.**
chahw^5 ohngm^1 // yahw^6 năy^5 lookp^2 nahw^5 em^1 koongm^3 thay^2 weh^4 wie^4 // khohngm^1 doo^4 shŭk^2 deh^4 hahkp^6 hănh^5 hăy^2 lam^5 vyehk^6
Hello, sir. Lately, I always feel sluggish and I don't have enough energy to study or work.

ÔNG BẢO **Trước hết, em hãy cho tôi biết thói quen ăn uống của em ra sao.**
trŭuhk^2 heht^2 em^1 hăy^3 chah^1 tohy^1 byeht^2 thahy^2 kwen^1 ăn^1 wohng^2 koouh^4 em^1 ra^1 shahw^1
First of all, tell me about your eating habits.

THẢO **Dạ, vào bữa sáng em thường ăn một cái bánh ngọt hay bột ngũ cốc và uống một ly sữa. Em ăn trưa với bánh mì thịt hay mì ăn liền. Thỉnh thoảng em có nấu ăn qua loa cho bữa tối, nhưng nhiều khi em chỉ ăn thức ăn đông lạnh vì đi làm về mệt quá.**
ya^6 vahw^5 bŭuh^3 shang^2 em^1 thŭuhng^5 ăn^1 moht^6 kie^2 bănh^2 ngaht^6 hăy^1 boht^6 ngoo^3 kohkp^2 va^5 wohng^2 moht^6 lee^1 shŭuh^3 // em^1 ăn^1 trŭuh^1 vuhy^2 bănh^1 mee^5 theet^6 hăy^1 mee^5 gahy^2 // theenh^4 thwang^4 em^1 kah^2 nohw^2 ăn^1 kwa^1 lwa^1 chah^1 bŭuh^3 tohy^2 // nhŭng^1 nhy-ehw^5 khee^1 em^1 chee^4 ăn^1 thŭk^2 ăn^1 dohngm^1 lănh^6 vee^5 dee^1 lam^5 veh^5 meht^6 kwa^2
For breakfast, I usually have a pastry or cereal and drink a glass of milk. I have a sandwich or instant ramen for lunch. I do make a quick dinner once in a while, but oftentimes I just eat frozen food because I am so tired after work.

ÔNG BẢO **Em nên giữ sự cân bằng giữa các loại thực phẩm có tinh bột, chất đạm và các loại mỡ tốt. Nhớ uống nhiều nước hằng ngày và đừng quên tập thể dục đều đặn cũng như ngủ đầy đủ nhé.**
em^1 nehn^1 yŭ^3 shŭ^6 kun^1 bang^{855} yŭuh^3 kak^2 lwie^6 thŭk^6 fum^4 kah^2 teenh^1 boht^6 chut^2 dam^6 va^5 kak^2 lwie^6 muh^3 toht^2// nhuh^2 wohng^2 nhyehw^5 nŭuhk^2 hăng^5 ngăy^5 // va^5 dŭng^5 kwehn^1 tup^6 theh^4 yookp^6 dehw^5 dăn^6 koongm^3 nhŭ^1 ngoo^4 day^5 doo^4 nhe^2
You should maintain a balance of foods that contain carbohydrates, protein and good fats. Remember to drink a lot of water every day, and don't forget to exercise regularly and get enough sleep.

KEY VOCABULARY 2

dạo này *adv*	lately	**đông lạnh** *adj*	frozen
uể oải *adj*	sluggish	**vì** *conj*	because
sức *n*	strength, energy	**giữ** *v*	to keep
đủ *adj*	enough	**sự cân bằng** *n*	balance
để *conj*	in order to	**giữa** *prep*	between; among
cho *v*	to give; to let	**thực phẩm** *n*	food product
thói quen *n*	habit	**tinh bột** *n*	carbs
thường *adv*	often; usually	**chất** *n*	substance
bánh ngọt *n*	pastry	**đạm** *n*	protein
bột ngũ cốc *n*	cereal	**loại** *n*	type; kind
ly *n*	glass	**mỡ** *n*	fat
bánh mì thịt *n*	sandwich	**tốt** *adj*	good
mì ăn liền *n*	instant ramen	**tập thể dục** *v*	to exercise
thỉnh thoảng *adv*	sometimes	**đều đặn** *adv*	regularly
qua loa *adv*	perfunctorily	**cũng như** *conj*	as well as
nhưng *conj*	but	**đừng** *adv*	for a negative command
nhiều khi *adv*	oftentimes	**đầy đủ** *adv*	sufficiently

IDIOMATIC EXPRESSIONS 2

đi làm về This expression contains two verbs of movement, **đi** "to go" and **về** "to return." Thus, **đi làm về** literally means "to go to work and back," that is, "to come home from work." Similar expressions include: **đi học về** "to come home from school," **đi chơi về** "to come home after hanging out," **đi ăn tiệc về** "to come home after a party."

CULTURE NOTES 2

In the dialogue, Thảo addresses Mr. Bảo as **ông** "sir" and calls herself as **em** "younger sibling." While **ông** is used to address middle-aged and older men in general, the term a speaker chooses for themselves depends on the estimated age gap between them and their interlocutor. Since Thảo thinks that Mr. Bảo is not old enough to be her father or uncle, instead of addressing herself as **con** "child" or **cháu** "niece," she chooses to use **em** during their talk.

GRAMMAR NOTES 2

II. Imperative forms

The imperative mood refers to the use of commands in everyday speech or in writing, in which verbs are used to express what a speaker wishes one or more people to do (or not to do). Different constructions are used to express the speaker's intentions, attitudes and emotions. The following are the most common imperative forms:

A. Verb + [*grammatical elements, if any*]
This is the simplest imperative form, often used in written directions or instructions. When used in speaking, this form may sound informal, curt or even disrespectful. In this form, a verb is used alone or followed by a particle, an object or a modifier.

(6) a. **Nằm xuống!** [*to a pet*]
năm^{5} swohng^{2}
Lie down!

b. **Quẹo phải ở đây.** [*on a street sign*]
kwew^{6} fie^{4} uh^{4} day^{1}
Turn right here.

c. **Thêm một muỗng đường.** [*in a recipe*]
thehm^{1} moht^{6} mwohng^{3} dŭuhng^{5}
Add a teaspoon of sugar.

d. **Uống một lần hai viên.** [*in a prescription*]
wohng^{2} moht^{6} lun^{5} hie^{1} vyehn^{1}
Take two pills at a time.

B. Subject + Verb [...]
To "tone down" a command, the speaker can add a subject (referring to the interlocutor(s)) before the verb.

(7) a. **Cháu thở mạnh.** [*doctor to a patient*]
chăw^{2} thuh^{4} mănh^{6}
(You) breathe hard.

b. **Các em đứng dậy.** [*teacher to students*]
kak^{2} em^{1} dŭng^{2} yay^{6}
(You guys) stand up.

C. (Subject) + Verb [...] + ĐI
When **đi** appears at the end of a command, the construction is equivalent to the English "Go ahead and (do something)," used for giving permission.

(8) a. **Em mặc áo vào đi.**
em^{1} măk^{6} ahw^{2} vahw^{5} dee^{1}
[You can] put your shirt back on.

b. **Cô vào đi.**
koh^{1} vahw^{5} dee^{1}
Come on in.

D. (Subject) + Verb [...] + NHÉ

Using the particle **nhé** (or **nghe** in the central and southern dialects), makes a command sound friendly. This construction, however, should be used only with family members, friends, or people the same age or younger than the speaker.

(9) a. **Anh điền mẫu đơn này nhé.**
ănh^{1} dyehn^{5} mohw^{3} năy^{5} nhe^{2}
Fill out this form, will you?

b. **Cô đợi một chút nghe.**
koh^{1} duhy^{6} moht^{6} choot^{2} nge^{1}
Wait a little bit, alright?

E. (Subject) + CỨ + Verb [...]

Roughly equivalent to "just," the particle **cứ** can be used after a subject and before a verb to encourage someone to do something.

(10) a. **Cứ ăn trước, tôi đang bận.**
kŭ^{2} ăn^{1} trŭuhk^{2} // tohy^{1} dang^{1} bun^{6}
Just eat first, I'm busy now.

b. Ông **cứ nói!**
ohngm^{1} kŭ^{2} nahy^{2}
Just say it!

F. (Subject) + HÃY + Verb [...]

The particle **hãy** makes a command sound either formal or emphatic or both.

(11) a. **Hãy hiến máu.**
hăy^{3} hyehn^{2} măw^{2}
Donate blood.

b. **Các anh chị hãy giữ gìn sức khoẻ cho tốt.**
kak^{2} ănh^{1} chee^{5} hăy^{3} yŭ^{3} yeen^{5} shŭk^{2} khwe^{4} chah^{1} toht^{2}
Stay healthy.

G. XIN + (Subject) + Verb [...]

Xin means "to ask, to beg." It is equivalent to "please" in a command.

(12) a. **Xin giữ im lặng.**
seen^{1} yŭ^{3} eem^{1} lăng^{6}
Please keep quiet.

b. **Xin quý vị đợi ở đây.**
seen^{1} kwee^{2} vee^{6} duhy^{6} uh^{4} day^{1}
Please wait here.

H. (Subject) + Verb [...] + GIÙM (Indirect object)

The adverb **giùm**, meaning "in someone else's stead," usually appears immediately after a verb or after its object(s) and modifier(s). An indirect object pronoun can optionally follow **giùm** to refer to the person the action is done for. This construction is equivalent to the English "Help (me/us) do (something)."

(13) a. **Mua giùm tôi một chai dầu gió xanh.**
moouh^{1} yoom^{5} tohy^{1} moht^{6} chie^{1} yohw^{5} yah^{2} sănh^{1}
Help me buy a flask of medicated oil.

b. **Con lấy hẹn đi bác sĩ cho mẹ thứ Sáu này giùm.**
kahn^{1} lay^{2} hen^{6} chah^{1} me^{6} dee^{1} bak^{2} shee^{3} thŭ^{2} shăw^{2} nay^{5}
Help me make a doctor's appointment this coming Friday.

I. MỜI + Direct object + Verb [...]

A command will sound polite or respectful when containing the verb **mời** "to invite," followed by a direct object that refers to the person or persons to whom the command is addressed.

(14) a. **Mời quý vị an toạ.**
muhy⁵ kwee² vee⁶ an¹ twa⁶
Please be seated.

b. **Mời bà vào phòng số 5.**
muhy⁵ ba⁵ vahw⁵ fahngm⁵ shoh² năm¹
Please come into Room 5.

J. (Subject) + ĐỪNG + Verb [...]

The verb **đừng** "to stop" rarely appears elsewhere than in negative commands. A sentence like **Tôi không đừng được**, for example, means "I can't help it."

(15) a. **Đừng hút thuốc trong khu vực này.**
dŭng⁵ hoot² thwok² trahngm¹ khoo¹ vŭk⁶ năy
Do not smoke in this area.

b. **Chị đừng quên uống thuốc sau bữa ăn.**
chee⁶ dŭng⁵ kwehn¹ wohng² thwohk² shăw¹ bŭuh³ ăn¹
Don't forget to take your medicine after a meal.

A command can contain two or more terms from the categories shown above, like the following:

(16) a. **Anh cứ thử dùng loại dầu nóng này đi nhé.**
ănh¹ kŭ² thŭ⁴ yoongm⁵ lwie⁶ yohw⁵ nahngm² năy⁵ dee¹nhe²
Just go ahead and try this hot oil, ok?

b. **Xin cô đừng quên gọi anh ấy giùm tôi.**
seen¹ koh¹ dŭng⁵ kwehn¹ gahy⁶ ănh¹ ay² yoom⁵ tohy¹
Please don't forget to call him for me.

 **READING**

THUỐC NAM

Ở Việt Nam, mỗi khi bệnh, người ta có thể tìm đến ba nguồn dược liệu: thuốc Tây (từ các nước Âu Mỹ), thuốc Bắc (từ Trung Hoa) và thuốc Nam (từ khắp nơi trong nước). Thuốc Nam dựa vào kinh nghiệm dân gian và y học cổ truyền Việt Nam, dùng dược thảo để chữa bệnh.

Nguyên liệu dùng để làm thuốc Nam là thảo mộc bản địa, bao gồm rau cải và hoa quả. Ở thôn quê, người ta dùng dược thảo tươi hay sấy khô để chữa các loại bệnh thông thường. Hiện nay, nhiều loại dược thảo được sản xuất dưới dạng thuốc nước hay thuốc viên theo tiêu chuẩn quốc tế.

Ngoài dược thảo, người Việt còn dùng nhiều loại dầu và thuốc đắp để chữa các bệnh ngoài da, như câu thành ngữ "Trong uống, ngoài thoa" thường nhắc nhở.

Các thầy thuốc Nam định bệnh bằng cách "chẩn mạch," ấn ba ngón tay giữa lên mạch máu ở cổ tay bệnh nhân để nghe khí huyết của họ. Ấn nhẹ, vừa hay mạnh là tuỳ thầy thuốc đang muốn chẩn đoán căn bệnh nào trong cơ thể của bệnh nhân.

thwohk2 nam1

uh4 vyeht5 nam1 mohy3 khee1 behnh6 // ngŭuhy5 ta1 kah2 theh4 teem5 dehn2 ba1 ngwohn5 yŭuhk6 lyehw6 // thwohk2 tay1 tŭ5 kak2 nŭuhk2 ohw1 mee3 // thwohk2 băk2 tŭ5 troongm1 hwa1 // va5 thwohk2 nam1 tŭ5 khăp2 nuhy1 trahngm1 nŭuhk2 // thwohk2 nam1 yŭuh6 vahw5 keenh1 ngyehm6 yun1 yan1 va5 ee1 hahkp6 koh4 trwyehn5 vyeht6 nam1 // yoongm5 yuhk6 thahw4 deh4 chŭuh3 behnh6

ngwyehn1 lyehw6 yoongm5 deh4 lam5 thwohk2 nam1 la5 thahw4 mohkp6 ban4 deeuh6 // bahw1 gohm5 răw1 kie4 va5 hwa1 kwa4 // uh4 thohn1 kweh1 ngŭuhy5 ta1 yoongm5 yŭuhk6 thahw4 tŭuhy1 hăy1 shay2 khoh1 deh4 chŭuh3 kak2 lwie6 behnh6 thohngm1 thŭuhng5 // nhyehw5 lwie6 yŭuhk6 thahw4 dŭuhk6 shan4 swut2 yŭuhy2 yang6 thwohk2 nŭuhk2 hăy1 thwohk2 vyehn1 thew1 tyehw1 chwun4 kwohk2 teh2

ngwie5 yŭuhk6 thahw4 ngŭuhy5 vyeht6 kahn5 yoongm5 nhyehw5 lwie6 yohw5 va5 thwohk2 dăp2 deh4 chŭuh3 kak2 behnh6 ngwie5 ya1, nhŭ1 kohw1 thănh5 ngŭ3 trahngm1 wohng2 ngwie5 thwa1 thŭuhng5 nhăk2 nhuh4

kak2 thay5 thwohk2 nam1 deenh6 behnh6 băng5 kăch2 chun4 măch6 // un2 ba1 ngahn2 tăy1 yŭuh3 lehn1 măch6 măw2 uh4 koh4 tăy1 behnh6 nhun1 deh4 nge1 khee2 hwyeht2 koouh4 hah6 // un2 nhe6 vŭuh5 hăy1 mănh6 la5 twee5 thay5 thwohk2 dang1 mwohn2 chŭn dwan2 kăn1 behnh6 nahw5 trahanm1 kuh1 theh4 koouh4 behnh6 nhun1

SOUTHERN MEDICINE

When sick, people in Vietnam can access three types of medicine: Western (from European and North American countries), Northern (from China) and Southern (from anywhere in Vietnam). Southern medicine is based on folk experience and traditional Vietnamese medicine, utilizing medicinal herbs to cure diseases.

Southern medicine is made from native plants, including vegetables, flowers and fruits. In the countryside, people use medicinal herbs, fresh or dried, to treat common diseases. Nowadays, many medicinal herbs are manufactured in liquid or pill form.

In addition to herbs, Vietnamese people also use several kinds of ointments and poultices to treat skin diseases, as the saying "Take medicine for the inside, apply ointment for the outside" often reminds us.

Southern-medicine physicians diagnose illnesses by "feeling pulses," pressing three middle fingers on the veins of the patient's wrist to feel their blood pressure. Whether to press lightly, moderately or strongly depends on the physician's attempt to diagnose a certain disease in the patient's body.

COMPREHENSION QUESTIONS

Answer the following questions in complete sentences, first orally, then in writing.

1. **Thuốc Tây, thuốc Bắc và thuốc Nam khác nhau như thế nào?** *What's the difference between Western medicine, Northern medicine and Southern medicine?*

   ____

2. **Thuốc Nam được làm từ các nguyên liệu gì?** *What is Southern medicine made from?*

   ____

3. **Bốn dạng của thuốc Nam là những dạng nào?** *What are the four forms of Southern medicine?*

   ____

4. **Người Việt dùng dầu và thuốc đắp để làm gì?** *What do Vietnamese use ointments and poultices for?*

   ____

5. **Các thầy thuốc Nam định bệnh bằng cách nào?** *How do Southern physicians diagnose diseases?*

   ____

PRACTICE

A. Listening comprehension 

Listen to the following commercial about a supplement and put a check mark above the correct answers in the following chart. Check all that apply.

Tên công ty *Company's name*			
	Thảo Mộc Nam Việt *Southern Vietnamese Herbs*	**Dược Thảo Nam Việt** *Southern Vietnamese Medicinal Herbs*	**Dược Thảo Việt Nam** *Vietnamese Medicinal Herbs*
Tên thuốc bổ *Supplement's name*			
	Sinh Lực *Vitality*	**Siêu Lực** *Super Power*	**Siêu Sinh Lực** *Super Vitality*
Nguyên liệu *Ingredients*			
	củ *roots*	**quả** *fruits*	**rau** *vegetables*
Dạng thuốc *Supplement's form*			
	viên *pill*	**tươi** *fresh*	**sấy khô** *dried*
Chỉ dẫn *Instructions*			
	mỗi ngày hai viên *two pills a day*	**mỗi ngày ba viên** *three pills a day*	**mỗi ngày một viên** *one pill a day*
	uống với sữa *taken with milk*	**uống với trà** *taken with tea*	**uống với nước** *taken with water*
	uống sau bữa ăn *taken after a meal*	**uống trước bữa ăn** *taken before a meal*	**uống trong bữa ăn** *taken during a meal*

B. Talking to a doctor in Vietnamese

Imagine you are talking to your doctor. Write complete sentences based on the English. Refer to the Functional Vocabulary section and/or a dictionary if necessary.

1. *I have a slight headache.*

____

2. *I don't sleep well at night.*

____

3. *My back hurts a lot.*

____

4. *How many of these pills do I take a day?*

____

5. *My left arm is so tired.*

____

6. *I don't exercise very often.*

____

7. *I have no appetite.*

____

8. *Do I need to take supplements?*

____

9. *I'm very afraid of shots.*

____

10. *I feel tired all the time.*

____

C. Making commands

Make commands in Vietnamese based on the suggestions in parentheses. Refer to the Functional Vocabulary section or a dictionary if necessary.

1. (*Exercise every day* – **HÃY** + ***Verb [...]***)

____

2. (*Do not smoke here* – **XIN ĐỪNG** + ***Verb [...]***)

____

3. (*Call the nurse for me* – ***Verb [...]*** + **GIÙM** + ***Indirect object***)

____

4. (*Continue to take this syrup* – ***Subject*** + **CỨ** + ***Verb [...]*** + **NHÉ**, *doctor speaking to a middle-aged woman*)

____

5. (*Step on this scale* – **MỜI** + ***Direct object*** + ***Verb [...]***, *nurse speaking to a male patient*)

____

6. (*Take these two pills* – ***Subject*** + ***Verb [...]*** + **ĐI**, *mother speaking to son*)

____

D. Vocabulary

Write the letters of the medicine brands in the left column in the brackets before the symptoms they treat in the right column. Refer to the Functional Vocabulary and/or a dictionary if necessary.

TÊN THUỐC *BRAND OF MEDICATION*	TRIỆU CHỨNG *SYMPTOM*	TÊN THUỐC *BRAND OF MEDICATION*	TRIỆU CHỨNG *SYMPTOM*
(a) Pepto Bismol®	[ ] 1. **Nhức đầu**	(f) Visine®	[ ] 6. **Đau bụng**
(b) Tylenol®	[ ] 2. **Mất ngủ**	(g) Salonpas®	[ ] 7. **Đỏ mắt**
(c) Robitussin®	[ ] 3. **Cúm**	(h) Ricola®	[ ] 8. **Đau lưng**
(d) Tamiflu®	[ ] 4. **Đau họng**	(i) Melatonin®	[ ] 9. **Nhức răng**
(e) Benadryl®	[ ] 5. **Ngứa**	(j) Orajel®	[ ] 10. **Ho**

PROVERB

MỘT NỤ CƯỜI BẰNG MƯỜI THANG THUỐC BỔ.

moht⁶ noo⁶ kŭuhy⁵ băng⁵ mŭuhy⁵ thang¹ thwohk² boh⁴

"A smile is worth ten packs of (herbal) supplements."

This old saying shows that people have long been aware of the importance of mental health.

The term **thang** "pack" refers exclusively to the treatments prescribed by Southern physicians, made up of medicinal herbs wrapped in paper. Depending on the severity of a disease, a patient might need to take one or more **thang**. **Một thang thuốc** means "a pack of (herbal) medicine," while **thuốc thang** is a compound noun meaning "medicine" in general. For example, **Bệnh này thì không cần thuốc thang gì cả** means "For this illness, no medications are needed."

 FUNCTIONAL VOCABULARY

DANH TỪ

sức khoẻ	health
sự an khang	well-being
bệnh	illness, disease
thuốc	medication
viên thuốc	pill
cổ họng	throat
thân	body
cúm	flu
cảm	cold
sốt	fever
bác sĩ	doctor
y tá	nurse
đầu	head
bụng	abdomen
lưng	back
cánh tay	arm
bàn tay	hand
mắt	eye
tai	ear
mũi	nose
miệng	mouth
đùi	leg
bàn chân	foot
bệnh viện	hospital

TÍNH TỪ

choáng váng	dizzy
mỏi nhừ	fatigued
uể oải	sluggish
buồn nôn	nauseated
mệt	tired
khoẻ	healthy, well
bệnh	sick

ĐỘNG TỪ

đau	to hurt
nhức đầu	to have a headache
nhức răng	to have a toothache
đau bụng	to have a stomachache
đau họng	to have a sore throat
đau lưng	to have a backache
bị bệnh	to be sick
bị cảm	to have a cold
bị cúm	to have the flu
nghẹt mũi	to have a stuffy nose
sổ mũi	to have a runny nose
ho	to cough
thở	to breathe
hắt hơi	to sneeze
nghỉ ngơi	to rest
tập thể dục	to exercise

Tôi thích bún bò hơn một chút.
I'm leaning toward the beef vermicelli.
THỰC ĐƠN
Anh chị đã sẵn sàng để gọi món ăn chưa ạ?
Are you ready to order?
Anh cho chúng tôi một tô phở gà và một tô bún bò.
Please give us one chicken noodle bowl and one beef vermicelli bowl.
PHỞ GIA TRUYỀN
Anh chị muốn uống gì không?
Would you like anything to drink?
Cho tôi một ly chanh muối, ít nước đá thôi.
One salted lime soda for me, not too much ice.
Còn tôi, một ly sữa đậu nành nóng.
For me, one hot soy milk.

CHAPTER 11

Foods and Beverages

Thức Ăn Và Thức Uống

DIALOGUE 1

Vũ and Hương are about to have lunch at a restaurant. They are looking at the menu and debating what to order.

HƯƠNG **Vũ định gọi món gì vậy?**
voo^3 deenh^6 gahy^6 mahn^2 yee^5 vay^5
What are you thinking of getting?

VŨ **Ừm, tôi đang phân vân giữa phở gà và bún bò đây. Còn Hương thì sao?**
ŭm^5 tohy^1 dang^1 fun^1 vun^1 yŭuh^3 fuh^4 va^5 boon^2 bah^5 day^1 // kahn^5 hŭuhng^1 thee^5 shahw^1
Hmm, I'm torn between chicken noodles and beef vermicelli. How about you?

HƯƠNG **Tôi thích bún bò hơn một chút. Hay là mình gọi cả hai món và chia với nhau nhé?**
tohy^1 theech^2 boon^2 bah^5 huhn^1 moht^6 choot^2 // hăy^1 la^5 meenh^5 gahy^5 ka^4 hie^1 mahn^2 va^5 cheeuh^1 vuhy^2 nhăw^1 nhe^2
I'm leaning toward the beef vermicelli. Or shall we order both, so we can share?

VŨ **Đồng ý. Như vậy chúng ta sẽ được thưởng thức cả hai món.**
dohngm^5 ee^2 // nhŭ^1 vay^6 choongm^2 ta^1 she^3 dŭuhk^6 thŭuhng^4 thŭk^2 ka^4 hie^1 mahn^2
Agreed. That way we'll be able to enjoy both dishes.

A male server approaches.

BỒI BÀN **Chào anh chị! Anh chị đã sẵn sàng để gọi món ăn chưa ạ?**
chahw^5 ănh^1 chee^6 // ănh^1 chee^6 da^3 shăn^3 shang^5 deh^4 gahy^6 mahn^2 ăn^1 chŭuh^1 a^6
Hello, guys! Are you ready to order?

HƯƠNG **Chào anh, anh cho chúng tôi một tô phở gà và một tô bún bò.**
chahw^5 ănh^1 // ănh^1 chah^1 choongm^2 tohy^1 moht^6 toh^1 fuh^4 ga^5 va^5 moht^6 toh^1 boon^2 bah^5
Hi! Please give us one chicken noodle bowl and one beef vermicelli bowl.

VŨ **Với hai cái tô không nữa nhé!**
vuhy² hie¹ kie² toh¹ khohngm¹ nŭuh³ nhe²
And two extra bowls, please.

BỒI BÀN **Dạ được. Anh chị muốn uống gì không?**
ya⁶ dŭuhk⁶ // ănh¹ chee⁶ mwohn² wohng² yee⁵ khohngm¹
Absolutely. Would you like anything to drink?

VŨ **Cho tôi một ly chanh muối, ít nước đá thôi.**
chah¹ tohy¹ moht⁶ lee¹ chănh¹ mwohy² // eet² nŭuhk² da² thohy¹
One salted lime soda for me, not too much ice.

HƯƠNG **Còn tôi, một ly sữa đậu nành nóng.**
kahn⁵ tohy¹ moht⁶ lee¹ shŭuh³ dohw⁶ nănh⁵ nahngm²
For me, one hot soy milk.

BỒI BÀN **Cám ơn anh chị. Chúng tôi sẽ mang mọi thứ ra ngay.**
kam² uhn¹ ănh¹ chee⁶ // choongm² tohy¹ she³ mang¹ mahy⁶ thŭ² ra¹ ngăy¹
Thank you. We'll bring everything out right away.

KEY VOCABULARY 1

bồi bàn *n*	server	**sẵn sàng** *adj*	ready
định *v*	to intend; to plan	**chưa** *adv*	not yet
gọi *v*	to call; to order	**không** *adj*	empty
phân vân *v*	to hesitate	**chanh** *n*	lime, lemon
phở gà *n*	chicken noodles	**muối** *n*	salt
bún bò *n*	beef vermicelli	**ít** *adj*	little, few
tô *n*	bowl	**nước đá** *n*	ice
một chút *adv*	a little	**thôi** *adv*	only
hay là *adv*	or; how about	**đậu nành** *n*	soy(bean)
cả hai *pron*	both	**mọi thứ** *pron*	everything
như vậy *adv*	so	**ngay** *adv*	right away

IDIOMATIC EXPRESSIONS 1

Chúng ta and **(chúng) mình** Both terms are the *inclusive we*, in this dialogue meaning "you and I," "we two" or "both of us." In other contexts, they can mean "all of us." The former is formal while the latter is informal. In Central and Southern Vietnam, the form **tụi mình** is usually used (both **chúng** and **tụi** being *plural markers*). As seen in the dialogue, the informal version is often shortened to just **mình**. On its own, **mình** means "I"; context will show whether it is being used as a singular or abbreviated plural form.

CULTURE NOTES 1

The term **bồi** derives from the English "(bus)boy." **Bồi bàn** means "waiter" (**bàn** is "table"). This term is now used alongside another term, **nhân viên phục vụ** "server."

The noun **cao-bồi** (from English "cowboy") was common in the sixties, in phrases like **phim cao-bồi** "western movies," **quần cao-bồi** "jeans." As an adjective, "**cao-bồi**" had a negative connotation; for example, **cử chỉ cao-bồi** "gang-like behavior."

GRAMMAR NOTES 1

I. Prepositions

Prepositions are called **giới từ** in Vietnamese. As in most languages, they are words that connect a verb to other elements in a sentence to indicate various grammatical and contextual relations between the former and the latter. In Vietnamese, a preposition precedes a noun, a pronoun, an adverb or a prepositional phrase, as illustrated by the following examples:

(1) a. **Chúng tôi ít ăn tráng miệng sau *bữa* ăn *tối*.** [**sau** + Noun]
choongm^2 *tohy*^{1} *eet*^{2} *ăn*^{1} *trang*^{2} *myehng*^{6} *shăw*^{1} *bŭuh*^{3} *ăn*^{1} *tohy*^{2}
We rarely have dessert after dinner.

b. **Ngày mai tôi sẽ đi ăn sáng với *anh ấy*.** [**với** + Pronoun]
ngăy^5 *mie*^{1} *tohy*^{1} *she*^{3} *dee*^{1} *ăn*^{1} *shang*^{2} *vuhy*^{2} *ănh*^{1} *ay*^{2}
I'll go out for breakfast with him tomorrow.

c. **Người Việt đã dùng đũa để ăn từ *xưa*.** [**từ** + Adverb]
ngŭuhy^5 *vyeht*^{6} *da*^{3} *yoongm*^{5} *doouh*^{3} *deh*^{4} *ăn*^{1} *tŭ*^{5} *sŭuh*^{1}
The Vietnamese have eaten with chopsticks since long ago.

d. **Cô ấy làm việc cho đến *trước giờ ăn trưa*.** [**cho đến** + Prepositional phrase]
koh^1 *ay*^{2} *lam*^{5} *vyehk*^{6} *chah*^{1} *dehn*^{2} *trŭuhk*^{2} *yuh*^{5} *ăn*^{1} *trŭuh*^{1}
She worked until before lunchtime.

In the examples above, the prepositions in Vietnamese translate neatly into their English counterparts. The use of prepositions, however, is not always straightforward across languages. Consider the following cases:

- The choice of prepositions can be different in Vietnamese and English:

(2) a. **Chim bay trên trời.** [**trên** means "above"]
cheem^1 *bay*^{1} *trehn*^{1} *truhy*^{5}
Birds are flying **in** the sky.

b. **Bố đâu rồi? – Bố đang nướng thịt ngoài sân sau.** [**ngoài** means "outside"]
boh^2 *dohw*^{1} *rohy*^{5} // *boh*^{2} *dang*^{1} *nŭuhng*^{2} *theet*^{6} *ngwie*^{5} *shun*^{1} *shăw*^{1}
Where's dad? – He's barbequing **in** the backyard.

- A number of verbs in Vietnamese come with a preposition, but their English equivalents do not:

(3) a. **Ai vừa nhắc đến món cà-ri vậy?** [**nhắc** "to mention" comes with **đến** "to"]
ie^1 vǔuh^5 nhăk^2 dehn^6 mahn^2 ka^5 ree^1 vay^6
Who just mentioned Ø curry?

b. **Chúng tôi đang bàn về việc tổ chức buổi tiệc cuối năm.** [**bàn** "to discuss" comes with **về** "about"]
choongm^1 tohy^1 dang^1 ban^5 veh^5 vyehk^6 toh^4 chŭk^2 bwohy^4 tyehk^6 kwohy^2 năm^1
We are discussing Ø the organization of the annual year-end party.

- A number of verbs in Vietnamese are not followed by a preposition, but their English equivalents are:

(4) a. **Chị đợi Ø tôi nấu xong nồi canh này nhé.** [**đợi** "to wait" does not require a preposition]
chee^6 duhy^6 tohy^1 nohw^2 sahngm^1 nohy^5 kănh^1 năy^5 nhe^2
Wait **for** me to finishing making this pot of soup, will you?

b. **Mẹ chăm sóc Ø vườn rau rất kỹ lưỡng.** [**chăm sóc** "to attend" does not require a preposition]
me^6 chăm^1 shahkp^2 vǔuhn^5 răw^1 rut^2 kee^3 lǔuhng^3
Mom attends **to** her vegetable garden very carefully.

Some prepositions are omitted if the omission will not cause a misunderstanding. In the following examples, the omittable prepositions are shown in parentheses:

(5) a. **Ba (của) tôi là một đầu bếp giỏi.** [**của** means "of"]
ba^1 koouh^4 tohy^1 la^5 moht^6 dohw^5 behp^2 yahy^4
My father is a great chef.

b. **Cô ấy gửi (cho) tôi một công thức nấu ăn hiếm.** [**cho** means "to"]
koh^1 ay^2 gǔy^3 chah^1 tohy^1 moht^6 kohngm^1 thŭk^2 nohw^2 ăn^1 hyehm^2
She has sent me a rare recipe.

The verb **đi** "to go" takes the preposition **đến** "to, toward" (or **tới**, in the southern and central dialects) when used in a literal sense:

(6) a. **Từ nhà cô đi đến chợ ABC là bao xa?**
tǔ^5 nha^5 koh^1 dee^1 dehn^2 chuh^6 a^1 beh^1 seh^1 la^5 bahw^1 sa^1
How far is it [to go] from your house to ABC Market?

b. **Đường nào ngắn nhất đi đến biển?**
dǔuhng^5 nahw^5 ngăn^2 nhut^2 dee^1 dehn^2 byehn^4
Which is the shortest way [to go] to the beach?

When used in fixed expressions, the preposition is usually omitted:

(7) a. **Cuối tuần nào tôi cũng đi chợ.**
kwohy^2 twun^5 nahw^5 tohy^1 koongm^3 dee^1 chuh^6
I go grocery shopping every weekend.

b. **Chiều nay mình đi biển không?**
chyehw^{5} năy^{1} meenh^{5} dee^{1} byehn^{4} khohngm^{1}
Shall we go to the beach this afternoon?

c. **Tuần trước chúng tôi đi xi-nê với nhau.**
twun^{5} trŭuhk^{2} choongm^{2} tohy^{1} dee^{1} see^{1} neh^{1} vuhy^{2} nhăw^{1}
We went to the movies together last week.

d. **Cô Lan thường đi chùa còn cô Mai thì đi nhà thờ.**
koh^{1} lan^{1} thŭuhng^{5} dee^{1} choouh^{5} kahn^{5} koh^{1} mie^{1} thee^{5} dee^{1} nha^{5} thuh^{5}
Miss Lan often goes to the temple while Miss Mai goes to church.

Coincidentally, some prepositions are also verbs:

(8) a. **Họ muốn đi bộ đến tiệm ăn.** [**đến**: preposition, "to"]
hah^{6} mwohn^{2} dee^{1} boh^{6} dehn^{2} tyehm^{6} ăn^{1}
They wanted to walk to the diner.

b. **Mấy giờ họ sẽ đến?** [**đến**: verb, "to come, to arrive"]
may^{2} yuh^{5} hah^{6} she^{3} dehn^{2}
What time will they come?

c. **Tôi chạy từ công viên về nhà.** [**về**: preposition, "back to"]
tohy^{1} chăy^{6} tŭ^{5} kohgn^{1} vyehn^{1} veh^{5} nha^{5}
I ran from the park back to my house.

d. **Tối nay anh có về nhà ăn cơm không?** [**về**: verb, "to return, to come back"]
tohy^{2} năy^{1} ănh^{1} kah^{2} veh^{5} nha^{5} ăn^{1} kuhm^{1} khohngm^{1}
Are you coming home for dinner this evening?

e. **Chị hâm dĩa thịt gà này cho tôi nhé.** [**cho**: preposition, "for"]
chee^{6} hum^{1} yeeuh^{3} theet^{6} ga^{5} năy^{5} chah^{1} tohy^{1} nhe^{2}
Warm up this plate of chicken for me, will you?

f. **Cám ơn cô đã cho tôi cái bánh thật ngon.** [**cho**: verb, "to give"]
kam^{2} uhn^{1} koh^{1} da^{3} chah^{1} tohy^{1} kie^{2} bănh^{2} thut^{6} ngahn^{1}
Thank you for giving me such a delicious cake.

Hôm nay tôi sẽ chỉ cho bạn làm món bánh xèo nhé.
Today I'll show you how to make crispy pancakes, OK?
Chúng ta cần 200 gram bột gạo, một muỗng cà-phê bột nghệ, nửa tách nước lọc...
We'll need 200 grams of rice flour, one teaspoon of turmeric powder, half a cup of water…
Còn về nhân thì mình có tôm và thịt heo...
As for the fillings, we'll have shrimp and pork…
Trước hết, chị trộn bột và nguyên liệu trong một cái tô lớn.
First off, you mix the flour and other ingredients in a large bowl.
Mình đảo chảo cho bột lan ra đều đặn... We're turning it around so that the batter spreads evenly…
Bánh xèo ăn chung với nhiều loại rau sống...
Crispy pancakes are eaten with several kinds of fresh vegetables…
Và chấm nước mắm tỏi ớt nữa!
And dipped in garlic-and-chili fish sauce, too!

DIALOGUE 2

Mỹ is teaching Hyung, her Korean co-worker, how to make her famous bánh xèo (Vietnamese crispy pancakes) in her apartment kitchen.

MỸ **Hyung à, hôm nay tôi sẽ chỉ cho bạn làm món bánh xèo nhé.**
hyung a5 // hohm1 năy1 tohy1 she3 chee4 chah1 chee6 lam5 mahn2 bănh2 sew5 nhe2
Hey Hyung, today I'll show you how to make crispy pancakes, OK?

HYUNG **Hay lắm! Nguyên liệu gồm có những gì vậy, Hoà?**
hăy1 lăm2 // ngwyehn1 lyehw6 gohm5 kah2 nhŭng3 yee5 vay6 hwa5
Sounds good. What are the ingredients?

MỸ **Này nhé, để làm 10 cái bánh xèo, về phần vỏ, chúng ta cần 200 gram bột gạo, một muỗng cà-phê bột nghệ, nửa tách nước lọc, một chút đường và một muỗng cà-phê muối.**
năy5 nhe2 // deh4 lam5 mŭuhy5 kie2 bănh2 sew5, veh5 fun5 vah4 // choong2 ta1 kun5 hie1 trăm1 gram1 boht6 gahw6 // moht6 mwohng3 ka5 feh1 boht6 ngeh6 // nŭuh4 tăch2 nŭuhk2 lahkp6 moht6 choot2 dŭuhng5 va5 moht6 mwohng3 ka5 feh1 mwohy2
Well, to make ten crêpes, for the batter [lit. crust], we'll need 200 grams of rice flour, one teaspoon of turmeric powder, half a cup of water, a pinch of sugar and one teaspoon of salt.

HYUNG **Còn về nhân thì mình có tôm, thịt heo, hành tây, hành lá và giá, phải không Mỹ?**
kahn5 veh5 nhun1 thee5 meenh5 kah2 tohm1 theet6 hew1 hănh5 tay1 hănh5 la2 va5 ya2 // fie4 khohngm1 mee3
And for the fillings, we'll use shrimp, pork, onion, green onion and bean sprouts, right, Mỹ?

MỸ **Chị nhớ hay đó! Trước hết, chị trộn bột và nguyên liệu trong một cái tô lớn. Sau đó, chị làm nóng chảo trên lửa vừa. Kế đến, chị đổ một phần tư tách bột đã trộn vào, rồi mình đảo chảo cho bột lan ra đều đặn như thế này.**
chee6 nhuh2 hăy1 dah2 // trŭuhk2 heht2 chee6 trohn6 boht6 va5 ngwyehn1 lyehw6 trahngm1 moht6 kie2 toh1 luhn2 // shăw1 dah2 chee6 lam5 nahngm2 chahw4 trehn1 lŭuh4 vŭuh5 // keh2 dehn2 chee6 doh5 moht6 fun5 tŭ1 tăch2 boht6 da3 trohn6 vahw5 // rohy5 meenh5 dahw5 chahw5 chah1 boht6 lan1 ra1 dehw5 dăn6 nhŭ1 theh2 năy5
You remember it well! First off, you mix the flour and other ingredients in a large bowl. Next, heat up this pan over medium heat. Next, pour ¼ cup of batter onto the pan, then turn it around so the batter spreads evenly, like this.

HYUNG **Hay quá! Bây giờ chúng ta cho nhân vào và dùng vá dẹt để gấp đôi cái bánh lại như tôi vẫn thấy, đúng không?**
hăy1 kwa2 // bay1 yuh5 choongm2 ta1 chah1 nhun1 vahw5 va5 yoongm5 va2 yet6 deh4 gup2 dohy1 kie2 bănh2 lie6 nhŭ1 tohy1 vun3 thay2 doongm2 khohngm1
Very interesting! Now we'll put the fillings in and use a spatula to fold the pancake in half, like I usually see them, right?

MỸ **Đúng vậy! Chắc chị đã biết, bánh xèo ăn chung với nhiều loại rau sống như cải xanh, bạc hà, xà-lách, tía tô và ngò.**

doongm^{2} vay^{6} // chăk^{2} chee^{6} da^{3} byeh^{2} // bănh^{2} sew^{5} ăn^{1} choongm^{1} vuhy^{2} nhyehw^{5} lwie^{6} răw^{1} shohngm^{2} nhŭ^{1} kie^{4} sănh^{1} bak^{6} ha^{5} sa^{5} lăch^{2} teeuh^{2} toh^{1} va^{5} ngah^{5}

That's right. As you probably know, crispy pancakes are eaten with several kinds of fresh vegetables and herbs such as mustard greens, mint, lettuce, perilla and cilantro.

HYUNG **Và chấm nước mắm tỏi ớt nữa! Cám ơn chị đã chỉ cho tôi làm món ăn độc đáo này của người Việt nhé!**

va^{5} nŭuhk^{2} măm^{2} tahy^{4} uht^{2} nŭuh^{3} // kam^{2} uhn^{1} chee^{5} da^{3} chee^{4} chah^{2} tohy^{1} lam^{5} mahn^{2} ăn^{1} dohkp^{6} dahw^{2} năy^{5} koouh^{4} ngŭuhy^{5} vyeht^{6} nhe^{2}

And dipped in garlic-and-chili fish sauce, too! Thank you for teaching me how to make this unique Vietnamese dish.

KEY VOCABULARY 2

bánh xèo *n*	crispy pancake	**làm nóng** *v*	to heat up
chỉ *v*	to show	**chảo** *n*	frying pan
nguyên liệu *n*	ingredient	**lửa** *n*	fire, flame
gồm có *v*	to consist of	**vừa** *adj*	medium
này nhé *interj*	well	**kế đến** *adv*	next
về phần *prep*	regarding	**đổ** *v*	to pour
vỏ *n*	crust; peel	**một phần tư** *n*	a quarter
bột *n*	flour, powder	**đảo** *v*	to turn around
muỗng cà-phê *n*	teaspoon	**lan** *v*	to spread
gạo *n*	rice	**đều đặn** *adv*	evenly
nghệ *n*	turmeric	**như thế này** *adv*	like this
nửa *n*	half	**dùng** *v*	to use
tách *n*	cup	**vá dẹt** *n*	spatula
nước lọc *n*	(filtered) water	**gấp đôi** *v*	to fold in half
một chút *n*	a little	**rau sống** *n*	fresh vegetable
đường *n*	sugar	**cải xanh** *n*	mustard greens
muối *n*	salt	**bạc hà** *n*	mint
còn về *prep*	as for	**xà-lách** *n*	lettuce
nhân *n*	filling	**tía tô** *n*	perilla
tôm *n*	shrimp	**ngò** *n*	cilantro
thịt heo *n*	pork	**chấm** *v*	to dip
hành tây *n*	onion	**nước mắm** *n*	fish sauce
hành lá *n*	green onion	**tỏi** *n*	garlic
giá *n*	bean sprout	**ớt** *n*	chili

trộn *v*	to mix	**độc đáo** *adj*	unique
tô *n*	bowl	**món ăn** *n*	dish

IDIOMATIC EXPRESSIONS 2

Hay lắm!
Hay quá!

Hay is an adjective meaning "good, great, interesting." As in the dialogue, a descriptive adjective such as this can simply be followed by an adverb of degree (**lắm** "very," **quá** "so," **thật** "really") to make a remark about something. A few other phrases are **đẹp lắm**! "very nice, very beautiful," **khó quá**! "so difficult," **ngon lắm**! "very delicious," **mặn quá**! "very salty," etc.

Hay also functions as an adverb meaning "well": **hát hay** "to sing well," **nhớ hay** "to remember well." The idiom **ăn vóc, học hay** (lit. "eating much and studying well") refers to young people, who are in their prime, full of health and energy.

CULTURE NOTES 2

Nước mắm is a dipping sauce that you can't miss in a Vietnamese meal. It is usually translated as "fish sauce" because it is normally made from various types of fish (mostly anchovies), although you can find **nước mắm** made from shrimp or squid (the generic term for any type of dipping sauce is **nước chấm**). Don't confuse "**nước mắm**" with **mắm**, which is brined or pickled fish (also shrimp, squid or crabs). Since Vietnam has over 3,000 kilometers of coastline washed by the East Sea, there are many, many types of **mắm**, such as **mắm thu** "brined mackerel," **mắm cá cơm** "brined anchovies," **mắm tôm chua** "brined shrimp," **mắm còng** "brined sand crabs," and **mắm mực** "brined squid," to name a few.

GRAMMAR NOTES 2

II. Conjunctions

A conjunction (**liên từ** in Vietnamese) is a word that joins together two elements of the same grammatical type (noun to noun or pronoun, adjective to adjective, verb to verb, phrase to phrase, clause to clause, sentence to sentence, etc.)

Coordinate conjunctions—such as **và** "and," **nhưng** "but," **hay** "or," **mà** "yet"—join two independent elements together:

(9) a. **Thực phẩm trong siêu thị này rất tươi <u>và</u> rẻ.**
thŭk^{6} fum^{4} trahngm^{1} shyehw^{1} thee^{6} năy^{5} rut^{2} tŭuhy^{1} va^{5} re^{4}
The food in this supermarket is very fresh and inexpensive.

b. **Thịt heo này nên kho <u>hay</u> nướng?**
theet^{6} hew^{1} năy^{5} nehn^{1} khah^{1} hăy^{1} nŭuhng^{2}
Should we braise or grill the pork?

c. **Tôi nêm món xào với rất ít muối mà nó vẫn mặn.**
tohy^{1} nehm^{1} mahn^{2} sahw^{5} vuhy^{2} rut^{2} eet^{2} mwohy^{2} ma^{5} nah^{2} vun^{3} măn^{6}
I seasoned this stir-fry with very little salt yet it still tastes salty.

d. **Cái bánh đó thơm nhưng lại không ngon.**
kie^{2} bănh^{2} dah^{2} thuhm^{1} nhŭng^{1} lie^{6} khohngm^{1} ngahn^{1}
That cake smells good, but it isn't tasty.

Subordinate conjunctions—such as **khi** "when," **vì** "because," **để** "so that," **nếu** "if," **mặc dầu** "although"—join a subordinate clause to a main clause in a complex sentence:

(10) a. **Nhớ vớt bánh phở ra khi nước bắt đầu sôi.**
nhuh^{2} vuht^{2} bănh^{2} fuh^{4} ra^{1} khee^{1} nŭuhk^{2} băt^{2} dohw^{5} shohy^{1}
Remember to scoop out the noodles when the water starts boiling.

b. **Em nên cất tô canh này vào tủ lạnh vì nó rất dễ thiu.**
em^{1} nehn^{1} kut^{2} toh^{1} kănh^{1} năy^{5} vahw^{5} too^{4} lănh^{5} vee^{5} nah^{2} rut^{2} yeh^{4} theew^{1}
You should put this bowl of soup in the fridge because it can spoil easily.

c. **Chị có dùng loại sữa này để làm sữa chua không?**
chee^{6} kah^{2} yoongm^{5} lwie^{6} shŭuh^{3} năy^{5} deh^{4} lam^{5} shŭuh^{3} choouh^{1} khohngm^{1}
Do you use this kind of milk to make yogurt?

d. **Nếu cô hầm thịt lâu hơn thì thịt sẽ mềm.**
nehw^{2} koh^{1} hum^{5} theet^{6} lohw^{1} huhn^{1} thee^{5} theet^{6} she^{3} mehm^{5}
If you stew the meat longer, it will be tender.

e. **Mặc dầu còn thiếu vài nguyên liệu, món gỏi vẫn khá thấm tháp.**
măk^{6} yohw^{5} kahn^{5} thyehw^{2} vie^{5} ngwyehn^{1} lyehw^{6} mahn^{2} gahy^{4} vun^{3} kha^{2} thum^{2} thap^{2}
Although missing a few ingredients, the salad was still pretty savory.

English speakers should pay special attention to the use of *conjunctions of time* as opposed to *prepositions of time* in Vietnamese, because most of these two types of words are used interchangeably in English. For example, while "before" is used both as a preposition and a conjunction, as in "We had lunch *before* 11am" and "We had lunch *before* they came," in Vietnamese the equivalents are, respectively, **Chúng tôi ăn trưa trước mười một giờ** and **Chúng tôi ăn trưa trước khi họ đến.** The following chart shows the differences between prepositions and conjunctions of time:

PREPOSITIONS & CONJUNCTIONS OF TIME						
Preposition	**vào** *in, on, at*	**trong** *during*	**trước** *before*	**sau** *after*	**từ** *from, since*	**đến** *to, until*
Conjunction	**khi** *when*	**trong khi** *while*	**trước khi** *before*	**sau khi** *after*	**từ khi** *since*	**đến khi** *until*

(11) a. **Nhà tôi thường ăn bữa tối trước sáu giờ.**
nha^{5} tohy^{1} thŭuhng^{5} ăn^{1} bŭuh^{3} tohy^{2} trŭuhk^{2} shăw^{2} yuh^{5}
My family usually has dinner before six o'clock.

b. **Mẹ luôn luôn dọn cơm tối sẵn sàng trước khi ba về.**
me6 lwohn1 lwohn1 yahn6 kuhm1 tohy2 trŭuhk2 khee1 ba1 veh5
Mom always has dinner ready before Dad comes home.

c. **Nhiều người có thói quen ngủ trưa một lát sau bữa ăn trưa.**
nhyehw5 ngŭuhy5 kah2 thahy2 kwen1 ngoo4 trŭuh1 moht6 lat2 shăw1 bŭuh3 ăn1 trŭuh1
Many people are used to taking a short nap after lunch.

d. **Tôi thường đi bách bộ sau khi ăn cơm tối.**
tohy1 thŭuhng5 dee1 băch2 boh6 shăw1 khee1 ăn1 kuhm1 tohy2
I often go for a walk after having dinner.

e. **Nhà hàng đó phục vụ điểm tâm từ bảy giờ sáng đến trưa.**
nha5 hang5 dah2 fookp6 voo6 dyehm4 tum1 tŭ5 băỹ yuh5 shang2 dehn2 trŭuh1
That restaurant serves breakfast from 7 a.m. until noon.

f. **Tiệm phở này mở cửa từ khi trời còn tối đến khi không còn khách vào nữa.**
tyehm6 fuh4 năy5 muh4 kŭuh4 tŭ5 khee1 truhy5 kahn5 tohy2 dehn2 khee1 khohngm1 kahn5 khăch2 vahw5 nŭuh3
This noodle shop is open from before dawn until customers stop coming.

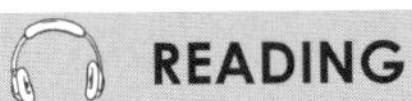

READING

CHỊ ĂN CƠM CHƯA?

Khi hỏi nhau câu này, thật ra người Việt không nhấn mạnh chữ "cơm" mà chỉ muốn biết người kia đã ăn chưa. Đó là vì cơm là món không thể thiếu trong các bữa ăn chính của người Việt.

Những hạt cơm trắng ngần, nóng hổi trong nồi là kết quả của sự lao động cực nhọc của người nông dân. Tất cả bắt đầu từ những hạt giống đã được ủ và gieo xuống các luống đất. Khi hạt nẩy mầm trở thành cây non, gọi là "mạ", người ta mang ra ruộng để cấy xuống đất. Mạ lớn lên trở thành "cây lúa". Hạt lúa chín gặt về, đập cho rời khỏi cành, gọi là "thóc". Thóc được cho vào cối giã ra, tách thành hai phần: phần vỏ gọi là "trấu" và phần hạt bên trong gọi là "gạo".

Có hai loại gạo chính: gạo tẻ, khi nấu chín trở thành "cơm", và gạo nếp, khi nấu chín trở thành "xôi". Gạo tẻ còn là nguyên liệu dùng làm ra nhiều loại thức ăn và thức uống khác như cháo, phở, bún, bánh cuốn, bánh tráng và cả rượu nữa.

chee6 ăn1 kuhm1 chŭuh1

khee1 hahy4 nhăw1 kohw1 năy5 // thut6 ra1 ngŭuhy5 vyeht6 khohngm1 nhun2 mănh6 chŭ3 kuhm1 ma5 chee4 mwohn2 byeht2 ngŭuhy5 keeuh1 da3 ăn1 chŭuh1 // dah2 la5 vee5 kuhm1 la5 mahn2 khohngm1 theh4 thyehw2 trahngm1 kak2 bŭuh3 ăn1 cheenh2 koouh4 ngŭuhy5 vyeht6

nhŭng3 hat6 kuhm1 trăng2 ngun5 nahngm2 hohy4 trahngm1 nohy5 la5 keh2 kwa4 loouh4 shŭ6 lahw1 dohngm6 kŭk6 nhahkp6 koouh4 ngŭuhy5 nohngm1 yun1 // tut2 ka4 băt2 dohw5 tŭ5 nhŭng3 hat6 yohngm2 da3 dŭuhk6 oo4 va5 yew1 swohng2 kak2 lwohng2 dut2 // khee1 hat6 nay4 mum5 truh4 thănh5 kay1 nahn1 // gahy6 la5 ma6 // ngŭuhy5 ta1 mang1 ra1 rwohng6 deh4 kay2 swohng2 dut2 // ma6 luhn2 kehn1 truh4 thănh5 kay1 loouh2 // hat6 loouh2 cheen2 găt6 veh5 dup6 chah1 ruhy5 khahy4 kănh5 gahy6 la5 thahkp2 // thahkp2 dŭuhk6 chah1 vahw5 kohy2 ya3 ra1, tăch2 thănh5 hie1 fun5 // fun5 vah4 gahy6 la5 trohw2 va5 fun5 hat6 behn1 trahngm1 gahy6 la5 gahw6

kah2 hie1 lwie6 gahw6 cheenh2 // gahw5 te4 khee1 nohw2 cheen2 truh4 thănh5 kuhm1 // va5 gahw6 nehp2 khee1 nohw2 cheen2 truh4 thănh5 sohy1 // gahw6 te4 kahn5 la5 ngwyehn1 lyehw6 yoongm5 lam5 ra1 nhyehw5 lwie6 thŭk2 ăn1 va5 thŭk2 wohng2 khak2 nhŭ1 // chahw2 fuh4 boon2 bănh2 kwohn2 bănh2 trang2 va5 ka4 rŭuhw6 nŭuh3

HAVE YOU EATEN STEAMED RICE YET?

When asking each other this question, Vietnamese people aren't literally asking about **cơm** or "steamed rice," but simply want to know if the other person has eaten or not. It's phrased this way because steamed rice is such an indispensable part of the main meals of the Vietnamese.

The steaming hot, white grains in the pot are the result of the farmer's arduous labor. Everything begins with the seeds, after incubation, being sown into furrows in the soil. When the seeds germinate into seedlings—called **mạ**—they are taken out to the fields and transplanted into the soil. Seedlings grow into rice plants. Ripe rice grains are harvested and threshed off the panicles—now called **thóc**. These grains are then put into mills for grinding, and are split into two parts: the husks are called **trấu** and the grains inside are **gạo**.

There are two main types of rice: regular white rice, which becomes **cơm** when cooked, and sticky rice, which becomes **xôi** when cooked. White rice is also used to make foods and beverages such as porridge, noodles, vermicelli, steamed pancakes and even liquor.

COMPREHENSION QUESTIONS

Answer the following questions in complete sentences, first orally, then in writing.

1. **Cây lúa non gọi là gì?** *What is a young rice plant called?*

   ____

2. **Hạt lúa đã đập rời khỏi cành gọi là gì?** *What do you call a rice grain already threshed off the panicle?*

   ____

3. **Hạt thóc được giã để tách ra thành hai phần nào?** *What are the two parts of a rice grain that's been milled?*

   ____

4. **Người ta dùng loại gạo nào để nấu thành cơm?** *Which type of rice is used to make steamed white rice?*

   ____

5. **Xôi được nấu bằng loại gạo nào?** *Which type of rice is steamed sticky rice made of?*

   ____

PRACTICE

A. Listening comprehension

Listen to the following description of **phở** and put a check mark above the terms you hear. Check all that apply.

PHỞ...NOMENAL!			
Loại món ăn *Type of dish*			
	Cơm *Rice*	**Xúp** *Soup*	**Bánh mì** *Bread*
Bánh *Noodles*			
	Mì *Egg noodles*	**Bún** *Vermicelli*	**Phở** *Rice noodles*
Nước dùng *Broth*			
	Xương heo *Pork bones*	**Xương gà** *Chicken bones*	**Xương bò** *Beef bones*
Rau *Veggies*			
	Bạc hà *Mint*	**Húng quế** *Basil*	**Ngò** *Cilantro*
Gia vị tươi *Fresh condiments*			
	Chanh *Limes*	**Ớt** *Jalapeños*	**Hương thảo** *Rosemary*
Tương *Sauces*			
	Tương đen *Hoisin sauce*	**Tương cà chua** *Ketchup*	**Tương đỏ** *Sriracha*
Gia vị *Spices*			
	Đinh hương *Cloves*	**Hồi** *Anise*	**Quế** *Cinnamon*

B. Prepositions and conjunctions

Complete the following sentences with a preposition or conjunction from the lists.

Prepositions:	về	bằng	cho	từ	với	của	như	vào	thay vì
Conjunctions:	khi	mà	hay	để	mặc dầu	vì	nếu	nên	

1. **Tôi không uống sữa được ____________ buổi sáng.**
   I can't drink milk in the morning.

2. **____________ món ăn cay quá, cô ấy sẽ không thấy ngon nữa.**
   If a dish is too spicy, she won't find it delicious anymore.

3. **Anh ấy không ăn hết chén canh ____________ canh nêm quá ngọt.**
   He didn't finish the bowl of soup because it was too sweet.

4. **Cô thường ăn rau luộc ____________ rau xào?**
   Do you usually eat boiled or stir-fried vegetables?

5. **Chúng tôi ít khi ăn cơm ______________ thịt vịt.**
We rarely eat rice with duck.

6. **Việt Nam nằm bên một bờ biển dài ______________ cá là món ăn rất phổ biến.**
Vietnam has a long coast, so fish is a very popular food.

7. **Ông có cảm tưởng gì ______________ món bánh mì thịt Việt Nam?**
What's your impression of Vietnamese sandwiches?

8. **Em tôi ăn chay ______________ rất thích thịt.**
My little brother is a vegetarian even though he likes meat a lot.

9. **Mẹ tôi thường nấu các loại canh khoai ______________ các loại rau.**
My mom often makes soups with root vegetables instead of leafy vegetables.

10. **Xà-lách là chữ mượn ______________ tiếng Pháp "salade" để chỉ tên một loại rau.**
"Xà-lách" is a word borrowed from French to name a kind of vegetable.

11. **Nước dùng của bún bò Huế được nấu ______________ xương bò và chân giò heo.**
Hue beef vermicelli broth is made with beef bones and pig's feet.

12. **Chè Việt Nam ăn cũng gần ______________ chè Thái hay chè Phi.**
Vietnamese sweet soups taste almost like Thai or Filipino sweet soups.

13. **______________ nước sôi, chị nhớ tắt bếp cho bánh phở chín đều.**
When the water boils, remember to turn off the stove and let the rice noodles finish cooking.

14. **Vị chua ______________ giấm làm tô mì gà thêm phần hấp dẫn.**
The sourness of vinegar makes this bowl of chicken egg noodles even tastier.

15. **Pha giùm tôi một chén nước mắm tỏi ớt ______________ ăn với món gỏi tôm này.**
Make me a bowl of fish sauce with garlic and chili to eat with this shrimp salad.

16. **Món cơm chiên đó là ______________ mấy đứa nhỏ.**
That fried rice dish is for the kids.

17. **Bắp nướng trông ngon quá ______________ lại thiếu mỡ hành!**
How delicious that grilled corn looks, but you're missing scallion oil!

C. Preposition or conjunction?

Circle the correct word (preposition or conjunction) in each of the following sentences.

1. **Không nên nói chuyện quá nhiều TRONG/TRONG KHI bữa ăn.**
You shouldn't talk too much during a meal.

2. **Con phải ăn TRƯỚC/TRƯỚC KHI tập thể dục.**
You should eat before exercising.

3. **SAU/SAU KHI ăn xong, tôi thường đi bộ cho mau tiêu cơm.**
After eating, I usually walk to digest the food faster.

4. **Tôi quan sát mẹ nấu món bún riêu TỪ/TỪ KHI đầu ĐẾN/ĐẾN KHI cuối.**
   I watched my mom make crab noodle soup from beginning to end.

5. **TỪ/TỪ KHI biết nấu ăn, cô ấy ăn toàn những món lành mạnh.**
   Since she knows how to cook, she has been eating only healthy dishes.

6. **ĐẾN/ĐẾN KHI mấy giờ tôi mới lấy con gà quay ra được?**
   When will I be able to take the roast chicken out of the oven?

7. **Bánh Trung Thu thường được bắt đầu bày bán VÀO/KHI tháng Sáu âm lịch.**
   Moon cakes are usually available for sale in the sixth month (of the lunar calendar).

D. Vocabulary

Choose the correct adjective for each of the underlined food items. Refer to the Functional Vocabulary section when necessary.

1. **Anh có ăn được ớt không?** (*chili*)
   a. chua b. cay c. ngọt d. đắng

2. **Tôi ít dùng đường trong các món ăn.** (*sugar*)
   a. mặn b. giòn c. ngọt d. mềm

3. **Cô đưa giùm tôi hũ muối.** (*salt*)
   a. nhạt b. sống c. tái d. mặn

4. **Chị có bao giờ ăn khổ qua chưa?** (*bitter melon*)
   a. đắng b. cay c. chua d. dai

5. **Cam ở Việt Nam có màu xanh lục.** (*orange*)
   a. giòn b. chua c. mặn d. dai

PROVERB

CƠM KHÔNG RAU NHƯ ĐAU KHÔNG THUỐC.

kuhm[1] khohngm[1] răw[1] nhŭ[1] dahw[1] khohngm[1] thwohk[2]

"Eating rice without vegetables is like being sick without medicine."

From the phrase **cơm không rau**, you might imagine (correctly) that meat was a luxury in Vietnam, at least in the old days when this saying became popular. Nowadays, people in the the city as well as the country grow their own vegetables to have fresh, safe produce. People believe as much in the health benefits of vegetables as they do in the effectiveness of medicine when they are sick.

 FUNCTIONAL VOCABULARY

DANH TỪ

cơm	steamed rice
gạo	uncooked rice
cháo	porridge
xôi	steamed sticky rice
phở	noodle soup
bún	vermicelli
mì	egg noodles
trứng	egg
thịt	meat
thịt gà	chicken
thịt heo	pork
thịt bò	beef
cá	fish
tôm	shrimp
hải sản	seafood
thức uống	beverage
chén	small bowl
tô	large bowl
chai	bottle
tách	cup
dĩa	plate
muỗng	spoon
nĩa	fork
dao	knife
đũa	chopstick
nước mắm	fish sauce
muối	salt
đường	sugar
tiêu	black pepper
ớt	chili
chanh	lime, lemon
rau	vegetable
món ăn	dish
trà	tea
sữa	milk
cà-phê	coffee
bia	beer
rượu	alcoholic beverage
nước đá	ice
kem	ice cream
chè	sweet soup
món tráng miệng	dessert

TÍNH TỪ

mặn	salty
ngọt	sweet
cay	spicy
chua	sour
đắng	bitter
nhạt	bland
mềm	tender
dai	chewy
giòn	crunchy
chín	cooked; ripe
sống	uncooked; unripe
tái	rare, half-cooked

ĐỘNG TỪ

luộc	to boil
chiên	to fry
xào	to stir-fry
hấp	to steam
nướng	to grill
quay	to roast
nấu ăn	to cook (in general)
ướp	to marinade
nêm	to season
nếm	to taste
húp	to drink (from a bowl)

Mấy đôi giày này trông có vẻ mời gọi quá!
These shoes over here look so tempting!

ĐẠI HẠ GIÁ 50%

Chà, mấy đôi này thì dễ thương thật!
Wow, these are really cute!

Thuỷ có cần mua món nào không?
Did you need to pick up anything?

CHAPTER 12

Shopping and Clothing

Đi Mua Sắm – Y Phục

DIALOGUE 1

Thuỷ and Ngọc are at Thương Xá Tự Do (Freedom Shopping Mall) on a weekend. They are telling each other about the things they want to buy.

THUỶ **Sao, hôm nay Ngọc định mua những gì đây?**
shahw^1 // hohm^1 năy^1 ngahkp^6 deenh^6 moouh^1 nhŭng^3 yee^5 day^1
So, what are you thinking of getting today?

NGỌC **Ngọc cũng chưa biết nữa. Ngọc rất cần thêm vài cái áo mới để đi làm, nhưng mấy đôi giày này trông có vẻ mời gọi quá!**
ngahkp^6 koongm^3 chŭuh^1 byeht^2 nŭuh^3 // ngahkp^6 rut^2 kun^5 thehm^1 vie^5 kie^2 ahw^2 muhy^2 deh^4 dee^1 lam^5 nhŭng^1 may^2 dohy^1 yăy^5 năy^5 trohngm^1 kah^2 ve^4 muhy^5 gahy^6 kwa^2
I'm not sure yet. I really need some new tops for work, but these shoes over here look so tempting!

THUỶ **Chà, mấy đôi này thì dễ thương thật!**
cha^5 // may^2 dohy^1 năy^5 thee^5 yeh^3 thŭuhng^1 thut^6
Wow, these are really cute!

NGỌC **Quyết định mua món gì lúc nào cũng khó cả. Còn Thuỷ thì sao? Thuỷ có cần mua món nào không?**
kwyeht^2 deenh^6 moouh^1 mahn^2 yee^5 lookp^2 nahw^5 koongm^3 khah^2 ka^4 // kahn^5 thwee^4 thee^5 shahw^1 // thwee^4 kah^2 kun^5 moouh^1 mahn^2 nahw^5 khohngm^1
It's always hard to decide what to buy. How about you? Did you need to pick up anything?

THUỶ **Thuỷ muốn xem thử những món đang bán hạ giá trong cửa tiệm đằng kia. Cái túi xách tay này của Thuỷ đã lỗi thời lắm rồi.**
thwee^4 mwohn^2 sem^1 thŭ^4 nhŭng^3 mahn^2 dang^1 ban^2 ha^6 ya^2 trahngm^1 kŭuh^4 tyehm^6 dăng^5 keeuh^1 // kie^2 tooy^2 săch^2 tăy^2 năy^5 koouh^4 thwee^4 da^3 lohy^3 thuhy^5 lăm^2 rohy^5
I wanted to check out the sale in the store over there. This handbag of mine is so out of fashion.

NGỌC **Ngọc cũng định ghé qua tiệm nữ trang một chút. Ngọc chưa có sợi dây chuyền nào để mang với áo đầm cả.**
ngahkp^6 koongm^3 deenh^6 ge^2 kwa^1 tyehm^6 nŭ^3 trang^1 moht^6 choot^2 // ngahkp^6 chŭuuh^1 kah^2 shuhy^6 yay^1 chwyehn^5 nahw^5 deh^4 mang^1 vuhy^2 ahw^2 dum^5 ka^4
I also planned to swing by a jewelry store. I don't have any necklaces to wear with my dresses.

THUỶ **Thuỷ rất hài lòng là chúng ta đã quyết định đến thương xá này. Nhìn thứ gì cũng muốn mua hết!**
thwee^4 rut^2 hie^5 lahngm^5 la^5 choongm^2 ta^1 da^3 kwyeht^2 deenh^6 dehn^2 thŭuhng^1 sa^2 năy^5 // nheen^5 thŭ^2 yee^5 koongm^4 mwohn^2 moouh^1 heht^2
I'm so glad that we decided to come to this shopping mall. Everything I see here is something I'd want to buy!

NGỌC **Chúng ta nên mua sắm vừa phải thôi để còn tiền ăn trưa nữa chứ!**
choongm^2 ta^1 nehn^1 moouh^1 shăm^2 vŭuh^5 fie^4 thohy^1 deh^4 kahn^5 tyehn^5 ăn^1 trŭuh^1 nŭuh^3 chŭ^2
We shouldn't shop too much, so we still have money left to grab lunch, right?

THUỶ **Nghe hay đó! Mình vào tiệm giày này trước rồi cùng qua các tiệm khác há!**
nge^1 hăy^1 dah^2 // meenh^5 vahw^5 tyehm^6 yăy^5 năy^5 trŭuhk^2 rohy^5 koongm^5 kwa^1 kak^2 tyehm^6 khak^2 ha^2
Sounds perfect! Let's go into this shoe shop and then we'll hit some other boutiques together.

KEY VOCABULARY 1

định *v*	to intend, to plan	**cửa tiệm** *n*	shop
vài *adj*	a few	**đằng kia** *adv*	over there
áo *n*	top, shirt	**túi xách tay** *n*	handbag
mấy *adj*	a few	**lỗi thời** *adj*	out of fashion
đôi *n*	pair	**tiệm nữ trang** *n*	jewelry store
giày *n*	shoe	**sợi** *n*	string
trông có vẻ *v*	to seem	**dây chuyền** *n*	necklace
mời gọi *adj*	inviting	**mang** *v*	to wear (accessories)
quá *adv*	too, so	**áo đầm** *n*	dress
dễ thương *adj*	cute, lovely	**hài lòng** *adj*	pleased
thật *adj* & *adv*	true; really	**thương xá** *n*	shopping mall

xem thử *v*	to check out	**mua sắm** *v*	to shop
bán hạ giá *v*	to be on sale	**vừa phải** *adv*	moderately

IDIOMATIC EXPRESSIONS 1

Sao? Used as an interjection, **sao** is roughly like "well" in English, an opener for a conversation with a touch of curiosity, because what follows is usually a question about something the other person has done or is going to do: **Sao, có gì lạ không?** "Well, what's new with you?"

When you ask **Anh nói sao?** ("What did you say?") instead of **Anh nói gì?**, it implies some element of surprise or disbelief at what has been said. If you apologize to someone and they say **Không sao đâu!** ("It's nothing"), they mean "No worries at all." If you fall or hurt yourself, someone can express their concern by asking **Cô có sao không**? which means "Are you okay?"

CULTURE NOTES 1

There are at least three verbs in Vietnamese that mean "to buy": **mua, sắm** and **buôn. Mua**, the most common of the three, means "to buy (something) in general," usually for short-term use or consumption: **mua thức ăn** "to buy food," **mua vé máy bay** "to buy a plane ticket," **mua hoa** "to buy flowers." **Sắm**, on the other hand, means "to buy (something) for long-term use or to keep as an asset": **sắm quần áo** "to buy clothes," **sắm xe** "to buy a car," **sắm đồ đạc** "to buy furniture or appliances." **Buôn**, used in business, means "to buy (something) for selling back at a profit" or "to trade": **buôn hàng hoá** "to trade merchandise," **buôn thực phẩm** "to trade foods," **buôn vải vóc** "to trade fabrics." This verb is commonly followed by the verb **bán** "to sell": **buôn bán hàng hoá, buôn bán thực phẩm, buôn bán vải vóc.**

GRAMMAR NOTES 1

I. Particles

Particles (**tiểu từ** in Vietnamese, meaning "small words") are words used in sentences either for a grammatical function or simply to add some nuance to what's being said. There are several ways to categorize particles, one of which is based on their position in a sentence.

A. Sentence-initial particles

- **Dạ**: This is a "respectful" particle that precedes an answer that can be just one word, a phrase or a full sentence. It is used when one is talking politely to peers or respectfully to superiors.

(1) a. **Dạ, phải,**
ya⁶ fie⁴
That's right.

b. **Dạ, không.**
ya⁶ khohngm¹
No.

c. **Dạ, có.**
ya⁶ kah²
Yes.

Saying **dạ** alone also means "yes" in a respectful way.

- **Thưa**: This word is originally a verb meaning "to speak respectfully." Used as a particle, it usually precedes a term of address or title before the speaker continues with what they have to say.

(2) a. **Thưa quý vị, ...**
thŭuh^1 kwee^2 vee^6
Ladies and gentlemen ...

b. **Thưa bà, bà cần gì?**
thŭuh^1 ba^5 // ba^5 kun^5 yee^5
Ma'am, what did you need?

c. **Thưa bác sĩ, tôi đau chỗ này lắm.**
thŭuh^1 bak^2 shee^3 // tohy^1 dăw^1 choh^3 năy^5 lăm^2
Doctor, I feel a lot of pain right here.

- **Kính**: Originally an adverb meaning "respectfully," **kính** becomes a particle when it precedes a verb at the beginning of a phrase or sentence:

(3) a. **Kính chào** ông **bà.**
keenh^2 chahw^5 ohngm^1 ba^5
Hello, sir and ma'am.

b. **Kính thưa quan khách, ...**
keenh^2 thŭuh^1 kwah^1 khăch^2
Esteemed guests ...

c. **Kính mời,**
keenh^2 muhy^5
Respectfully inviting ...

B. Sentence-medial particles

- **Lại**: This particle appears before a verb or an adjective in the second clause of a compound or complex sentence to show a contrast between the first and the second part.

(4) a. **Lan không ưa đội nón, còn Mai lại ghét đeo vòng.**
lan^1 khohngm^1 ŭuh^1 dohy^6 nahn^2 // kahn^5 mie^1 lie^6 get^2 dew^1 vahngm^5
Lan doesn't like wearing hats, and Mai hates wearing bracelets.

b. **Cái áo vét hơi rộng, còn cái quần lại dài quá.**
kie^2 ahw^2 vet^2 huhy^1 rohngm^6 // kahn^5 kie^2 kwun^5 lie^6 yie^5 kwa^2
The jacket is a bit too big, whereas the pants are very long.

- **Mà**: When following the subject of a subordinate clause, **mà** expresses a hypothetical situation:

(5) **Cái váy này mà bằng da chắc đẹp lắm!**
kie^2 văy^2 năy^5 ma^5 băng^5 ya^1 chăk^2 dep^6 lăm^2
If this skirt were made of leather, it would look very nice!

Mà also appears after an indefinite word to make the sentence sound either rhetorical or emphatic:

(6) a. **Ai mà không thích mang loại dép đó!**
ie^1 ma^5 khohngm^1 theech^2 mang^1 lwie^6 yep^2 dah^2
Who would not like wearing that type of flip-flops?

b. **Ở đâu mà có bán đồ len đẹp như vậy?**
uh^4 *dohw*^{1} *ma*^{5} *kah*^{2} *ban*^{2} *doh*^{5} *len*^{1} *dep*^{6} *nhŭ*^{1} *vay*^{6}
Where on earth do they sell such beautiful woolen clothing?

c. **Làm sao mà chị móc được cái mũ này?**
lam^5 *shahw*^{1} *ma*^{5} *chee*^{6} *mahkp*^{2} *dŭuhk*^{5} *kie*^{2} *moo*^{3} *năy*^{5}
How could you have crocheted this cap?

- **Thì**: In a sentence with an emphasized element appearing at the beginning, **thì** follows this element to make the emphasis even stronger:

(7) a. **Thời trang thì giới trẻ luôn luôn ưa chuộng.**
thuhy^5 *trang*^{1} *thee*^{5} *yuhy*^{2} *tre*^{4} *lwohn*^{1} *lwohn*^{1} *ŭuh*^{1} *chwohng*^{6}
Fashion is something young people always like.

b. **Lúc nào thì cô ấy chẳng diện!**
lookp^2 *nahw*^{5} *thee*^{5} *koh*^{1} *ay*^{2} *chăng*^{4} *yehn*^{6}
When does she not dress up?

c. **Đồ thể thao đẹp và bền thì có thể mua trong tiệm này.**
doh^5 *theh*^{4} *thahw*^{1} *dep*^{6} *va*^{5} *behn*^{5} *thee*^{5} *kah*^{2} *theh*^{4} *moouh*^{1} *trahngm*^{1} *tyehm*^{6} *năy*^{5}
Nice and durable sports clothes can be bought in this shop.

- **Có**: This particle serves as an emphatic element when it comes before a verb, an adjective or an adverb of manner.

(8) a. **Tôi có mặc thử cái áo đầm đó nhưng không mua.**
tohy^1 *kah*^{2} *măk*^{6} *thŭ*^{4} *kie*^{4} *ahw*^{2} *dum*^{5} *dah*^{2} *nhŭng*^{1} *khohngm*^{1} *moouh*^{1}
I did try that dress on but didn't buy it.

b. **Anh ấy có mua sắm ở tiệm này nhiều lần rồi.**
ănh^1 *ay*^{2} *kah*^{2} *moouh*^{1} *shăm*^{2} *uh*^{4} *tyehm*^{6} *năy*^{5} *nhyehw*^{5} *lun*^{5} *rohy*^{5}
He has indeed shopped in this store several times.

c. **Nhà may đó có nổi tiếng thật nhưng tôi lại không thích.**
nha^5 *măy*^{1} *dah*^{2} *kah*^{2} *nohy*^{4} *tyehng*^{2} *nhŭng*^{1} *tohy*^{1} *lie*^{6} *khohngm*^{1} *theech*^{2}
That tailor's shop is well known indeed, yet I don't like it.

- **Giùm**: When a verb is followed by the particle **giùm**, together they mean "to help to do (something)." Its usage is also roughly similar to saying "please" in an imperative sentence.

(9) a. **Mẹ vá giùm con cái áo sơ-mi này.**
me^6 *va*^{2} *yoom*^{5} *kahn*^{1} *kie*^{2} *ahw*^{2} *shuh*^{1} *mee*^{1} *năy*^{5}
Mom, please mend this shirt for me.

b. **Mua giùm tôi một cái cà-vạt xanh nhé.**
moouh^1 *yoom*^{5} *tohy*^{1} *moht*^{6} *kie*^{2} *ka*^{5} *vat*^{6} *sănh*^{1} *nhe*^{2}
Please buy a blue tie for me.

c. **Tuần trước cô ấy đan giùm chúng tôi mấy cái khăn quàng.**
twun^{5} trŭuhk^{2} koh^{1} ay^{2} dan^{1} yoom^{5} choongm^{2} tohy^{1} may^{2} kie^{2} khăn^{1} kwang^{5}
She helped knit a couple of scarfs for us last week.

C. Sentence-final particles

- **À**: Following a person's name or term of address, this particle helps to attract their attention:

(10) a. **Hồng à, chị đã đem cái váy đi sửa chưa?**
hohngm^{5} a^{5} // chee^{6} da^{3} dem^{1} kie^{2} văy^{2} dee^{1} shŭuh^{4} chŭuh^{1}
Hey Hong, have you taken the skirt to have it altered?

b. **Mẹ à, con vừa sấy quần áo xong rồi.**
me^{6} a^{5} // kahn^{1} vŭuh^{5} shay^{2} kwun^{5} ahw^{2} sahngm^{1} rohy^{5}
Mom, I've just dried the clothes.

À is also used as a tag, turning a statement into a question:

(11) a. **Hôm nay tiệm giày đang có nhiều món bán hạ giá à?**
hohm^{1} năy^{1} tyehm^{6} yăy^{5} dang^{1} kah^{2} nhyehw^{5} mahn^{2} ban^{2} ha^{6} ya^{2} a^{5}
The shoe shop has some sales today, doesn't it?

b. **Chị không mua gì cả à?**
chee^{6} khohng^{1} moouh^{1} yee^{5} ka^{4} a^{5}
You didn't buy anything, did you?

- **Ạ**: When used toward a superior, **ạ** adds a touch of respect to a sentence:

(12) a. **Cái áo choàng này của ông, phải không ạ?**
kie^{2} ahw^{2} chwang^{5} năy^{5} koouh^{4} ohngm^{1} // fie^{4} khohngm^{1} a^{6}
This coat is yours, isn't it?

b. **Loại áo len đó không bán hạ giá đâu ạ.**
lwie^{6} ahw^{2} len^{1} dah^{2} khohngm^{1} ban^{2} ha^{6} ya^{2} dohw^{1} a^{6}
The sweaters with those designs are not on sale.

This particle can also be used when speaking to an equal (to show politeness) or to an inferior or younger person (to show affection). In this usage, **ạ** usually comes after a name or term of address:

(13) a. **Tôi không thích loại vải này, cô ạ.**
tohy^{1} khohngm^{1} theech^{2} lwie^{6} vie^{4} năy^{5} koh^{1} a^{6}
(*To a female salesperson*) I don't like this kind of fabric.

b. **Bà mặc cái áo dài này rất vừa, cháu ạ.**
ba^{5} măk^{6} kie^{2} ahw^{1} yie^{5} năy^{5} rut^{2} vŭuh^{5} chăw^{2} a^{6}
(*To a granddaughter*) This dress fits me perfectly.

- **Nhé**: This particle is used frequently in several northern dialects. Its southern counterpart is **nghe**. It adds a friendly tone to an imperative sentence.

(14) a. **Em vào bên trong mặc thử cái** áo **khoác này** <u>**nhé**</u>**.**
em[1] vahw[5] behn[1] trahngm[1] măk[6] thŭ[4] kie[2] ahw[2] khwak[2] năy[5] nhe[2]
Come on back and try this jacket on, okay?

b. **Chị nhớ mua giùm em một đôi găng tay** <u>**nghe**</u>**!**
chee[6] nhuh[2] moouh[1] yoom[5] em[1] moht[6] dohy[1] găng[1] tăy[1] nge[1]
Please remember to buy me a pair of gloves.

- **Vậy**: To "tone down" a question, speakers add this particle at the end. Its northern counterpart is **thế**.

(15) a. **Cái áo thun vàng giá bao nhiêu** <u>**vậy**</u>**?**
kie[2] ahw[2] thoon[1] vang[5] ya[2] bahw[1] nhyehw[1] vay[6]
How much does the yellow T-shirt cost?

b. **Tại sao đôi giày bốt này đắt** <u>**thế**</u>**?**
tie[6] shahw[1] dohy[1] yăy[5] boht[2] năy[5] dăt[2] theh[2]
Why are these boots so expensive?

- **Chứ**: A sentence sounds emphatic with this particle at the end:

(16) a. *Question*: **Anh không thích cái quần soọc này sao?**
ănh[1] khohngm[1] theech[2] kie[2] kwun[5] shok[6] năy[5] shahw[1]
Don't you like these shorts?

Answer: **Tôi thích** <u>**chứ**</u>**!**
tohy[1] theech[2] chŭ[2]
I do like them!

b. *Speaker A*: **Tôi thấy màu vải này không đẹp.**
tohy[1] thay[2] măw[5] vie[4] năy[5] khohngm[1] dep[6]
I don't find this color fabric pretty.

Speaker B: **Tôi thấy nó đẹp** <u>**chứ**</u>**!**
tohy[1] thay[2] nah[2] dep[6] chŭ[2]
I do find it pretty!

- **Nhỉ/Há**: The first particle is common in northern dialects and the second in southern dialects. They appear at the end of a comment or remark, roughly equivalent to the English "huh":

(17) a. **Đôi guốc này lạ** <u>**nhỉ**</u>**!**
dohy[1] gwohk[2] năy[5] la[6] nhee[4]
These clogs look interesting, huh.

b. **Thương xá này có nhiều tiệm sang quá** <u>**há**</u>**!**
thŭuhng[1] sa[2] năy[5] kah[2] nhyehw[5] tyehm[6] shang[1] kwa[2] ha[2]
This shopping mall has so many elegant stores, huh.

Ông đang tìm mua món gì vậy?
What are you looking to pick up?

Tôi đang kiếm một cái áo khoác mới.
I'm on the hunt for a new jacket.

Ở chỗ áo khoác đằng kia có nhiều loại đẹp lắm.
There are some great options over by the outerwear section.

Tôi đang để mắt đến cái áo khoác màu đen kia kìa
I'm eyeing that black jacket over there.

Tôi đang định mua vài cái quần jeans mới.
I'm thinking of grabbing some new jeans.

Tôi cũng cần thêm một ít sơ-mi.
I also need a few more shirts.

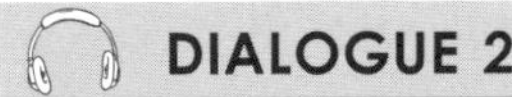

DIALOGUE 2

Thịnh runs into Hoàng in a men's store. They are discussing a few things they wanted to get.

THỊNH **Ủa, hôm nay ông cũng đi sắm đồ ở đây há? Ông đang tìm mua món gì vậy?**
oouh^4 // hohm^1 năy^1 ohngm^1 koongm^4 dee^1 shăm^2 doh^5 uh^4 day^1 ha^2 // ohngm^1 dang^1 teem^5 moouh^1 mahn^2 yee^5 vay^6
Ah, are you shopping here today too? What are you looking to pick up?

HOÀNG **Chào ông! Tôi đang kiếm một cái áo khoác mới. Cái nào mỏng mỏng và hợp thời trang nữa.**
chahw^5 ognm^1 // tohy^1 dang^1 kyehm^2 moht^6 kie^2 ahw^2 khwak^2 muhy^2 // kie^2 nahw^5 mahngm^4 mahngm^4 va^5 huhp^6 thuhy^5 trang^1 nŭuh^3
Hey dude, I'm on the hunt for a new jacket. Something lightweight and stylish.

THỊNH **Ừ, ở chỗ áo khoác đằng kia có nhiều loại đẹp lắm. Ông có thấy cái nào ông thích không?**
ŭ^5 // uh^4 choh^3 ahw^2 khwak^2 dăng^5 keeuh^1 kah^2 nhyehw^5 lwie^6 dep^6 lăm^2 // ohngm^1 kah^2 thay^2 kie^2 nahw^5 ohngm^1 theech^2 khohngm^1
There are some great options over by the outerwear section. Have you seen anything you like?

HOÀNG **Có, tôi đang để mắt đến cái áo khoác màu đen kia kìa. Trông nó rất sang và chắc sẽ hợp với mấy cái quần tôi đang có. Còn ông muốn mua cái gì đây?**
kah^2 // tohy^1 dang^1 deh^4 măt^2 dehn^2 kie^2 ahw^2 khwak^2 măw^5 den^1 keeuh^1 keeuh^5 // trohngm^1 nah^2 rut^2 shang^1 va^5 chăk^2 she^3 huhp^6 vuhy^2 may^2 kie^2 kwun^5 tohy^1 dang^1 kah^2 // kahn^2 ohngm^1 mwohn^2 moouh^1 kie^2 yee^5 day^1
Yeah, I'm eyeing that black jacket over there. It looks pretty slick and will likely go well with the pants I'm getting. And you, what did you want to get?

THỊNH **À, tôi đang định mua vài cái quần jeans mới. Mấy cái tôi có đã khá sờn cả rồi. Ông thấy cái quần màu xanh đậm này được không?**
a^5 // tohy^1 dang^1 deenh^6 moouh^1 vie^5 kie^2 kwun^5 jeans muhy^2 // may^2 kie^2 tohy^1 kah^2 da^3 kha^2 shuhn^5 ka^4 rohy^5 // ohngm^1 thay^2 kie^2 kwun^5 măw^5 sănh^1 dum^{66} năy^5 dŭuhk^6 khohngm^1
Oh, I'm thinking of grabbing some new jeans. Mine are getting a bit worn out. How do you like this dark blue pair?

HOÀNG **Ừ, tôi thấy nó đẹp đó! Loại ống rộng này bây giờ đang rất hợp thời.**
ŭ^5 // tohy^1 thay^2 nah^2 dep^6 dah^2 // lwie^6 ognm^2 rohngm^6 bay^1 yuh^5 dang^1 rut^2 huhp^6 thuhy^5
Well, I think they're nice. This flared style is very much in.

THỊNH **Chắc tôi cũng cần thêm một ít sơ-mi. Áo bây giờ cũng không còn bó sát người như trước nữa, đúng không?**
chăk^2 tohy^1 koongm^3 kun^5 thehm^1 moht^6 eet^2 shuh^1 mee^1 // ahw^2 bay^1 yuh^5 koongm^3 khohngm^1 kahn^5 bah^2 shat^2 ngŭuhy^5 nhŭ^1 trŭuhk^2 nŭuh^3 // doongm^2 khohngm^1
I also need a few more shirts. Nowadays they're not tight-fitting like before, are they?

HOÀNG **Đúng vậy. Nhiều lúc chạy theo thời trang cũng mệt lắm! Mua quần kiểu mới thì lại cần có áo kiểu mới, rồi đến giày hay nịt cũng phải kiểu mới luôn!**
doongm² vay⁶ // nhyehw⁵ lookp² chăy⁶ thew¹ thuy trang¹ koongm³ meht⁶ lăm² // moouh¹ kwun⁵ kyehw⁴ muhy² thee⁵ lie⁶ kun⁵ kah² ahw² kyehw⁴ muhy² // rohy⁵ dehn² yăy⁵ hăy¹ neet⁶ koongm³ fie⁴ kyehw⁴ muhy² lwohn¹
Yeah. It's so tiring to keep up with fashion! Getting a new pair of stylish pants calls for a new stylish shirt, and then your shoes and belt will have to be the new style, too.

THỊNH **Nhưng ăn mặc lỗi thời thì lại chẳng có cô nào nhìn đến, cũng khổ lắm, ông ạ.**
nhŭng¹ ăn¹ măk⁶ lohy⁴ thuhy⁵ thee⁵ lie⁶ chăng⁴ kah² koh¹ nahw⁵ nheen⁵ dehn² // koongm³ khoh⁴ lăm²
Yet if you dress out of style, no lady will look at you twice, which is sad!

HOÀNG **Ông nói phải. Thôi thì chúng ta cứ sắm sửa một ít, vì không phải ngày nào chúng ta cũng đối đãi tử tế với chính mình như thế này được đâu!**
ohngm¹ nahy² fie⁴ // thohy¹ thee⁵ choongm² ta¹ kŭ² shăm² shŭuh⁴ moht⁶ eet² // vee⁵ khohngm¹ fie⁴ ngăy⁵ nahw⁵ choongm² ta¹ koongm³ dohy² die³ tŭ⁴ teh² vuhy² cheenh² meenh⁵ nhŭ¹ theh² năy⁵ dŭuhk⁶ dohw¹
Touché. Well, let's just get a few things, since it's not every day that we can treat ourselves like this.

KEY VOCABULARY 2

kiếm *v*	to look for	**một ít** *adj*	some
áo khoác *n*	jacket	**bó sát người** *adj*	tight-fitting
mỏng *adj*	thin	**nhiều lúc** *adv*	many a time
hợp thời trang *adj*	fashionable	**chạy theo** *v*	to keep up with
để mắt *v*	to eye	**thời trang** *n*	fashion
sang *adj*	classy; slick	**kiểu** *n*	design; model
chắc *adj*	maybe; sure	**nịt** *n*	belt
hợp *adj*	suitable, matching	**luôn** *adv*	at the same time
khá *adj & adv*	good; fairly	**ăn mặc** *v*	to dress (in general)
sờn *adj*	worn	**như thế này** *expr*	like this
cả *adj*	all	**khổ** *adj*	suffering
đậm *adj*	dark (color)	**sắm sửa** *v*	to shop (in general)
ống rộng *adj*	flared (pants)	**đối đãi** *v*	to treat
hợp thời *adj*	trendy	**chính mình** *pron*	oneself

IDIOMATIC EXPRESSIONS 2

mỏng mỏng A descriptive adjective or adverb said twice is "full reduplication," in which its meaning is diminished. Thus, **mỏng** means "thin," while **mỏng mỏng** means "kind of thin." Some other examples include **vàng vàng** "yellowish," **nhẹ nhẹ** "gently." The reduplication process can be partial, with the reduplicative word having a different tone: **mong mỏng**, or sharing only one or two similar sound segments with the main word: **mỏng manh** "fragile." When an onomatopoeic adjective is reduplicated, however, the effect is augmented: **ầm ầm** "roaring," **đùng đùng** "rumbling," **ào ào** "noisy."

CULTURE NOTES 2

When friends talk, they can use several pronouns for informal address. Two male friends can use **ông** for "you," and **tôi** for "I" or "me." Two female friends can use **bà** for "you," and also use **tôi** for "I" or "me." In many regions of central and south Vietnam, the very informal and colloquial form **tui** is used instead of **tôi**. In the north, one hears **cậu** for "you" and **tớ** for "I" or "me," regardless of whether the friends are male or female. The most casual forms, used only among very close friends, are **mày** "you" and **tao** "I/me"; in other contexts these terms can sound extremely rude or disrespectful.

GRAMMAR NOTES 2

II. Interjections

Interjections in Vietnamese are generally divided into two main categories: *vocative* (to call someone or to respond to a call) and *emotive* (to express emotion or reaction). Below are the most common interjections useful for beginners:

A. Vocative interjections

- **Ơi**: Follows a name or a term of address to get someone's attention.

(18) a. **Cô Hoa ơi!**
koh^{1} hwa^{1} uhy^{1}
Hey Miss Hoa!

b. **Mẹ ơi!**
me^{6} uhy^{1}
Hey Mom!

If the person being called is nowhere in sight, the vocative **à** is added for a stronger effect:

c. **cô Hoa ơi, cô Hoa à!**
koh^{1} hwa^{1} uhy^{1} // koh^{1} hwa^{1} a^{5}

- **Này**: Also used for getting attention, **này** can be used alone or followed by a term of address:

(19) a. **Này, đằng kia có một tiệm bán kính mắt rất sang trọng đó!**
nǎy^{5} // dǎng^{5} keeuh^{1} kah^{2} mot^{6} tyehm^{5} ban^{2} keenh^{2} mat^{82} rut^{2} trahngm^{6} dah^{2}
Hey, there's a very elegant eyewear store over there.

b. **Này cháu, gần đây có chỗ nào sửa quần áo không?**
năy^5 chăw^2 // gun^5 day^1 kah^2 choh^3 nahw^5 shŭuh^4 kwun^5 ahw^2 khohngm^1
Hey young man, is there an alteration shop nearby?

- **Dạ**: Besides being a particle of respect as introduced earlier in this chapter, **dạ** is also used to respond when called by someone (said with a rising intonation):

(20) *Speaker A*: **Con ơi!**
kahn^1 uhy^1
Hey child!

Speaker B: **Dạ?**
ya^6
Yes?

The saying **Gọi dạ, bảo vâng** means "When someone calls you, say '**dạ**,' and when you are told to do something, say '**vâng**.'" This is shown in the example below, with **vâng** serving as an interjection showing obedience (**vâng** is also a verb meaning "to obey").

(21) *Speaker A*: **Hưng ơi!**
hŭng^1 uhy^1
Hey Hung!

Speaker B: **Dạ?**
ya^6
Yes?

Speaker A: **Nhớ lấy đồ giặt ủi nhé!**
nhuh^2 lay^2 doh^5 yăt^6 ooy^4 nhe^2
Remember to pick up the clothes at the dry cleaners.

Speaker B: **Vâng.**
vung^1
Yes.

In the Central and South regions of Vietnam, however, speakers would answer with **dạ** in both cases.

B. Emotive interjections

- **A**: Used when you see a friend unexpectedly or when you are able to remember something:

(22) a. **A! Lâu ngày không gặp cô há.**
a^1 // lohw^1 ngăy^5 khohng^1 găp^6 koh^1 ha^2
Ah, I haven't seen you for a long time.

b. **A! Tôi nhớ ra rồi!**
a^1 // tohy^1 nhuh^2 ra^1 rohy^5
Ah, I remember it now!

- **Á**: Expresses pain or shock.

(23) a. **Á! Có cái gì đâm vào tay tôi!**
a^2 // kie^2 yee^5 dum^1 vahw^5 tăy^1 tohy^1
Ouch! Something just poked my hand.

b. **Á! Chuyện gì lạ vậy?**
a^2 // chwyehn^6 yee^5 la^6 vay^6
What (on earth) happened?

- **À**: Used when changing the subject or adding a comment or afterthought:

(24) a. **À! Anh đã đặt mua cái quần tây trên mạng chưa?**
a^{5} // ănh^{1} da^{3} dăt^{6} moouh^{1} kie^{2} kwun^{5} tay^{1} trehn^{1} mang^{6} chŭuh^{1}
So, have you ordered the pants online yet?

b. **À! Cô đừng quên cái áo len trên xô-pha nhé.**
a^{5} // koh^{1} dŭng^{5} kwehn^{1} kie^{2} ahw^{2} len^{1} trehn^{1} soh^{1} fa^{1} nhe^{2}
Oh, and don't forget your sweater on the sofa.

- **Chà**: Expresses that you find something beautiful, cute, special, etc.

(25) a. **Chà! Chiếc nhẫn này đẹp thật!**
cha^{5} // chyehk^{2} nhun^{3} năy^{5} dep^{6} thut^{6}
Aw! This ring is really cute!

b. **Chà! Hôm nay anh diện bảnh lắm!**
cha^{5} // hohm^{1} năy^{1} ănh^{1} yehn^{6} bănh^{4} lăm^{2}
Wow! You're dressed so sharp today!

- **Hở**: Expresses confusion or bewilderment:

(26) a. **Hở? Cô nói sao?**
huh^{4} // koh^{1} nahy^{2} shahw^{1}
Huh? What did you say?

b. **Hở? Cái đồng hồ này mà chỉ có một trăm ngàn thôi à?**
huh^{4} // kie^{2} dohngm^{5} hoh^{5} năy^{5} ma^{5} chee^{4} kah^{2} moht^{6} trăm^{1} ngan^{5} thohy^{1} a^{5}
Wait, what? This watch only costs one hundred thousand (dong)?

- **Thôi**: Originally a verb meaning "to stop," but also serves as an interjection:

(27) a. **Thôi! Đừng mua thêm món gì nữa!**
thohy^{1} // dŭng^{5} moouh^{1} thehm^{1} mahn^{2} yee^{5} nŭuh^{3}
Whoa, don't buy anything anymore!

b. **Thôi, giở nón ra đi!**
thohy^{1} // yuh^{4} nahn^{2} ra^{1} dee^{1}
Hey, take off your hat.

- **Ủa**: Expresses surprise:

(28) a. **Ủa, sao cô không mặc áo len?**
oohuh^{4} // shahw^{1} koh^{1} khohngm^{1} măk^{6} ahw^{2} len^{1}
Gee, why aren't you wearing a sweater?

b. **Ủa, cái sơ-mi trắng của tôi đâu rồi?**
oouh^{4} // kie^{2} shuh^{1} mee^{1} trăng^{2} koouh^{4} tohy^{1} dohw^{1} rohy^{5}
Oh, where's my white shirt?

READING

CHIẾC ÁO DÀI VIỆT NAM

Nếu người Nhật có chiếc *kimono*, người Đại Hàn có chiếc *hanbok*, người Hoa có chiếc *xường xám* hay người Cam Bốt có chiếc *sampot*, thì người Việt cũng hãnh diện có chiếc *áo dài* nổi tiếng trên thế giới.

Tiền thân của chiếc áo dài ngày nay là áo ngũ thân (trong thế kỷ XIX), là loại áo có hai tà sau, hai tà trước, cùng một tà nhỏ nằm bên dưới. Vào khoảng thập niên 1930, chiếc áo dài đã được cải tiến, chỉ còn hai tà chính, phía trước và phía sau, mặc với quần xa-tanh hay lụa.

Không chỉ dành cho phụ nữ, áo dài cũng được đàn ông và trẻ em mặc, nhất là trong các dịp lễ lạt hay hội hè. Phụ nữ thường mặc áo dài với nón lá, còn đàn ông mặc với khăn đóng trong các ngày lễ truyền thống.

Chiếc áo dài là niềm cảm hứng không bao giờ cạn đối với thơ văn, ca nhạc, hội hoạ, nhiếp ảnh hay điện ảnh. Các cuộc thi "hoa hậu áo dài" vẫn thường được tổ chức ở khắp ba miền đất nước cũng như trong các cộng đồng người Việt ở hải ngoại.

chyehk^2 ahw^2 yie^5 vyeht^6 nam^1

nehw^2 ngŭuhy^5 nhut^6 kah^2 chyehk^2 kee^1 moh^1 noh^1 // ngŭuhy^5 die^6 han^5 kah^2 chyehk^2 han^1 bok^2 // ngŭuhy^5 hwa^1 kah^2 chyehk^2 suhng^5 sam^2 // ngŭuhy^5 kam^1 boht^2 kah^2 chyehk^2 sam^1 pot^2 // thee^5 ngŭuhy^5 vyeht^6 koongm^4 hănh^3 yehn^6 kah^2 chyehk^2 ahw^2 yie^5 nohy^4 tyehng^2 trehn^1 theh^2 yuhy^2

tyehn^5 thun^1 koouh^4 chyehk^2 ahw^2 yie^5 ngăy^5 năy^1 la^5 ahw^2 ngoo^3 thun^1 trahngm^1 theh^2 kee^4 hie^1 mŭuhy^1 // la^5 lwie^6 ahw^2 kah^2 hie^1 ta^5 shăw^1 // hie^1 ta^5 trŭuhk^2 // koongm^5 moht^6 tas^5 nhah^4 năm^5 behn^1 yŭuhy^2 // vahw^5 khwang^4 thup^6 nyehn^1 moht^6 ngan^5 cheen^2 trăm^1 ba^1 mŭuhy^1 // chyehk^2 ahw^2 yie^5 da^3 dŭuhk^6 kie^4 tyehn^2 // chee^4 kahn^5 hie^1 ta^5 cheenh^2 // feeuh^2 trŭuhk^2 va^5 feeuh^2 shăw^1 // măk^6 vuhy^2 kwun^5 sa^1 tănh^1 hăy^1 loouh^6

khohngm^1 chee^4 yănh^5 chah^1 foo^6 nŭ^3 // ahw^1 yie^5 koong^3 dŭuhk^6 dan^5 ohngm^1 va^5 tre^4 em^1 măk^6 // nhut^2 la^5 trahngm^1 kak^2 yeep^6 leh^3 lat^6 hohy^6 he^5 // foo^6 nŭ^3 thŭuhng^5 măk^6 ahw^2 yie^5 vuhy^2 nahn^2 la^2 // kahn^5 dan^5 ohngm^1 măk^6 vuhy^2 khăn^1 dahngm^2 trahngm^1 kak^2 ngăy^5 leh^3 trwyehn^5 thohgnm^2

chyehk^2 ahw^2 yie^5 la^5 nyehm^5 kam^4 hŭng^2 khohngm^1 bahw^1 yuh^5 kan^6 dohy^2 vuhy^2 thuh^1 văn^1 // ka^1 nhak^6 // hohy^6 hwa^6 // nhyehp^2 ănh^4 hăy^1 dyehn^6 ănh^4 // kak^2 kwohk^6 thee^1 hwa^1 hohw^6 ahw^2 yie^5 vun^3 thŭuhng^5 dŭuhk^6 toh^4 chŭk^2 uh^4 khăp^2 ba^1 myehn^5 dut^2 nŭuhk^2 koongm^3 nhŭ^1 trahngm^1 kak^2 kohngm^6 dohngm^5 ngŭuhy^5 vyeht^6 hie^4 ngwie^6

VIETNAMESE TRADITIONAL DRESS

If Japanese have the *kimono*, Koreans have the *hanbok*, Chinese have the *cheongsam* and Cambodians have the *sampot*, the Vietnamese are also proud to have the world-famous *ao dai*.

The predecessor of today's *ao dai* was the five-panel dress (in the 19th century), a version with two back flaps, two front flaps, and a small flap underneath. Around the 1930s, the *ao dai* was redesigned to have only two main flaps, front and back, worn with satin or silk pants.

Not just for women, the *ao dai* is also worn by men and children, especially during holidays or festivals. Women often wear the *ao dai* with conical hats, while men wear it with turbans during traditional holidays.

The *ao dai* is an endless inspiration for poetry, songs, paintings, photography and cinema. "Miss Ao Dai" contests are held frequently throughout the three regions of the country as well as in overseas Vietnamese communities.

COMPREHENSION QUESTIONS

Answer the following questions in complete sentences, first orally, then in writing.

1. **"Áo dài" nghĩa đen là gì?** *What does "ao dai" literally mean?*

   ____

2. **Thoạt đầu, chiếc áo dài có mấy tà?** *At first, how many flaps did the ao dai have?*

   ____

3. **Áo dài được cải tiến vào năm nào?** *In what year was the ao dai redesigned?*

   ____

4. **Ngoài phụ nữ ra, những ai khác thường mặc áo dài?** *Besides women, who else wears the ao dai?*

   ____

5. **Chiếc áo dài gợi cảm hứng cho những ngành nghệ thuật nào?** *To which kinds of art does the ao dai provide inspiration?*

   ____

PRACTICE

A. Listening comprehension 

The following is a radio commercial. Listen to the recording and circle the correct answer to each of the questions below:

1. **Đợt hạ giá là dành cho mặt hàng nào?** *What kind of merchandise is the sales event for?*
   a. **đồ gia dụng** – *home appliances*
   b. **y phục** – *clothing*
   c. **đồ điện tử** – *electronics*
   d. **trái cây** – *fruit*

2. **Đợt hạ giá diễn ra trong mùa nào?** *In which season will the event take place?*
   a. **mùa xuân** – *spring*
   b. **mùa hè** – *summer*
   c. **mùa thu** – *fall*
   d. **mùa đông** – *winter*

3. **Tiệm bán hạ giá tên là gì?** *What is the name of the boutique having the sales event?*
   a. **Thời Trang** 12
   b. **Thời Trang** 21
   c. **Thời Trang** 24
   d. **Thời Trang** 20

4. **Mặt hàng nào KHÔNG được nhắc đến trong phần quảng cáo?** *What kind of merchandise is NOT mentioned in the commercial?*
   a. **áo khoác** – *jackets*
   b. **áo len** – *sweaters*
   c. **giày bốt** – *boots*
   d. **áo choàng** – *coats*

5. **Giá hạ được bao nhiêu phần trăm?** *What is the discount offered in the sale?*
   a. 20%
   b. 30%
   c. 40%
   d. 50%

6. **Đợt hạ giá kéo dài trong bao lâu?** How long does the sale last?
   a. **một tuần** – *one week*
   b. **hai tuần** – *two weeks*
   c. **ba tuần** – *three weeks*
   d. **bốn tuần** – *four weeks*

B. Particles

Write sentences in Vietnamese based on the English prompt in parentheses, adding a particle as suggested. Do not use a particle more than once.

1. (*Tell your mom that you don't need to wear a sweater* – Use a sentence-initial respectful particle)

   ____

2. (*Ask a salesclerk if this red dress is not on sale* – Use a sentence-final "tag" particle)

   ____

3. (*Ask a seamstress to alter your new skirt* – Use a sentence-medial particle meaning "help")

   ____

4. (*Tell a female customer that the shop doesn't have a large size for those pants* – Use a sentence-initial respectful particle)

   ____

5. (*Say that this fabric is durable* – Use a sentence-final particle for emphasis)

____

6. (*Tell a child that you like her hat a lot* – Use a sentence-final particle of endearment)

____

C. Interjections

Fill in the blanks with an interjection as suggested in parentheses.

1. ____________! **Cái đồng hồ này trông sang quá!** (*admiration*)
   This watch looks so elegant!

2. **Cô** ____________! **Ở đây có bán vớ len không, cô?** (*vocative*)
   Miss, do you carry woolen socks here?

3. ____________! **Sao anh không đeo cà-vạt?** (*surprise*)
   Why aren't you wearing a tie?

4. ____________! **Tuần sau thương xá này có nhiều tiệm bán hạ giá lắm.** (*change of topic*)
   Next week many stores in this mall will have a sale.

5. ____________! **Tôi có nhiều áo sơ-mi rồi.** (*refusal*)
   I already have so many shirts.

6. ____________? **Đôi giày này mà giá hai triệu à?** (*bewilderment*)
   Do these shoes really cost two million (dong)?

D. Vocabulary

There are several verbs in Vietnamese meaning "to wear," depending on the type of clothing, object or accessory. Put the nouns provided in the correct column for the corresponding verbs. Refer to the Functional Vocabulary section for help with the vocabulary.

Nouns	**áo đầm** "dress" – **nước hoa** "perfume" – **quần tây** "pants" – **râu** "beard" – **nịt** "belt" – **hoa tai** "earrings" – **nhẫn** "ring" – **khăn quàng** "scarf" – **dây chuyền** "necklace" – **vớ** "socks" – **tóc dài** "long hair" – **vòng đeo tay** "bracelet" – **nón** "hat" – **giày** "shoes" – **áo khoác** "jacket" – **găng tay** "gloves" – **đồng hồ** "watch" – **khăn đóng** "turban" – **kính** "glasses" – **kem chống nắng** "sunscreen"					
Verbs	**mặc**	**mang**	**đeo**	**để**	**bôi**	**đội**

 **PROVERB**

ĂN LẤY CHẮC, MẶC LẤY BỀN.

ăn^{1} lay^{2} chăk^{2} măk^{6} lay^{2} behn^{5}

"Choose filling foods to eat and durable fabrics to wear."

This proverb reflects the mentality of low- and middle-income people in Vietnam, where more than half of the population make their living in agriculture, forestry or fishing. During the century when Vietnam was a French colony, people used to quote the famous French playwright Molière: "You should eat to live, not live to eat." For many, the purpose of clothing is also to keep warm rather than to be vain, although another expression suggests a different view: **ăn ngon, mặc đẹp** "eating well and dressing nice."

FUNCTIONAL VOCABULARY

DANH TỪ

áo	top (*garment*)
áo sơ-mi	shirt, blouse
áo len	sweater
áo khoác	jacket
áo choàng	coat
áo đầm	dress
áo dài	Vietnamese dress
áo thun	t-shirt
áo lót	undershirt
quần tây	pants
quần soọc	shorts
quần lót	briefs; panties
nón	hat
mũ	cap
kính	eyeglasses
nịt	belt
đồng hồ	watch; clock
nhẫn	ring
vòng đeo tay	bracelet
hoa tai	earrings
khăn quàng	scarf
giày	shoe
giày bốt	boot
dép	flip-flop
guốc	clog
vớ	sock
dây chuyền	necklace
thương xá	shopping mall

TÍNH TỪ

rẻ	inexpensive; cheap
đắt/mắc	expensive
rộng	wide; loose
chật	narrow; tight
vừa	fitting
dài	long
ngắn	short
dày	thick
bền	durable
tạm thời	temporary

ĐỘNG TỪ

mặc	to wear (*clothing*)
mang	to wear (*scarfs, footwear*)
đội	to wear (*headwear*)
đeo	to wear (*jewelry*)
để	to wear (*hair, beard*)
bôi	to wear (*perfume, lotion*)
trả giá	to haggle
hạ giá	to discount
mua sắm	to shop
ăn mặc	to dress (*in general*)
mặc thử	to try on

TRẠNG TỪ

đằng kia	over there
nhiều lúc	many a time
luôn	at the same time
vừa phải	moderately
thật	really, truly
khá	fairly

Anh có đọc một số bài điểm phim.
I've read some reviews about this movie.
Em rất thích hai tài tử chí trong cuốn phim này.
I like the two leading act very much.
Phim này đã đoạt giải Cành Cọ Vàng tại Đại Hội Điện Ảnh Cannes năm nay.
This movie won the Golden Palm at this year's Cannes Film Festival.
PALME D'OR
FESTIVAL DE CANNES
Anh lại muốn phim được chuyển âm ra tiếng Việt.
But I prefer movies dubbed in Vietnamese.
Em thích xem phim nói tiếng Pháp có phụ đề tiếng Anh.
I like to watch movies in French with English subtitles.
Anh mong là chúng ta sẽ không thất vọng về cuốn phim này.
I hope we won't be disappointed about this one.

CHAPTER 13

Entertainment and the Arts

Giải Trí Và Nghệ Thuật

DIALOGUE 1

Nhân and his girlfriend Hạnh are in a movie theater, waiting to see a movie that everyone is talking about.

HẠNH **Chắc anh đã nghe nhiều người nói về cuốn phim ly kỳ này lắm rồi, phải không? Em nghĩ là mình sẽ rất thích.**
chăk^{2} ănh^{1} da^{3} nge^{1} nhyehw^{5} ngŭuhy^{5} nahy^{2} veh^{5} kwohn^{2} feem^{1} lee^{1} kee^{5} năy^{5} lăm^{2} rohy^{5} // fie^{4} khohngm^{1} // em^{1} ngee^{3} la^{5} meenh^{5} she^{3} rut^{2} theech^{2}
You must have heard so many people talk about this thriller, right? I think we'll like it a lot.

NHÂN **Ừ, anh có đọc một số bài điểm phim. Họ khen nó lắm, nhưng chúng ta phải xem mới biết thực hư ra sao. Anh thấy hào hứng lắm!**
ŭ^{5} // ănh^{1} kah^{2} dahkp^{6} moht^{6} shoh^{2} bie^{5} dyehm^{4} feem^{1} // hah^{5} khen^{1} nah^{2} lăm^{2} // nhŭng^{1} choongm^{2} ta^{1} fie^{4} sem^{1} muhy^{2} byeht^{2} thŭk^{6} hŭ^{1} ra^{1} shahw^{1} // ănh^{1} thay^{2} hahw^{5} hŭng^{2} lăm^{2}
Yeah, I've read some movie reviews. Everyone says it's amazing, but we'll have to see it for ourselves to know the truth. I'm really excited!

HẠNH **Em cũng vậy. Lâu rồi mình không đi xem phim với nhau. Em rất thích hai tài tử chính trong cuốn phim này.**
em^{1} koongm^{3} vay^{6} // lohw^{1} rohy^{5} meenh^{5} khohngm^{1} dee^{1} sem^{1} feem^{1} vuhy^{2} nhăw^{1} // em^{1} rut^{2} theech^{2} hie^{1} tie^{5} tŭ^{4} cheenh^{2} trahngm^{1} kwohn^{2} feem^{1} năy^{5}
Me too. It's been a while since we've been to the movies together. I like the two leading actors in this movie a lot.

NHÂN **Còn anh thì hết sức ngưỡng mộ ông đạo diễn. Phim này đã đoạt giải Cành Cọ Vàng tại Đại Hội Điện Ảnh Cannes năm nay đó em!**
kahn^{5} ănh^{1} thee^{5} heht^{2} shŭk^{2} ngŭuhng^{3} moh^{6} ohngm^{1} dahw^{6} yehn^{3} // feem^{1} năy^{5} da^{3} dwat^{6} yie^{4} kănh^{5} kah^{6} vang^{5} tie^{6} die^{6} hohy^{6} dyehn^{6} ănh^{4} kan^{1} năm^{1} năy^{1} dah^{2} em^{1}
Personally, I really admire the director. This movie won the Golden Palm at this year's Cannes Film Festival, you know.

HẠNH **Em thích xem phim nói tiếng Pháp có phụ đề tiếng Anh để có thể học thêm cả hai thứ tiếng như phim này.**
em^1 theech^2 sem^1 feem^2 nahy^2 tyehng^2 fap^2 kah^2 foo^6 deh^5 tyehng^2 ănh^1 deh^4 kah^2 theh^4 hahkp^6 thehm^1 ka^4 hie^1 thŭ^2 tyehng^2 nhŭ^1 feem^1 năy^5
I like to watch movies in French with English subtitles like this one, so I can practice both languages.

NHÂN **Anh lại muốn phim được chuyển âm ra tiếng Việt cho dễ hiểu.**
ănh^1 lie^6 mwohn^2 feem^1 dŭuhk^6 chwyehn^4 um^1 ra^1 tyehng^2 vyeht^6 chah^1 yeh^3 hyehw^4
But I wish it was dubbed in Vietnamese so it was easy to understand.

HẠNH **Như vậy thì làm sao mình có thể biết rõ được các diễn viên có diễn tả trọn vẹn vai trò của họ hay không?**
nhŭ^1 vay^6 thee^5 lam^5 shahw^1 meenh^5 kah^2 theh^4 byeht^2 rah^4 dŭuhk^6 kak^2 yehn^3 vyehn^1 kah^2 yehn^3 ta^4 trahn^6 ven^6 vie^1 trah^5 koouh^4 hah^6 hăy^1 khohngm^1
Then how would we know for sure if the actors were playing their roles well?

NHÂN **Em có lý! Dù sao đi nữa thì anh cũng mong là chúng ta sẽ không thất vọng về cuốn phim này.**
em^1 kah^2 lee^2 // yo^5 shahw^1 dee^1 nŭuh^3 thee^5 ănh^1 koongm^3 mahngm^1 la^5 choongm^2 ta^1 she^3 khohngm^1 thut^2 vahngm^6 beh^5 kwohn^2 feem^1 năy^5
You're right. Anyway, I hope we won't be disappointed by this movie.

KEY VOCABULARY 1

phim *n*	film, movie	**đoạt giải** *v*	to win an award
bài điểm phim *n*	movie review	**đại hội điện ảnh** *n*	film festival
khen *v*	to praise	**phụ đề** *n*	subtitles
hào hứng *adj*	excited	**chuyển âm** *v*	to dub (*a language*)
đi xem phim *v*	to go to the movies	**diễn viên** *n*	actor
tài tử *n*	movie actor	**diễn tả** *v*	to interpret
chính *adj*	main	**trọn vẹn** *adv*	completely
phim ly kỳ *n*	thriller	**vai trò** *n*	role
hết sức *adv*	extremely	**dù sao đi nữa** *expr*	at any rate
ngưỡng mộ *v*	to admire	**thất vọng** *adj*	disappointed
đạo diễn *n*	movie director	**như vậy thì** *adj*	then, so

IDIOMATIC EXPRESSIONS 1

biết thực hư ra sao "To know whether something is real or unreal." This idiom is used when you want to check something out for yourself. **Thực** is used in compound words like **thực tế** "reality," **thực hiện** "to realize," and **thực chất** "essence." **Hư** appears in **hư không** "nil" and **hư cấu** "fictional." The adjective "surreal" is best translated into Vietnamese as **nửa thực nửa hư** ("partly real, partly unreal).

có lý "Logical, reasonable." **Vô lý** is "illogical, unreasonable," **phi lý** is "absurd," and **hợp lý** is "rational, justifiable." **Lý lẽ** is "reason, logic." The expression **hợp tình hợp lý** means "reasonably and satisfactorily."

CULTURE NOTES 1

For "actor" or "actress," two words can be used: **diễn viên** is more versatile, for it can refer to both a movie actor or a stage actor. **Tài tử**, on the other hand, mostly refers to movie actors or actresses and also appears with the noun **điện ảnh** "cinema" in the compound **tài tử điện ảnh**. To specify gender, you can say **nam tài tử** or **nam diễn viên** for actors and **nữ tài tử** or **nữ diễn viên** for actresses. The verb **diễn xuất** means "to act" or "to perform."

GRAMMAR NOTES 1

I. "Được" and "bị"

These two words have different grammatical functions and, consequently, different meanings. Both can serve as *auxiliary verbs* in passive sentences, which will be discussed in Grammar Notes 2 of this chapter. Other functions and meanings of these words include:

A. "Được" and "bị" as "linking verbs," equivalent to "to be"

As linking verbs, **được** and **bị** work like **là** or **thì** when used with adjectives, but with a touch of nuance. **Được** goes with adjectives deemed "favorable" and **bị**, with adjectives considered "unfavorable."

(1) a. **Chúc ông bà luôn được hạnh phúc và khoẻ mạnh.**
chookp^{2} ohng^{1} ba^{5} lwohn^{1} dŭuhk^{6} hănh^{6} kookp^{2} va^{5} khwe^{4} mănh^{6}
(I) wish you to be always happy and healthy.

b. **Ông nội tôi đang bị bệnh nặng.**
ohngm^{1} nohy^{6} tohy^{1} dang^{1} bee^{6} behnh^{6} năng^{6}
My grandfather is gravely ill.

B. "Được" and "bị" as particles

The sense of "favorability" and "unfavorability" in these words also holds when they serve as particles preceding a verb.

(2) a. **Tuần sau tôi được đi nghe hoà nhạc.**
twun^{5} shăw^{1} tohy^{1} dŭuhk^{6} dee^{1} nge^{1} hwa^{5} nhak^{6}
Next week I get to go to a concert.

b. **Cô ấy bị xem vở kịch đó nhiều lần rồi.**
koh^{1} ay^{2} bee^{6} sem^{1} vuh^{4} keech^{6} dah^{2} nhyehw^{5} lun^{5} rohy^{5}
She had to see that play several times.

Được also expresses *permission* when preceding a verb and *ability* when following it:

(3) a. **Đạo diễn nói các diễn viên được nghỉ hai tiếng để ăn trưa.**
dahw^{6} *yehn*^{3} *nahy*^{2} *kak*^{2} *yehn*^{3} *vyehn*^{1} *dŭuhk*^{6} *ngee*^{4} *hie*^{1} *tyehng*^{2} *deh*^{4} *ăn*^{1} *trŭuh*^{1}
The director said that actors are allowed to take a two-hour lunch break.

b. **Chị có hiểu được hết phụ đề bằng tiếng Anh của phim này không?**
chee^{6} *kah*^{2} *hyehw*^{4} *dŭuhk*^{6} *heht*^{2} *foo*^{6} *deh*^{5} *băng*^{5} *tyehng*^{2} *ănh*^{1} *koouh*^{4} *feem*^{1} *năy*^{5} *khohngm*^{1}
Are you able to understand all the English captions in this movie?

C. "Được" as an interjection

When said alone in response to a request for permission or simply to show consent, **được** is equivalent to "okay."

(4) a. *Speaker A*: **Tối nay con đi xi-nê nhé, mẹ?**
tohy^{2} *năy*^{1} *kahn*^{1} *dee*^{1} *see*^{1} *neh*^{1} *nhe*^{2} *me*^{6}
May I go to the movies tonight, Mom?

Speaker B: **Được, con ạ.**
dŭuhk^{6} *kahn*^{1} *a*^{6}
Okay, dear.

b. *Speaker A*: **Cho tôi mượn cái đĩa hát này nhé?**
chah^{1} *tohy*^{1} *mŭuhn*^{6} *kie*^{2} *deeuh*^{3} *hat*^{2} *năy*^{5} *nhe*^{2}
May I borrow this record?

Speaker B: **Được.**
dŭuhk^{5}.
Okay.

Tác phẩm của họ không khác gì một cuộc đối thoại giữa sáng tạo và kỹ thuật.
Their works is truly a dialogue between creativity and technique.

DIALOGUE 2

Khoa, a college professor, and his wife Trang, a fashion designer, are at a painting, photography and sculpture exhibit.

KHOA **Em thấy bức tượng này ra sao? Điêu khắc gia đã nắm bắt được điệu bộ của nhân vật một cách hết sức tài tình!**
em^{1} thay^{2} bŭk^{2} tŭuhng^{6} năy^{5} ra^{1} shahw^{1} // dyehw^{1} khăk^{2} ya^{1} da^{3} năm^{2} băt^{2} dŭuhk^{6} dyehw^{6} boh^{6} koouh^{4} nhun^{1} vut^{6} moht^{6} kăch^{2} heht^{2} shŭk^{2} tie^{5} teenh^{5}
What do you think about this statue here? The sculptor has captured the character's gesture so skillfully!

TRANG **Tuyệt thật đó, anh! Cách sử dụng kết cấu và hình dạng của nghệ sĩ này gây nhiều cảm hứng lắm!**
twyeht^{6} thut^{6} dah^{2} ănh^{1} // kăch^{2} shŭ^{4} yoongm^{6} keht^{2} kohw^{2} va^{5} heenh^{5} yang^{6} koouh^{4} ngeh^{6} shee^{3} năy^{5} gay^{1} nhyehw^{5} kam^{4} hŭng^{2} lăm^{2}
It's wonderful indeed! The way the artist uses texture and form is so inspiring!

KHOA **Rõ ràng là nghệ thuật có thể gợi ra nhiều cảm xúc và suy nghĩ. Em có để ý đến màu sắc của bức tranh bên trái không? Màu của nó dường như cũng thay đổi theo ánh sáng vậy.**
rah^{4} rang^{5} la^{5} ngeh^{6} thwut^{6} kah^{2} theh^{4} guhy^{6} ra^{1} nhyehw^{5} kam^{4} sookp^{2} va^{5} shwee^{1} ngee^{3} // em^{1} kah^{2} deh^{4} ee^{2} dehn^{2} măw^{5} shăk^{2} koouh^{4} bŭk^{2} trănh^{1} behn^{1} trie^{2} khohng^{1} // ma^{8}w^{5} koouh^{4} nah^{2} yŭuhng^{5} nhŭ^{1} koongm^{3} thăy^{1} dohy^{4} thew^{1} ănh^{2} shang^{2} vay^{6}
Art can truly evoke so many emotions and thoughts. Did you notice the colors in the painting on the left? They seem to change along with the light.

TRANG **Có, anh ạ. Nó làm em nghĩ đến những loại vải em thường dùng, cũng có thể đổi màu theo độ sáng tối khác nhau.**
kah^{2} ănh^{1} a^{6} // nah^{2} lam^{5} em^{1} ngee^{3} dehn^{2} nhŭng^{3} lwie^{6} vie^{4} em^{1} thŭuhng^{5} yoongm^{5} // koong^{3} kah^{2} theh^{4} dohy^{4} măw^{5} thew^{1} doh^{6} shang^{2} tohy^{2} khak^{2} nhăw^{1}
Yes, I saw that too. It reminds me of the fabrics I usually work with, which also can transform under different lighting.

KHOA **Anh rất thích nghe em nói đã tìm thấy cảm hứng như thế nào từ nghệ thuật. Bây giờ chúng ta qua xem khu triển lãm nhiếp ảnh nhé.**
ănh^{1} ryt^{2} theech^{2} nge^{1} em^{1} nahy^{2} da^{3} teem^{5} thay^{2} kam^{4} hŭng^{2} nhŭ^{1} theh^{2} nahw^{5} tŭ^{5} ngeh^{6} thwut^{6} // bay^{1} yuh^{5} choongm^{2} ta^{1} kwa^{1} sem^{1} khoo^{1} tryehn^{4} lam^{3} nhyehp^{2} ănh^{4} nhe^{2}
I love hearing how you draw inspiration from art. Shall we check out the photography section now?

TRANG **Tất nhiên rồi! Em rất hiếu kỳ muốn biết các nhiếp ảnh gia ghi lại những khoảnh khắc và cảm xúc qua ống kính của họ ra sao.**
tut^{2} nhyehn^{1} rohy^{5} // em^{1} rut^{2} hyehw^{2} kee^{5} mwohn^{2} byeht^{2} kak^{2} nhyehp^{2} ănh^{4} ya^{1} gee^{1} lie^{6} nhŭng^{3} khwănh^{4} khăk^{2} va^{5} kam^{4} sookp^{2} kwa^{1} ohng^{2} keenh^{2} koouh^{4} hah^{6} ra^{1} shahw^{1}
Absolutely! I'm curious to see how the photographers have captured moments and emotions through their lenses.

KHOA **Cái hay của người nghệ sĩ là tác phẩm của họ không khác gì một cuộc đối thoại giữa sáng tạo và kỹ thuật, giống như những gì chúng ta đang theo đuổi trong nghề nghiệp của mình vậy.**
kie^{2} hăy^{1} koouh^{4} ngŭuhy^{5} ngeh^{6} shee^{3} la^{5} tak^{2} fum^{4} koouh^{4} hah^{6} khohng^{1} khak^{2} yee^{5} moht^{6} kwohk^{6} dohy^{2} thwie^{6} yŭuh^{3} shang^{2} tahw^{6} va^{5} kee^{3} thwut^{6} // yohng^{2} nhŭ^{1} nhŭng^{3} yee^{5} choong^{2} ta^{1} dang^{1} thew^{1} dwohy^{4} trahngm^{1} ngheh^{5} ngyehp^{6} koouh^{4} meenh^{5} vay^{6}
One thing I love about artists is that their work is a dialogue between creativity and technology, just like what we're pursuing in our own professions.

KEY VOCABULARY 2

bức *cl*	(*for photo, painting, statue*)	**tranh** *n*	painting
điêu khắc gia *n*	sculptor	**theo** *prep*	according to
nắm bắt *v*	to capture	**độ** *n*	degree; level
điệu bộ *n*	gesture	**tìm thấy** *v*	to find
nhân vật *n*	character	**khu** *n*	zone, section
tài tình *adj*	skillful	**triển lãm** *v*	exhibition
tuyệt (vời) *adj*	wonderful	**nhiếp ảnh** *n*	photography
cách *n*	way, manner	**tất nhiên rồi** *adv*	of course!
sử dụng *v*	to utilize	**hiếu kỳ** *adj*	curious
kết cấu *n*	structure	**nhiếp ảnh gia** *n*	photographer
hình dạng *n*	form	**ghi lại** *v*	to record
nghệ sĩ *n*	artist	**khoảnh khắc** *n*	moment
gây *v*	to cause	**ống kính** *n*	lens
cảm hứng *n*	inspiration	**qua** *prep*	through
rõ ràng *adj/adv*	clear(ly)	**tác phẩm** *n*	works
nghệ thuật *n*	arts	**không khác gì** *expr*	not all that different
gợi *v*	to evoke	**đối thoại** *n*	dialogue
cảm xúc *n*	emotion	**sáng tạo** *n*	creativity
suy nghĩ *n*	thought	**kỹ thuật** *n*	technology
để ý *v*	to pay attention	**giống như** *adj*	similar to
màu sắc *n*	color (in general)	**theo đuổi** *v*	to pursue
tượng *n*	statue	**nghề nghiệp** *n*	career

IDIOMATIC EXPRESSIONS 2

Tuyệt thật đó! **Thật** means "really, indeed," and **đó** is a colloquial particle used with comments. You can replace **tuyệt** "wonderful" with other descriptive adjectives when talking expressively about something: **Hay thật đó!** "It's interesting indeed!" **Lạ thật đó!** "It's unusual indeed!" **Vui thật đó!** "It's really fun!"

Tất nhiên rồi! **Rồi** means "already." However, when it comes at the end of expressions containing an adjective or adverb, **rồi** functions as a particle and simply emphasizes the words it accompanies. Some other similar expressions include **Chắc chắn rồi!** "Sure/Certainly!" **Nhất định rồi!** "Absolutely!" **Dĩ nhiên rồi!** "Naturally!" **Đúng rồi!** "Correct!"

CULTURE NOTES 2

A majority of vocabulary that is considered "standard" in Vietnamese belongs to the northern dialects since originally the country extended only to what is now most of northern Vietnam. For example, the term for "photo/picture" is **ảnh** (northern), as opposed to **hình** (central and southern), with the former considered the standard term. "To take a picture" is **chụp ảnh** in the northern regions and **chụp hình** in the central and southern regions. **Hình**, meanwhile, also means "shape," as in **hình vuông** "square (shape)," **hình tròn** "round shape/circle," and **hình chữ nhật** "rectangle." With this meaning, **hình** is the standard term in all dialects. When used together as a compound noun, **hình ảnh** means "image" or "illustration," as in **Cuốn sách này có nhiều hình ảnh đẹp** "This book has many beautiful illustrations." In this case there is no distinction between dialects; the word is used nationwide.

GRAMMAR NOTES 2

II. Passive sentences

Passive sentences in Vietnamese are expressed with two constructions, neither of which is similar to English passive sentences. Pay attention to word order in the passive sentences in the following examples.

The first passive construction is the most common, expressing the idea that the subject of the sentence receives or is affected by the action done by someone or caused by something (the "agent" of action). The auxiliary verb **được** is used when the main verb expresses a "favorable" action, or simply an action without any nuance, while its counterpart **bị** appears before a verb expressing an "unfavorable" action.

The formula of this passive construction is: [subject + **được/bị** + agent complement + main verb].

(5) a. *Active sentence*: **Khán giả khen ngợi cuốn phim đầu tay của Lê Sơn.**
khan^{2} ya^{4} khen^{1} nguhy^{6} kwohn^{2} feem^{1} dohw^{5} tăy^{1} koouh^{4} leh^{1} shuhn^{1}
Viewers have praised Le Son's directorial debut.

b. *Passive sentence*: **Cuốn phim đầu tay của Lê Sơn <u>được</u> khán giả khen ngợi.**
kwohn^{2} feem^{1} dohw^{5} tăy^{1} koouh^{4} leh^{1} shun^{1} dŭuhk^{6} khan^{2} ya^{4} khen^{1} nguhy^{6}
Le Son's directorial debut was praised by viewers.

c. *Active sentence*: **Nhiều nhà phê bình chê bức tranh này.**
nhyehw^{5} nha^{5} feh^{1} beenh^{5} cheh^{1} bŭk^{2} trănh^{1} năy^{5}
Many critics have criticized this painting.

d. *Passive sentence*: **Bức tranh này <u>bị</u> nhiều nhà phê bình chê.**
bŭk² trănh¹ năy⁵ bee⁶ nhyehw⁵ nha⁵ feh¹ beenh⁵ cheh¹
This painting has been criticized by many critics.

When an action implies a sense of achievement, result or consequence, another passive construction is usually preferred, in which the auxiliary verb is **là** and the preposition **do** "by" follows it.

The formula of this passive construction is: [subject + **là do** + agent complement + main verb].

(6) a. *Active sentence*: **Một điêu khắc gia người Việt đã nặn bức tượng đó.**
moht⁶ dyehw¹ khăc² ya¹ ngŭuhy⁵ vyeht⁶ da³ năn⁶ bŭk² tŭuhn⁶ dah²
A Vietnamese sculptor created that statue.

b. *Passive sentence*: **Bức tượng đó là do một điêu khắc gia người Việt nặn.**
bŭk² tŭuhng⁶ dah² la⁵ yah¹ moht⁶ dyehw¹ khăc² ya¹ ngŭuhy⁵ vyeht⁶ năn⁶
That statue was created by a Vietnamese sculptor.

c. *Active sentence*: **Một tổ chức bất vụ lợi thành lập viện bảo tàng thành phố.**
moht⁶ toh⁴ chŭk² but² voo⁶ luhy⁶ thănh⁵ lup⁶ vyehn⁶ bahw⁴ tang⁵ thănh⁵ foh²
A non-profit organization established the municipal museum.

d. *Passive sentence*: **Viện bảo tàng thành phố là do một tổ chức bất vụ lợi thành lập.**
vyehn⁶ bahw⁴ tang⁵ thănh⁵ foh² la⁵ yah¹ moht⁶ toh⁴ chŭk² but² voo⁶ lohy⁶ thănh⁵ lup⁶
The municipal museum was established by a non-profit organization.

READING

SÂN KHẤU CẢI LƯƠNG

Miền Bắc có nghệ thuật hát chèo (có nghĩa là "trào phúng"), miền Trung có hát bội (có nghĩa là "điệu bộ"), còn ở miền Nam, nghệ thuật sân khấu phổ biến nhất là cải lương. Đây là một hình thức ca kịch dựa vào nghệ thuật đờn ca tài tử và dân ca của miền đồng bằng sông Cửu Long. Động từ "cải lương" có nghĩa là "sửa đổi cho tốt đẹp hơn".

Cải lương ra đời vào khoảng đầu thế kỷ thứ XX. Tuy có phần chịu ảnh hưởng của hát chèo và hát bội, cải lương mới lạ và lôi cuốn hơn hai bộ môn nghệ thuật kia. Đó là nhờ cải lương đã thêm âm nhạc vào các tuồng hát, đồng thời phân chia một vở tuồng thành nhiều màn và cảnh như trong các vở ca nhạc kịch của người Pháp trong thời kỳ thuộc địa.

Trong khi hát chèo và hát bội không lan truyền vào miền Nam, cải lương lại được giới thiệu rộng rãi ở miền Trung và miền Bắc. Gần đây, cải lương có phần yếu thế trước sự phổ biến của truyền hình và điện ảnh. Tuy vậy, các nhà biên kịch, đạo diễn và diễn viên cải lương luôn nổ lực để bảo tồn một nghệ thuật truyền thống độc đáo của miền Nam nói riêng và Việt Nam nói chung.

shun¹ khohw² kie⁴ lŭuhng¹

myehn⁵ băk² kah² ngeh⁶ thwut⁶ hat²² chew⁵ // kah² ngeeuh⁵ la⁵ trahw⁵ foongm² // myehn⁵ troongm¹ kah² hat²² bohy⁶ // kah² ngeeuh³ la⁵ dyehw⁶ boh⁶ // kahn⁵ uh⁴ myehn⁵ nam¹ ngeh⁶ hwut⁶ shun¹ khohw² foh⁴ byehn² nhut² la⁵ kie⁴ lŭuhng¹ // day¹ la⁵ moht⁶ heenh⁵ thŭk² ka¹ keech⁶ yŭuh⁶ vahw⁵ ngeh⁶ thwut⁶ duhn⁵

ka^1 tie^5 tŭ^4 va^5 yun^1 ka^1 koouh^4 myehn^5 dohng^5 băng^5 shohngm^1 kŭw^4 lahngm^1 // dohngm^6 tŭ^5 kie^4 lŭuhng^1 kah^2 ngeeuh^3 la^5 shŭuh^4 dohy^4 chah^1 toht^2 dep^6 huhn^1

kie^5 lŭuhng^1 ra^1 duhy^5 vahw^5 khwang^4 dohw^5 theh^2 kee^4 thŭ^2 hie^1 mŭuhy^1 // twee^1 kah^2 fun^5 cheew^6 ănh^4 hŭuhng^4 koouh^4 hat^{2}chew^5 va^5 hat^2 bohy^6 // kie^4 lŭuhng^1 muhy^2 la^6 va^5 lohy^1 kwohn^2 huhn^1 hie^1 boh^5 mohn^1 ngeh^6 thwut^6 keeuh^1 // dah^2 la^5 nhuh^5 kie^4 lŭuhng^1 da^3 thehm^1 um^1 nhak^6 vahw^5 kak^2 twohng^5 hat^2 // dohng^5 thuhy^5 fun^1 cheeuh^1 moht^6 vuh^4 twohng^5 thănh^5 nhyehw^5 man^5 va^5 kănh^4 nhŭ^1 trahngm^1 kak^2 vuh^4 nhak^6 keech^6 koouh^4 ngŭuhy^5 fap^2 trahngm^1 thuhy^5 kee^5 thwohk^6 deeuh^6

trahngm^1 khh^1 hat^2 chew^5 va^5 hat^2 bohy^6 khognm^1 lan^1 trwyehn^5 vahw^5 myehn^5 nam^1 //kie^4 lŭuhng^1 lie^6 dŭuhk^5 yuhy^2 thyehw^6 rohngm^6 rie^3 uh^4 myehn^5 troongm^1 va^5 myehn^5 băk^2 // gun^5 day^1 kie^4 lŭuhng^1 kah^2 fun^5 yehw^2 theh^2 trŭuhk^2 shŭ^6 foh^4 byehn^2 koouh^4 trwyehn^5 heenh^5 va^5 dyehn^6 ănh^4 // twee^1 vay^6 kak^2 nha^5 byehn^1 keech^6 dahw^6 yehn^3 va^5 yehn^3 vyehn^1 kie^4 lŭuhng^1 lwohn^1 noh^4 lŭk^6 deh^4 bahw^4 tohn^5 moht^5 ngeh^6 thwut^6 trwyehn^5 thohng^2 dohkp^6 dahw^2 koouh^4 myehn^5 nam^1 nahy^2 ryehng^1 va^5 vyeht^6 nam^1 nahy^2 choongm^1

REFORMED THEATER

The North has Chèo theater ("satirical theater"), the Central region has Bội theater ("gesture theater"), and in the South, the most popular performing art is Cải Lương. This is a form of theater based on the folk music and songs of the Mekong Delta. The verb "**cải lương**" means "to change for the better."

Cải Lương was born around the beginning of the twentieth century. Although somewhat influenced by Chèo theater and Bội theater, Cải Lương was novel and more appealing than the other two forms. That's because Cải Lương added music to its shows, which were divided into many acts and scenes like the French musicals of the colonial period.

While Chèo and Bội theater did not spread to the south, Cải Lương was widely introduced in the central and northern regions. Recently, Cải Lương has struggled to compete with television and cinema. However, Cải Lương writers, directors and actors strive to preserve this unique traditional art of the south in particular and Vietnam in general.

COMPREHENSION QUESTIONS

Answer the following questions in complete sentences, first orally, then in writing.

1. **Kể ra ba hình thức sân khấu chính ở Việt Nam.** *Name the three main forms of theater in Vietnam.*

   ____

2. **Tên gọi "cải lương" có nghĩa là gì?** *What does the name "***cải lương***" mean?*

   ____

3. **Hai yếu tố mới nào đã được thêm vào các tuồng cải lương?** *Which two new elements were added to reformed theater?*

   ____

4. **Tại sao cải lương được xem là phổ biến nhất trong các hình thức sân khấu?** *Why is reformed theater considered the most popular of all the theater forms?*

   ____

5. **Nguyên nhân cải lương trở nên yếu thế trong thời gian gần đây là gì?** *Why has reformed theater become disadvantaged lately?*

   ____

PRACTICE

A. Listening comprehension

Listen to the TV commercial and choose the correct answers to the questions below:

1. **Tiết mục quảng cáo là về:** *The commercial is for:*
   a. **một cuốn phim** – *a movie*
   b. **một chương trình truyền hình** – *a television show*
   c. **một vở kịch** – *a play*
   d. **một vở cải lương** – *a reformed theater show*

2. **Đây là một tác phẩm của nhóm nào?** *Whose production is this?*
   a. **Đất Việt**
   b. **Nước Việt**
   c. **Quốc Việt**
   d. **Tiếng Việt**

3. **Chủ đề của tác phẩm là gì?** *What is the theme of the production?*
   a. **văn hoá** – *culture*
   b. **lịch sử** – *history*
   c. **nghệ thuật** – *arts*
   d. **tình cảm** – *romance*

4. **Giặc Nguyên từ đâu đến?** *Where did the Nguyen invaders come from?*
   a. **phương Đông** – *the east*
   b. **phương Tây** – *the west*
   c. **phương Nam** – *the south*
   d. **phương Bắc** – *the north*

5. **Nguyễn Nam là ai?** *Who is Nguyen Nam?*
   a. **diễn viên** – *actor*
   b. **nhà viết kịch** – *playwright*
   c. **đạo diễn** – *director*
   d. **nhà văn** – *writer*

6. **Có thể mua vé bằng cách nào?** *How are tickets purchased?*
   a. **qua mạng** – *online*
   b. **tại cửa** – *at the door*
   c. **tại Thư Viện Thành Phố** – *at the City Library*
   d. (a) and (b)

B. ĐƯỢC and BỊ

Translate the following sentences, adding **được** or **bị** in the correct position as suggested:

1. I watched a very bad horror movie last week. (**bị**)

____

2. He won't play the piano tonight because he's got a cold. (**bị**)

____

3. Are you able to understand the dialogues in that play? (**được**)

____

4. Mom, may I turn on the TV now? (**được**)

____

5. The art exhibition was successful thanks to those well-known artists. (**được**)

____

C. Passive sentences

Change the active sentences below into passive form.

1. *Active sentence:* **Chúng tôi đã quay cuốn phim này trong ba tháng.** *We filmed this movie in three months.* (Use the **được** construction).

   Passive sentence: _______________________________

2. *Active sentence:* **Nhà văn Trần Việt viết vở kịch "Giữ Vững Sơn Hà".** *Novelist Trần Việt wrote the play Safeguarding Our Fatherland.* (Use the **là do** construction)

   Passive sentence: _______________________________

3. *Active sentence:* **Ai đóng vai người mẹ trong bộ phim truyền hình đó?** *Who played the mother in that TV series?* (Use the **là do** construction)

   Passive sentence: _______________________________

4. *Active sentence:* **Hoạ sĩ miêu tả cảnh hoàng hôn thật sâu lắng.** The artist depicted the sunset scene quite profoundly. (Use the **được** construction)

   Passive sentence: _______________________________

5. *Active sentence:* **Bóng tối làm mờ đi nhiều nét trên khuôn mặt cô trong bức ảnh này.** *Shadows blur many traits of your face in this photo.* (Use the **bị** construction)

   Passive sentence: _______________________________

D. Vocabulary

Fill in the blanks in the following sentences in Vietnamese with the correct words in the list provided below:

đạo diễn giải điêu khắc gia đóng phim
diễn tuồng nhiếp ảnh gia điện ảnh khán giả

1. **Người ta dùng chữ "màn ảnh nhỏ" để nói về vô tuyến truyền hình và "màn ảnh lớn" để nói về ________________.** *The term "small screen" is used to refer to television and the term "big screen," to ________________.*
2. **"Tài tử" là người ________________ chứ không đóng kịch.** *An "actor" performs in a movie and not in a ________________.*
3. **Hoạ sĩ vẽ tranh, còn ________________ thì nặn tượng.** *An artist paints, while a ________________ creates statues.*
4. ________________ **là những người xem một tác phẩm nghệ thuật.** ________________ *are people who watch or look at a work of art.*
5. **Người chụp hình chuyên nghiệp gọi là ________________.** *A person who takes photos professionally is called ________________.*
6. ________________ **là người làm một kịch bản trở nên sống động qua một cuốn phim hay một vở kịch.** ________________ *is a person who brings a script to life as a movie or a play.*
7. ________________ **cải lương đòi hỏi cả diễn xuất lẫn giọng hát.** ________________ *in reformed theater requires both acting and singing.*
8. **Bức ảnh này đã đoạt ________________ nhất trong cuộc thi nhiếp ảnh toàn quốc.** *This photo won the Grand ________________ in the national photography competition.*

PROVERB

ĂN CƠM CHÚA, MÚA TỐI NGÀY.

ăn^{1} kuhm^{1} choouh^{2} moouh^{2} tohy^{2} ngăy^{5}

"Those who are fed by a lord must dance for him day and night."

This proverb reflects a historical period in Vietnam when kings and lords ruled. The term **chúa** "lord" was common between the early 17th century and the late 18th century, when the country—then called **Đại Việt**—was divided into **Đàng Ngoài** "the Outer Region," (present-day northern Vietnam), controlled by the **Chúa Trịnh**, and **Đàng Trong** "the Inner Region," (present-day central and southern Vietnam), ruled by the **Chúa Nguyễn**. War raged between the two powers for almost a century before the country was finally reunited following the loss of **Chúa Nguyễn's** forces.

Similar to the English saying "Do as you are paid to do," with a touch of sarcasm added by the image of "dancing," this proverb hints at things that you reluctantly do simply because you are forced to do them to make a living.

 FUNCTIONAL VOCABULARY

DANH TỪ

phim	movie, film
tài tử	movie actor
diễn viên	actor (*movie or play*)
đạo diễn	director
phim ly kỳ	thriller
phim kinh dị	horror movie
phim tình cảm	romantic movie
phim hành động	action movie
phim hài hước	comedy movie
phim thời sự	documentary
điện ảnh	cinema
rạp chiếu phim	movie theater
rạp hát	theater (*building*)
màn ảnh	screen
sân khấu	stage; theater (*art*)
kịch	play
hội hoạ	painting (*art*)
điêu khắc	sculpture
nhiếp ảnh	photography
tranh	painting (*artwork*)
tượng	statue
hình/ảnh	photo
giải (thưởng)	award, prize
khán giả	audience
đại hội	festival

TÍNH TỪ

hào hứng	excited
thất vọng	disappointed
tài tình	talented, skillful
tuyệt vời	wonderful
rõ ràng	clear; obvious
hiếu kỳ	curious
hay	good, interesting
dở	bad, awful
hấp dẫn	exciting

ĐỘNG TỪ

quay phim	to film
đóng phim	to act (*in a movie*)
đóng vai	to play (*a role*)
đóng kịch	to act (*in a play*)
diễn tuồng	to act (*in an opera*)
đi xem phim	to go to a movie
chụp hình/ảnh	to take a picture
vẽ	to draw, to paint
hát	to sing
múa	to dance (*in general*)
khiêu vũ	to dance (*ballroom*)
đánh đàn	to play a string instrument
thổi kèn	to play a wind instrument
đánh trống	to play the drums
sơn	to cover with paint

TRUYỀN HÌNH VIỆT NAM

Tôi rất hiếu kỳ về các phong tục cưới hỏi ở Việt Nam.
I'm very curious about wedding traditions in Vietnam.

Nghi lễ đầu tiên gọi là "lễ dạm ngõ".
The first ritual is called a "proposal ceremony."

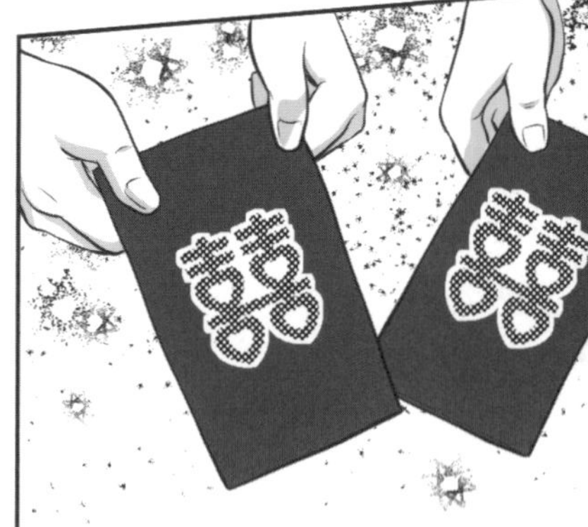

CHAPTER 14

Family and Traditions

Gia Đình Và Truyền Thống

DIALOGUE 1

Megan, a TV journalist, is asking Trúc, a Vietnamese college student, about wedding traditions in Vietnam on a talk show in America.

MEGAN **Chào chị Trúc! Khỏi nói chị cũng biết là tôi rất hiếu kỳ về phong tục cưới hỏi ở Việt Nam.**
chahw^{5} chee^{6} trookp^{2} // khahy^{2} nahy^{2} chee^{6} koongm^{3} byeht^{2} la^{5} tohy rut^{2} hyehw^{2} kee^{5} veh^{5} fahnngm^{1} tookp^{6} kŭuhy^{2} hahy^{4} uh^{4} vyeht^{6} nam^{1}
Hello Trúc! It goes without saying that I'm very curious about wedding traditions in Vietnam.

TRÚC **Chị Megan à, ở nước tôi, việc cưới hỏi có liên quan đến cả hai gia đình chứ không riêng gì đôi trai gái. Nghi lễ đầu tiên gọi là "lễ dạm ngõ", lúc gia đình đàng trai đến nhà gia đình đàng gái để xin phép cho mối quan hệ giữa đôi trai gái được công nhận.**
chee^{6} megan a^{5} // uh^{4} nŭuhk^{2} tohy^{1} // vyehk^{6} kŭuhy^{2} hahy^{4} kah^{2} lyehn^{1} kwan^{1} dehn^{2} ka^{4} hie^{1} ya^{1} deenh^{5} chŭ^{2} khognm^{1} ryehng^{1} yee^{5} dohy^{1} trie^{1} gie^{2} // ngee^{1} leh^{3} dohw^{5} tyehn^{1}gahy^{5} la^{5} leh^{3} yam^{6} ngah^{3} // lookp^{2} ya^{1} deenh^{5} dang^{5} trie^{1} dehn^{2} nha^{5} ya^{1} deenh^{5} dang^{5} gie^{2} deh^{4} seen^{1} fep^{2} chah^{1} mohy^{2} kwan^{1} heh^{6} yŭuh^{3} dohy^{1} trie^{1} gie^{2} dŭuhk^{6} kohngm^{1} nhun^{6}
Hey Megan! In my country, weddings involve both families, rather than just the couple themselves. The first ritual is called a "proposal ceremony," where the man's family comes to the woman's family to ask permission for the couple's relationship to be recognized.

MEGAN **Ừm, chuyện này thì ở nước Mỹ không bao giờ xảy ra! Kế đến là gì nữa hở chị?**
ŭm^{5} chwyehn^{6} năy^{5} thee^{5} uh^{4} nŭuhk^{2} mee^{3} khohngm^{1} bahw^{1} yuh^{5} săy^{4} ra^{1} // keh^{2} dehn^{2} la^{5} yee^{5} nŭuh^{3} huh^{4} chee^{6}
Hmm, that would never happen in America! What's next then?

TRÚC **Nghi lễ kế tiếp là "đám hỏi", lúc nhà trai lại sang nhà gái, lần này mang trầu cau để làm sính lễ, tượng trưng cho sự kết hợp của đôi trai gái, chính thức hỏi cưới người con gái cho con trai của mình.**

ngee^1 leh^3 keh^2 tyehp^2 la^5 dam^2 hhahy^4 // lookp^2 nha^5 trie^1 lie^6 shang^1 nha^5 gie^2 // lun^5 năy^5 mang^1 trohw^5 kahw^1 deh^4 lam^5 sheenh^2 leh^3 // tüuhng^6 trüng^1 chah^1 shü^6 keht^2 huhp^6 koouh^4 dohy^1 trie^1 gie^2 // cheenh^2 thük^2 hahy^4 küuhy^2 ngüuhy^5 kahn^1 gie^2 chah^1 kahn^1 trie^1 koouh^4 meenh^5

The next ritual is an engagement ceremony, when the man's family once again comes to the woman's family, this time bringing betel leaves and areca nuts as offerings that symbolize the union of the couple, formally asking for the woman's hand.

MEGAN **Rồi cuối cùng là đến đám cưới, phải không chị?**

rohy^5 kwohy^2 koongm^5 la^5 dehn^2 dam^2 küuhy^2 // fie^4 khohngm^1 chee^6

Then eventually comes the wedding ceremony, correct?

TRÚC **Phải, và lần nào nhà trai cũng phải sang nhà gái! Nhà trai lại mang sính lễ qua nhà gái để xin "rước dâu", nghĩa là đón cô dâu về nhà chồng. Trong buổi lễ này, cha mẹ đàng gái tặng cô dâu "của hồi môn". Sau đó, chú rể và cô dâu lạy trước bàn thờ gia tiên cùng cha mẹ hai bên để tỏ lòng hiếu kính.**

fie^4 va^5 lun^5 nahw^5 nha^5 trie^1 koongm^4 fie^4 shang^1 nha^5 gie^2 // nha^5 trie^1 lie^6 mang^1 sheenh^2 leh^3 kwa^1 nha^5 gie^2 deh^4 seen^1 rüuhk^2 yohw^1 // ngeeuh^3 la^5 doahn^2 koh^1 yohw^1 veh^5 nha^5 chohngm^5 // trahngm^1 bwohy^4 leh^3 năy^5 // cha^1 me^6 dang^5 gie^2 tăng^6 koh^1 yohw^1 koouh^4 hohy^5 mohn^1 // shăw^1 dah^2 choo^2 reh^4 va^5 koh^1 yohw^1 lăy^6 trüuhk^2 ban^5 thuh^5 ya^1 tyehn^1 koongm^5 cha^1 me^6 hie^1 behn^1 deh^4 tah^4 lahngm^5 hyehw^2 keenh^2

That's right, and every time, the groom's family has to come to the bride's family! They again bring offerings to her house to ask permission to "pick up the bride," or bring her to the groom's house. During this ceremony, the bride's parents give her a dowry. Afterwards, the groom and the bride bow before the family ancestor altar, then before the two sets of parents to show their respect and gratitude.

MEGAN **Còn tiệc cưới thì sao? Có khác với các tiệc cưới ở đây không, chị?**

khạn tyehk^6 küuhy^2 thee^5 shahw^1 // kah^2 khak^2 vuhy^2 kak^2 tyehk^6 küuhy^2 uh^4 day^1 khohngm^1 chee^6

How about the wedding banquet? Is it any different from those over here?

TRÚC **Nói chung thì không khác gì lắm đâu! Chỉ có điều là thân nhân, bạn bè và khách mời thường mừng đôi vợ chồng mới cưới bằng tiền mặt thay vì quà cáp như ở đây.**

nahy^2 choongm^1 thee^5 khohngm^1 khak^2 yee^5 lăm^2 dohw^1 // chee^4 kah^2 dyehw^5 la^5 thun^1 nhun^1 ban^6 be^5 va^5 khăch^2 muhy^5 thüuhng^5 müng^5 dohy^1 vuh^6 chohngm^5 muhy^2 küuhy^2 băng^5 tyehn^5 măt^6 thăy^1 vee^5 kwa^5 kap^2 nhü^1 uh^4 day^1

In general, there's not too much of a difference. The only thing is that relatives, friends and guests customarily give cash to the newlyweds instead of presents.

 KEY VOCABULARY 1

khỏi nói *expr*	it goes without saying	**đón** *v*	to pick up (*a person*)
phong tục *n*	custom	**tặng** *v*	to gift
cưới hỏi *n*	engagement and marriage	**cô dâu** *n*	bride
liên quan tới *adj*	concerning	**chú rể** *n*	groom
đôi trai gái *n*	unmarried couple	**vợ** *n*	wife
nghi lễ *n*	ritual	**chồng** *n*	husband
lễ dạm ngõ *n*	proposal ceremony	**của hồi môn** *n*	dowry
đàng trai *n*	the man's family	**lạy** *v*	to prostrate
đàng gái *n*	the woman's family	**bàn thờ** *n*	altar
xin phép *v*	to ask for permission	**gia tiên** *n*	ancestors
mối quan hệ *n*	relationship	**cha** *n*	father
công nhận *v*	to recognize	**mẹ** *n*	mother
xảy ra *v*	to happen	**tỏ** *v*	to show
đám hỏi *n*	engagement ceremony	**lòng hiếu kính** *n*	respect and gratitude
đám cưới *n*	wedding	**tiệc cưới** *n*	wedding reception
mang *v*	to bring	**nói chung** *expr*	generally speaking
trầu cau	betel leaves and areca nuts	**chỉ có điều là** *expr*	it's just that
sính lễ *n*	offering	**thân nhân** *n*	relatives
tượng trưng cho *v*	to symbolize	**bạn bè** *n*	friends
sự kết hợp *n*	union	**khách mời** *n*	guest
chính thức *adv*	officially	**mừng** *v*	to celebrate; to gift
hỏi cưới *v*	to ask someone's hand for marriage	**mới cưới** *adj*	newlywed
sang *v*	to come over	**tiền mặt** *n*	cash
rước dâu *v*	to pick up the bride	**thay vì** *prep*	instead of
nghĩa là *expr*	that is to say	**quà cáp** *n*	presents

IDIOMATIC EXPRESSIONS 1

Khỏi nói [chị] cũng biết là... "It goes without saying that..." When using this expression, replace the personal pronoun according to the person(s) you are speaking with. **Khỏi nói anh cũng biết là một đám cưới Việt Nam bao gồm rất nhiều tục lệ** "It goes without saying that a Vietnamese wedding consists of many customs."

CULTURE NOTES 1

After marriage, a good number of Vietnamese women live with their husband's family. This living arrangement is called **làm dâu** "to assume the responsibility of a daughter-in-law," which can create conflicts between them and the mother-in-law. Less often, a married man lives with his wife's family, which is termed **gửi rể** "to entrust (the wife's family) with a son-in-law." The concept behind **gửi** implies only a temporary arrangement in comparison to that of the married woman.

GRAMMAR NOTES 1

I. Compound sentences

A compound sentence consists of two independent sentences joined together by a coordinating conjunction. There are two types of coordinating conjunctions: simple conjunctions and correlative conjunctions.

A. Compound sentences with simple coordinating conjunctions
The most common conjunctions of this type include **và/còn** "and" (with **còn** expressing a contrast), **nhưng** "but," **mà** "yet," **hay/hoặc** "or" (with **hoặc** only used in affirmative or negative sentences, not in questions) and **vì vậy** "so."

(1) a. **Anh Trung sẽ bưng quả trầu cau, và anh Hải sẽ bưng quả trái cây.**
ănh^1 troongm^1 she^3 bŭng^1 kwa^4 trohw^5 kăw^1 // va^5 ănh^1 hie^4 she^3 bŭng^1 kwa^4 trie^2 kay^1
Trung will carry a box of betel leaves, and Hải, a box of fruits.

b. **Mâm có hình tròn và phẳng, còn quả là hộp tròn.**
mum^1 kah^2 heenh^5 trahn^5 va^5 făng^4 // kahn^5 kwa^4 la^5 hohp^6 trahn^5
Mâm is a flat, round tray, and **quả** is a round box.

c. **Tôi đã gửi thiệp mời đám cưới cho họ, nhưng chưa thấy họ trả lời.**
tohy^1 da^3 gŭy^4 thyehp^6 muhy^5 dam^2 kŭuhy^2 chah^1 hah^6 // nhŭng^1 chŭuh^1 thay^2 hah^6 tra^4 luhy^5
I have sent them a wedding invitation, but I still haven't gotten a response.

d. **Chúng tôi không hợp tuổi, mà vẫn quyết định cưới nhau.**
choongm^2 tohy^1 khohngm^1 huhp^6 twohy^4 // ma^5 vun^3 kwyeht^2 deenh^6 kŭuhy^2 nhăw^1
Our zodiac signs are not a good match, yet we still decided to get married.

e. **Cô Hoa sẽ đến chọn mua áo cưới ở tiệm hay cô sẽ đặt mua một cái qua mạng.**
koh^1 hwa^1 she^3 dehn^2 chahn^6 moouh^1 ahw^2 kŭuhy^2 uh^4 tyehm^6 // hăy^1 koh^1 she^3 dăt^6 moouh^1 moht^6 kie^2 kwa^2 mang^6
Hoa will go to a shop to pick out a wedding dress, or she will buy one online.

f. **Tháng Tám là tháng bắt đầu mùa cưới, vì vậy chúng tôi định làm đám cưới vào dịp Trung Thu này.**
thang^2 tam^2 la^5 thang^2 băt^2 dohw^5 moouh^5 kŭuhy^2 // vee^5 vay^6 choongm^2 tohy^1 ddenh^5 lam^5 dam^2 kŭuhy^2 vahw^5 yeep^6 troongm^1 thoo^1 năy^5
The eighth month starts the wedding season, so we plan to have our wedding this coming Mid-Autumn holiday.

B. Compound sentences with correlative conjunctions

Conjunctions of this type used in compound sentences include **hoặc là ... hoặc là ...** "either ... or ...," **không ... mà cũng không ...** "neither ... nor ...," **không những ... mà còn ...** "not only ... but also ...," **vừa ... thì cũng ...** "no sooner ... than ..."

(2) a. **Hoặc là anh viết điện thư cho cô ấy, hoặc là em gọi điện thoại cho cô ấy, để mời cô ấy đến dự đám hỏi của chúng ta.**
hwăk6 la5 ănh1 vyeht2 dyehn6 thŭ1 chah1 koh1 ay2 // hwăk5 la5 em1 gahy6 dyehn6 thwie6 chah1 koh1 ay2 // deh4 muhy5 koh1 ay2 dehn2 yŭ6 dam2 hahy4 koouh4 choongm2 ta1
Either you'll email her or I'll call her to invite her to our engagement party.

b. **Ở Việt Nam, người vợ không lấy họ của người chồng, mà người chồng cũng không lấy họ của người vợ.**
uh4 vyeht6 nam1 // ngŭuhy5 vuh6 khohngm1 lay2 hah6 koouh4 ngŭuhy5 chohngm5 // ma5 ngŭuhy5 chohngm5 koong3 khohngm1 lay2 hah6 koouh4 ngŭuhy5 vuh6
In Vietnam, neither does a wife take her husband's last name, nor does the husband take his wife's name.

c. **Văn hóa cũ của Việt Nam đòi hỏi không những người con dâu lo cho chồng mà còn phải săn sóc cả cha mẹ chồng.**
văn1 hwa2 koo3 koouh4 vyeht6 nam1 dahy5 hahy4 khohngm1 nhŭng3 ngŭuhy5 kahn1 yohw1 lah1 chah1 chohngm5 ma5 kahn5 fie4 shăn1 shahkp2 ka4 cha1 me6 chohngm5
In the past, Vietnamese culture expected not only that a daughter-in-law attend to her husband but also that she take care of her parents-in-law.

d. **Nhà trai vừa đến trước ngõ của nhà gái thì một tràng pháo cũng nổ vang chào mừng mọi người.**
nha5 tri1 vŭuh5 dehn2 trŭuhk2 ngah3 koouh4 nha5 gie2 thee5 moht6 trang5 fahw2 koongm3 noh4 vang1 chahw5 mŭng5 mahy6 ngŭuhy5
No sooner had the groom's family arrived at the gate of the bride's house than a round of firecrakers exploded to welcome them.

"Tết Nguyên Đán", có nghĩa là "buổi sáng sớm đầu năm". "Tết Nguyên Đán" means "New Year's early morning."

Gia đình nào cũng dọn dẹp nhà cửa sạch sẽ. Every family cleans their home thoroughly.

Chúng tôi làm bánh chưng và bánh tét. We make sticky rice cakes in square or cylindrical shapes.

Chúng tôi trang hoàng phòng khách với nhiều loại hoa. We decorate our living room with colorful flowers.

DIALOGUE 2

Jimmy, a podcaster, is talking to Tâm, a young Vietnamese engineer, about the Vietnamese Lunar New Year.

JIMMY **Chào anh Tâm! Trong chương trình hôm nay, mời anh kể một vài đặc điểm của Tết Âm Lịch ở Việt Nam cho thính giả của tôi nghe nhé.**
chahw^{5} ănh^{1} tum^{1} // trahngm^{1} chŭuhng^{1} treenh^{5} hohm^{1} năy^{1} // muhy^{5} ănh^{1} keh^{4} moht^{6} vie^{5} dăk^{6} dyehm^{4} kooh^{4} teht^{2} um^{1} leech^{6} uh^{4} vyeht^{6} nam^{1} chah^{1} theenh^{2} ya^{4} koouh^{4} tohy^{1} nge^{2} nhe^{2}
Hello Tâm! In today's program, please tell my listeners about some of the special features of the Vietnamese Lunar New Year.

TÂM **Dạ, ngày lễ quan trọng nhất này của chúng tôi có tên chính thức là "Tết Nguyên Đán", có nghĩa là "buổi sáng sớm đầu năm", nhằm vào tháng Giêng, tháng đầu tiên theo lịch mặt trăng, thường là vào tháng Hai của dương lịch.**
ya^{6} ngăy^{5} leh^{3} kwan^{1} trahngm^{6} nhut^{2} năy^{5} koouh^{4} choongm^{2} tohy^{1} kah^{2} tehn^{1} cheenh^{2} thŭk^{2} la^{5} teht^{2} ngwyehn^{1} dan^{2} // kah^{2} ngeeuh^{3} la^{5} bwohy^{4} shang^{2} shuhm^{2} dohw^{5} năm^{1} // nhăm^{5} vahw^{5} thang^{2} yehng^{1} // thang^{2} dohw^{5} tyehn^{1} thew^{1} leech^{6} măt^{6} trăng^{1} // thŭuhng^{5} la^{5} vahw^{5} thang^{2} hie^{1} yŭuhng^{1} leech^{6}
Sure, this very important holiday of ours has the official name **Tết Nguyên Đán**, which means "New Year's early morning." It falls on the first month of the lunar calendar, usually during February according to the solar calendar.

JIMMY **Xin anh cho chúng tôi biết một số chi tiết về ngày lễ đặc biệt này.**
seen^{1} ănh^{1} chah^{1} choongm^{2} tohy^{1} byeht^{2} moht^{6} shoh^{2} chee^{1} tyeht^{2} veh^{5} ngăy^{5} leh^{3} dăk^{6} byeht^{6} năy^{5}
Please tell us more about this special holiday.

TÂM **Gia đình nào cũng dọn dẹp nhà cửa sạch sẽ để xua đi những điều không may mắn và làm mâm cơm cúng tổ tiên trong mấy ngày Tết. Chúng tôi sắm quần áo mới, trang hoàng phòng khách với nhiều loại hoa xuân và nấu những món ăn truyền thống.**
ya^{1} deenh^{5} nhaw^{5} koongm^{3} yahn^{6} yep^{6} nha^{5} kŭuh^{4} shăch^{6} she^{3} deh^{4} soouh^{1} dee^{1} nhŭng^{3} dyehw^{1} khohngm^{1} măy^{1} măn^{2} va^{5} lam^{5} mum^{1} kuhm^{1} koongm^{2} toh^{4} tyehn^{1} trahngm^{1} may^{2} ngăy^{5} teht^{2} // choongm^{2} tohy^{1} shăm^{2} kwun^{5} ahw^{2} muhy^{2} // trang^{1} hwang^{5} fahngm^{5} khăch^{2} vuhy^{2} nhyehw^{5} lwie^{6} hwa^{1} swun^{1} va^{5} nohw^{2} nhŭng^{3} mahn^{2} ăn^{1} trwyehn^{5} thohngm^{2}
Every family cleans their home thoroughly to sweep away bad luck, and makes offerings to their ancestors during the New Year holiday. We buy new clothes, decorate our living room with spring flowers and cook traditional foods.

JIMMY **Những món ăn ngày Tết đó là gì ạ?**
nhŭng^{3} mahn^{2} ăn^{1} ngăy^{5} teht^{2} dah^{2} la^{5} yee^{5} a^{6}
What are those Tết foods?

TÂM **Chúng tôi làm bánh chưng, đặc sản của miền Bắc, và bánh tét, món Tết của miền Nam. Tuy khác nhau về hình dạng và hương vị, hai loại bánh này đều dùng nguyên liệu giống nhau là gạo nếp và thịt heo, gói trong lá dong hay lá chuối.**

choongm[2] tohy[1] lam[5] bănh[2] chŭng[1] dăk[6] shan[4] koouh[4] myehn[5] băk[2] va[5] bănh[2] tet[2] // mahn[2] teht[2] kooh[4] myehn[5] nam[1] // twee[1] khak[2] nhăw[1] veh[5] heenh[5] yang[6] va[5] hŭuhng[1] vee[6] // hie[1] lwie[6] bănh[2] năy[5] dehw[5] yoongm[5] ngwyehn[1] lyehw[6] yohngm[2] nhăw[1] la[5] gahw[6] nehp[2] va[5] theet[6] hew[1] // gahy[2] trahngm[1] la[2] yahngm[1] hăy[1] la[2] chwohy[2]

We make square sticky rice cakes, a specialty of the north, and round sticky rice cakes, the southern version. Although different in shape and flavor, both types of cake use similar ingredients, such as sticky rice and pork, and are wrapped in phrynium leaves and banana leaves.

JIMMY **Nghe ngon quá há! Còn về những tập tục ngày Tết thì sao, hở anh?**

nge[1] ngahn[1] kwa[2] ha[2] // kahn[5] veh[5] nhŭng[3] tup[6] tookp[6] ngăy[5] teht[2] thee[5] shahw[1] huh[4] ănh[1]

That sounds very delicious! How about some practices observed during Tết?

TÂM **Chúng tôi thường thăm viếng, chúc tụng họ hàng và bạn bè vào ngày đầu năm. Người lớn mừng tuổi trẻ em với tiền mới trong phong bao đỏ. Con cháu cung kính chúc ông bà, cha mẹ dồi dào sức khoẻ và sống lâu trăm tuổi.**

choongm[2] tohy[1] thŭuhng[5] thăm[1] vyehng[2] chookp[2] toongm[6] hah[6] hang[5] va[5] ban[6] be[5] vahw[5] ngăy[5] dohw[5] năm[1] // ngŭuhy[5] luhn[2] mŭng[5] twohy[4] tre[4] em[1] băng[5] tyehn[5] muhy[2] trahngm[1] fahngm[1] bahw[1] dah[4] // kahn[1] chăw[2] koongm[1] keenh[2] chookp[2] ohngm[1] ba[5] cha[1] me[6] yohy[5] yahw[5] shŭk[2] khwe[4] va[5] shohngm[2] lohw[1] trăm[1] twohy[4]

We usually visit relatives and friends to wish them a happy New Year. Adults celebrate children growing older with lucky money in red envelopes. Young people respectfully wish their parents and grandparents good health and longevity.

JIMMY **Ngày Tết của các bạn nhấn mạnh ý nghĩa quan trọng của gia đình. Cám ơn anh Tâm đã cho chúng tôi biết nhiều điều thú vị về một nét văn hoá của các bạn nhé!**

ngăy[5] teht[2] koouh[4] kak[2] ban[6] nhun[2] mănh[6] ee[2] ngeeuh[3] kwan[1] trahngm[6] koouh[4] ya[1] deenh[5] // kam[2] uhn[1] ănh[1] tum[1] da[3] chah[1] choongm[2] tohy[1] byeht[2] nhyehw[5] dyehw[5] thoo[2] vee[6] veh[5] moht[6] net[2] văn[1] hwa[2] koouh[4] kak[2] ban[6] nhe[2]

Your Tết holiday emphasizes the significance of family. Thank you, Tâm, for telling us several interesting things about one of your cultural traditions.

KEY VOCABULARY 2

mời *v*	to invite	**thu** *n*	autumn
Tết *n*	Lunar New Year	**đông** *n*	winter
kể *v*	to tell	**truyền thống** *adj*	traditional
một vài *adj*	a few	**bánh chưng** *n*	square sticky rice cake
đặc điểm *n*	characteristic	**bánh tét** *n*	round sticky rice cake
thính giả *n*	listener	**tuy** *conj*	although
ngày lễ *n*	holiday	**hương vị** *n*	flavor

quan trọng *adj*	important	**chuối** *n*	banana
nhất *adj*	first; most	**gạo nếp** *n*	sticky rice
nhằm vào *v*	to fall on, to coincide with	**gạo tẻ** *n*	white rice (not sticky)
dương lịch *n*	solar calendar	**tập tục** *n*	customary pratice
âm lịch *n*	lunar calendar	**chúc (tụng)** *v*	to wish
dọn dẹp *v*	to clean up	**ngày đầu năm** *n*	New Year's Day
sạch sẽ *adj*	clean	**người lớn** *n*	adult
xua đi *v*	to sweep away	**trẻ em** *n*	children
điều *n*	thing, matter	**dồi dào** *adj*	abundant
may mắn *adj*	lucky	**sống lâu trăm tuổi**	to live to be 100
mâm cơm *n*	tray of food	**nhấn mạnh** *v*	to emphasize
cúng *v*	to make offerings (*to the deceased*)	**ý nghĩa** *n*	significance
tổ tiên *n*	ancestors	**thú vị** *adj*	delightful
trang hoàng *v*	to decorate	**nét** *n*	trait, feature
xuân *n*	spring	**văn hoá** *n*	culture
hạ *n*	summer	**cám ơn/cảm ơn**	thank you

IDIOMATIC EXPRESSIONS 2

Gia đình nào cũng...

To emphasis an element in a sentence, you can use an indefinite expression refering to it followed by the word **cũng** (sometimes with other elements in between): **Chiều ba mươi Tết, gia đình nào cũng đã sẵn sàng đón xuân vào nhà** "On Lunar New Year's Eve, every family is ready to ring Tết in." More examples with this constructions: **Ai cũng thích ăn mứt vào ngày Tết** "Everyone loves eating candied fruit during Tết." **Cái gì ở chợ tết tôi cũng muốn mua** "Anything at the Tết fair, I'd love to buy." **Ở đâu cũng có bán loại pháo này** "They sell this kind of firecracker everywhere." **Năm nay thế nào tôi cũng cố về quê ăn Tết với gia đình** "I'll try to come home to celebrate Tết with my family no matter what." **Khu bán hoa Tết lúc nào cũng đông người mua** "There are lots of buyers at the Tết flower zone at any given time."

CULTURE NOTES 2

Tết in Vietnam is as important as Christmas in America. People buy good food and new clothes for the whole family on this significant occasion. This is also an opportunity for people to see whether a family is well-to-do or not. The proverb **Giàu nghèo ba mươi Tết mới hay** means "You can't know whether a family is rich or not until the thirtieth of the twelfth month." In other words, just by looking at how elaborately a house is decorated and how much food is displayed on the main altar, you'll know if the family is well-off or not.

GRAMMAR NOTES 2

II. Complex sentences

A complex sentence consist of two clauses, the main clause and the subordinate clause. A subordinate clause usually begins with a subordinating conjunction or, simply put, a "connector." There are three types of subordinate clauses: noun clauses, adjective clauses and adverb clauses.

A. Complex sentences containing noun clauses

A subordinate noun clause usually functions as an object of a verb in the main clause. The most common connector is **rằng** "that" (or **là**, in spoken Vietnamese). In the spoken language, **rằng** or **là** is often omitted.

(3) a. **Ai cũng biết rằng không nên quét nhà vào ngày đầu năm.**
ie^1 koongm^3 byeht^2 răng^5 khohngm^1 nehn^1 kwet^2 nha^5 vahw^5 ngăy^5 dohw^5 năm^1
Everyone knows that you should not sweep the floors on New Year's Day.

b. **Anh tin là tuổi chúng ta hợp nhau để trở thành vợ chồng.**
ănh^1 teen^1 la^5 twohy^4 choongm^2 ta^1 huhp^6 nhăw^1 deh^4 truh^4 thănh^5 vuh^6 chohngm^5
I believe that our zodiac signs are in synch for us to become husband and wife.

Indirect questions are also a type of noun clause. An indirect yes-no question contains **có... không/chưa** and an indirect specific question begins with an interrogative word:

(4) a. **Bà Xuân hỏi tôi đã có gia đình chưa.**
ba^5 swun^1 hahy^4 tohy^1 da^3 kah^2 ya^1 deenh^5 chŭuh^1
Mrs. Xuân asked me if I was married or not.

b. **Loan rất muốn biết khi nào Nhân sẽ cầu hôn với cô.**
lwan^1 rut^2 mwohn^2 byeht^2 khee^1 nahw^5 nhun^1 she^4 kohw^5 hohn^1 vuhy^2 koh^1
Loan really wants to know when Nhân will propose to her.

B. Complex sentences containing adjective clauses

A subordinate adjective clause describes or explains a noun in the main clause. The connector introducing an adjective clause is **mà** "who, whom, which, that, whose" (which can be omitted in some cases).

(5) a. **Người đàn bà (mà) anh gặp hôm qua là mợ của tôi.**
ngŭuhy^5 dan^5 ba^5 ma^5 ănh^1 găp^6 hohm^1 kwa^1 la^5 muh^6 koouh^4 tohy^1
The woman [whom] you met yesterday is my maternal uncle's wife.

b. **Vấn đề (mà) làm anh lo lắng đã được giải quyết xong.**
vun^2 deh^5 ma^5 lam^5 ănh^1 lah^1 lăng^2 da^3 dŭuhk^6 yie^4 kwyeht^2 sahngm^1
The problem that was worrying you has been resolved.

c. **Ông giám đốc công ty mà vợ là phụ tá giám đốc vừa từ chức.**
ohngm^1 yam^2 dohkp^2 kohngm^1 tee^1 ma^5 vuh^6 la^5 foo^6 ta^2 yam^2 dohkp^2 vŭuh^5 tŭ^5 chŭk^2
The company director whose wife is assistant director has just resigned.

C. Complex sentences containing adverb clauses

A subordinate adverb clause modifies the verb in the main clause to indicate time, place, reason, result, purpose, condition, comparison, manner or concession. The most common connectors for each of the above-mentioned categories are, respectively, **khi** "when," **nơi** "where," **vì** "because," **để** "so that," **nếu** "if," **là** "than," **như** "as," and **và tuy** "although." The main clause usually comes before the adverb clause, but for emphasis, an adverb clause can begin a complex sentence.

(6) a. **Ông nội tôi đã mất trước khi tôi ra đời.**
ohngm^1 nohy^1 tohy^1 da^3 mut^2 trŭuhk^2 khee^1 tohy^1 ra^1 duhy^5
My paternal grandfather passed away before I was born.

b. **Tôi thích sống nơi có nhiều cảnh đẹp thiên nhiên.**
tohy^1 theech^2 shohngm^2 nuhy^1 kah^2 nhyehw^5 kănh^4 dep^6 thyehn^1 nhyehn^1
I'd like to live where there is lots of natural scenery.

c. **Mẹ Lan rất thương Lan vì cô là con út.**
me^6 lan^1 rut^2 thŭuhng^1 lan^1 vee^5 koh^1 la^5 kahn^1 oot^2
Lan's mom loves her very much because she is the youngest child.

d. **Cô Thuý gọi cho mẹ chồng để báo cho bà biết là cô sắp có con.**
koh^1 thwee^2 gahy^6 chah^1 me^6 chohngm^5 deh^4 bahw^2 chah^1 ba^5 byeht^2 la^5 koh^1 shăp^2 kah^2 kahn^1
Thuý called her mother-in-law to tell her that she was going to have a baby.

e. **Nếu có con trai, Hưng sẽ đặt tên cho con là Thịnh.**
nehw^2 kah^2 kahn^1 trie^1 // hŭng^1 she^3 dăt^6 tehn^1 chah^1 khán la^5 theenh^6
If he has a son, Hưng will name him Thịnh.

f. **Cha mẹ thương con cái nhiều hơn là chúng tôi tưởng.**
cha^1 me^6 thŭuhng^1 kahn^1 kie^2 nhyehw^5 huhn^1 la^5 choongm^2 tohý tŭuhng^4
Our parents love us more than we can imagine.

g. **Người Việt về thăm nhà ngày Tết cũng như người Mỹ đoàn tụ dịp Giáng Sinh.**
ngŭuhy^5 vyeht^6 veh^5 thăm^1 nha^5 ngăy^5 teht^2 koongm^3 nhŭ^1 ngŭuhy^5 mee^3 dwan^5 too^6 yeep^6 yang^2 sheenh^1
Vietnamese people come home for Tết just as Americans gather together at Christmas.

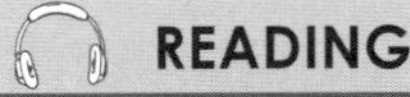
READING

GIA ĐÌNH VIỆT NAM

Cách xưng hô trong gia đình của người Việt khá phức tạp. Bên người cha gọi là "bên nội" (tức là bên của "những người trong nhà"), còn bên người mẹ gọi là "bên ngoại" (hay là bên của "những người ngoài"). Việc phân chia này dựa theo quan niệm lâu đời (và hết sức lỗi thời) là "trọng nam khinh nữ".

Về bên ngoại, anh hay em trai của người mẹ gọi là "cậu", còn chị hay em gái của mẹ gọi là "dì". Còn bên nội, anh của người cha gọi là "bác", còn em trai của cha gọi là "chú". Chị hay em gái của cha đều gọi là "cô". Rắc rối hơn nữa là những cách xưng hô này có thể thay đổi theo từng vùng trong nước, hay ngay cả theo từng gia đình.

Quan hệ gia đình có ý nghĩa quan trọng đến nỗi người Việt dùng các danh từ chỉ liên hệ huyết thống để xưng hô với nhau, thay vì dùng đại danh từ nhân xưng như nhiều ngôn ngữ khác. Chẳng hạn như trong tiếng Anh, khi một người con nói: "I love you" với mẹ, người mẹ đáp lại: "I love you, too", trong khi trong tiếng Việt, người con nói: "Con thương mẹ", thì người mẹ thường trả lời: "Mẹ cũng thương con".

Không hiếm những gia đình ở Việt Nam có đến bốn thế hệ chung sống với nhau, bao gồm ông bà cố (nội hay ngoại), ông bà nội hay ông bà ngoại, cha mẹ và con cái. Nhiều người con khi đã có gia đình vẫn sống chung với cha mẹ. Trong nhiều trường hợp, ông bà hay cha mẹ, dù đã già yếu, vẫn ở với con cháu để được tận tình chăm sóc.

ya^{1} deenh^{5} vyeht^{6} nam^{1}

kăch^{2} sŭng^{1} hoh^{1} trahngm^{1} ya^{1} deenh^{5} koouh^{4} ngŭuhy^{5} vyeht^{6} kha^{2} fŭk^{2} tap^{6} // behn^{1} ngŭuhy^{5} cha^{1} gahy^{6} la^{5} behn^{1} nohy^{6} // tŭk^{2} la^{5} behn^{1} koouh^{4} nhŭng^{3} ngŭuhy^{5} trahnm^{1} nha^{5} // kahn^{5} behn^{1} ngŭuhy^{5} me^{6} gahy^{6} la^{5} behn^{1} ngwie^{6} // hăy^{1} la^{5} behn^{1} koouh^{4} nhŭng^{3} ngŭuhy^{5} ngwie^{5} // vyehk^{6} fun^{1} cheeuh^{1} năy^{5} yŭuh^{6} thew^{1} kwan^{1} nyehm^{6} lowh^{1} duhy^{5} // va^{5} heht^{2} shŭk^{2} lohy^{3} thuhy^{5} // la^{5} trahngm^{6} nam^{1} kheenh^{1} nŭ^{3}

veh^{5} behn^{1} ngwie^{6} // ănh^{1} hăy^{1} em^{1} trie^{1} koouh^{4} ngŭuhy^{5} me^{6} gahy^{6} la^{5} kohw^{6} // kahn^{5} chee^{6} hăy^{1} em^{1} gie^{2} koouh^{4} me^{6} gahy^{6} la^{5} yee^{5} // kahn^{5} behn^{1} nohy^{6} // ănh^{1} koouh^{4} ngŭuhy^{5} cha^{1} gahy^{6} la^{5} bak^{2} // kahn^{5} em^{1} trie^{1} koouh^{4} cha^{1} gahy^{6} la^{5} choo^{2} // chee^{6} hăy^{1} em^{1} gie^{2} koouh^{4} cha^{1} dehw^{5} gahy^{6} la^{5} koh^{1} // răk^{2} rohy^{2} huhn^{1} nŭuh^{3} la^{5} nhŭng^{3} kăch^{2} sŭng^{1} hoh^{1} năy^{5} kah^{2} theh^{4} thăy^{1} dohy^{4} thew^{1} tŭng^{5} voongm^{5} trahngm^{1} nŭuhk^{2} // hăy^{1} ngăy^{1} ka^{4} thew^{1} tŭng^{5} ya^{1} deenh^{5}

kwan^{1} heh^{6} ya^{1} deenh^{5} kah^{2} ee^{2} ngeeuh^{3} kwan^{1} trahngm^{6} dehn^{2} nohy^{3} ngŭuhy^{5} vyeht^{6} yoongm^{5} kak^{2} yănh^{1} tŭ^{5} chee^{4} lyehn^{1} heh^{6} hwyhet^{2} thohngm^{2} deh^{4} sŭng^{1} hoh^{1} vuhy^{2} nhăw^{1} // thăy^{1} vee^{5} yoongm^{5} die^{6} yănh^{1} tŭ^{5} nhun^{1} sŭng^{1} nhŭ^{1} nhyehw^{5} ngohn^{1} ngŭ^{3} khak^{2} // chăng^{4} han^{6} nhŭ^{1} trahngm^{1} tyehng^{2} ănh^{1} // khee^{1} moht^{6} ngŭuhy^{5} kahn^{1} nahy^{2} i love you vuhy^{2} me^{5} // ngŭuhy^{5} me^{6} dap^{2} lie^{6} i love you too // trahngm^{1} khee^{1} trahngm^{1} tyehng^{2} vyeht^{5} // ngŭuhy^{5} kahn^{1} nahy^{2} kahn^{1} thŭuhn^{1} me^{6} thee^{5} ngŭuhy^{5} me^{6} thŭuhng^{5} tra^{4} luhy^{5} me^{6} koongm^{4} thŭuhng^{1} kahn^{1}

khohngm^{1} hyehm^{2} nhŭng^{3} ya^{1} deenh^{5} vyeht^{6} nam^{1} kah^{2} dehn^{2} bohn^{2} theh^{2} heh^{6} choongm^{1} shohngm^{2} vuhy^{2} nhăw^{1} // bahw^{1} gohm^{5} ohngm^{1} ba^{5} koh^{2} // nohy^{6} hăy^{1} ngwie^{6} // ohngm^{1} ba^{5} nohy^{6} hăy^{1} ohngm^{1} ba^{5} ngwie^{6} // cha^{1} me^{6} va^{5} kahn^{1} kie^{2} // nhyehw^{5} ngŭuhy^{5} kahn^{1} khee^{1} da^{3} kah^{2} ya^{1} deenh^{5} vun^{3} shohngm^{2} choong^{1} vuhy^{2} cha^{1} me^{6} // trahngm^{1} nhyehw^{5} trŭuhng^{5} huhp^{6} // ohngm^{1} ba^{5} hăy^{1} cha^{1} me^{6} // yoo^{5} da^{3} ya^{5} yehw^{2} // vun^{3} uh^{4} vuhy^{2} kahn^{1} chăw^{2} deh^{4} dŭuhk^{6} tun^{6} teenh^{5} chăm^{1} shahkp^{2}

THE VIETNAMESE FAMILY

Vietnamese people's way of addressing family members is quite complicated. The father's side is called the **bên nội** (that is, the "internal side" or "insiders"), while the mother's side is called the **bên ngoại** (the "external side" or the "outsiders"). This discriminatory language is based on the long-standing (and extremely outdated) concept of respecting men more than women.

On the maternal side, the mother's brother, older or younger, is called **cậu**, and the mother's sister, older or younger, is called **dì**. On the paternal side, the father's older brother is called **bác**, and his younger brother is called **chú**. The father's sister, older or younger, is called **cô**. To make matters worse, terms of address can vary from region to region, or even from family to family.

Family relationships are so important that Vietnamese people use nouns that indicate kinship to address each other instead of personal pronouns as in many other languages. For example, in English, when a child says "I love you" to his mother, the mother replies "I love you, too." In Vietnamese, by contrast, a child literally says "Child loves mom," and their mother responds "Mom loves child, too."

It's not rare for some families in Vietnam to have up to four generations living under the same roof, including great-grandparents (paternal or maternal), grandparents (paternal or maternal), parents and children. Some children, once married, still live with their parents. In many cases, grandparents or parents, in their old age or sickness, still live with their children and grandchildren to receive dedicated care from them.

COMPREHENSION QUESTIONS

Answer the following questions in complete sentences, first orally, then in writing.

1. **Tại sao gia đình người mẹ gọi là "bên ngoại"?** *Why is the mother's family called "the external side"?*

____

2. **Giữa "cậu" và "chú", từ ngữ nào cho thấy người đó là bên cha hay bên mẹ, và từ ngữ nào cho thấy người đó là lớn hơn hay nhỏ hơn cha hay mẹ?** *Between* **cậu** *and* **chú**, *which term reveals that the person belongs to the mother's or the father's side, and which term indicates that he is older or younger than the parent?*

____

____

3. **Đại danh từ nhân xưng trong tiếng Việt phần lớn thật ra là thuộc từ loại nào?** *Which word class do most personal pronouncs in Vietnamese actually belong to?*

____

4. **Dùng như đại danh từ, chữ "con" có thể chỉ hai ngôi nào trong văn phạm?** *When* **con** *is used as a pronoun, what two grammatical persons can it refer to?*

____

5. **Một gia đình Việt Nam có thể có đến bao nhiêu thế hệ cùng sống chung?** *Up to how many generations of a Vietnamese family can live together?*

____

PRACTICE

A. Listening comprehension

Listen to the wedding announcement and invitation and put a check mark in cells where an item in the leftmost column matches an item in the top row. Some vertical items can match more than one vertical item.

	Cha mẹ Chú rể *Groom's parents*	**Cha mẹ cô dâu** *Bride's parents*	**Chú rể** *Groom*	**Cô dâu** *Bride*	**Lễ cưới** *Wedding ceremony*	**Tiệc cưới** *Wedding reception*	**Nhà Thờ** *Church*	**Nhà hàng** *Restaurant*	**Thiệp phúc đáp** *RSVP*
Đồng Khánh									
Nguyễn Văn Thảo									
Thánh Linh									

4/26/26									
Nguyễn Thị Bảo									
Trần Văn Huy									
12/25/25									
Trần Quốc Việt									

B. Compound sentences

Translate the following English sentence pairs into Vietnamese, then join them with the coordinating conjunction given in parentheses. When the subject in both conjuncts is the same, the one in the second conjunct can be omitted.

1. *At this restaurant (a) we can book a wedding reception (b) we can throw a birthday party* (**hay** "or")

   ____

   ____

2. *(a) This is a photo of the groom's family (b) this a a photo of the bride's family* (**còn** "and")

   ____

   ____

3. *(a) We had a wedding ceremony (b) we didn't have an engagement ceremony* (**nhưng** "but")

   ____

   ____

4. *(a) Our wedding reception had no singing (b) our wedding reception had no dancing* (**mà cũng không** "nor")

   ____

   ____

5. *(a) I will order a white wedding cake (b) I will hire a band* (**và** "and")

____

____

6. *(a) It was quite cold that day (b) the wedding ceremony still took place on the beach* (**mà** "yet")

____

____

7. *(a) Vietnamese couples prefer money as a wedding gift (b) we remind each other to not buy any presents* (**vì vậy** "so")

____

____

C. Complex sentences

Match each main clause in the left column to a subordinate clause in the right column to form complex sentences. Write them in the space provided below. Omit the subject in the subordinate clause if it is the same as the subject in the main clause.

MAIN CLAUSE	SUBORDINATE CLAUSE
Mẹ tôi sinh đứa con đầu lòng *My mom had her first-born*	**để nối dõi tông đường.** *so they will continue the family line*
Tôi muốn gặp ông giám đốc *I'd like to meet with the director*	**vì chú còn độc thân.** *because he is still single.*
Chú Bình rất thương chúng tôi *Uncle Bình loves us very much*	**nếu bạn đã có gia đình.** *if you are married.*
Đây là cô em họ *This is the little cousin*	**là những gì các bạn biết được qua sách vở.** *than what you know through books.*
Hãy bỏ qua câu hỏi này *Skip this question*	**nơi ông đã sống trong thời thơ ấu.** *where he lived during his childhood.*
Nhiều gia đình muốn có con trai *Many families want to have sons*	**mà vợ là bác sĩ ở bệnh viện thành phố.** *whose wife is a doctor at the city hospital.*
Gần đây, các nhà xã hội học nhận thấy *Of late, sociologists find*	**như các bạn thấy ở trong nước.** *as the families you see in Vietnam.*
Họ đang định xin một đứa con nuôi *They plan to adopt a child*	**nên chị rất cưng chiều em.** *so she pampers her very much.*

MAIN CLAUSE	SUBORDINATE CLAUSE
Con trai của ông Vũ ao ước được đến *Mr. Vũ wishes to go*	**rằng giới trẻ Việt Nam thích sống độc thân hơn.** *Vietnamese youths prefer to stay single.*
Gia đình người Việt ở nước ngoài cũng gắn bó *Vietnamese expat families are as close-knit*	**mà tôi đã giới thiệu với anh qua điện thư.** *whom I introduced to you via email.*
Chị Lan chỉ có một đứa em gái *Lan only has a younger sister*	**khi bà mới 25 tuổi.** *when she was just 25 years old.*
Giới trẻ Việt Nam phóng khoáng về tình yêu hơn *Vietnamese youths are more open-minded about love*	**tuy đã có ba người con.** *although they already have three kids.*

1. ______________________________

2. ______________________________

3. ______________________________

4. ______________________________

5. ______________________________

6. ______________________________

7. ______________________________

8. ______________________________

9. ______________________________

10. ______________________________

11. ______________________________

12. ______________________________

D. Vocabulary

Do the following **ô chữ** "crossword puzzle," referring to the Functional Vocabulary Section if necessary. Many of the words selected for this puzzle are kinships terms used to refer to or address family members. Include all the necessary accent marks.

ACROSS – NGANG	DOWN – DỌC
1. Son-in-law	1. Father's younger brother
4. Being single	2. Groom's side
6. Father's older brother	3. Another term for **mẹ**
8. Younger sibling	5. Bride's side
9. Romantic feeling	7. To raise (*a child*)
12. Grandparents	8. Younger sister
13. Son of your parent's older sibling	10. Relatives
15. Antonym of "young"	11. Sibling's child
16. Paternal grandfather	14. Older brother
17. Male spouse	15. Household consisting of parents and children
18. Older sister's husband	16. Maternal grandfather
21. Mother's sister (older or younger)	17. Older brother's wife
22. Widowed	19. Biological (*family member*)
23. Father	20. Jealous (*romantically*)
24. Fiancée	

PROVERB

MỘT GIỌT MÁU ĐÀO HƠN AO NƯỚC LÃ.

moht^{6} yaht^{6} măw^{2} dahw^{5} huhn^{1} ahw^{1} nŭuhk^{2} la^{3}

"A drop of blood is better than a pondful of water."

Besides emphasizing the importance of family, this proverb also depicts a cultural aspect of life in the Vietnamese countryside: Most houses have a large backyard that includes a pond where people raise fish, shrimp or snails, and even do laundry by the edge. In poetry and songs, ponds are a familiar image and a source of inspiration. The first two verses of a popular folk poem are: **Đêm qua ra đứng bờ ao/Trông cá, cá lặn, trông sao, sao mờ...** "Last night by the pond (I) stood musing/Watching the fish hiding and the stars dimming..."

FUNCTIONAL VOCABULARY

DANH TỪ

cha	father
mẹ	mother
con	child (in the family)
con trai	son; boy
con gái	daughter; girl
anh	older brother
chị	older sister
em	younger sibling
em trai	younger brother
em gái	younger sister
cậu	uncle (mother's side)
dì	maternal aunt
chú	paternal uncle (*father's younger brother*)
ông nội	paternal grandfather
bà nội	paternal grandmother
ông ngoại	maternal grandfather
bà ngoại	maternal grandmother
ông cố	great-grandfather
bà cố	great-grandmother
anh họ	cousin; son of your parent's older sibling
chị họ	cousin; daughter of your parent's older sibling
em họ	cousin; child of your parent's younger sibling
cháu trai	nephew; grandnephew
cháu gái	niece; grandniece
vợ	wife
chồng	husband
cô dâu	bride
chú rể	groom
bạn trai	boyfriend
bạn gái	girlfriend
tình yêu	love
vị hôn thê	fiancée (woman)
vị hôn phu	fiancé (man)
họ hàng	relatives
đám hỏi	engagement ceremony
đám cưới	wedding ceremony
cha/mẹ chồng	father-/mother-in-law (*man's side*)
cha/mẹ vợ	father-/mother-in-law (*woman's side*)
con dâu	daughter-in-law
con rể	son-in-law
cha/mẹ nuôi	adoptive father/mother
con nuôi	adoptive child
cha dượng	stepfather
mẹ kế	stepmother

TÍNH TỪ

có vợ	married (*man*)
có chồng	married (*woman*)
độc thân	single
ly dị	divorced
goá	widowed
ly thân	separated
ruột	biological (*relation*)
cùng cha khác mẹ	with the same father but a different mother
cùng mẹ khác cha	with the same mother but a different father
nuôi	adoptive
có hiếu	devoted (child to parents)
đính hôn	engaged (to be married)
có bầu	pregnant
giận	mad, angry
ghen	jealous
hạnh phúc	happy
có gia đình	married
mồ côi	orphaned

ĐỘNG TỪ

dạy dỗ	to bring up
trông	to look after
chăm sóc	to care for
lớn lên	to grow up
yêu/thương	to love
nhớ	to miss (a person)
cưới/lấy vợ	to marry (a woman)
lấy chồng	to marry (a man)
hỏi cưới	to propose marriage
ghét	to hate
có con	to have a child
nuôi	to raise (a child)
giáo dục	to educate

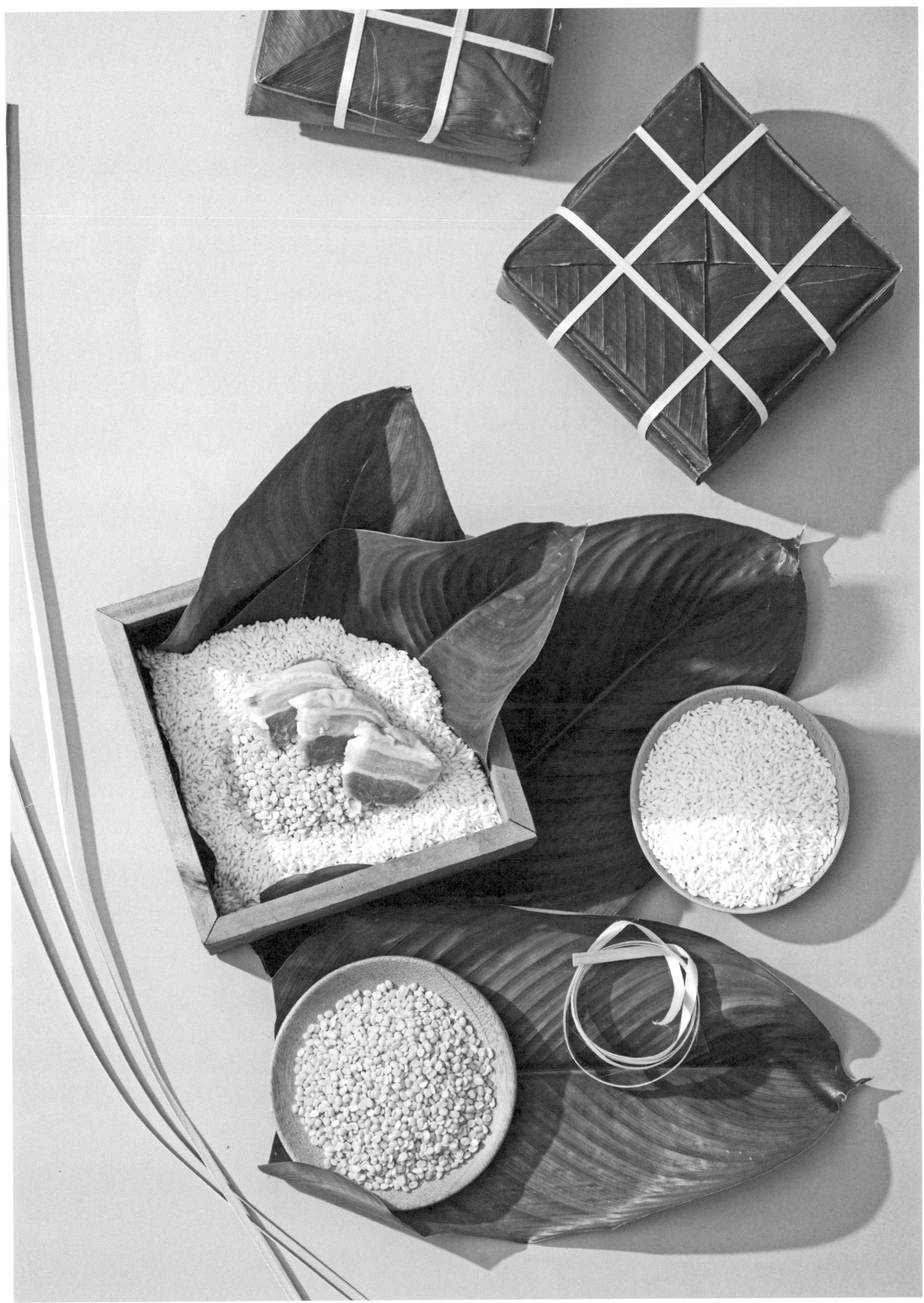

Appendices

Pronunciation Guide

This guide shows how selected letters and numbers are conventionally used to help English-speaking learners pronounce Vietnamese words, phrases and sentences in the book.

For simplicity's sake, where possible, words with the high-level tone (bearing no accent marks in the spellings and showing number 1 in the pronunciation guides) are chosen for examples.

TONES

TONE MARK	TONE DESCRIPTION	NUMBER USED FOR TONE	WORD EXAMPLE	PRONUNCIATION GUIDE
None	mid-high, level	1	**la**	*la*^{1}
´	high, rising	2	**lá**	*la*^{2}
~	mid-high rising, glottalized	3	**lã**	*la*^{3}
ˀ	mid-low, rising	4	**lả**	*la*^{4}
ˋ	mid-low, falling	5	**là**	*la*^{5}
.	low-falling, glottalized	6	**lạ**	*la*^{6}

CONSONANTS 

SPELLING	PRONUNCIATION GUIDE	WORD EXAMPLE	PRONUNCIATION GUIDE
b	*b*	**ba**	*ba*^{1}
c, k, q	*k*	**ca, kê, qui**	*ka*^{1}, *keh*^{1}, *kwi*^{1}
ch	*ch*	**cha**	*cha*^{1}
d, gi	*y*	**da, gia**	*ya*^{1}
đ	*d*	**đa**	*da*^{1}
g, gh	*g*	**ga, ghe**	*ga*^{1}, *ge*^{1}
h	*h*	**ha**	*ha*^{1}
kh	*kh*	**kha**	*kha*^{1}
l	*l*	**la**	*la*^{1}
m	*m*	**ma**	*ma*^{1}
n	*n*	**na**	*na*^{1}
ng, ngh	*ng*	**nga, nghe**	*nga*^{1}, *nge*^{1}
nh	*nh*	**nha**	*nha*^{1}
p	*p*	**họp**	*hahp*^{6}
ph	*f*	**pha**	*fa*^{1}

SPELLING	PRONUNCIATION GUIDE	WORD EXAMPLE	PRONUNCIATION GUIDE
r	*r*	ra	*ra*[1]
s	*sh*	sa	*sha*[1]
t	*t*	ta	*ta*[1]
th	*th*	tha	*tha*[1]
tr	*tr*	tra	*tra*[1]
v	*v*	va	*va*[1]
x	*s*	xa	*sa*[1]

VOWELS

SPELLING	PRONUNCIATION GUIDE	WORD EXAMPLE	PRONUNCIATION GUIDE
i, y	*ee*	ly	*lee*[1]
ê	*eh*	lê	*leh*[1]
e	*e*	le	*le*[1]
a	*a*	la	*la*[1]
ă	*ă*	lăn	*lăn*[1]
â	*u*	lân	*lun*[1]
o	*ah*	lo	*lah*[1]
ô	*oh*	lô	*loh*[1]
ơ	*uh*	lơ	*luh*[1]
u	*oo*	lu	*loo*[1]
ư	*ŭ*	lư	*lŭ*[1]

DIPHTHONGS

SPELLING	PRONUNCIATION GUIDE	WORD EXAMPLE	PRONUNCIATION GUIDE
ai	*ie*	cai	*kie*[1]
ao	*ahw*	cao	*kahw*[1]
ay	*ăy*	cay	*kăy*[1]
au	*ăw*	cau	*kăw*[1]
ây	*ay*	cây	*kay*[1]
âu	*ohw*	câu	*kohw*[1]
eo	*ew*	keo	*kew*[1]
êu	*ehw*	kêu	*kehw*[1]
ia	*eeuh*	kia	*keeuh*[1]
iê, yê	*yeh*	kiêng, yên	*kyehng*[1], *yehn*[1]

SPELLING	PRONUNCIATION GUIDE	WORD EXAMPLE	PRONUNCIATION GUIDE
iu	*eew*	hiu	*heew*^{1}
oi	*oy*	coi	*koy*^{1}
ôi	*ohy*	côi	*kohy*^{1}
ơi	*uhy*	cơi	*kuhy*^{1}
ua	*oouh*	cua	*koouh*^{1}
oa, ua	*wa*	loa, qua	*lwa*^{1}, *kwa*^{1}
oă, uă	*wă*	loăn, quăn	*lwăn*^{1}, *kwăn*^{1}
uâ	*wu*	quân	*kwun*^{1}
oe, ue	*we*	loe, que	*lwe*^{1}, *kwe*^{1}
uê	*weh*	quê	*kweh*^{1}
uy	*wee*	quy	*kwee*^{1}
ui	*ooy*	cui	*kooy*^{1}
uô	*woh*	luôn	*lwohn*^{1}
uơ	*wuh*	quơ	*kwuh*^{1}
ưa, ươ	*ŭuh*	cưa, lươn	*kŭuh*^{1}, *lŭuhn*^{1}
ưi	*ŭy*	ngửi	*ngŭy*^{4}
ưu	*ŭw*	lưu	*lŭw*^{1}

TRIPHTHONGS 

SPELLING	PRONUNCIATION GUIDE	WORD EXAMPLE	PRONUNCIATION GUIDE
yêu, iêu	*yehw*	tiêu	*tyehw*^{1}
uôi	*wohy*	xuôi	*swohy*^{1}
ươi	*ŭuhy*	tươi	*tŭuhy*^{1}
ươu	*ŭuhw*	hươu	*hŭuhw*^{1}
uya	*weeuh*	khuya	*khweeuh*^{1}
uyu	*weew*	khuỷu	*khweew*^{4}
oai, uai	*wahy*	khoai	*khwahy*^{1}
oay, uay	*wăy*	quay	*kwăy*^{1}
uây	*way*	quây	*kway*^{1}
uao	*wahw*	quào	*kwahw*^{5}
uau	*wăw*	quạu	*kwăw*^{6}
oeo, ueo	*wew*	ngoèo	*ngwew*^{5}
uyê	*wyeh*	quyên	*kwyehn*^{1}

Listening Comprehension Transcripts and Translations

CHAPTER 3

Chào mừng mọi người đến Sài Gòn. Tôi là Vinh, giám đốc công ty Vina. Xin giới thiệu các vị khách của chúng ta hôm nay: Giáo sư Minh, từ Nha Trang vào, luật sư Thuý, từ Huế vào, Kỹ sư Long, từ Tây Ninh lên, và bác sĩ Vy, từ Đà Lạt xuống. Mong chúng ta có một cuộc hội thảo thành công.

Welcome, everyone, to Saigon. I am Vinh, the director of Vina Company. Let me introduce our guests today: Professor Minh, coming from Nha Trang; Lawyer Thúy, coming from Huế; Engineer Long, coming from Tây Ninh; and Doctor Vy, coming from Đà Lạt. I hope we'll have a successful conference.

CHAPTER 4

Kính chào quý vị khán giả. Đây là bản tin thời tiết từ thành phố Sài Gòn. Sáng nay trời khá nóng với nhiệt độ trung bình là 30 độ C. Trời ít mây, gió nhẹ và nắng ráo. Vào buổi chiều sẽ có vài cơn mưa rào nên nhiệt độ sẽ hạ thấp hơn ban sáng. Buổi tối trời quang đãng và có trăng. Xin cám ơn quý vị đã theo dõi bản tin của chúng tôi.

Greetings to our audience. This is the weather report from Saigon. This morning, the weather is quite hot, with an average temperature of 30°C. The sky is mostly clear, with light winds and dry conditions. In the afternoon, there will be some scattered showers, causing the temperature to drop compared to the morning. In the evening, the sky will be clear with the moon visible. Thank you for watching our report.

CHAPTER 5

Hãng điện tử Vinatronics đang tuyển dụng một chức giám thị. Đây là một công việc tạm thời trong một năm. Hồ sơ cần có một đơn xin việc, một bản tóm tắt cá nhân, một bản điểm và một bài luận văn ngắn. Xin gửi hồ sơ điện tử về bà Nguyễn Ngọc Minh, thư ký phòng nhân sự, qua địa chỉ minhnguyen@gmail.org. Hạn chót nhận đơn là cuối tháng này.

Vinatronics Electronics Company is hiring a supervisor. This is a temporary job for one year. The application must include a cover letter, a resumé, a transcript and a short essay. Please send your electronic application to Mrs. Nguyễn Ngọc Minh, HR department secretary, at minhnguyen@gmail.org. The application deadline is the end of this month.

CHAPTER 6

Kính chào quý vị thính giả. Đây là phần thông báo của đài phát thanh Cộng Hoà. Vào thứ Hai, ngày 6, tháng 10, năm 2025, nhằm ngày 15 tháng 8 âm lịch, năm Ất Tỵ, trường đại học Âu Cơ sẽ tổ chức một buổi phát quà Tết Trung Thu cho các em thiếu nhi lúc 7:30 tối tại khuôn viên của trường. Chúng tôi đã chuẩn bị 500 phần quà, gồm 375 bánh nướng và 125 bánh dẻo, 400 chiếc lồng đèn và 100 món đồ chơi. Xin quý vị đưa con em đến trường vào ngày giờ nói trên để chúng ta cùng vui đón Tết Trung Thu. Xin cám ơn quý vị.

Greetings to our listeners. This is an announcement from Republic Radio Station. On Monday, October 6, 2025, which corresponds to the 15th day of the 8th lunar month, Year of the Snake (Ất Tỵ), Âu Cơ University will host a Mid-Autumn Festival gift-giving event for children at 7:30 PM on the university campus. We have prepared 500 gift sets, including 375 baked mooncakes and 125 soft mooncakes, 400 lanterns, and

100 toys. We kindly invite you to bring your children to the university at the indicated date and time so we can celebrate the Mid-Autumn Festival together. Thank you.

CHAPTER 7

1. Năm nay anh bao nhiêu tuổi?
2. Anh có phải là người Mỹ không?
3. Anh học ở trường nào?
4. Anh sống ở thành phố nào?
5. Anh học tiếng Pháp hay tiếng Tây Ban Nha?
6. Anh đang học năm thứ ba, phải không?
7. Anh có đi làm ngoài giờ học không?
8. Anh thường học bài ở đâu?

1. *How old are you (this year)?*
2. *Are you American?*
3. *What school do you go to?*
4. *What city do you live in?*
5. *Do you study French or Spanish?*
6. *You are in your third year, aren't you?*
7. *Do you work besides going to school?*
8. *Where do you often study?*

CHAPTER 8

Hôm nay là Chủ Nhật trong gia đình của Thảo. Mọi người đều bận rộn với công việc của mình. Ba đang đọc báo tại bàn ăn. Mẹ đang làm bữa ăn sáng trong nhà bếp. Huy đang tập thể dục trong phòng gia đình. Thảo đang rửa mặt trong phòng tắm. Bảo đang thay quần áo trong phòng ngủ. Con chó đang chơi với quả banh. Chỉ có con mèo là còn ngủ trên xô-pha.

Today is Sunday in Thảo's family. Everyone is busy with their own tasks. Dad is reading the newspaper at the dining table. Mom is making breakfast in the kitchen. Huy is exercising in the family room. Thảo is washing up in the bathroom. Bảo is getting dressed in the bedroom. The dog is playing with a ball. Only the cat is still sleeping on the sofa.

CHAPTER 9

Xin hân hạnh giới thiệu với quý vị chương trình du dịch đặc biệt mùa hè 3 ngày 2 đêm đến Phú Quốc của Công Ty Du Lịch Việt Á. Chương trình trọn vẹn này bao gồm:

- Chuyến bay khứ hồi từ Sài Gòn đến Phú Quốc của Hàng Không Việt Nam.
- Phòng giường đôi trong khu nghỉ mát 4 sao.
- Bao gồm bữa sáng và bữa trưa.
- Đi du thuyền qua 4 đảo.
- Thăm viếng nhiều chùa và bãi biển.
- Giá vé du lịch cho mỗi khách: 2.950.000đ.
- Giá vé máy bay khứ hồi cho mỗi khách: 385.000đ.

We are pleased to introduce a special three-day, two-night summer tour to Phú Quốc from Việt Á Travel Company. This all-inclusive package includes:

- *Round-trip flight from Saigon to Phú Quốc on Vietnam Airlines*
- *A double-bed room at a 4-star resort*
- *Breakfast and lunch included*
- *A boat tour to four islands*
- *Visits to various temples and beaches*
- *Tour package price per guest: 2,950,000 VND*
- *Round-trip airfare per guest: 385,000 VND*

CHAPTER 10

Quý vị muốn có đầy đủ sức khoẻ để vui sống và làm việc có hiệu quả? Xin mời dùng thử thuốc bổ Siêu Sinh Lực của công ty Dược Thảo Nam Việt. Thuốc được bào chế từ hai nguyên liệu trong thiên nhiên như rau và quả dưới dạng thuốc viên, bao gồm nhiều sinh tố và chất khoáng. Mỗi ngày uống ba lần, mỗi lần một viên với nhiều nước và uống sau bữa ăn.

Do you want to have excellent health so you can enjoy life and work effectively? Try SuperPower supplements from Nam Việt Herbal Medicine Company. This supplement is made from two natural ingredients, vegetables and fruits, in tablet form, and contains various vitamins and minerals. Take one tablet three times a day with plenty of water, after meals.

CHAPTER 11

Món phở Việt Nam là một loại xúp thơm ngon, đậm đà, gồm có nước dùng nấu bằng xương bò hay gà, bánh phở và thịt xắt mỏng. Kèm theo đó là vài loại rau tươi như ngò, húng quế, giá, chanh và ớt. Hai loại tương thường ăn với phở là tương đen và tương đỏ. Nét đặc biệt của phở là sự pha trộn giữa các thứ gia vị thơm như hồi, đinh hương, hành tây, gừng và quế, mang lại một món ăn bổ dưỡng, ngon lành, phổ biến khắp Việt Nam và nhiều nơi trên thế giới.

Vietnamese phở is a delicious and flavorful soup consisting of broth made from beef or chicken bones, rice noodles and thinly sliced meat. It is served with fresh herbs such as cilantro and basil, bean sprouts, lime and chili. Two common sauces eaten with phở are hoisin sauce and chili sauce. What makes phở special is the blend of aromatic spices like star anise, cloves, onion, ginger and cinnamon, creating a nutritious and delicious dish that is popular throughout Vietnam and many places around the world.

CHAPTER 12

Mùa đông sắp đến. Quý vị phải giữ ấm với phong cách riêng của mình! Bắt đầu từ cuối tuần này, tiệm Thời Trang 21 của chúng tôi sẽ có đợt bán hạ giá y phục mùa đông, nơi thời trang gặp gỡ sự ấm áp với giá cả sẽ làm quý vị hài lòng.

Từ các loại áo len Cashmere đến đủ kiểu áo choàng sang trọng, hay giày bốt vừa thanh lịch vừa tiện dụng... chúng tôi đều có đầy đủ!

Trong bốn tuần sắp tới, quý vị sẽ được hưởng giá hạ đến 40% cho nhiều loại y phục mùa đông, kể cả khăn quàng, găng tay, vớ và nhiều thứ khác. Hàng chọn lọc của chúng tôi sẽ làm quý vị trông lịch lãm, cảm thấy thoải mái và ấm áp suốt mùa đông năm nay.

Quý vị hãy đến ngay, vì đợt hạ giá này chỉ có giới hạn. Cái lạnh sẽ ở lại trong một thời gian dài, nhưng cơ hội tiết kiệm của quý vị sẽ kết thúc rất sớm.

Winter is coming. You should stay warm in your own unique style! Starting this weekend, our Fashion 21 store will have a winter clothing sale, where fashion meets warmth at prices that will satisfy you.

From cashmere sweaters to elegant coats and stylish yet practical boots . . . we have it all!

For the next four weeks, you will enjoy up to 40% off on many winter clothing items, including scarves, gloves, socks and more. Our selected pieces will make you look elegant, feel comfortable and stay warm throughout this winter.

Come visit us now, as this sale is limited. The cold will stay for a long time, but your chance to save will end very soon!

CHAPTER 13

Hân hạnh giới thiệu vở tuồng "Hội Nghị Diên Hồng" của đoàn cải lương Đất Việt sẽ ra mắt khán giả trong bốn tuần lễ nữa. Đây là một ca kịch phẩm độc đáo làm sống lại những mẫu chuyện lịch sử chưa hề được kể lại về tinh thần bất khuất của tổ tiên chúng ta quyết tâm chống lại giặc Nguyên từ phương bắc. Với một dàn diễn viên hùng hậu và đạo diễn tài ba Nguyễn Nam, "Hội Nghị Diên Hồng" sẽ đưa quý vị vào một thế giới của tình yêu, lòng căm phẫn, sự phản trắc và lòng can đảm. Xin đừng bỏ qua vở tuồng hiếm có này. Vé có thể đặt qua trang mạng của chúng tôi hay mua tại cửa. Quý vị sẽ rất thích thú được cùng chúng tôi sống lại một thời kỳ oanh liệt trong lịch sử nước Nam.

We are proud to feature the play The Diên Hồng Conference *by the Đất Việt traditional opera troupe, which will premiere for audiences in four weeks. This unique opera brings to life historical stories that have never been told before, highlighting the indomitable spirit of our ancestors in their determination to resist the Mongol invaders from the north.*

With a powerful cast and the talented director Nguyễn Nam, The Diên Hồng Conference will immerse you in a world of love, anger, betrayal and courage. Don't miss this rare performance! Tickets can be reserved through our website or purchased at the door. You will thoroughly enjoy reliving a heroic period in the history of Vietnam with us.

CHAPTER 14

Ông Bà Trần Văn Huy và Ông Bà Nguyễn Văn Thảo – Trân trọng báo tin lễ thành hôn của con chúng tôi là Trần Quốc Việt (trưởng nam) và Nguyễn Thị Bảo (thứ nữ). Hôn lễ sẽ được cử hành vào lúc 10 giờ sáng Chủ Nhật, ngày 26 tháng Tư năm 2026 tại nhà thờ Thánh Linh – Số 8 Đường Tự Do - thành phố Sài Gòn.

Sau hôn lễ, kính mời quý vị đến tham dự tiệc cưới tại nhà hàng Đồng Khánh, số 4 đường Độc Lập, Sài Gòn vào lúc 6 giờ tối cùng ngày. Sự hiện diện của quý vị sẽ là một niềm vinh hạnh lớn cho hai gia đình chúng tôi.

Xin vui lòng gửi thiệp phúc đáp trước ngày 25 tháng Mười Hai năm 2025. Trân trọng cám ơn quý vị.

We, Mr. and Mrs. Trần Văn Huy and Mr. and Mrs. Nguyễn Văn Thảo, are pleased to announce the wedding of our children, Trần Quốc Việt (the eldest son) and Nguyễn Thị Bảo (the younger daughter). The wedding ceremony will be held at 10:00 AM on Sunday, April 26, 2026, at the Holy Spirit Church – 8 Tự Do Street, Saigon.

After the wedding, we cordially invite you to join us for the wedding reception at Đồng Khánh Restaurant, 4 Độc Lập Street, Saigon, at 6:00 PM on the same day. Your presence will be a great honor to both of our families.

Please kindly RSVP by December 25, 2025. We sincerely thank you.

Answer Key to Practice Exercises

CHAPTER 1

A. Vowel letter recognition

	a	ă	â	e	ê	i	o	ô	ơ	u	ư	y
1						✓						
2												✓
3		✓										
4										✓		
5				✓								
6								✓				
7	✓											
8											✓	
9			✓									
10							✓					
11									✓			
12					✓							

B. Single consonant letter recognition

1.	m	**(n)**	l
2.	**(b)**	p	v
3.	t	**(đ)**	c
4.	**(g)**	d	r
5.	**(x)**	s	c

6.	h	**(k)**	g
7.	n	**(r)**	m
8.	đ	b	**(t)**
9.	r	l	**(d)**
10.	**(p)**	v	đ

C. Double and triple consonant letter recognition

1. kh
2. ng
3. tr
4. ch
5. ngh
6. nh
7. ph
8. th
9. gi
10. gh

D. Word recognition

1. tư
2. sa
3. cho
4. xô
5. ghe
6. tri
7. khê
8. nơ
9. măng
10. nhu
11. lân
12. kê
13. đi
14. do
15. phu
16. nga
17. thư
18. bơ
19. vô
20. lu

CHAPTER 2

A. Vowel recognition

1	ban	băn	bân	bơn
2	con	cân	côn	cơn
3	lung	lưng	long	lông
4	minh	manh	măn	mân
5	sen	sên	sinh	sanh

B. Diphthong recognition

1	cai	cay	cây	coi
2	mau	mao	mâu	môi
3	nêu	nao	neo	nâu
4	hiên	heo	hêu	hiu
5	tưa	tua	tuôn	tuân

C. Triphthong recognition

1	quai	quay	quây	quau
2	nghiêu	ngươu	ngoao	người
3	khoeo	khuyu	khuya	khuyên
4	liêu	luyên	loai	loay
5	tươi	tuôi	tiêu	tuyên

D. Consonant recognition

1	sai	chai	dai	xai
2	bai	phai	mai	vai
3	hai	khai	cai	gai
4	tai	thai	đai	lai
5	nai	nhai	ngai	mai

E. Tone recognition

1	tiên	tiền	tiến	tiện
2	bông	bổng	bỗng	bống
3	đai	đài	đãi	đại
4	lâu	lầu	lẩu	lậu
5	lánh	lành	lãnh	lạnh
6	tình	tỉnh	tĩnh	tính

CHAPTER 3

A. Listening comprehension

	People	*Profession*	*Hometown*
1	Bà Thuý	luật sư	Huế
2	Ông Long	kỹ sư	Tây Ninh
3	Anh Vinh	giám đốc	Sài Gòn
4	Cô Vy	bác sĩ	Đà Lạt
5	Ông Minh	giáo sư	Nha Trang

B. The verb LÀ

1. họ
2. tên đệm
3. người Việt
4. giáo sư
5. vui tính

C. Personal pronouns

1. tôi
2. anh ấy
3. chúng tôi
4. cháu
5. cháu
6. các cháu

D. Vocabulary

(1) chào; (2) là; (3) người; (4) sinh viên; (5) học; (6) dạy; (7) khó; (8) nói

CHAPTER 4

A. Listening comprehension

Report location			c. Sài Gòn	
Morning temperature				d. 30°C
Cloudiness			c. a little	
Wind condition	a. light			
Sun condition				d. dry
Afternoon weather		b. rainy		
Evening weather	a. clear			
Night sky			c. moonlit	

B. Weather expressions

1. Trời có vẻ sắp mưa, phải không?
2. Vào mùa này thì trời thường ẩm ướt.
3. Hôm qua trời có nhiều sương mù.
4. Dường như trời sẽ có bão lớn.
5. Chiều nay trời trông thật u ám.
6. Tối nay trời thấy khá lạnh.
7. Sáng nay trời đẹp.

C. Aspect markers

1. Chương trình dự báo thời tiết sắp bắt đầu.
2. Bây giờ tuyết đang rơi ở Minnesota à?
3. Chiều mai trời sẽ rất u ám.
4. Anh đã xem hàn thử biểu để biết nhiệt độ hôm nay chưa?
5. Trời vừa có mưa phùn.

D. Vocabulary

1. Khí hậu ở tiểu bang California rất dễ chịu.
2. Tôi hy vọng ngày mai sẽ đẹp trời để chúng ta đi biển.
3. Vào mùa này, thời tiết thường thay đổi khá bất ngờ.
4. Hôm nay nhiệt độ cao nên tôi phải mở máy lạnh.
5. Việc dự báo thời tiết không phải lúc nào cũng chính xác.
6. Nhiều vùng cao nguyên miền Bắc có tuyết vào mùa đông.

CHAPTER 5

A. Listening comprehension

	a.	b.	c.
Company	điện tử		
Position		giám thị	
Job type			tạm thời
Document NOT needed	thư giới thiệu		
Send application to			thư ký
Send application via	điện thư		
Deadline		cuối tháng	

B. Classifiers

1. căn
2. người
3. cái
4. cây – cuốn
5. trái
6. con
7. tòa
8. chiếc
9. bài

C. Demonstrative adjectives

1. Cuốn sách nhỏ này không mắc lắm.
2. Cây viết mới đó không phải là của tôi.
3. Con mèo lớn đó tên là Mimi.
4. Chiếc xe đạp cũ kia giá bao nhiêu?
5. Ngôi nhà đẹp này ở gần biển.

D. Vocabulary

(1) người; (2) thư ký; (3) tòa; (4) xe; (5) đi làm; (6) sống; (7) nhà; (8) lớn; (9) đi dạo; (10) chó

CHAPTER 6

A. Listening comprehension

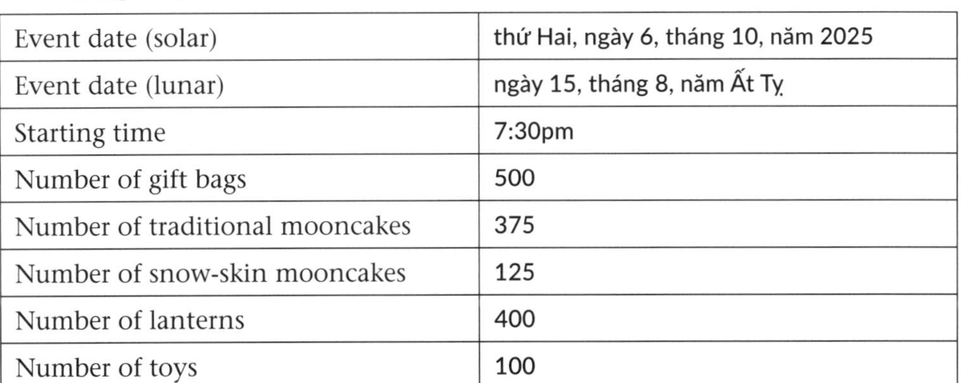

Event date (solar)	thứ Hai, ngày 6, tháng 10, năm 2025
Event date (lunar)	ngày 15, tháng 8, năm Ất Tỵ
Starting time	7:30pm
Number of gift bags	500
Number of traditional mooncakes	375
Number of snow-skin mooncakes	125
Number of lanterns	400
Number of toys	100

B. Basic math in Vietnamese!

1. 140 + 39 = 179
   Một trăm bốn mươi cộng (với) ba mươi chín bằng một trăm bảy mươi chín.
2. 263 – 98 = 165
   Hai trăm sáu mươi ba trừ (đi) chín mươi tám bằng một trăm sáu mươi lăm.
3. 72 × 41 = 2.952
   Bảy mươi hai nhân (với) bốn mươi mốt bằng hai ngàn chín trăm năm mươi hai.
4. 1.879.860 ÷ 15 = 125.324
   Một triệu tám trăm bảy mươi chín ngàn tám trăm sáu mươi chia (cho) mười lăm bằng một trăm hai mươi lăm ngàn ba trăm hai mươi bốn.
5. 25,30 × 250 = 6.325
   Hai mươi lăm phẩy ba mươi nhân (với) hai trăm năm mươi bằng sáu ngàn ba trăm hai mươi lăm.

C. Telling time –Mấy giờ rồi?

1a. Tám giờ bốn mươi lăm phút sáng.
1b. Chín giờ kém mười lăm phút sáng.
2a. Năm giờ ba mươi phút chiều.
2b. Năm giờ rưỡi chiều.
3. Một giờ hai mươi lăm phút trưa.
4. Bảy giờ mười hai phút tối.
5a. Mười hai giờ khuya.
5b. Nửa đêm.
6a. Mười giờ ba mươi bảy phút đêm.
6b. Mười một giờ kém hai mươi ba phút đêm.

D. Vocabulary

1. Một tháng thường có bốn tuần (lễ).
2. Năm nay ông ấy bao nhiêu tuổi?
3. Một năm có ba trăm sáu mươi lăm ngày.
4. Theo âm lịch, năm nay là năm gì?
5. Chúng ta sẽ gặp nhau lúc mấy giờ?
6. Cô ấy sinh vào năm nào?
7. Một thế kỷ là một trăm năm.
8. Ngày tây là ngày tính theo dương lịch.

CHAPTER 7

A. Listening comprehension

Câu hỏi	Câu trả lời
1	Tôi mười chín tuổi.
2	Phải, tôi là người Mỹ.
3	Tôi học ở Đại Học Quốc Gia.
4	Tôi sống ở Đà Nẵng.
5	Tôi học tiếng Pháp.
6	Không, tôi đang học năm thứ hai.
7	Không, tôi không đi làm.
8	Tôi học bài ở thư viện.

B. Interrogative words

1. Thư viện thành phố cách ngân hàng Chase bao xa?
2. Cô ấy đi mua sắm với ai?
3. Con trai cô mấy tuổi?
4. Khi nào họ sẽ đi ăn với nhau?
5. Ngày mai các anh đi đâu?
6. Thành phố Tampa thuộc tiểu bang nào?
7. Tại sao anh ấy học tiếng Anh?
8. Chiếc xe này giá bao nhiêu?
9. Hôm nay chị thế nào?
10. Trường đại học này tên là gì?
11. Từ nhà anh lái xe đến trường mất bao lâu?

C. Types of questions

1. Ngân Hàng Thành Phố nằm trên đường nào?
2. Cô cần đô-la hay euro?
3. Hôm nay hối suất đồng yen có cao không?
4. Đồng nhân dân tệ là của Trung Quốc, phải không?
5. Đây có phải là quầy đổi ngoại tệ không?
6. Tại sao anh muốn mua lệnh phiếu?

D. Vocabulary

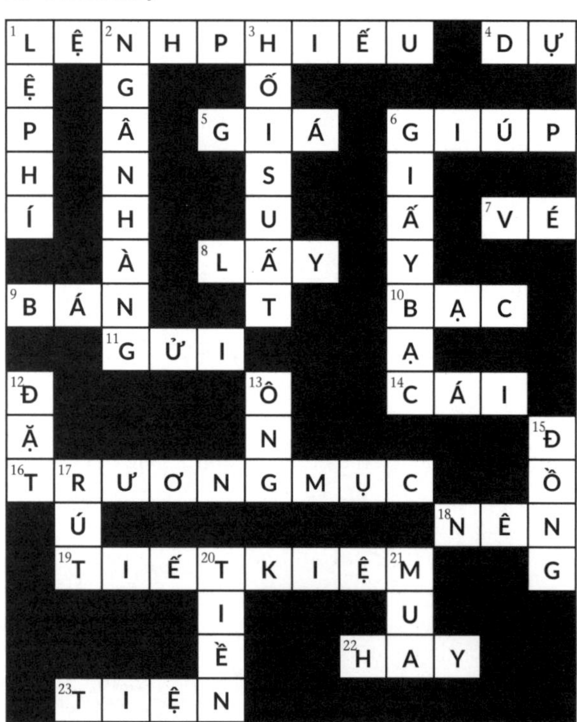

CHAPTER 8

A. Listening comprehension 

Activity	People/Pets
Ngủ trên xô-pha	con mèo
Thay quần áo trong phòng ngủ	Bảo
Rửa mặt trong buồng tắm	Thảo
Đọc báo tại bàn ăn	Ba
Chơi với quả banh	con chó
Tập thể dục trong phòng gia đình	Huy
Làm bữa ăn sáng trong nhà bếp	Mẹ

B. Emphatic negative expressions

1b. Trong nhà tôi không ai mà không đi ngủ sớm.
2b. Không có gì trong nhà bếp mà không sạch sẽ và gọn gàng.
3b. Không đâu mà không có công viên để người dân đến chơi.
4b. Không thế nào mà tôi không ăn trái cây tráng miệng.
5b. Không bao giờ mà em gái tôi không rửa chén sau bữa ăn.

C. Adverbs of manner and degree

1b. Anh tôi giặt quần áo một cách kỹ lưỡng lắm.
2b. Tôi thường phải nấu ăn một cách hơi vội vàng.
3b. Chị có tập thể dục một cách thật đều đặn không?
4b. Các em của cô xếp quần áo một cách gọn gàng quá.
5b. Con chúng tôi luôn luôn học một cách khá chăm chỉ.

D. Vocabulary

	Item	*Associated verb*
1	giường	đi ngủ
2	lời nhắn	nhắn tin
3	điện thoại	gọi điện thoại
4	khăn	lau mặt
5	áo quần	giặt đồ
6	đồng hồ báo thức	thức giấc
7	bãi cỏ	cắt cỏ
8	vòi hoa sen	tắm

	Item	*Associated verb*
9	thùng rác	đổ rác
10	sách	đọc sách
11	bàn chải răng	đánh răng
12	nồi	nấu ăn
13	bàn ủi "	ủi đồ
14	phim	xem phim
15	tóc	gội đầu

CHAPTER 9

A. Listening comprehension

Tên công ty *Company's name*	✓		
	Việt Á *Viet-Asia*		

Thời gian du lịch *Tour length*			✓ 3 ngày 2 đêm *3 days & 2 nights*
Địa điểm du lịch *Travel destination*		✓ Phú Quốc	
Chuyến bay *Flight*	✓ khứ hồi *round trip*		
Hãng hàng không *Airline*			✓ Việt Nam *Vietnam*
Khu nghỉ mát *Resort*		✓ 4 sao *four-star*	
Phòng *Room*	✓ giường đôi *double bed*		
Bữa ăn bao *Meal included*	✓ bữa sáng *breakfast*	✓ bữa trưa *lunch*	
Nơi KHÔNG thăm viếng *Place NOT visited*			✓ sòng bài *casinos*
Giá tổng cộng *Total price*			✓ 3.335.000đ

B. The verb THÌ

1. Thị xã Sapa thì nổi tiếng về ruộng bậc thang.
2. Khí hậu ở vùng này thì lý tưởng cho ngành du lịch.
3. Người dân địa phương thì lúc nào cũng thân thiện với du khách nước ngoài.
4. Ngày nay xe lửa Xuyên Việt thì rất hiện đại.
5. Thời tiết ở thành phố ven biển này thì thường khó đoán trước, phải không?

C. Verbs of movement

1. Ngày mai đoàn du khách ở Sapa sẽ xuống Hà Nội.
2. Từ Hà Nội vào Huế bằng xe lửa mất bao nhiêu tiếng đồng hồ?
3. Giá vé máy bay từ Nha Trang lên Pleiku thì không mắc lắm.
4. Cuối tuần này chúng tôi sẽ qua Cam Bốt và về lại Sài Gòn vào thứ Tư.
5. Họ sẽ từ Cà Mau lên Sài Gòn, rồi sau đó ra Nha Trang bằng xe đò.

D. Vocabulary

1. b. phi trường
2. c. nghỉ hè
3. d. đi bộ
4. a. khu nghỉ mát
5. c. giấy thông hành
6. d. chuyến đi
7. a. hướng dẫn viên
8. c. thẻ lên máy bay

CHAPTER 10

A. Listening comprehension

Tên công ty *Company's name*		✓	
	Thảo Mộc Nam Việt *Southern Vietnamese Herbs*	Dược Thảo Nam Việt *Southern Vietnamese Medicinal Herbs*	Dược Thảo Việt Nam *Vietnamese Medicinal Herbs*
Tên thuốc bổ *Supplement's name*			✓
	Sinh Lực *Vitality*	Siêu Lực *Super Power*	Siêu Sinh Lực *Super Vitality*
Nguyên liệu *Ingredients*		✓	✓
	củ *roots*	quả *fruits*	rau *vegetables*
Dạng thuốc *Supplement's form*	✓		
	viên *pill*	tươi *fresh*	sấy khô *dried*
Chỉ dẫn *Instructions*		✓	
	mỗi ngày hai viên *two pills a day*	mỗi ngày ba viên *three pills a day*	mỗi ngày một viên *one pill a day*
			✓
	uống với sữa *taken with milk*	uống với trà *taken with tea*	uống với nước *taken with water*
	✓		
	uống sau bữa ăn *taken after a meal*	uống trước bữa ăn *taken before a meal*	uống trong bữa ăn *taken during a meal*

B. How do you say these things in Vietnamese to your doctor?

1. Tôi hơi nhức đầu.
2. Ban đêm tôi ngủ không ngon.
3. Lưng tôi đau lắm.
4. Thuốc này tôi uống một ngày mấy viên?
5. Cánh tay trái của tôi mỏi lắm.
6. Tôi không tập thể dục thường xuyên.
7. Tôi ăn không ngon miệng.
8. Tôi có cần uống thuốc bổ không?
9. Tôi rất sợ bị chích thuốc.
10. Lúc nào tôi cũng cảm thấy mệt mỏi.

C. Making commands

1. Hãy tập thể dục hằng ngày.
2. Xin đừng hút thuốc ở đây.
3. Gọi y tá giùm tôi.
4. Cô cứ tiếp tục uống loại xi-rô này nhé.
5. Mời anh đứng lên cái cân này.
6. Con uống hai viên thuốc này đi.

D. Vocabulary

Tên thuốc *Brand of medication*	Triệu chứng *Symptom*
(a) Pepto Bismol®	[b] 1. Nhức đầu
(b) Tylenol®	[i] 2. Mất ngủ
(c) Robitussin®	[d] 3. Cúm
(d) Tamiflu®	[h] 4. Đau họng
(e) Benadryl®	[e] 5. Ngứa
(f) Visine®	[a] 6. Đau bụng
(g) Salonpas®	[f] 7. Đỏ mắt
(h) Ricola®	[g] 8. Đau lưng
(i) Melatonin®	[j] 9. Nhức răng
(j) Orajel®	[c] 10. Ho

CHAPTER 11

A. Listening comprehension

PHỞ...NOMENAL!			
Loại món ăn *Type of dish*		✓	
		Xúp *Soup*	
Bánh *Noodles*			✓
			Phở *Rice noodles*
Nước dùng *Broth*		✓	✓
		Xương gà *Chicken bones*	Xương bò *Beef bones*
Rau *Veggies*		✓	✓
		Húng quế *Basil*	Ngò *Cilantro*
Gia vị tươi *Fresh condiments*	ü	✓	
	Chanh *Limes*	Ớt *Jalapeños*	
Tương *Sauces*	ü		✓
	Tương đen *Hoisin sauce*		Tương đỏ *Sriracha*
Gia vị *Spices*	✓	✓	✓
	Đinh hương *Cloves*	Hồi *Anise*	Quế *Cinnamon*

B. Prepositions and conjunctions.

1. Tôi không uống sữa được vào buổi sáng.
2. Nếu món ăn cay quá, cô ấy sẽ không thấy ngon nữa.
3. Anh ấy không ăn hết chén canh vì canh nêm quá ngọt.
4. Cô thường ăn rau luộc hay rau xào?
5. Chúng tôi ít khi ăn cơm với thịt vịt.
6. Việt Nam nằm bên một bờ biển dài nên cá là món ăn rất phổ biến.
7. Ông có cảm tưởng gì về món bánh mì thịt Việt Nam?
8. Em tôi ăn chay mặc dầu rất thích thịt.
9. Mẹ tôi thường nấu các loại canh khoai thay vì các loại rau.
10. Xà-lách là chữ mượn từ tiếng Pháp "salade" nhưng để chỉ tên một loại rau.
11. Nước dùng của bún bò Huế được nấu bằng xương bò và chân giò heo.
12. Chè Việt Nam ăn cũng gần như chè Thái hay chè Phi.
13. Khi nước sôi, chị nhớ tắt bếp cho bánh phở chín đều.
14. Vị chua của giấm làm tô mì gà thêm phần hấp dẫn.
15. Pha giùm tôi một chén nước mắm tỏi ớt để ăn với món gỏi tôm này.
16. Món cơm chiên đó là cho mấy đứa nhỏ.
17. Bắp nướng trông ngon quá mà lại thiếu mỡ hành!

C. Preposition or conjunction?

1. Không nên nói chuyện quá nhiều TRONG bữa ăn.
2. Con phải ăn TRƯỚC KHI tập thể dục.
3. SAU KHI ăn xong, tôi thường đi bộ cho mau tiêu cơm.
4. Tôi quan sát mẹ nấu món bún riêu TỪ đầu ĐẾN cuối.
5. TỪ KHI biết nấu ăn, cô ấy ăn toàn những món lành mạnh.
6. ĐẾN mấy giờ tôi mới lấy con gà quay ra được?
7. Bánh Trung Thu thường được bắt đầu bày bán VÀO tháng Sáu âm lịch.

D. Vocabulary

1. b. cay
2. c. ngọt
3. d. mặn
4. a. đắng
5. b. chua

CHAPTER 12

A. Listening comprehension

1. b. y phục
2. d. mùa đông
3. b. Thời Trang 21
4. a. áo khoác
5. c. 40%
6. d. bốn tuần

B. Particles

1. Dạ, con không cần mặc áo len.
2. Cái áo đầm đỏ này không bán hạ giá à?
3. Cô sửa giùm cái váy mới của tôi.
4. Thưa bà, tiệm chúng tôi không có cỡ lớn cho những cái quần đó.
5. Vải này bền lắm chứ!
6. Cô thích cái nón của cháu lắm, cháu ạ.

C. Interjections

1. Chà! Cái đồng hồ này trông sang quá!
2. Cô ơi! Ở đây có bán vớ len không, cô?
3. Ủa! Sao anh không đeo cà-vạt?
4. À! Tuần sau thương xá này có nhiều tiệm bán hạ giá lắm.
5. Thôi! Tôi có nhiều áo sơ-mi rồi.
6. Hở? Đôi giày này mà giá hai triệu à?

D. Vocabulary

Verbs	mặc	mang	đeo	để	bôi	đội
Nouns	áo đầm quần tây áo khoác	nịt khăn quàng vớ giày găng tay kính	hoa tai nhẫn dây chuyền vòng đeo tay đồng hồ	râu tóc dài	nước hoa kem chống nắng	nón khăn đóng

CHAPTER 13

A. Listening comprehension

1. d. một vở cải lương
2. a. Đất Việt
3. b. lịch sử
4. d. phương bắc
5. c. đạo diễn
6. d. (a) and (b)

B. ĐƯỢC and BỊ

1. Tuần trước tôi bị xem một cuốn phim kinh dị rất dở.
2. Tối nay anh ấy sẽ không chơi dương cầm vì bị cảm.
3. Cô có hiểu được các đối thoại trong vở kịch đó không?
4. Mẹ ơi, con mở tivi lên được không?
5. Buổi triển lãm nghệ thuật được thành công nhờ những nghệ sĩ nổi tiếng đó.

C. Passive sentences

1. Cuốn phim này đã được chúng tôi quay trong ba tháng.
2. Vở kịch "Giữ Vững Sơn Hà" là do nhà văn Trần Việt viết.
3. Vai người mẹ trong bộ phim truyền hình đó là do ai đóng?
4. Cảnh hoàng hôn được hoạ sĩ miêu tả thật sâu lắng.
5. Nhiều nét trên khuôn mặt cô trong bức ảnh bị bóng tối làm mờ đi.

D. Vocabulary

1. điện ảnh
2. đóng phim
3. điêu khắc gia
4. khán giả
5. nhiếp ảnh gia
6. đạo diễn
7. diễn tuồng
8. giải

CHAPTER 14

A. Listening comprehension

	Cha mẹ Chú rể *Groom's parents*	Cha mẹ cô dâu *Bride's parents*	Chú rể *Groom*	Cô dâu *Bride*	Lễ cưới *Wedding ceremony*	Tiệc cưới *Wedding reception*	Nhà Thờ *Church*	Nhà hàng *Restaurant*	Thiệp phúc đáp *RSVP*
Đồng Khánh						✓		✓	
Nguyễn Văn Thảo		✓							
Thánh Linh					✓		✓		
26/4/26					✓				
Nguyễn Thị Bảo				✓					
Trần Văn Huy	✓								
25/12/25									✓
Trần Quốc Việt			✓						

B. Compound sentences

1. Ở nhà hàng này chúng ta có thể đặt tiệc cưới hay tổ chức sinh nhật.
2. Đây là một tấm hình gia đình chú rể, còn đây là hình gia đình cô dâu.
3. Chúng tôi làm lễ cưới nhưng không làm đám hỏi.
4. Tiệc cưới của chúng tôi không có hát mà cũng không có khiêu vũ.
5. Tôi sẽ đặt một cái bánh cưới màu trắng và thuê một ban nhạc.
6. Hôm đó trời rất lạnh mà lễ cưới vẫn diễn ra trên bãi biển.
7. Đôi tân hôn thích tiền mặt hơn quà cưới, vì vậy chúng tôi nhắc nhau đừng mua quà cáp gì cả.

C. Complex sentences

1. Mẹ tôi sinh đứa con đầu lòng khi bà mới 25 tuổi.
2. Tôi muốn gặp ông giám đốc mà vợ là bác sĩ ở bệnh viện thành phố.
3. Chú Bình rất thương chúng tôi vì chú còn độc thân.
4. Đây là cô em họ mà tôi đã giới thiệu với anh qua điện thư.
5. Hãy bỏ qua câu hỏi này nếu bạn đã có gia đình.
6. Nhiều gia đình muốn có con trai để nối dõi tông đường.
7. Gần đây, các nhà xã hội học nhận thấy rằng giới trẻ Việt Nam thích sống độc thân hơn.
8. Họ đang định xin một đứa con nuôi tuy đã có ba người con.
9. Con trai của ông Vũ ao ước được đến nơi ông đã sống trong thời thơ ấu.
10. Gia đình người Việt ở nước ngoài cũng gắn bó như các bạn thấy ở trong nước.
11. Chị Lan chỉ có một đứa em gái nên chị rất cưng chiều em.
12. Giới trẻ Việt Nam phóng khoáng về tình yêu hơn là những gì các bạn biệt được qua sách vở.

D. Vocabulary

Vietnamese-English Glossary

A/Ă/Â

à *part – interrogative*

ạ *part – polite*

ai *pron* who • ***ai đó?*** who is it?

anh 1 *n* brother; *pron* you (*male*) **2 Anh** – English • ***nước Anh*** England • ***tiếng Anh*** English language • ***người Anh*** Briton

anh ấy *pron* he • ***các anh ấy*** they/them (*male*)

anh/chị/em họ *n* cousin

áo *n* top (*garment*)

áo choàng *n* coat

áo dài *n* Vietnamese traditional dress

áo đầm *n* dress

áo khoác *n* blazer

áo len *n* sweater

áo lót *n* undershirt

áo sơ-mi *n* shirt

áo tắm *n* bathing suit

áo thun *n* T-shirt

áo vét *n* suit jacket

ăn *v* to eat • ***ăn sáng*** to have breakfast • ***ăn trưa*** to have lunch • ***ăn tối*** to have dinner • ***ăn kiêng*** to be on a diet

ăn mặc *v* to dress (*in general*)

âm lịch *n* lunar calendar • ***Tết Âm Lịch*** Lunar New Year

ấm *adj* warm, lukewarm

ầm ĩ *adj* boisterous

ẩm thấp *adj* humid

B

ba *n* **1** father **2** three • ***thứ ba*** third • ***thứ Ba*** Tuesday

bà *n* **1** ma'am **2** grandmother **3** *pron* you (*female*)

bà cố *n* great-grandmother

bà ngoại *n* maternal grandmother

bà nội *n* paternal grandmother

bác (gái) *n* wife of "**bác trai**"

bác (trai) *n* paternal uncle (*older than father*)

bác sĩ *n* doctor • ***đi bác sĩ*** to go to the doctor

bạc *n* silver • ***tiền bạc*** money

bài hát *n* song

bài học *n* lesson

bài tập *n* exercise • ***bài tập ở nhà*** homework

bãi biển *n* beach

ban đêm *n* night; nighttime

ban ngày *n* day; daytime

bán *v* to sell • ***bán hạ giá*** to have a sale

bán thời gian *adj* part-time

bàn *n* table • ***bàn giấy*** desk

bàn chân *n* foot

bàn tay *n* hand

bàn thờ *n* altar

bản tin *n* news report

bản tóm tắt cá nhân *n* resumé

bạn *n* friend • ***bạn gái*** girlfriend • ***bạn trai*** boyfriend

banh *n* ball • ***đá banh*** to play soccer

bánh *n* cake • ***bánh ngọt*** pastry • ***bánh xe*** tire

bánh chưng *n* square sticky rice cake

bánh mì *n* bread

bánh tét *n* cylindrical rice cake

bánh xèo *n* crispy pancake

bao *v* to cover; to include • ***bao gồm*** including

bao giờ *interr adv* when • ***không bao giờ*** never

bao nhiêu *interr adj/adv* how many; how much • ***cuốn sách này bao nhiêu tiền?*** how much is this book?

bảo hiểm *n* insurance • ***bảo hiểm sức khỏe*** health insurance

bão *n* storm

bay *v* to fly • ***chuyến bay*** flight

bắc *adj* northern • ***miền Bắc*** the North

băng qua đường *v* to cross the street

bằng 1 *adj* equal **2** *prep* by • ***bằng máy bay*** by airplane

bắt đầu *v* to start

bận (rộn) *adj* busy

bây giờ *adv* now

bên *n* side • ***bên phải của*** *prep* on the right of • ***bên trái của*** *prep* on the left of

bền *adj* durable

bệnh *n* disease, sickness; *adj* sick • ***bị bệnh*** to be sick

bệnh nhân *n* patient
bệnh viện *n* hospital
bệnh xá *n* clinic
bi quan *adj* pessimistic
bị *v* to be (*in unfavorable situations*) • ***bị phạt*** to be punished
bia *n* beer
biến đổi khí hậu *n* climate change
biển *n* sea • ***bãi biển*** beach • ***bờ biển*** coast • ***Biển Đông*** the East Sea
bình cắm hoa *n* flower vase
bình thường *adj* normal
bó sát người *adj* tight-fitting
bò *n* cow • ***thịt bò*** beef
bọc *v* to cover; to wrap
bố/ba/cha *n* father
bố chồng *n* father-in-law (*of the woman*)
bố vợ *n* father-in-law (*of the man*)
bôi *v* to wear (*perfume*); to apply (*ointment, lotion*)
bồi bàn *n* server
bột *n* flour, powder • ***bột ngũ cốc*** cereal • ***bột yến mạch*** oatmeal
bún *n* rice vermicelli • ***bún bò*** beef vermicelli
bụng *n* abdomen, belly • ***bị đau bụng*** to have a stomachache
bữa (ăn) sáng *n* breakfast
bữa (ăn) tối *n* dinner
bữa (ăn) trưa *n* lunch
buổi chiều *n* late afternoon
buổi sáng *n* morning
buổi tối *n* evening
buổi trưa *n* early afternoon
buồn *adj* sad • ***nỗi buồn*** sadness
buồn ngủ *adj* sleepy
buồn nôn *adj* nauseated
buồng tắm *n* bathroom
bức *cl for photo, painting, statue* • ***bức tranh*** painting • ***bức ảnh*** photo
bưu điện *n* post office

C

cá *n* fish • ***câu cá*** to fish
cá nhân *adj* personal, individual
cà *n* tomato • ***cà tím*** eggplant
cà-phê *n* coffee • ***cà-phê đen*** black coffee • ***cà-phê sữa đá*** iced coffee with milk
cả *adj* all • ***cả hai*** both • ***tất cả*** all
các anh *pron* you (*male/plural*)
các anh ấy *pron* they (*male*)
các bà *pron* you (*female/plural*)
các bà ấy *pron* they (*female*)
các chị *pron* you (*female/plural*)
các chị ấy *pron* they (*female*)
các ông *pron* you (*male/plural*)
các ông ấy *pron* they (*male*)
cách 1 *n* way, manner • ***bằng cách nào?*** how? in what way? **2** *adv* away (*from*) • ***cách nhau*** apart
cam *n, adj* orange • ***nước cam*** orange juice
cảm *n* cold • ***bị cảm*** to have a cold
cảm giác *n* sensation
cảm hứng *n* inspiration
cảm ơn/cám ơn *interj* thanks
cảm thấy *v* to feel • ***cô cảm thấy thế nào?*** how are you feeling?
cảm tưởng *n* impression
cảm xúc *n* emotion
cánh *n* wing
cánh tay *n* arm
cảnh sát *n* police officer
cảnh *n* scenery
cạnh *pron* next to
cao *adj* tall • ***chiều cao*** height
cao nguyên *n* highlands
cạo râu *n* to shave
cay *adj* spicy
cắt cỏ *v* to cut the grass; to mow the lawn
cần *v* to need • ***ông cần gì?*** how can I help you?
cầu hôn *v* to propose (*marriage*)
câu *n* sentence • ***câu hỏi*** question • ***câu trả lời*** answer
cậu *n* maternal uncle
cha *n* father • ***cha dượng*** stepfather
cha mẹ *n* parents
cha/mẹ chồng *n* father-/mother-in-law (*man's side*)
cha/mẹ nuôi *n* adoptive father/mother
cha/mẹ vợ *n* father-/mother-in-law (*woman's side*)
chai *n* bottle
chanh *n* lime, lemon • ***nước chanh*** lemonade
cháo *n* porridge
chào 1 *v* to greet **2** *interj* hello; goodbye
chảo *n* frying pan
cháu 1 (trai/gái) *n* nephew/niece **2** grandson/granddaughter

chạy *v* to run

chắc *adj* **1** maybe **2** sure • ***anh có chắc không?*** are you sure?

chân *n* foot • ***ngón chân*** toe • ***móng chân*** toenail

chất *n* substance • ***phẩm chất*** quality

chật *adj* **1** tight **2** narrow

chè *n* sweet soup (*dessert*)

chén *n* small bowl

chết *v* to die

chi tiết *n* detail; information

chị 1 *n* sister; **2** *pron* you/female

chị ấy *pron* she • ***các chị ấy*** they (*female*)

chỉ1 *v* to show • ***chỉ đường*** to show the way

chỉ2 *adv* only • ***chỉ có điều là*** it's just that

chia *v* to divide

chiên *v* to fry

chim *n* bird

chín[1] *adj* cooked; ripe

chín[2] *adj, n* nine • ***chín tuổi*** nine years old

chính *adj* main • ***chính mình*** oneself

chính thức *adj* official

cho 1 *n* to give **2** *prep* for

chó *n* dog

choáng váng *adj* lightheaded, dizzy

chọn *v* to choose

chóng mặt *adj* dizzy

chỗ *n* place • ***chỗ làm*** workplace • ***chỗ nào?*** where?

chồng *n* husband • ***chồng sắp cưới*** fiancé

chợ *n* market • ***đi chợ*** to go grocery shopping

chú *n* paternal uncle (*younger than father*)

chú rể *n* groom

chua *adj* sour • ***cà chua*** tomato • ***sữa chua*** yogurt

chùa *n* Buddhist temple

chuẩn bị *v* to prepare

chúc (tụng) *v* to wish • ***Chúc Mừng Năm Mới!*** Happy New Year!

chung *adv* together, collectively

chung quanh *prep* around

chúng nó *pron* they (*kids*)

chúng ta *pron* we (*inclusive*)

chúng tôi *pron* we (*exclusive*)

chuối *n* banana • ***nải chuối*** bunch of bananas

chụp hình/ảnh *v* to take a picture

chuyên về *v* to specialize in

chuyến du lịch *n* trip

chuyển *v* to transfer

chuyển âm *v* to dub (*a movie*)

chuyện *n* matter; story • ***có chuyện gì vậy?*** what's the matter?

chứ *part* **1** *interrogative* • ***cô sẽ đến chứ?*** you will come, won't you? **2** *emphatic* • ***truyện này hay chứ!*** this story is good indeed

chưa *adv* not yet • ***chưa tính*** excluding, not to mention

chương trình *n* program

có *v* **1** to have **2** there is/there are **3** *adv* yes • ***có chứ!*** why yes!

có bầu *adj* pregnant

có chồng *v* to be married (*for a woman*)

có con *v* to have a child

có gia đình *adj* married

có hiếu *adj* devoted (*child to parents*)

có lý *v* to make sense • ***cô nói có lý*** you're right

có mặt *v* to be present

có thể *v* to be able to, can • ***không thể*** cannot

có vẻ *v* to appear, to seem

có vợ *v* to be married (*for a man*)

con gái *n* **1** girl **2** daughter

con trai *n* **1** boy **2** son

con dâu *n* daughter-in-law

con nuôi *adj* adoptive child

con rể *n* son-in-law

còn[1] *adv* still • ***còn sớm*** still early

còn[2] *conj* and, as for • ***còn anh thì sao?*** how about you?

cô *n* **1** paternal aunt **2** Miss; *pron* you/female

cô dâu *n* bride

cô ấy *pron* she

cổ *n* neck

cổ họng *n* throat

công việc *n* work; job

công viên *n* park

công nhân *n* worker

công nhận *v* to recognize

công ty *n* company

công viên *n* park

cộng *v* to add

cỡ *n* size • ***cỡ nào?*** what size?

cởi ra *v* to take off (*clothing*)

cơm *n* steamed rice • ***cơm chiên*** fried rice

cũ *adj* old • ***bạn cũ*** old friend

của *prep* of • ***của ai*** *interr adj* whose

của hồi môn *n* dowry

cúm *n* flu • ***bị cúm*** to have the flu

cung điện *n* royal palace
cúng *v* to make offerings (*to the deceased*)
cùng *adv* together • ***cùng cha khác mẹ*** with the same father but a different mother • ***cùng mẹ khác cha*** with the same mother but a different father
cũng *adv* also • ***tôi cũng vậy*** me too
cũng như *conj* as well as
cuộc phỏng vấn *n* interview
cuộc sống *n* life
cuối cùng *adj, adv* last, final(ly)
cuối tuần *n* weekend
cửa *n* door
cửa sổ *n* window
cửa tiệm *n* shop
cưới hỏi *n* engagement and marriage
cưới/lấy vợ *v* to marry (*a woman*)

D

dạ dày *n* stomach
dai *adj* chewy
dài *adj* long • ***chiều dài*** length
dám *v* dare • ***tôi không dám*** I dare not
dao *n* knife • ***dao lam*** razor
dạo này *adv* lately
dấu *n* mark • ***dấu chấm hỏi*** question mark • ***dấu chấm than*** exclamation mark
dày *adj* thick • ***bề dày*** thickness
dạy *v* to teach
dạy dỗ *v* to bring up (*a child*)
dây *n* string, cord
dây chuyền *n* necklace • ***đeo dây chuyền*** to wear a necklace
dậy *v* to get up • ***thức dậy*** to wake up
dép *n* flip-flops
dễ *adj* easy
dễ thương *adj* cute, lovely
dì *n* maternal aunt
diễn ra *v* to take place
diễn tuồng *v* to act (*in an opera*)
diễn viên *n* actor
dọn dẹp *v* to clean up
doanh nhân *n* businessman
dồi dào *adj* plentiful, abundant
dở *adj* bad; tasteless
du khách *n* tourist
du lịch *n* traveling, tourism
du ngoạn *v* to go sightseeing
dùng *v* **1** to use **2** to have (*meal, food*) • ***nước dùng*** broth
dự báo *v* to forecast • ***dự báo thời tiết*** weather forecast
dưới *prep* below; under
dượng *n* husband of "**cô**" or "**dì**" • ***cha dượng*** stepfather

Đ

đám cưới *n* wedding
đám giỗ *n* death anniversary
đám hỏi *n* engagement ceremony
đàn *n* string instrument • ***đánh đàn*** to play a string instrument
đàn bà *n* woman
đàn ông *n* man
đang *part* – *indicates an on-going action* • ***cô đang làm gì đó?*** what are you doing?
đánh răng *v* to brush one's teeth
đau 1 *v* to hurt **2** *adj* painful
đau bụng *v* to have a stomachache
đau cổ họng *v* to have a sore throat
đau lưng *v* to have a backache
đã *part* – *indicates a completed action* • ***tôi đã làm bài xong*** I have finished my homework
đắt *adj* expensive
đầu *n* head • ***tôi nhức đầu*** I have a headache
đen *adj* black • ***cà-phê đen*** black coffee
đèn giao thông *n* traffic lights
đẹp *adj* beautiful
đếm *v* to count • ***số đếm*** cardinal number
đền *n* temple
đến *v* to come; to arrive
đi *v* **1** to go • ***bạn đi đâu vậy?*** where are you going? **2** to leave, to depart • ***khi nào ông đi?*** when are you leaving?
đi bộ *v* to walk
đi câu *v* to go hunting
đi dạo *v* to go for a walk
đi làm *v* to go to work
đi mua sắm *v* to go shopping
đi ngủ *v* to go to bed
đi săn *v* to go hunting
đĩa *n* plate • ***rửa chén đĩa*** to wash the dishes
điện thoại *n* telephone • ***điện thoại cầm tay*** cell phone • ***gọi điện thoại*** to make a phone call
đó 1 *adj* that **2** *adv* there • ***ai đó?*** who's there?
đỏ *adj* red

đói *adj* hungry• ***tôi đói bụng quá!*** I'm so hungry!
đội *v* to wear (*on the head*) • ***đội nón*** to wear a hat
đối diện *prep* opposite
đồng hồ *n* watch, clock • ***đồng hồ báo thức*** alarm clock
đũa *n* chopstick • ***đôi đũa*** pair of chopsticks
đường *n* **1** street **2** sugar

E

em chồng *n* husband's younger sibling
em cùng cha khác mẹ/em cùng mẹ khác cha *n* half-sibling (*younger*)
em dâu *n* sister-in-law (*younger brother's wife*)
em gái *n* younger sister
em họ *n* first cousin (*child of mom's or dad's younger sibling*)
em rể *n* brother-in-law (*younger sister's husband*)
em trai *n* younger brother
em vợ *n* wife's younger sibling
êm *adj* smooth
êm đềm *adj* peaceful, tranquil

G

gà *n* chicken • ***phở gà*** chicken noodle soup
gần *adv, prep* near • ***gần đây*** lately
gầy *adj* skinny
ghế *n* chair • ***ghế bành*** armchair
ghi tên *v* to check in; to register
gì *interr pron* what • ***anh tên gì?*** what's your name?
gia đình *n* family
giá *n* price • ***giá hạ*** discount price
Giáng Sinh *n* Christmas • ***Chúc Mừng Giáng Sinh!*** Merry Christmas!
giáo sư *n* professor
giáo viên *n* teacher
giày *n* shoe • ***giày cao gót*** high heels
giặt *v* to wash (*clothes*) • ***máy giặt*** washer • ***tiệm giặt ủi*** drycleaner's
giây *n* second • ***đợi một giây!*** wait a second!
giấy nhập cảnh *n* visa
gió *n* wind • ***trời gió quá!*** it's so windy!
giờ *n* hour; o'clock • ***mấy giờ rồi?*** what time is it?
giúp *v* to help • ***giúp tôi với!*** help me!
giữa *prep* **1** between **2** in the middle of
gọi *v* **1** to call **2** to order (*food, drinks*)

H

hãng hàng không *n* airline
hành lý *n* luggage
hắt hơi *v* to sneeze
heo *n* pig; pork • ***heo quay*** roasted pig
hiểu *v* to understand • ***tôi không hiểu chữ này*** I don't understand this word
ho *v* to cough • ***thuốc ho*** cough medicine
họ **1** *pron* they **2** *n* last name
học sinh *n* student, pupil
hồng *adj* pink • ***hoa hồng*** rose
hơi *adv* kind of • ***bài tập này hơi khó*** this exercise is kind of hard
hút bụi *v* to vacuum • ***máy hút bụi*** vacuum cleaner
hút thuốc *v* to smoke • ***cấm hút thuốc*** no smoking allowed

K

khách sạn *n* hotel
khám *v* to examine • ***khám bệnh*** to examine a patient
khát *adj* thirsty • ***cô có khát nước không?*** are you thirsty?
khăn quàng *n* scarf
khoẻ *adj* well, healthy • ***sức khoẻ*** health
không *adv* no, not • ***không có chi*** you are welcome • ***không ai*** nobody • ***không (có) gì*** nothing • ***không bao giờ*** never
kia *adj* that... over there • ***đằng kia*** over there
kiên nhẫn *adj* patient
kính *n* eyeglasses • ***kính mát*** sunglasses
kỹ sư *n* engineer

L

là **1** *v* to be • ***anh là ai?*** who are you? **2** *conj (informal)* that • ***Tôi nghĩ là anh nói đúng*** I think that you're right
lạc quan *adj* optimistic
lái xe *v* to drive
làm *v* **1** to do • ***các em đang làm gì đó?*** what are you guys doing? **2** to make • ***làm ơn*** please
làm đám cưới *v* to have a wedding
làm việc *v* to work
lạnh *adj* cold • ***nước lạnh*** water • ***máy lạnh*** air conditioner • ***tủ lạnh*** refrigerator
lau chùi *v* to clean, to wipe
lấy chồng *v* to get married (*for a woman*)
lấy vợ *v* to get married (*for a man*)
lễ *n* holiday • ***nghỉ lễ*** to have a holiday off

lễ Phật Đản *n* Buddha's Birthday holiday
lớn *adj* big • ***người lớn*** adult
luật sư *n* lawyer
lưng *n* back
lưỡi *n* tongue
ly *n* glass

M

mang *v* **1** to bring, to carry **2** to wear (*accessories*) • ***mang kính*** to wear glasses
mang thai *v* to be pregnant
màu *n* color • ***màu gì?*** what color?
máy bay *n* airplane • ***đi máy bay*** to fly
máy rút tiền *n* ATM
mặc *v* to wear (*clothing*) • ***mặc quần áo*** to get dressed
mặc vào *v* to put on (*clothing*)
mặn *adj* salty
mắt *n* eye • ***nhắm mắt*** to close one's eyes
mặt *n* face • ***rửa mặt*** to wash one's face
mặt trăng *n* moon
mặt trời *n* sun
mất *v* **1** to lose **2** to pass away
mây *n* cloud • ***trời có nhiều mây*** it's cloudy
mấy *interr adj* how many • ***hôm nay thứ mấy?*** what's today?
mẹ/má *n* mother
mẹ chồng *n* mother-in-law (*of the woman*)
mẹ vợ *n* mother-in-law (*of the man*)
mèo *n* cat
mệt *adj* tired • ***mỏi mệt*** fatigued
mì *n* egg noodles • ***mì ăn liền*** instant noodles
miệng *n* mouth • ***món tráng miệng*** dessert
món *n* **1** item **2** dish
mợ *n* wife of "**cậu**"
mới **1** *adj* new **2** *adv* newly • ***mới cưới*** newly wed
mời *v* to invite • ***thiệp mời*** invitation card
mùa *n* season • ***mùa học*** academic term
mùa đông *n* winter
mùa hè/mùa hạ *n* summer • ***nghỉ hè*** to be on summer vacation
mùa thu *n* autumn • ***Tết Trung Thu*** Mid-Autumn Festival
mùa xuân *n* spring
mũi *n* nose • ***lỗ mũi*** nostril
muốn *v* to want • ***ước muốn*** wish
muỗng *n* spoon • ***muỗng canh*** tablespoon • ***muỗng cà-phê*** teaspoon
mưa *n, v* (to) rain • ***trời đang mưa lớn*** it's raining hard

N

này *adj* this • ***cái này là cái gì?*** what is this?
năm *n* **1** five • ***thứ Năm*** Thursday **2** year • ***năm ngoái*** last year
nằm *v* **1** to lie **2** to be located
nắng **1** *n* sunlight **2** *adj* sunny • ***trời nắng quá*** it's very sunny
nặng *adj* **1** heavy **2** grave, serious
nâu *adj* brown
nấu ăn *v* to cook
ngã tư *n* intersection
ngày *n* day • ***ngày lễ*** *n* holiday
ngày tháng *n* date
ngắn *adj* short (*lengthwise*)
ngân hàng *n* bank • ***thẻ ngân hàng*** ATM card
nghẹt mũi *v* to have a stuffy nose
nghề *n* profession • ***anh làm nghề gì?*** what do you do for a living?
nghỉ *v* **1** to rest, to break **2** to be off (*work*)
nghỉ ngơi *v* to rest, to relax
ngoài *adv, prep* outside • ***ngoài ra*** *adv* besides
ngoại tệ *n* foreign currency
ngoạn cảnh *v* to sightsee
ngon *adj* delicious
ngọt *adj* sweet
ngón tay *n* finger
ngực *n* chest
nhà *n* house • ***ở nhà*** at home
nhà hàng *n* restaurant
nhà thờ *n* church
nhỏ *adj* small
nhức đầu *v* to have a headache
nĩa *n* fork
nó *pron* it, he/she (*child*)
nón *n* hat • ***nón lá*** conical hat
nóng *adj* hot
nôn *v* to throw up
nước *n* **1** water **2** country
nước đá *n* ice
nước ngọt *n* soda, soft drink

Ô

ôm *v* to hug
ốm *adj* **1** sick **2** skinny

ôn *v* to review
ồn *adj* noisy
ông *n* **1** sir, mister **2** *pron* you/male
ông bà *n* **1** grandparents **2** Mr. and Mrs.
ông cố *n* great-grandfather
ông ngoại *n* maternal grandfather
ông nội *n* paternal grandfather

Ơ

ở *v* to be at; to live in
ở nhà *v* to stay home
ơi *part (vocative)* • ***mẹ ơi!*** mom!
ơn *n* favor • ***cảm/cám ơn*** thank you
ớt *n* chili • ***tương ớt*** chili sauce

P

phần *n* portion, part
phi công *n* pilot
phi trường *n* airport
phiếu *n* coupon • ***phiếu giảm giá*** discount coupon
phim *n* movie, film • ***xem phim*** to watch a movie
phòng *n* room • ***phòng khách*** living room • ***phòng ngủ*** bedroom • ***phòng tắm*** bathroom
phòng cấp cứu *n* emergency room
phổi *n* lung
phở *n* rice noodles
phút *n* minute

Q

qua **1** *v* to cross, to come over **2** *adj* past • ***tuần qua*** last week
quá *adv* so • ***đẹp quá!*** so beautiful!
quà *n* gift • ***tặng quà*** to give a gift
quả *n/cl* fruit • ***quả cam*** orange
quần tây *n* pants, trousers
quẹo *v* to make a turn
quét nhà *v* to sweep the floors
quên *v* to forget • ***đừng quên*** don't forget
quý *adj* precious • ***quý vị*** you all (*formal*)

R

ra **1** *adv* out • ***bước ra*** to step out **2** *v* to go out
rạp chiếu phim *n* movie theater
rau *n* vegetable • ***rau cải*** vegetables
răng *n* tooth • ***nhức răng*** to have a toothache
râu *n* beard • ***cạo râu*** to shave
rẻ *adj* affordable, inexpensive • ***rẻ tiền*** cheap
rộng *adj* **1** loose **2** wide • ***chiều rộng*** width
rửa chén *v* to wash the dishes

S

sao *pron* what • ***anh nói sao?*** what did you say? • ***tại sao?*** why? • ***không sao*** no worries
sau *adv, prep* behind; after
sắp *part indicates a planned action (soon)* • ***trời sắp mưa*** it's going to rain
sẽ *part indicates a planned action (later)* • ***ngày mai sẽ có mưa lớn*** it will rain hard tomorrow
siêng năng *adj* hard-working
siêu thị *n* supermarket
sinh *v* **1** to give birth **2** to be born • ***cô sinh năm nào?*** what year were you born in?
sinh nhật *n* birthday • ***quà sinh nhật*** birthday present
sinh viên *n* college student
số *n* number • ***anh mang giày số mấy?*** what size shoes do you wear?
sổ mũi *v* to have a runny nose
sống *v* to live • ***ông sống ở thành phố nào?*** what city do you live in?
sốt *n* fever • ***bị sốt cao*** to have a high fever
sớm *adj* **1** early • ***dậy sớm*** to get up early **2** soon
sữa *n* milk • ***cà-phê sữa đá*** iced coffee with milk
sức khoẻ *n* health
sức mạnh *n* strength
sưng *adj* swollen

T

tách *n* cup
tai *n* ear • ***hoa/bông tai*** earring
táo *n* apple
tập thể dục *v* to exercise
tên *n* name • ***tên đệm*** middle name • ***anh tên là gì?*** what's your name?
Tết Nguyên Đán *n* Lunar New Year holiday
Tết Trung Thu *n* Mid-Autumn festival
tháng *n* month • ***tháng mấy?*** what month? • ***tháng trước*** last month • ***tháng tới/sau*** next month
thành phố *n* city
thay quần áo *v* to get dressed
thăm *v* to visit
thấp *adj* short (*person*); low
thì **1** *v* to be • ***hôm nay thì tôi bận lắm*** I'm really busy today **2** *adv* then • ***vậy thì sao?*** then what?
thím *n* wife of "**chú**"

thịt *n* meat • ***bánh mì thịt nguội*** cold cut sandwich
thông hành *n* passport
thông minh *adj* smart
thời gian *n* time • ***thời gian qua nhanh quá!*** time does fly!
thời tiết *n* weather • ***hôm nay thời tiết thế nào?*** what's the weather like today?
thuốc *n* medication • ***thuốc bổ*** supplements
thuyền *n* boat
thư viện *n* library
thức ăn *n* food
thức giấc *v* to wake up
thức uống *n* beverage
thực đơn *n* menu
thương xá *n* shopping mall
tiệm ăn *n* eatery
tiền *n* money
tim *n* heart
tím *adj* purple • ***cà tím*** eggplant
tô *n* bowl
tôi *pron* I/me • ***cái này là của tôi*** this is mine
tôm *n* shrimp
trả *v* to pay • ***trả lời*** to answer
trả phòng *v* to check out
trang điểm *v* to put on make up
trắng *adj* white
trễ *adj, adv* late
trên *prep, adv* above; over
trong *prep, adv* inside
trước *prep, adv* **1** in front (of) **2** before
tuần (lễ) *n* week • ***cuối tuần*** weekend
tuổi *n* age • ***anh bao nhiêu tuổi?*** how old are you?

U

ủi *v* to iron • ***ủi đồ*** to iron clothes • ***bàn ủi*** iron
uống *v* to drink
uống thuốc *v* to take medication
ừ *adv* yes (*informal*)
ướt *adj* wet

V

và *conj* and
vai *n* shoulder
vào 1 *v* to enter • ***vào đây!*** come in! **2** *prep* in, on, at (*time*) • ***vào mấy giờ?*** at what time? • ***vào ngày nào?*** on what day? • ***vào tháng nào?*** in what month?
vàng *adj* **1** yellow **2** gold
váy *n* skirt • ***váy ngắn*** miniskirt
vé *n* ticket • ***vé khứ hồi*** two-way ticket
viện bảo tàng *n* museum
viết bi *n* ball point pen
viết chì *n* pencil
viết *v* to write • ***viết thư*** to write a letter
vớ *n* sock • ***đôi vớ*** pair of socks • ***mang vớ*** to wear socks
vợ *n* wife • ***cưới vợ*** to marry (*for a man*)
vui tính *adj* funny
vừa 1 *part indicates a recently completed action* • ***tôi vừa ngủ dậy*** I've just woken up **2** *adj* medium • ***cỡ vừa*** medium size **3** *adj* fitting • ***cái áo này không vừa với tôi*** this shirt doesn't fit me

X

xa *prep, adv* far (from) • ***bao xa?*** how far?
xám *adj* gray
xanh dương *adj* blue
xanh lục *adj* green
xe buýt *n* bus • ***trạm xe buýt*** bus stop
xe đạp *n* bicycle • ***đi xe đạp*** to ride a bicycle
xe đò *n* charter bus
xe hơi *n* car
xe lửa *n* train • ***ga xe lửa*** train station
xem *v* **1** to look at **2** to watch • ***xem truyền hình*** to watch TV
xếp hàng *v* to stand in line
xin lỗi *interj* pardon, excuse me
xoài *n* mango
xôi *n* sticky rice

Y

y khoa *n* medicine (*branch of science*) • ***đại học y khoa*** medical school
y sĩ *n* physician
y tá *n* nurse
ý *n* idea • ***ý anh là sao?*** what's your point? • ***cố ý*** intentional • ***đồng ý*** to agree • ***vô ý*** careless
ý định *n* intention
ý kiến *n* opinion
ý nghĩ *n* thought
ý nghĩa *n* meaning, significance
yên *adj* peaceful • ***yên ổn*** safe • ***yên tâm*** worry-free
yêu *v* to love • ***người yêu*** loved one • ***tình yêu*** love • ***yêu quý*** to cherish
yếu *adj* weak

English-Vietnamese Glossary

A

a *art* một • ***a person*** một người • ***an orange*** một trái cam

ability *n* khả năng

able *adj* có thể

about *adj* 1 v • ***what about?*** về chuyện gì? 2 khoảng • ***about two days*** khoảng hai ngày

above *adj* & *adv* trên • ***above average*** trên trung bình

accept *v* chấp nhận, chấp thuận

account *n* trương mục • ***savings account*** trương mục tiết kiệm • ***checking account*** trương mục ngân phiếu

across *prep* qua, băng qua

act *n* hành động

activity *n* hoạt động, sinh hoạt

actually *adv* thật ra, đúng ra

add *v* cộng, thêm vào

address *n* địa chỉ

adult *n* người lớn

affect *v* ảnh hưởng đến

after *prep* & *conj* sau, sau khi

again *adv* lại, nữa • ***do it again*** làm lại đi

against *prep* chống lại

age *n* tuổi • ***how old are you?*** anh bao nhiêu tuổi?

agency *n* văn phòng, chi nhánh

agent *n* nhân viên, người đại diện

ago *adv* cách đây, về trước • ***two years ago*** cách đây hai năm

agree *v* đồng ý

ahead *adv* phía trước • ***go ahead*** xin tự nhiên

air *n* không gian, không khí

all *adj* tất cả, mọi

allow *v* cho phép

almost *adv* hầu như

alone *adv* một mình

along *prep* dọc theo

already *adv* rồi, xong

also *adv* cũng

although *conj* mặc dầu

always *adv* luôn luôn, lúc nào cũng...

American *adj* & *n* (người) Mỹ, thuộc về Mỹ

among *prep* giữa, trong số

amount *n* số tiền

and *conj* và, với • ***mother and daughter*** hai mẹ con

animal *n* thú vật, con vật

another *adj* khác • ***another time*** lúc khác

answer *v* trả lời

any *adj* 1 bất cứ • ***any time*** bất cứ lúc nào 2 nào • ***do you have any questions?*** cô có câu hỏi nào không?

anyone *pron* ai, bất cứ ai, bất cứ người nào • ***I didn't see anyone*** tôi không thấy ai cả

anything *pron* gì, bất cứ cái gì, bất cứ điều gì • ***did you buy anything?*** anh có mua cái gì không?

apply *v* áp dụng, ứng dụng

area *n* vùng, khu

arm *n* cánh tay

around *prep* & *adv* chung quanh, vòng vòng • ***to run around*** chạy vòng vòng

arrive *v* đến • ***what time will the flight arrive?*** mấy giờ máy bay đến?

art *n* nghệ thuật, mỹ thuật

artist *n* nghệ sĩ, hoạ sĩ

as *conj* như • ***as soon as possible*** càng sớm càng tốt

ask *v* hỏi • ***to ask a question*** đặt câu hỏi

at *prep* 1 tại, ở • ***at home*** ở nhà 2 vào, vào lúc • ***at two o'clock*** vào lúc hai giờ

attention *n* sự chú ý, sự để ý • ***attention!*** xin chú ý!

audience *n* khán giả, cử toạ

available *adj* có, có sẵn, rảnh • ***when are you available to do this?*** khi nào ông rảnh để làm việc này?

avoid *v* tránh

away *adv* 1 cách • ***twenty meters away*** cách hai mươi mét 2 khỏi • ***get away from here*** ra khỏi chỗ này

B

baby *n* em bé

back *n* lưng • ***in the back of*** phía sau

bad *adj* xấu, dở, tồi

bag *n* bao, túi

ball *n* banh, bóng

bank *n* ngân hàng, nhà băng • ***bank account*** trương mục ngân hàng

bar *n* quán rượu

be *v* là, thì, bị, được • ***be patient*** hãy kiên nhẫn

beat *v* đánh, gõ

beautiful *adj* xinh, đẹp

because *conj* vì, bởi vì

become *v* trở nên, trở thành

bed *n* giường • ***bedroom*** phòng ngủ

before *prep* & *adv* trước, trước khi

begin *v* bắt đầu

behind *prep* & *adv* sau

believe *v* tin, tin tưởng

best *adj* & *adv* nhất, tốt nhất

better *adj* & *adv* tốt hơn, hay hơn

between *prep* giữa

big *adj* to, lớn

bill *n* 1 hoá đơn 2 giấy bạc

billion *adj* & *n* tỷ • ***billionaire*** tỷ phú

bit *n* chút, tí • ***just a little bit*** chỉ một chút thôi

black *adj* & *n* (màu) đen

blood 1 *n* máu 2 *adj* ruột • ***blood sister*** chị ruột

blue *adj* & *n* (màu) xanh dương

board *n* bảng

body *n* thân thể, cơ thể

book *n* sách • ***bookstore*** tiệm sách

born *adj* sinh • ***when were you born?*** anh sinh năm nào?

both *adj* & *pron* cả hai

box *n* hộp

boy *n* con trai • ***boyfriend*** bạn trai

break *n* sự nghỉ ngơi, sự gián đoạn • ***let's take a break*** chúng ta hãy nghỉ một chút

bring *v* mang đến, đem theo

brother *n* anh • ***older brother*** anh • ***younger brother*** em trai

build *v* xây, cất, xây dựng

building *n* toà nhà

business *n* 1 việc buôn bán, cơ sở thương mại 2 công việc

but 1 *conj* nhưng, mà 2 *prep* ngoại trừ

buy *v* mua, sắm

by *prep* 1 bằng, do, trước • ***by bus*** bằng xe buýt • ***by whom?*** do ai? 2 trước • ***by ten o'clock*** trước mười giờ

C

call *v* kêu, gọi

camera *n* máy chụp hình, máy quay phim

can[1] *n* thùng, lon • ***a can of beer*** lon bia

can[2] *v* có thể • ***can I help you?*** ông cần gì?

capital *n* thủ đô

car *n* xe, xe hơi

card *n* 1 thẻ • ***credit card*** thẻ tín dụng 2 thiệp • ***greeting card*** thiệp mừng 3 bài • ***to play cards*** chơi bài

care *v* săn sóc, chăm sóc • ***take care*** giữ gìn sức khoẻ nhé

career *n* nghề nghiệp, sự nghiệp

carry *v* mang, xách, khiêng, bồng

case *n* trường hợp • ***just in case*** phòng khi

catch *v* bắt, chụp • ***to catch a cold*** bị cảm

cause *v* gây ra, khiến

cell phone *n* điện thoại cầm tay

center *n* trung tâm

certain *adj* chắc chắn

chair *n* ghế

chance *n* cơ hội, dịp • ***by chance*** tình cờ

change *v* thay đổi

charge *v* tính tiền

check[1] *v* kiểm soát, kiểm tra

check[2] *n* ngân phiếu • ***to cash a check*** đổi ngân phiếu ra tiền mặt

child *n* 1 trẻ con 2 con cái

choice *n* sự chọn lựa

choose *v* chọn, lựa

church *n* nhà thờ, thánh đường

citizen *n* công dân • ***citizenship*** quốc tịch

city *n* thành phố

class *n* lớp học

clear *adj* 1 trong suốt 2 rõ ràng

close *v* đóng, khép • ***the store is closed*** tiệm đã đóng cửa

cold 1 *adj* lạnh 2 bệnh cảm • ***I have a cold*** tôi bị cảm

college *n* trường cao đẳng

color *n* màu, màu sắc • ***what's your favorite color?*** cô thích màu gì nhất?

come *v* đến, lại • ***come here!*** lại đây!

commercial *adj* thương mại

common *adj* 1 chung 2 thông thường

community *n* cộng đồng

company *n* công ty

compare *v* so sánh

computer *n* máy điện toán

concern *v* quan tâm, lo lắng • ***I'm very concerned*** tôi rất lo lắng

condition *n* điều kiện, tình trạng

continue *v* tiếp tục

control *v* điều khiển, kiểm soát

cost *v* giá • ***how much does this house cost?*** căn nhà này giá bao nhiêu?

could *v* có thể • ***could you help me with this?*** anh giúp tôi việc này nhé!

country *n* nước, quốc gia

couple *n* đôi, cặp, vài • ***a couple of days*** vài ngày

course *n* khoá học, lớp học

cover *v* che, phủ

culture *n* văn hoá

cup *n* **1** tách **2** cúp, giải • ***the World Cup*** Giải Túc Cầu Thế Giới

current *adj* hiện thời, hiện hành

customer *n* khách hàng

cut *v* cắt, chặt

D

dark *adj* tối, tối tăm • ***darkness*** bóng tối

daughter *n* con gái • ***daughter-in-law*** con dâu

day *n* ngày • ***all day long*** suốt ngày • ***every day*** hằng ngày

dead *adj* chết

death *n* sự chết • ***death anniversary*** ngay giỗ

decide *v* quyết định

deep *adj* sâu, sâu sắc

degree *n* **1** độ, mức **2** bằng cấp

describe *v* miêu tả, mô tả

design *n* kiểu mẫu • ***fashion designer*** nhà vẽ kiểu

despite *prep* mặc, bất chấp

detail *n* chi tiết

determine *v* quyết tâm

develop *v* phát triển

die *v* chết

different *adj* khác, khác nhau

diffcult *adj* khó, khó khăn

dinner *n* bữa ăn tối

direction *n* hướng, phương hướng

director *n* giám đốc

discover *v* khám phá, phát giác

discuss *v* thảo luận, bàn bạc

disease *v* bệnh

do *v* làm • ***don't do it*** đừng làm chuyện đó

doctor *n* **1** bác sĩ **2** tiến sĩ

dog *n* chó

door *n* cửa • ***the house next door*** nhà bên cạnh

down *adv* xuống

draw *v* vẽ • ***drawing*** hình vẽ

dream *v* nằm mơ, mơ ước

drive *v* lái • ***driver*** tài xế, người lái xe

drop *v* đánh rơi, làm rớt

drug *n* thuốc • ***drugstore*** tiệm thuốc tây

during *prep* trong, suốt • ***during winter*** suốt mùa đông

E

each *adj* & *pron* mỗi • ***each and every one*** tất cả mọi người

early *adj* & *adv* sớm

east *n* & *adj* (hướng) đông, (miền) đông • ***the East Sea*** Biển Đông

easy *adj* dễ, dễ dàng • ***take it easy*** hãy bình tĩnh

eat *v* ăn • ***what would you like to eat?*** cô muốn ăn món gì?

economy *n* nền kinh tế

education *n* giáo dục

eight *n* & *adj* (số) tám

either **1** *adj* mỗi, nào • ***either side*** mỗi bên **2** *conj* hoặc • ***either this or that*** hoặc cái này hoặc cái kia **3** *adv* cũng (không) • ***I don't like it, either*** tôi cũng không thích cái đó

else *adj* khác, nữa • ***what else?*** còn gì nữa không? • ***anywhere else*** bất cứ nơi nào khác

employee *n* nhân viên, người làm

end *n* phần cuối, đoạn kết

enjoy *v* hưởng, thưởng thức

enough *adj* & *adv* đủ • ***that's enough*** thôi đủ rồi

enter *v* vào, đi vào • ***entrance*** lối vào

entire *adj* cả, toàn thể • ***the entire world*** cả thế giới

environment *n* môi trường

especially *adv* đặc biệt, nhất là

even *adv* ngay cả, ngay đến, thậm chí

evening *n* buổi tối

event *n* sinh hoạt, sự kiện

ever *adv* bao giờ • ***have you ever been to Vietnam?*** cô có bao giờ đi Việt Nam chưa?

every *adj* mỗi, mọi

everyone *pron* mỗi người, mọi người

everything *pron* mỗi thứ, mọi thứ, mọi việc

exactly *adv* đúng, một cách chính xác

example *n* ví dụ • ***for example*** ví dụ như

exist *v* hiện hữu, tồn tại, sinh tồn

expect *v* mong, đợi

experience *n* kinh nghiệm
expert *n* chuyên viên, chuyên gia
explain *v* giải thích, cắt nghĩa
eye *n* mắt • ***keep an eye on*** để mắt tới

F

face *n* mặt • ***face to face*** mặt đối mặt
fail *v* 1 thất bại 2 làm thất vọng, phụ lòng
fall 1 *v* rơi, ngã, té 2 *n* mùa thu
family *n* gia đình, nhà
far *adj* & *adv* xa • ***how far is it from here?*** từ đây đến đó là bao xa?
fast *adj* & *adv* nhanh, mau
father *n* cha, ba, bố • ***father and son*** hai cha con • ***father-in-law*** cha vợ, cha chồng
feel *v* cảm thấy • ***how are you feeling?*** ông cảm thấy thế nào?
few *adj* ít • ***he has very few friends*** anh ấy có rất ít bạn • ***within a few days*** trong vòng mấy ngày
fill *v* làm cho đầy, điền • ***fill in the blanks*** điền vào chỗ trống
film *n* phim • ***to watch a film*** xem phim
final *adj* cuối, chót
finally *adv* cuối cùng
find *v* tìm thấy, tìm ra
fine *adj* tốt, hay • ***I'm fine, thank you*** tôi khoẻ, cám ơn anh
finger *n* ngón tay
finish *v* kết thúc, làm xong
fire *n* lửa, hoả hoạn
first *adj* đầu tiên, thứ nhất • ***the first time*** lần đầu tiên
fish *n* cá • ***fish sauce*** nước mắm
five *adj* & *n* (số) năm
floor *n* 1 nền nhà, sàn nhà 2 tầng • ***first floor*** tầng trệt
fly *v* bay
follow *v* theo sau, theo dõi
food *n* thức ăn, thực phẩm
foot *n* bàn chân • ***to go on foot*** đi bộ
for *prep* cho, dành cho, để • ***what is this for?*** cái này để làm gì?
force *n* sức mạnh
foreign *adj* ngoại quốc, nước ngoài • ***foreign language*** ngoại ngữ • ***foreigner*** người ngoại quốc
forget *v* quên • ***forgetful*** hay quên
form *n* 1 hình dạng, hình thức 2 mẫu đơn
four *adj* & *n* (số) bốn
free *adj* 1 tự do 2 rảnh rỗi 3 miễn phí
friend *n* bạn • ***best friend*** bạn thân
from *prep* từ • ***where are you from?*** anh là người nước nào?
front *n* phía trước, đằng trước
full *adj* 1 đầy 2 no, no nê
future *n* tương lai

G

game *n* trò chơi, cuộc đấu
garden *n* vườn
gas *n* 1 xăng 2 ga, khí đốt
general *adj* chung, tổng quát, khái quát • ***in general*** nói chung
get *v* lấy, có được
girl *n* con gái • ***girlfriend*** bạn gái
give *v* cho, đưa • ***give me that*** đưa cái đó cho tôi
glass *n* 1 kính • ***glass door*** cửa kính 2 ly • ***glass of water*** ly nước • ***eyeglasses*** kính đeo mắt
go *v* đi • ***go ahead!*** cứ việc!
good *adj* tốt, hay • ***good morning, sir*** chào ông
great *adj* hay, tuyệt
green *adj* xanh lục, xanh lá cây • ***greens*** rau cải
group *n* nhóm
grow *v* 1 mọc 2 trồng 3 lớn lên
guess *v* đoán • ***I guess so*** tôi nghĩ vậy

H

hair *n* tóc, lông • ***hairdresser*** thợ làm tóc
half *adj* & *n* nửa, rưỡi • ***half an hour*** nửa giờ, nửa tiếng • ***a dollar and a half*** một đô-la rưỡi
hand *n* bàn tay • ***handy man*** người đàn ông tháo vát
happen *v* xảy ra, xảy đến • ***what happened?*** có chuyện gì vậy?
happy *adj* vui, mừng • ***Happy New Year!*** Chúc Mừng Năm Mới!
hard *adj* 1 cứng 2 khó 3 *adv* nhiều • ***he worked very hard*** anh ấy làm việc nhiều lắm
have *v* 1 có • ***we have no time to do that*** chúng tôi không có thì giờ để làm việc đó 2 đã • ***she has met with John*** cô ấy đã gặp John
head *n* đầu • ***to have a headache*** bị nhức đầu
health *n* sức khoẻ • ***health insurance*** bảo hiểm sức khoẻ, bảo hiểm y tế
healthy *adj* mạnh khoẻ
hear *v* nghe • ***I can't hear you*** tôi không nghe anh nói gì cả

heart *n* tim • ***to know by heart*** thuộc lòng

heavy *adj* nặng, nặng nề

help *v* giúp, giúp đỡ • ***help! help!*** cứu tôi với!

her *pron* cô ấy, chị ấy, bà ấy

here *adv* đây, ở đây • ***here you go*** đây này

high *adj* cao • ***high wind*** gió lớn

him *pron* anh ấy, ông ấy

his *adj* của anh ấy, của ông ấy

hit *v* đánh, đập

hold *v* giữ • ***hold on*** chờ một chút

home *n* nhà • ***at home*** ở nhà

hope *v* mong, hy vọng • ***I hope so, too*** tôi cũng hy vọng như thế

hospital *n* bệnh viện, nhà thương

hot *adj* **1** nóng **2** cay

hotel *n* khách sạn

hour *n* giờ, tiếng • ***after-hours*** sau giờ làm việc

house *n* nhà • ***housework*** việc nhà

how *adv* thế nào, ra sao • ***how have you been?*** dạo này anh ra sao?

however *adv* tuy nhiên, tuy vậy

huge *adj* to lớn

human *adj* con người • ***human beings*** loài người

hundred *adj* & *n* trăm • ***hundreds of people*** hàng trăm người

husband *n* chồng • ***husband and wife*** hai vợ chồng

I

I *pron* tôi, em, con, cháu

idea *n* ý, ý kiến • ***I had no idea*** tôi không hay biết gì cả

if *conj* nếu, giá như • ***if you please*** xin ông vui lòng

image *n* hình, ảnh

important *adj* quan trọng

in *prep* ở, tại, vào, trong • ***in this case*** trong trường hợp này

include *v* gồm có, bao gồm

increase *v* tăng lên, gia tăng

individual *n* cá nhân

industry *n* kỹ nghệ, công nghiệp

information *n* tin tức, chi tiết • ***for more information*** để biết thêm chi tiết

inside *prep* & *adv* trong, bên trong

instead *adv* thay vì, thay vào đó

interest *n* sự quan tâm, sự chú ý

interesting *adj* hay, lôi cuốn, thú vị

interview *n* cuộc phỏng vấn

into *prep* vào

issue *n* vấn đề

it *pron* nó, điều đó • ***that's it*** đúng vậy!

item *n* món

its *adj* của nó

J

jacket *n* áo khoác • ***suit jacket*** áo vét

jam *n* sự mắc kẹt, sự tắc nghẽn • ***traffic jam*** sự kẹt xe

job *n* việc, công việc, việc làm • ***to apply for a job*** xin việc

jog *v* chạy bộ

join *v* gia nhập, vào

jump *v* nhảy

just *adv* **1** chỉ • ***just a bit*** chỉ một chút thôi **2** vừa, mới • ***they've just left*** họ vừa đi khỏi

K

keep *v* giữ • ***keep out!*** tránh ra!

key *n* chìa khoá

kid *n* đứa nhỏ • ***my kids*** các con của tôi

kind[1] *n* loại, thứ • ***what kind of drink would you like?*** cô muốn uống gì?

kind[2] *adj* tử tế, tốt bụng • ***it's very kind of you*** anh tử tế quá

kitchen *n* nhà bếp

know *v* biết • ***you know what?*** anh biết không? • ***who knows*** ai biết được

knowledge *n* kiến thức

knowledgeable *adj* hiểu biết

L

land *n* đất, đất đai

language *n* ngôn ngữ, tiếng

large *adj* to, lớn

last *adj* cuối, chót • ***last but not least*** cuối cùng nhưng không kém phần quan trọng

late *adj* & *adv* muộn, trễ

later *adj* sau này, về sau • ***sooner or later*** sớm muộn gì

laugh *v* cười

law *n* luật, luật lệ

lawyer *n* luật sư

learn *v* học, học hỏi

least *adj* ít nhất

leave *v* **1** ra đi, rời khỏi **2** để lại, bỏ lại

left *adj* trái, bên trái • ***left-handed*** thuận tay trái

leg *n* chân, đùi

less *adv* kém, ít hơn • ***more or less*** xấp xỉ

let *v* để, để cho • ***let's go!*** chúng ta đi thôi!

letter *n* 1 chữ, chữ cái 2 thư

level *n* mức độ, trình độ

lie *v* 1 nằm 2 nói dối

life *n* cuộc sống, cuộc đời

light[1] *n* ánh sáng, đèn

light[2] *adj* 1 sáng 2 nhẹ

like[1] *v* thích, mến

like[2] *prep* như, giống như

line *n* đường, hàng • ***to stand in line*** sắp hàng

list *n* danh sách

listen *v* nghe, lắng nghe

little *adj* ít, nhỏ

live *v* sống • ***where do you live?*** anh sống ở đâu?

long *adj* dài, lâu • ***how long will it take?*** việc này sẽ mất bao lâu?

look *v* nhìn • ***to look for*** tìm, kiếm

lose *v* mất, làm mất

lot *n* nhiều • ***a lot of money*** nhiều tiền

love *n* tình yêu, tình thương • ***I love you*** anh yêu em *(man to woman)*, em yêu anh *(woman to man)*

low *adj* thấp

M

machine *n* máy

magazine *n* tạp chí • ***monthly magazine*** nguyệt san

main *n* chính

make *v* làm

man *n* đàn ông

manager *n* giám đốc, quản lý

many *adj* nhiều • ***how many children do you have?*** ông bà có bao nhiêu người con?

market *n* chợ • ***supermarket*** siêu thị

material *n* vật liệu

matter *n* vấn đề • ***what's the matter?*** có chuyện gì vậy?

may *v* có thể, được phép • ***may I come in?*** tôi vào được không?

maybe *adv* có lẽ, có thể

me *pron* tôi, em, con, cháu

mean *v* có nghĩa là, muốn nói • ***what does this word mean?*** chữ này có nghĩa là gì? • ***what do you mean by that?*** anh nói vậy nghĩa là gì?

medical *adj* y tế • ***medical care*** chăm sóc y tế

meet *v* gặp, gặp gỡ • ***nice to meet you*** hân hạnh được biết cô

meeting *n* cuộc họp

member *n* hội viên, thành viên

message *n* tin nhắn • ***do you want to leave a message for her?*** ông có muốn nhắn cô ấy điều gì không?

method *n* cách, phương pháp

middle *adj* giữa • ***in the middle of nowhere*** không biết đang ở chỗ nào

might *v* có thể • ***I might run a bit late*** tôi có thể đến trễ một chút

military *adj & n* quân đội

million *n* triệu • ***millionaire*** triệu phú

mind *v* phiền • ***would you mind if I sat here?*** tôi ngồi đây có phiền đến ông không?

minute *n* phút

miss *v* 1 lỡ, mất • ***he missed the 8 o'clock bus*** anh ấy lỡ chuyến xe buýt tám giờ 2 nhớ • ***we miss them so much*** chúng tôi nhớ họ lắm

model *n* 1 kiểu, mẫu 2 người mẫu thời trang

modern *adj* tân thời, hiện đại • ***modern times*** thời nay

moment *n* chốc lát, giây lát • ***just a moment*** xin đợi một chút

money *n* tiền, tiền bạc

month *n* tháng • ***monthly*** hằng tháng, mỗi tháng một lần

more *adj & adv* nhiều hơn, thêm, nữa • ***the more the better*** càng nhiều càng tốt

morning *n* buổi sáng • ***yesterday morning*** sáng hôm qua • ***tomorrow morning*** sáng mai

most *adj & adv* nhiều nhất, phần lớn • ***most of all*** nhất là

mother *n* mẹ, má • ***stepmother*** mẹ kế • ***mother-in-law*** mẹ vợ, mẹ chồng

mouth *n* miệng, mồm

move *v* 1 cử động 2 xê dịch, di chuyển, dọn

movie *n* phim • ***movie theater*** rạp chiếu phim, rạp xi-nê

much *adj & adv* nhiều • ***thank you so much!*** cám ơn anh nhiều lắm!

music *n* nhạc, âm nhạc

must *v* phải • ***you must come on time*** các anh chị phải đến đúng giờ

my *adj* của tôi, của em, của con, của cháu • ***my pleasure*** rất hân hạnh

N

name *n* tên • ***what's your name?*** tên anh là gì? • ***first name*** tên • ***last name*** họ • ***middle name*** tên đệm

nation *n* quốc gia

natural *adj* tự nhiên

nature *n* thiên nhiên

near *prep* & *adv* gần

necessary *adj* cần thiết

need *v* cần • ***needless to say*** không cần nói cũng biết

never *adv* • ***better late than never*** thà trễ còn hơn không bao giờ

new *adj* mới • ***brand new*** mới toanh

news *n* tin tức • ***breaking news*** tin giờ chót

newspaper *n* báo • ***daily newspaper*** nhật báo

next *adj* kế tiếp, kế bên

nice *adj* tử tế, đáng mến

night *n* ban đêm • ***good night*** ngủ ngon nhé

nine *adj* & *n* (số) chín

no *adj* & *adv* không • ***no problem*** không có chi

none *pron* không gì, không ai • ***none of them came*** bọn họ chẳng ai đến cả

north *adj* & *n* (hướng) bắc, (miền) bắc

not *adv* không • ***something is not right*** có điều gì không ổn

note *n* điều ghi chú

nothing *pron* không có gì • ***I saw nothing in there*** tôi thấy trong đó không có gì cả

notice *v* để ý

now *n* bây giờ, hiện giờ • ***right now*** ngay bây giờ • ***nowadays*** ngày nay

number *n* số, con số • ***telephone number*** số điện thoại • ***even number*** số chẵn • ***odd number*** số lẻ

O

of *prep* của • ***the economy of Vietnam*** nền kinh tế của Việt Nam

off *prep* & *adv* 1 khỏi, ra khỏi • ***to be off duty*** khỏi trực 2 đi, ra • ***he took 10% off*** ông ấy bớt đi mười phần trăm

offer *v* mời, đề nghị

office *v* văn phòng

officer *n* sĩ quan; cảnh sát viên; viên chức

official *adj* chính thức

often *adv* thường, thường xuyên • ***how often do you go shopping?*** cô có thường đi mua sắm không?

old *adj* 1 cũ 2 già • ***how old are you?*** anh bao nhiêu tuổi?

on *prep* trên, vào • ***on time*** đúng giờ • ***on and off*** lúc có lúc không

once *adv* một lần • ***once and for all*** một lần cuối cùng rồi thôi

one *adj* & *n* một • ***one day at a time*** chuyện ngày nào lo ngày ấy

only 1 *adj* duy nhất, một • ***only child*** con một 2 *adv* chỉ, chỉ có

open *v* & *adj* mở • ***is the library open today?*** hôm nay thư viện có mở cửa không?

opportunity *n* cơ hội, dịp may

or *conj* hay, hoặc • ***rain or shine*** dù mưa hay nắng

order *v* 1 ra lệnh, yêu cầu 2 gọi (*food, drink*) • ***what would you like to order?*** bà muốn gọi món gì?

other *adj* khác • ***other things*** những điều khác

our *adj* của chúng tôi, của chúng ta

out *prep* & *adv* ra, ra ngoài, ra khỏi • ***to go out*** đichơi

outside *adj, prep* & *adv* bên ngoài, ở ngoài, ngoài • ***to go outside*** đi ra ngoài

over 1 *prep* & *adv* trên 2 *adj* hết • ***it's over*** hết rồi

owner *n* chủ, chủ nhân

P

page *n* trang, trang giấy

pain *n* sự đau đớn, sự đau khổ

paint *v* sơn, vẽ

paper *n* giấy

parent *n* cha, mẹ • ***parents*** cha mẹ • ***grandparents*** ông bà

part *n* phần, bộ phận • ***to take part in*** tham gia

partner *n* bạn, người cùng làm việc

party *n* buổi tiệc • ***birthday party*** tiệc sinh nhật

pass *v* đi qua, vượt qua

past *prep* qua, qua khỏi • ***go past the bridge*** đi qua khỏi cây cầu

patient[1] *adj* kiên nhẫn • ***be patient*** hãy kiên nhẫn

patient[2] *n* người bệnh, bệnh nhân

pay *v* trả, trả tiền • ***to pay one's debt*** trả nợ

peace *n* hoà bình; sự yên tĩnh

people *n* người, người ta

perhaps *adv* có lẽ

period *n* 1 thời kỳ, thời gian 2 dấu chấm

person *n* người

personal *adj* cá nhân, riêng tư

phone *n* điện thoại • ***phone call*** cú điện thoại

pick *v* chọn, lấy, hái

picture *n* hình, tranh, ảnh • ***to take a picture*** chụp ảnh

piece *n* mẩu, miếng, mảnh • ***a piece of paper*** một mảnh giấy

place *n* nơi, chỗ, chốn • ***to go places*** đi đây đi đó

plan *n* chương trình, kế hoạch

plant *v* trồng • ***to plant trees*** trồng cây

play *v* chơi, đùa giỡn • ***to play the piano*** chơi dương cầm

police *n* cảnh sát • ***police officer*** cảnh sát viên • ***police station*** đồn cảnh sát

politics *n* chính trị

poor *adj* 1 nghèo 2 tồi, kém 3 tội nghiệp • ***poor you!*** tội anh quá!

popular *adj* phổ thông, phổ biến

position *n* vị trí, địa vị

possible *adj* có thể • ***as soon as possible*** càng sớm càng tốt

power *n* 1 sức mạnh, quyền lực 2 nguồn điện

practice *v* thực hành, tập luyện

prepare *v* chuẩn bị, sửa soạn

present *n* 1 hiện tại • ***at present*** hiện giờ 2 quà tặng

president *n* chủ tịch, giám đốc, tổng thống

pretty[1] *adj* xinh, dễ thương

pretty[2] *adv* khá, cũng • ***pretty good*** cũng hay

price *n* giá, giá cả • ***at any price*** với bất cứ giá nào

private *adj* tư, riêng tư

probably *adv* có lẽ, có thể

problem *n* vấn đề, chuyện rắc rối • ***is there a problem?*** có rắc rối gì không?

process *n* tiến trình

product *n* sản phẩm

professor *n* giáo sư

program *n* chương trình

project *n* dự án, đề án

property *n* tài sản

protect *v* bảo vệ, che chở

prove *v* chứng minh, chứng tỏ

provide *v* cung cấp, cho

public *adj* công, công cộng • ***the public*** công chúng

pull *v* kéo, giật

purpose *n* mục đích • ***on purpose*** cố tình

push *v* đẩy, xô

put *v* đặt, để

Q

quality *n* phẩm chất • ***best quality*** phẩm chất thượng hạng

question *n* câu hỏi, vấn đề • ***out of the question*** không thành vấn đề

quickly *adv* nhanh chóng

quit *v* bỏ, từ bỏ • ***to quit smoking*** bỏ hút thuốc

quite *adv* rất, hoàn toàn

R

race *n* cuộc chạy đua

raise *v* nâng lên, làm cao lên

rate *n* tỷ lệ • ***at any rate*** dù sao đi nữa • ***exchange rate*** tỷ giá hối đoái, hối suất

rather *adv* phần nào, thà • ***to die rather than quit*** thà chết còn hơn là bỏ cuộc • ***would rather*** thích (làm gì) hơn

reach *v* đến, đạt đến

read *v* đọc • ***reader*** độc giả

ready *adj* sẵn sàng

real *adj* thật, có thật

really *adv* thật, thật là • ***really?*** thật vậy sao?

reason *n* lý do

receive *v* nhận, tiếp nhận

recent *adj* mới, mới đây

recognize *v* nhận ra, thừa nhận

record *n* sổ sách

red *adj* đỏ

reduce *v* giảm, bớt

relationship *n* mối quan hệ

religion *n* tôn giáo

remain *v* còn lại, vẫn • ***she remained silent*** cô ấy vẫn im lặng

remember *v* nhớ

remove *v* lấy đi

report *v* tường trình, thuật lại, báo cáo

require *v* yêu cầu, đòi hỏi

respond *v* trả lời, đáp

responsibility *n* bổn phận, nhiệm vụ

rest *v* nghỉ ngơi • ***restroom*** phòng vệ sinh

result *n* kết quả • ***as a result*** kết quả là

return *v* về, trở về, trở lại

rich *adj* giàu, phong phú

right *adj* phải, đúng • ***is it right?*** đúng không?

rise *v* nổi lên, dâng lên, mọc lên • ***sunrise*** bình minh

road *n* đường

rock *n* đá

role *n* vai trò • ***to play a role*** đóng vai

room *n* phòng, chỗ

rule *n* luật lệ • ***as a rule*** theo lệ

run *v* chạy, chảy

S

safe *adj* an toàn, bình an • ***safe and sound*** bình an vô sự

same *adj* giống, giống nhau

save *v* 1 cứu, cứu giúp 2 để dành, dành dụm

say *v* nói • ***you don't say!*** anh nói thật sao?

school *n* trường, trường học • ***elementary school*** trường tiểu học • ***high school*** trường trung học

score *n* điểm, tỷ số

sea *n* biển • ***seashore*** bờ biển

season *n* mùa

seat *n* chỗ ngồi • ***please take a seat*** xin mời bà ngồi

second[1] *adj* thứ nhì, thứ hai • ***on second thought*** sau khi suy nghĩ lại

second[2] *n* giây • ***just a second*** đợi một giây

section *n* khu, khu vực, phần

security *n* sự an toàn

see *v* thấy • ***you see?*** anh thấy chưa?

seek *v* tìm, kiếm

seem *v* có vẻ, dường như • ***so it seems*** dường như là vậy

sell *v* bán

send *v* gởi • ***to send a text message*** gởi một tin nhắn, nhắn tin

sense *n* 1 giác quan 2 ý nghĩa, nghĩa lý • ***that doesn't make sense*** vô lý quá

serious *adj* nghiêm chỉnh, nghiêm trọng

serve *v* phục vụ • ***dinner is served*** bữa ăn tối đã dọn ra

service *n* sự phục vụ

set *v* sắp, xếp, đặt • ***you're all set*** việc của anh đã xong xuôi

seven *adj* & *n* bảy

several *adj* vài, một số, nhiều

shake *v* rung, lắc, run • ***to shake hands with someone*** bắt tay ai

share *v* chia, san sẻ

she *pron* cô ấy, chị ấy, bà ấy

shoot *v* 1 bắn 2 quay (*movie*)

short *adj* 1 ngắn 2 thấp

should *v* nên • ***what should I do now?*** bây giờ tôi nên làm gì đây?

shoulder *n* vai

show *v* chỉ, cho thấy

side *n* bên, phe • ***side by side*** bên nhau

sign *v* ký, ký tên • ***signature*** chữ ký

similar *adj* giống, tương tự

simple *adj* đơn giản, giản dị

since *adv* & *conj* từ đó, từ khi • ***ever since*** kể từ dạo đó

sing *v* hát, ca • ***singer*** ca sĩ

single *adj* 1 đơn, chiếc 2 độc thân • ***single parent*** cha/mẹ độc thân

sister *n* chị, em gái • ***older sister*** chị • ***younger sister*** em gái • ***half-sister*** chị/em cùng cha khác mẹ *or* cùng mẹ khác cha

sit *v* ngồi • ***sit down!*** ngồi xuống!

situation *n* tình trạng, tình hình, hoàn cảnh

six *adj* & *n* sáu

size *n* cỡ • ***what size shoes do you wear?*** ông mang giày số mấy?

skill *n* tài năng, kỹ năng

skin *n* da • ***skin disease*** bệnh ngoài da

small *adj* nhỏ, bé

smile *v* mỉm cười, cười

so *adv* 1 như vậy, như thế • ***is that so?*** vậy sao? 2 quá, lắm • ***the food is so good!*** thức ăn ngon quá!

society *n* xã hội

soldier *n* lính, quân nhân

some *adj* vài, một ít • ***some time*** một thời gian, ít lâu

someone *pron* ai, người nào

something *pron* gì, điều gì

sometimes *pron* đôi khi, thỉnh thoảng

son *n* con trai • ***eldest son*** con trai cả • ***only son*** con trai duy nhất

song *n* bài hát, bài ca

soon *adv* sớm, chóng • ***see you soon*** hẹn sớm gặp lại cô nhé

sound *n* âm thanh, tiếng

south *adj* & *n* (hướng) nam, (miền) nam

space *n* không gian, chỗ, chỗ trống

speak *v* nói, nói chuyện • ***do you speak Vietnamese?*** anh có nói tiếng Việt không?

special *adj* đặc biệt

specific *adj* cụ thể, rõ ràng

speech *n* lời nói, bài diễn văn

spend *v* 1 trải qua 2 tiêu, xài • ***to spend a lot of money*** tiêu tiền nhiều

sport *n* thể thao

spring *n* mùa xuân

staff *n* nhân viên

stage *n* sân khấu

stand *v* đứng • ***stand up!*** đứng dậy!

star *n* ngôi sao

start *v* bắt đầu • ***let's get started*** chúng ta bắt đầu nhé!

state *n* 1 tình trạng 2 tiểu bang

station *n* 1 nhà ga • ***train station*** ga xe lửa 2 đài • ***radio station*** đài phát thanh

stay *v* ở, ở lại • ***how long will you stay?*** anh sẽ ở lại bao lâu?

step *n* bước • ***step by step*** từng bước một

still *adv* vẫn, còn • ***the night is still young*** còn sớm mà

stop *v* dừng, ngừng, thôi

store *n* tiệm, cửa hiệu

story *n* chuyện, truyện

street *n* đường • ***what street is your house on?*** nhà anh ở đường nào?

strong *adj* mạnh, khoẻ

student *n* học sinh, sinh viên • ***college student*** sinh viên đại học

study *v* học, nghiên cứu

stuff *n* điều, việc • ***all kinds of stuff*** đủ thứ cả

style *n* kiểu, cách, phong thái

subject *n* chủ đề, đề tài

success *n* thành công

such *adj* như thế, như vậy • ***such as*** như là, ví dụ như

suddenly *adv* thình lình, đột nhiên

suffer *v* bị, chịu, đau khổ

suggest *v* yêu cầu, đề nghị

summer *n* mùa hè, mùa hạ • ***summer vacation*** kỳ nghỉ hè

support *v* 1 ủng hộ 2 nuôi nấng, chu cấp

sure *adj* chắc, chắc chắn

system *n* hệ thống

T

table *n* bàn

take *v* lấy. cầm lấy

talk *v* nói, nói chuyện

task *n* nhiệm vụ, phận sự, việc làm

tax *n* thuế • ***to pay taxes*** đóng thuế

teach *v* dạy, giảng dạy

teacher *n* giáo viên

team *n* đội, toán, nhóm

technology *n* kỹ thuật

television *n* vô tuyến truyền hình

tell *v* bảo, kể

ten *adj* & *n* mười

term *n* thời hạn, học kỳ

test *n* 1 sự thử nghiệm 2 bài thi

than *conj* so với • ***more than ever before*** hơn bao giờ hết

thank *v* cám ơn • ***thanks a lot*** cám ơn nhiều

that 1 *adj* đó, đấy, ấy • ***in that moment*** trong khoảnh khắc đó 2 *conj* rằng, là • ***she thought that she was right*** cô ấy nghĩ rằng mình đúng 3 *pron* mà • ***all the things that you said*** tất cả những điều mà ông nói

the *art* người, cái, con, etc. • ***the TV in the kitchen*** cái ti-vi trong nhà bếp

their *adj* của họ, của chúng nó

them *pron* họ, chúng nó

then *adv* rồi, thì • ***and then what?*** rồi sao nữa?

there *adv* 1 đó, ở đó • ***who's there?*** ai đó? 2 có • ***how many people are there in the meeting?*** có bao nhiêu người trong buổi họp?

these *adj* & *pron* những... này, mấy... nay • ***it's been very warm these days*** mấy hôm nay trời nóng quá

they *pron* họ, chúng nó • ***who are they?*** họ là ai?

thing *n* điều, vật, việc • ***how are things?*** mọi việc thế nào?

think *v* nghĩ, suy nghĩ • ***what do you think about the situation?*** ông nghĩ sao về tình hình này?

third *adj* thứ ba

this *adj* & *pron* này, cái này, điều này • ***what's this?*** cái này là cái gì?

those *adj* & *pron* những... đó

though 1 *adv* tuy vậy, dù vậy 2 *conj* mặc dầu, tuy

thought *n* ý nghĩ

thousand *adj* & *n* nghìn, ngàn • ***thousands of dollars*** hàng ngàn đô-la

three *adj* & *n* (số) ba

through 1 *adv* kỹ càng • ***I'll think it through*** tôi sẽ suy nghĩ kỹ về chuyện đó 2 *prep* qua, xuyên qua

throw *v* quăng, ném

time *n* 1 thời gian, thì giờ • ***what time is it?*** mấy giờ rồi? 2 lần • ***how many times have you been here?*** cô đã đến đây mấy lần rồi?

to *prep* đến • ***from A to Z*** từ đầu đến cuối

today *n* & *adv* hôm nay • ***what's today's date?*** hôm nay là ngày tháng mấy?

together *adv* cùng, cùng nhau, với nhau

tonight *n* & *adv* tối nay, đêm nay

too *adv* 1 cũng • ***we like it, too*** chúng tôi cũng thích nó 2 quá • ***it's too much*** quá đáng

top *n* đỉnh, đầu • ***on top of that*** ngoài ra

total *n* tổng số, tổng cộng

tough *adj* 1 khó, đầy thử thách 2 bền bỉ, dai, dẻo dai

toward *prep* về phía

town *n* phố, thị xã

trade *n* thương mại, việc buôn bán

traditional *adj* truyền thống

travel *v* du lịch, đi xa

treat *v* 1 đối xử 2 chữa (bệnh)

tree *n* cây • ***apple tree*** cây táo

trip *n* chuyến đi • ***have a good trip!*** chúc anh đi chơi vui vẻ! chúc thượng lộ bình an!

trouble *n* chuyện rắc rối • ***the trouble is that*** rắc rối ở chỗ là

true *adj* thật. có thật • ***is it true?*** có thật không?

truth *n* sự thật • ***to tell the truth*** nói thật

try *v* **1** cố gắng **3** thử • ***try this dress on*** mặc thử cái áo đầm này đi

turn *v* rẽ, quẹo, quay • ***turn left here*** rẽ trái ở đây

two *adj* & *n* (số) hai

type *n* loại, kiểu • ***what type of car do you like?*** ông thích loại xe gì?

U

under *prep* dưới, bên dưới • ***underage*** vị thành niên

understand *v* hiểu • ***I don't understand*** tôi không hiểu

ugly *adj* xấu, xấu xí

unfair *adj* không công bằng, bất công

unit *n* đơn vị, cái

unnecessary *adj* không cần thiết

until *prep* & *conj* cho đến, cho đến khi • ***we will not call you until after midnight*** sau nửa đêm chúng tôi mới gọi anh

up *prep* & *adv* lên • ***please speak up!*** xin nói lớn lên!

upon *prep* trên, vào, khi • ***upon receiving this letter*** khi nhận được bức thư này

urgent *adj* khẩn cấp, khẩn thiết • ***urgent care*** chăm sóc khẩn cấp

us *pron* chúng tôi, chúng ta

use *v* dùng, sử dụng

useful *adj* có ích, tiện lợi

usually *adj* thường, thông thường

V

vague *adj* không rõ ràng

valid *adj* có giá trị, hợp lệ • ***valid license*** giấy phép hợp lệ

value *n* giá trị

van *n* xe khách

various *adj* khác nhau, nhiều • ***for various reasons*** vì nhiều lý do khác nhau

vary *v* thay đổi

vegetable *n* rau

vegetarian *adj* & *n* (người) ăn chay

very *adv* rất, lắm • ***very good!*** hay lắm!

view *v* xem, coi

visit *v* thăm, thăm viếng

voice *n* giọng, giọng nói • ***I've lost my voice*** tôi bị mất giọng

vote *v* bầu cử, bỏ phiếu

W

wait *v* đợi, chờ • ***waiting room*** phòng đợi

walk *v* đi, bước, đi bộ

wall *n* tường, vách

want *v* muốn • ***do you want to say something?*** anh muốn nói gì không?

war *n* chiến tranh

watch[1] *v* xem, coi, theo dõi • ***to watch TV*** xem truyền hình, coi ti-vi • ***watch out!*** coi chừng!

watch[2] *n* đồng hồ đeo tay • ***smart watch*** đồng hồ thông minh

water *n* nước

way *n* **1** lối đi • ***go this way*** đi lối này **2** cách, cách thức • ***in what way?*** bằng cách nào?

we *pron* chúng tôi, chúng ta

wear *v* mang, mặc, đội, đeo, để, bôi, xức • ***to wear sunglasses*** mang kính mát • ***to wear a ring*** đeo nhẫn • ***to wear flip-flops*** mang dép • ***to wear shorts*** mặc quần cộc • ***to wear one's hair long*** để tóc dài • ***to wear perfume*** bôi nước hoa

week *n* tuần, tuần lễ • ***long weekend*** cuối tuần có ngày lễ • ***have a good weekend!*** chúc cuối tuần vui vẻ!

weight *n* sức nặng, cân nặng

well **1** *adj* khoẻ • ***I am very well*** tôi khoẻ lắm **2** *adv* giỏi, hay, đẹp, khá • ***she sings pretty well*** cô ấy hát khá hay

west *adj* & *n* (hướng) tây, (miền) tây

what *adj* & *pron* gì, sao • ***what did you say?*** cô nói sao? • ***what day is it today?*** hôm nay là thứ mấy?

whatever *adj* & *pron* bất cứ cái gì, bất cứ điều gì • ***whatever!*** sao cũng được!

when *conj* khi, khi nào • ***when are you guys leaving?*** khi nào các anh đi?

where *adv* đâu, ở đâu • ***where are you going now?*** bây giờ ông đi đâu? • ***where are you now?*** hiện giờ anh đang ở đâu?

whether *conj* có... hay không • ***We don't know whether they will come or not*** chúng tôi không biết họ có đến không

which *adj* & *pron* nào, cái nào • ***which one do you prefer?*** chị thích cái nào hơn?

while **1** *conj* trong khi, trong lúc • ***he left while I was sleeping*** anh ấy ra đi lúc tôi đang ngủ **2** *n* một lát, một chốc • ***we chatted for a while*** chúng tôi nói chuyện trong một lát

white *adj* & *n* (màu) trắng

who *pron* ai, người nào, mà • ***excuse me, who are you?*** xin lỗi, ông là ai? • ***the man who called you didn't leave a message*** người mà gọi anh không để lại lời nhắn

whole *adj* & *n* toàn thể, trọn, cả • ***the whole month*** cả tháng • ***as a whole*** nói chung

why *adv* tại sao, vì sao • ***why did you do that?*** tại sao bà lại làm thế?

wide *adj* rộng • ***far and wide*** khắp nơi

wife *n* vợ • ***whose wife is she?*** bà ấy là vợ của ai?

will *v* sẽ, định, muốn • ***I will call you soon*** tôi sẽ gọi anh ngay

win *v* thắng, chiến thắng

wind *n* gió

window *n* cửa sổ • ***please close the window*** đóng giùm cửa sổ lại

wish *v* chúc, ước, mong • ***I wish you all the best*** chúc anh mọi sự tốt đẹp

with *prep* với • ***with pleasure*** xin sẵn lòng, rất hân hạnh

without *prep* không có, thiếu • ***it goes without saying*** rõ ràng là

woman *n* đàn bà, phụ nữ

wonder *v* thắc mắc, tự hỏi • ***no wonder*** thảo nào

word *n* chữ, tiếng, lời, từ ngữ • ***what does this word mean?*** chữ này nghĩa là gì? • ***to be at a loss for words*** không nói được lời nào

work *v* **1** làm việc • ***to go to work*** đi làm **2** chạy, hoạt động • ***the clock is not working*** đồng hồ không chạy, đồng hồ đứng

worker *n* thợ, công nhân

world *n* thế giới • ***around the world*** khắp thế giới

worry *v* lo, lo lắng • ***don't worry*** đừng lo

would *v* sẽ, muốn • ***how would you like your steak?*** anh muốn món thịt như thế nào?

write *v* viết, viết thư

wrong *adj* sai, trái • ***to tell right from wrong*** biết phân biệt phải trái

Y

yard *n* sân • ***backyard*** sân sau • ***front yard*** sân trước

year *n* năm • ***every year*** hằng năm • ***all year long*** suốt năm

yellow *adj* & *n* (màu) vàng

yes *adv* vâng, dạ, ừ

yet *adv* **1** còn, vẫn • ***there is much yet to do*** còn nhiều việc phải làm • ***not yet*** chưa, chưa xong **2** tuy, nhưng, mà • ***it is unbelievable, yet true*** khó tin nhưng có thật

you *pron* anh, chị, cô, ông, bà, em, con, cháu • ***how are you doing?*** anh thế nào?

young *adj* trẻ

your *adj* của anh, của chị, của ông, của bà

yourself *pron* chính anh, chính chị, chính ông, chính bà • ***you said it yourself*** chính anh đã nói như vậy

Z

zealous *adj* hăng hái, sốt sắng, háo hức

zebra *n* ngựa vằn

Zen *n* thiền

zero *adj* & *n* (số) không • ***zero degrees*** không độ

zest *n* sự thú vị, sự thích thú • ***the story lacks zest*** truyện không thú vị

zipper *n* dây kéo

zone *n* vùng, khu vực • ***time zone*** múi giờ

zoo *n* sở thú

"Books to Span the East and West"

Tuttle Publishing was founded in 1832 in the small New England town of Rutland, Vermont [USA]. Our core values remain as strong today as they were then—to publish best-in-class books which bring people together one page at a time. In 1948, we established a publishing outpost in Japan—and Tuttle is now a leader in publishing English-language books about the arts, languages and cultures of Asia. The world has become a much smaller place today and Asia's economic and cultural influence has grown. Yet the need for meaningful dialogue and information about this diverse region has never been greater. Over the past seven decades, Tuttle has published thousands of books on subjects ranging from martial arts and paper crafts to language learning and literature—and our talented authors, illustrators, designers and photographers have won many prestigious awards. We welcome you to explore the wealth of information available on Asia at **www.tuttlepublishing.com**.

Published by Tuttle Publishing, an imprint of Periplus Editions (HK) Ltd.

www.tuttlepublishing.com

Illustrations by Le Nguyen and UnoDay Studio

Library of Congress Publication Data in process

ISBN 978-0-8048-5772-7

29 28 27 26 25
10 9 8 7 6 5 4 3 2 1 2508UM

Printed in Malaysia

Distributed by

North America, Latin America & Europe
Tuttle Publishing
364 Innovation Drive, North Clarendon
VT 05759-9436 U.S.A.
Tel: 1 (802) 773-8930
Fax: 1 (802) 773-6993
info@tuttlepublishing.com
www.tuttlepublishing.com

Japan
Tuttle Publishing
Yaekari Building 3rd Floor
5-4-12 Osaki Shinagawa-ku, Tokyo 141 0032
Tel: (81) 3 5437-0171
Fax: (81) 3 5437-0755
sales@tuttle.co.jp
www.tuttle.co.jp

Asia Pacific
Berkeley Books Pte. Ltd.
3 Kallang Sector #04-01, Singapore 349278
Tel: (65) 6741-2178
Fax: (65) 6741-2179
inquiries@periplus.com.sg
www.tuttlepublishing.com

GPSR representative
Matt Parsons matt.parsons@upi2mbooks.hr
UPI-2M PLUS d.o.o., Medulićeva 20
10000 Zagreb, Croatia